THE CAMBRIDGE COMPANION TO
FRANKENSTEIN

The Cambridge Companion to Frankenstein consists of sixteen original essays on Mary Shelley's novel by leading scholars, providing an invaluable introduction to *Frankenstein* and its various critical contexts. Theoretically informed but accessibly written, this volume relates *Frankenstein* to various social, literary, scientific and historical contexts, and outlines how critical theories such as ecocriticism, posthumanism and queer theory generate new and important discussion in illuminating ways. The volume also explores the cultural afterlife of the novel including its adaptations in various media such as drama, film, television, graphic novels, and literature aimed at children and young adults. Written by an international team of leading experts, the essays provide new insights into the novel and the various critical approaches which can be applied to it. The volume is an essential guide to students and academics who are interested in *Frankenstein* and who wish to know more about its complex literary history.

ANDREW SMITH is Reader in Nineteenth-Century English Literature at the University of Sheffield. His 18 books include *Gothic Death 1740–1914: A Literary History* (2016), *The Ghost Story 1840–1920: A Cultural History* (2010), *Gothic Literature* (2007, revised 2013), *Victorian Demons* (2004) and *Gothic Radicalism* (2000). He edits, with Benjamin Fisher, the award winning series 'Gothic Literary Studies' and 'Gothic Authors: Critical Revisions', published by the University of Wales Press. He also edits, with William Hughes, 'The Edinburgh Companions to the Gothic' series, published by Edinburgh University Press. He is a past President of the International Gothic Association.

A complete list of books in the series is at the back of the book.

D1260610

THE CAMBRIDGE COMPANION TO
FRANKENSTEIN

EDITED BY
ANDREW SMITH

CAMBRIDGE
UNIVERSITY PRESS

University Printing House, Cambridge CB2 8BS, United Kingdom

One Liberty Plaza, 20th Floor, New York, NY 10006, USA

477 Williamstown Road, Port Melbourne, VIC 3207, Australia

4843/24, 2nd Floor, Ansari Road, Daryaganj, Delhi - 110002, India

79 Anson Road, #06-04/06, Singapore 079906

Cambridge University Press is part of the University of Cambridge.

It furthers the University's mission by disseminating knowledge in the pursuit of education, learning and research at the highest international levels of excellence.

www.cambridge.org
Information on this title: www.cambridge.org/9781107450608

© Cambridge University Press 2016

First published 2016

A catalogue record for this publication is available from the British Library

ISBN 978-1-107-08619-7 Hardback
ISBN 978-1-107-45060-8 Paperback

Cambridge University Press has no responsibility for the persistence or accuracy of URLs for external or third-party internet websites referred to in this publication, and does not guarantee that any content on such websites is, or will remain, accurate or appropriate.

For Diane Long Hoeveler
In Memoriam

CONTENTS

CONTENTS

ILLUSTRATIONS

NOTES ON CONTRIBUTORS

PATRICK BRANTLINGER is James Rudy Professor (Emeritus) from Indiana University. He served as Editor of *Victorian Studies* from 1980 to 1990. Among his publications are *Rule of Darkness: British Literature and Imperialism* (1988); *The Reading Lesson: Mass Literacy as Threat in Nineteenth-Century British Fiction* (1998); *Dark Vanishings: Discourse on the Extinction of Primitive Races* (2003); *Crusoe's Footprints: Cultural Studies in Britain and America* (1990); *Taming Cannibals: Race and the Victorians* (2011); and, most recently, *States of Emergency: Essays on Culture and Politics* (2013).

KAREN COATS is Professor of English at Illinois State University. She is author of *Looking Glasses and Neverlands: Lacan, Desire, and Subjectivity in Children's Literature* (2004), and co-editor of *The Gothic in Children's Literature: Haunting the Borders* (2007) and the *Handbook of Research on Children's and Young Adult Literature* (2011).

ADRIANA CRACIUN is University of California Presidential Chair at the University of California, Riverside, and has previously taught at the University of London and the University of Nottingham. She is the author of numerous works on British literature and culture, the history of exploration, and material textuality. Her most recent books are *Writing Arctic Disaster: Authorship and Exploration* (2016) and *The Material Cultures of Enlightenment Arts and Sciences* (with Simon Schaffer, 2016).

GEORGE E. HAGGERTY is Distinguished Professor and Chair of English at the University of California, Riverside. His recent publications include *Horace Walpole's Letters: Masculinity and Friendship in the Eighteenth-Century* (2011); *Queer Gothic* (2006); *Music and Sexuality in Britten: Selected Essays of Philip Brett* (2006); and *The Blackwell Companion to LGBTI/Q Studies* (with Molly McGarry, 2007). He is currently at work on a biography of Horace Walpole.

DIANE LONG HOEVELER was Professor of English at Marquette University, Milwaukee, Wisconsin. Books include *The Gothic Ideology: Religious Hysteria and*

Anti-Catholicism in British Popular Fiction, 1770–1870 (2014), as well as *Gothic Riffs: Secularizing the Uncanny in the European Imaginary, 1780–1820* (2010). In addition, she authored *Gothic Feminism* (1998) and *Romantic Androgyny* (1990). In addition to publishing some 65 articles on a variety of literary topics, she co-authored a critical study of *Charlotte Brontë*, and edited or co-edited another 20 books on a variety of topics in the Gothic and women's literature. She served as President of the International Conference of Romanticism from 2001–2003, and co-editor of the *European Romantic Review*.

JERROLD E. HOGLE is University Distinguished Professor in English at the University of Arizona. A former President of the International Gothic Association, holder of Guggenheim and Mellon research fellowships, and winner of the Distinguished Scholar Award from the Keats–Shelley Association of America, he has published widely on Romantic and Gothic literature. His books include *The Undergrounds of The Phantom of the Opera* (2002) and *The Cambridge Companion to the Modern Gothic* (2014).

MARK JANCOVICH is Professor of Film and Television Studies at the University of East Anglia. He is the author of several books: *Horror* (1992); *The Cultural Politics of the New Criticism* (1993); *Rational Fears: American Horror in the 1950s* (1996); and *The Place of the Audience: Cultural Geographies of Film Consumption* (with Lucy Faire and Sarah Stubbings, 2003). He is also the editor of several collections: *Approaches to Popular Film* (with Joanne Hollows, 1995); *Horror, The Film Reader* (2001); *Quality Popular Television: Cult TV, the Industry and Fans* (with James Lyons, 2003); and *Defining Cult Movies: The Cultural Politics of Oppositional Taste* (with Antonio Lazaro-Reboll, Julian Stringer and Andrew Willis, 2003). He was the founder of *Scope: An Online Journal of Film Studies*; and is currently writing a history of horror in the 1940s.

CATHERINE LANONE is Professor of English Literature at the University of Paris 3-Sorbonne Nouvelle. She has worked on the Franklin expedition and representations of the Arctic. She has published a book on Emily Brontë (*Wuthering Heights: un vent de sorcière* (2000)), and articles on Mary Shelley, Charlotte and Emily Brontë, Charles Dickens and Margaret Atwood, among others. Her latest book, written with Corinne Bigot, *Sunlight and Shadows, Past and Present: Alice Munro's Dance of the Happy Shades* (2014), includes a study of Munro's displacement of Gothic motifs.

TIMOTHY MORTON is Rita Shea Guffey Chair in English at Rice University, Texas. He gave the Wellek Lectures in Theory in 2014 and has collaborated with Björk. He is the author of *Dark Ecology: For a Logic of Future Coexistence* (forthcoming); *Nothing: Three Inquiries in Buddhism* (forthcoming); *Hyperobjects: Philosophy and Ecology after the End of the World* (2013); *Realist Magic: Objects, Ontology, Causality* (2013); *The Ecological Thought* (2010); *Ecology without Nature*

(2007); eight other books and 130 essays on philosophy, ecology, literature, music, art, design and food. He blogs regularly at www.ecologywithoutnature.blogspot .com.

ANDY MOUSLEY is Professor of Critical Theory and Renaissance Literature at De Montfort University, Leicester. Recent publications include *Literature and the Human* (2013) and *Re-Humanising Shakespeare*, 2nd edn (2015). He is the co-author (with Martin Halliwell) of *Critical Humanisms* (2003), and has published articles on humanism, literary humanism and posthumanism in the journals *Textual Practice, Shakespeare* and *postmedieval.*

CHRISTOPHER MURRAY is Senior Lecturer in English and Film Studies at the University of Dundee. He leads a Comics Studies Masters course, and is Director of the Scottish Centre for Comics Studies. He has published on Alan Moore and Grant Morrison, horror comics, and comics and propaganda. He is co-editor of *Studies in Comics* (Intellect) and *UniVerse Comics*, and co-organizer of the International Comics and Graphic Novel conference.

FARRAN NORRIS SANDS currently teaches at the University of Houston – Downtown. She holds a PhD in English Studies from Illinois State University, where she completed a dissertation titled 'Dr. Frankenstein's Hideous Progeny: A Typology of the Mad Scientist in Contemporary Young Adult Novels and Computer Animated Film' in 2015. She is currently writing about adaptations of mad scientists in young adult novels.

DAVID PUNTER is Professor of English at the University of Bristol. He is a poet, writer and academic, and has published extensively on topics including the Gothic, Romantic literature, contemporary writing, literary theory, metaphor and modernity. His published books include *The Literature of Terror: A History of Gothic Fictions from 1765 to the Present Day* (1980); *The Hidden Script: Writing and the Unconscious* (1985); *The Romantic Unconscious: A Study in Narcissism and Patriarchy* (1989); *Gothic Pathologies: The Text, the Body and the Law* (1998); *Writing the Passions* (2000); *Postcolonial Imaginings: Fictions of a New World Order* (2000); *The Influence of Postmodernism on Contemporary Writing: An Interdisciplinary Study* (2005); *Metaphor* (2007); *Modernity* (2007); *Rapture: Literature, Addiction, Secrecy* (2009); and *The Literature of Pity* (2014). His next book will be *The Gothic Condition: Terror, History, Psyche*, to be published in 2016.

CHARLES E. ROBINSON, Emeritus Professor of English at the University of Delaware, has published a number of books and articles on the Shelleys, Byron, Hazlitt and other English Romantic writers. His editions include *Mary Shelley's Collected Tales and Stories* (1976); *The Mary Shelley Reader* (1990); *Mary Shelley's Proserpine and Midas* (1992); *The Frankenstein Notebooks* (2 vols., 1996);

and *The Original Frankenstein* (Bodleian, 2008; Vintage, 2009). He is currently preparing a new edition of *The Letters of William Hazlitt*.

ANDREW SMITH is Reader in Nineteenth-Century English Literature at the University of Sheffield. His 18 published books include *Gothic Death 1740–1914: A Literary History* (2016); *The Ghost Story 1840–1920: A Cultural History* (2010); *Gothic Literature* (2007, revised 2013); *Victorian Demons* (2004); and *Gothic Radicalism* (2000). He is editor, with Benjamin Fisher, of the award winning series 'Gothic Literary Studies' and 'Gothic Authors: Critical Revisions', published by the University of Wales Press. With William Hughes he edits the series 'Edinburgh Companions to the Gothic'. With Anna Barton he edits the series 'Rethinking the Nineteenth Century' for Manchester University Press. He is a past President of the International Gothic Association.

LISA VARGO is Professor and Head of the Department of English, University of Saskatchewan, Saskatoon. She has produced editions of Mary Shelley's *Lodore* (1997); Mary Shelley's *Spanish and Portuguese Lives* (2002); and Thomas Love Peacock's *Nightmare Abbey* (2007). She has published a number of essays on women Romantic writers, and her ongoing research interests include the Shelley circle and Anna Barbauld.

ANGELA WRIGHT is Professor of Romantic Literature at the University of Sheffield and currently co-President of the International Gothic Association. She is the author of *Gothic Fiction* (2007); *Britain, France and the Gothic: The Import of Terror* (2013, pbk 2015); and co-editor (with Dale Townshend) of *Ann Radcliffe, Romanticism and the Gothic* (2014) and *Romantic Gothic: An Edinburgh Companion* (2015). Her study *Mary Shelley* will be published by the University of Wales Press in 2016, and she is undertaking research for a new project, provisionally entitled *Fostering Romanticism*.

ACKNOWLEDGMENTS

I edited this volume during a period of research leave from the University of Sheffield in the Spring term of 2015 and I am grateful for the support provided by colleagues on the School of English's Research Strategy Committee. I would also like to thank Mark Faulkner, Anna Barton and Valerie Hobbs who took over my administrative duties at this time. In particular I would like to thank my colleague Angela Wright for suggesting this volume to me and for Linda Bree at Cambridge University Press for her enthusiastic adoption of it. I would also like to thank Deborah Hey for her excellent copy-editing of the final typescript.

Whilst preparing the final typescript one of the contributors, Diane Long Hoeveler, sadly passed away. She was much admired both as a scholar and as an individual. She will be much missed and this volume is respectfully dedicated to her.

I would also like to thank my wife, Joanne Benson, for her love, tolerance and support throughout the editing of this book and other projects completed during the period of research leave.

NOTE ON THE TEXT

The contributors refer to the 1818 edition of *Frankenstein* edited by Marilyn Butler, published by Oxford University Press in 1998. Contributors make reference to authors by their full name unless it is obvious when a writer may be referred to by their forename. Shortened titles are used in the notes after first quotation. The Chronology was previously published in *The Cambridge Companion to Mary Shelley* edited by Esther Schor in 2003 and is reproduced by kind permission of Cambridge University Press.

1797   (30 Aug.) Mary Wollstonecraft Godwin born in London, daughter
       of William Godwin and Mary Wollstonecraft.
       (10 Sept.) Wollstonecraft dies of puerperal fever.

1801   (21 Dec.) Godwin remarries, to Mary Jane Clairmont. Mary God-
       win is raised in Somers Town (near London); her family household
       consists of her father, stepmother, half-sister (Fanny Imlay, daughter
       of Wollstonecraft and Gilbert Imlay) and step-siblings Mary Jane
       (Claire) Clairmont and Charles Clairmont.

1808   Publishes first story, 'Mounseer Nongtongpaw' (M. J. Godwin and
       Co.).

1812   (7 June) Travels to Dundee to live with the Baxter family until the
       following spring.
       (11 Nov.) Briefly meets Percy Bysshe Shelley (b. 4 Aug. 1792) and
       his wife, Harriet Westbrook Shelley.

1814   (May) Meets Percy Shelley again; a friendship develops.
       (28 June) Elopes with Percy Shelley to the Continent, with Claire
       Clairmont.
       (July–Aug.) Travels in France, Germany, Switzerland, Holland.
       (Sept.) They return to England. During the next two months, Percy
       Shelley resides in London, dodging creditors.

1815   (22 Feb.) Gives birth to her first daughter, who dies 6 March.
       (Aug.) Moves to Bishopsgate, Windsor.

1816   (24 Jan.) Gives birth to a son, William.
       (May) Travels with Percy Shelley and Claire Clairmont, who is preg-
       nant with Byron's child, to Geneva. They live near Byron and Poli-
       dori.
       (16 June) Begins writing *Frankenstein*. (July) Visit to Chamonix.

(Sept.) Returns to London, with Percy Shelley and Claire Clairmont in Bath.

(9 Oct.) Fanny Imlay commits suicide.

(10 Dec.) Harriet Shelley's pregnant body is found in the Serpentine, Hyde Park, London; five days later, Percy Shelley is informed about her suicide.

(30 Dec.) Marriage to Percy Shelley in St. Mildred's Church, London.

1817   (12 Jan.) Claire Clairmont gives birth to Alba, later Allegra, Byron.

(Mar.) Percy Shelley loses custody of his children, Charles and Ianthe. Mary Shelley moves to Marlow.

(14 May) Completes *Frankenstein.*

(2 Sept.) Gives birth to a daughter, Clara.

(Nov.) Publishes *History of a Six Weeks' Tour*, a collaboration with Percy Shelley (T. Hookham and C. and J. Ollier).

1818   (1 Jan.) *Frankenstein; or, The Modern Prometheus* published (Lackington, Hughes, Harding, Mavor, & Jones).

(11 Mar.) Family departs for Continent; arrives in Milan 4 April.

(June) At Bagni di Lucca.

(24 Sept.) Clara Shelley dies in Venice.

(Nov.–Dec.) Travel to Rome and Naples; they remain in Naples until the following February.

1819   (5 Mar.–June) In Rome, where William Shelley dies of malaria on 7 June.

(17 June) Move to Livorno (Leghorn).

(Aug.) Begins writing *Matilda.*

(2 Oct.) Move to Florence.

(12 Nov.) Gives birth to Percy Florence.

1820   (26 Jan.) Move to Pisa.

(Feb.) Finishes *Matilda.*

(Mar.) Begins *Castruccio, Prince of Lucca*; Godwin later renames it *Valperga.*

(Apr.–May) Composes *Proserpine and Midas.*

(Oct.) After relocating several times, move to Pisa.

1821   (Aug.–Dec.) Finishes and revises [*Valperga*: or,] *Castruccio.*

1822   (19 Apr.) Allegra Byron dies from typhus.

(16 June) Miscarriage; haemorrhage arrested when Percy Shelley places her in a vat of icy water.

(8 July) Percy Shelley drowns in the Gulf of Spezia.

(Sept.) Moves to Genoa.

1823   (Feb.) Publishes *Valperga* (Henry Colburn and Richard Bentley).

(23 Apr.) 'Madame d'Houtetot' appears in *The Liberal*, 3, 67–83.

(29 July) Opening night of *Presumption, or, The Fate of Franken-stein*, a play by Richard Brinsley Peake; Mary Shelley sees it on 28 August.

(30 July) 'Giovanni Villani' appears in *The Liberal*, 4, 281–97.

(25 Aug.) With Percy Florence, returns to London.

(Aug.) Second edition of *Frankenstein* appears.

1824   (Mar.) 'On Ghosts' appears in *London Magazine*, 9, 253–6.

(19 Apr.) Byron dies at Missolonghi in Greece. (Spring) Begins *The Last Man*.

(June) Publishes her edition of Percy Shelley's *Posthumous Poems*; enraged, Sir Timothy Shelley threatens to withdraw Percy Florence Shelley's allowance if she again brings Percy Shelley's name before the public.

1825   (25 June) Refuses marriage proposal from American dramatist John Howard Payne.

1826   (23 Jan.) Publishes *The Last Man* (Henry Colburn).

(Oct.) 'The English in Italy"' appears in *Westminster Review*, 6, 325–41.

(Dec.) 'A Visit to Brighton' appears in *London Magazine*, n.s. 6, 460–6.

1827   (June) Agrees to help Thomas Moore with his biography of Byron.

(July) Helps secure passports for friends Isabel Robinson, her illegit-imate child and her partner, 'Sholto Douglas' (Mary Diana Dods); the three elope to Paris.

1828   (Jan.) Begins *The Fortunes of Perkin Warbeck*.

(Mar.) Begins writing for the *Keepsake*, to which she will contribute for ten years.

(Apr.) In Paris with Douglases; meets Prosper Mérimée; contracts smallpox.

1829   (Jan.) 'Illyrian Poems – Feudal Scenes', review of works by Mérimée, published in *Westminster Review*, 10, 71–81.

1830   (18 Jan.) Moore publishes Volume I of his *Letters and Journals of Lord Byron: With Notices of his Life*.

(13 May) *Perkin Warbeck, A Romance* published (Colburn and Bentley).

(Nov.–Dec.) 'Transformation' in the *Keepsake* for publication in 1831 edition (18–39).

1831 (Jan.) Begins *Lodore*. Volume II of Moore's *Byron* published.

(Nov.) Publishes revised third edition of *Frankenstein*, with 'Author's Introduction', in Bentley's Standard Novels series (Colburn and Bentley).

1832 (8 Sept.) William Godwin, Jr (born 28 Mar. 1803, son of William and Mary Jane Clairmont Godwin) dies of cholera.

(29 Sept.) Percy Florence enters Harrow; the following May, Mary Shelley moves there.

1835 (Feb.) Publishes Volume I of *Lives of the Most Eminent Literary and Scientific Men of Italy, Spain and Portugal* (Longman).

(Apr.) Publishes *Lodore* (Richard Bentley).

(Oct.) Publishes Volume II of *Lives of...Men of Italy, Spain and Portugal*.

1836 (23 Mar.) Removes Percy Florence Shelley from Harrow; together, they relocate to Regent's Park, London.

(7 Apr.) William Godwin dies.

1837 (Feb.) Publishes *Falkner, A Novel* (Saunders and Otley)

(Sept.–Oct.) Publishes Volume III of *Lives of...Men of Italy, Spain and Portugal*.

(10 Oct.) Percy Florence Shelley enters Trinity College, Cambridge.

1838 (Aug.) Publishes Volume I of *Lives of the Most Eminent Literary and Scientific Men of France* (Longman). Sir Timothy Shelley relents, allowing publication of his son's poems, but not a biographical memoir. Mary Shelley instead writes extensive notes.

1839 (Jan.–May) Her four-volume edition of Percy Shelley's *Poetical Works* appears, with prefaces and notes (Moxon).

(Aug.) Publishes Volume II of *Lives of...Men of France*.

(Nov.) One-volume edition of Percy Shelley's *Poetical Works* (Moxon).

(Dec.) Publishes two-volume edition of Percy Shelley's *Essays and Letters from Abroad, Translations and Fragments* (Moxon).

1840 (22 June) Arrives in Paris with her son and his Cambridge friends for continental tour; travel through Germany and Switzerland, summer in Italian lakes; arrive Milan on 11 Sept.

Late September, Percy Florence Shelley and friends depart for England; Mary Shelley travels to Paris, where she remains through December.

1841   (Jan.) Returns to London.
(Feb.) Percy Florence Shelley graduates from Cambridge.
(17 June) Death of Mary Jane Godwin.

1842   (30 June–Aug.) With her son and friends, second tour of Continent: Kissingen (baths), Berlin, Dresden, Venice, Florence, Rome, Paris.
(July–Aug.) In Paris; meets Ferdinando Luigi Gatteschi and other Italian exiles.

1844   (24 Apr.) Death of Sir Timothy Shelley; Percy Florence Shelley inherits baronetcy and estate.
(July) Publishes two-volume *Rambles in Germany and Italy in 1840, 1842, and 1843* (Moxon).

1845   (Sept.) Gatteschi threatens to expose her letters to him; blackmail attempt foiled.

1846   (Mar.) 'Attack', probably of severe back pain; possibly also chest pain.

1848   (22 June) Percy Florence Shelley marries Jane St. John, a young widow.
(Oct.) Complains of headaches; probably symptoms of a brain tumour. Intermittently ill until her death.

1850   (17 Dec.) Diagnosis of brain tumor.

1851   (1 Feb.) Mary Shelley dies at age fifty-three at home in London.
(8 Feb.) Buried in Bournemouth with her parents, who were exhumed from St. Pancras at Lady Jane Shelley's request.

ANDREW SMITH

Introduction

Mary Shelley's account of the dream which inspired *Frankenstein* has become almost as well known as the novel itself. She recounts that after days of being unable to conjure a tale in the wake of the infamous ghost story contest at the Villa Diodati in the summer of 1816, she went to bed after listening to Byron and Shelley discussing some fashionable, and at the time scientifically respectable, ideas about how life might be animated from dead matter:

> ...we retired to rest. When I placed my head on my pillow, I did not sleep, nor could I be said to think. My imagination, unbidden, possessed and guided me, gifting the successive images that arose in my mind with a vividness far beyond the usual bounds of reverie. I saw – with shut eyes, but acute mental vision – I saw the pale student of unhallowed arts kneeling beside the thing he had put together. I saw the hideous phantasm of a man stretched out, and then, on the working of some powerful engine, show signs of life, and stir with an uneasy, half-vital motion.[1]

Shelley's self-reflexive 1831 account of her genesis of the 1818 novel locates *Frankenstein* within a highly ambivalent model of Romantic authorship. If we are to take her retrospective account of 1816 at face value then we should note that her 1831 Introduction indicates an anxiety about creativity which is echoed in Victor Frankenstein's plight as he too struggles with the creation of 'the transient existence of the hideous corpse which he had looked upon as the cradle of life' (p. 196). As the 'pale student' becomes hunted and haunted by his creation so Mary claims that she was, try as she might, unable to cast of the power of this dream, 'I could not...easily get rid of my hideous phantom; still it haunted me' despite her attempts to return to 'my tiresome, unlucky ghost story!' (p. 196), that she had been working on. The tale therefore seems to be the product of a cursed imagination that becomes reflected in Victor's ambivalent attitude towards his creation. For Mary the dream provides both a troubling inspiration and an antidote to 'that blank incapacity of invention which is the greatest misery of authorship, when dull nothing replies to our anxious invocations' (p. 195). Mary was under pressure after an evening in which Byron, his physician Dr John Polidori, Percy Shelley, Mary and her stepsister Claire Clairmont (who was also Byron's pregnant mistress) had spent an evening reading aloud from J. B. Eyriès's *Fantasmagoriana*, a French translation of German Gothic tales. This recital led Byron to propose that '"We will each write a ghost story"' (p. 194). Mary, the daughter of two well-known radical authors, Mary Wollstonecraft and William Godwin, was clearly conscious of the cumulative pressure on her to succeed as a writer. Indeed she notes that Percy was eager to test whether the 18-year-old Mary might have a hidden capability for authorship. Mary records:

> He was forever inciting me to obtain literary reputation, which even on my own part I cared for then, though since I have become infinitely indifferent to it. At this time he desired that I should write, not so much with the idea that I could produce any thing worthy of notice, but, that he might himself judge how far I possessed the promise of better things hereafter. (p. 193)

It is therefore clear that Mary felt subject to considerable scrutiny at this time and the ghost story writing competition added to this pressure with her noting that in subsequent days she was asked '"Have you thought of a story?"... and each morning I was forced to reply with a mortifying negative' (p. 195). Until she has her dream.

This sketch of the origins of *Frankenstein* indicates how ideas about creativity shaped the genesis of the novel which in turn dwells on the dangers of creativity. Romanticism, broadly defined, emphasized the importance of the creative imagination which had links to a model of freedom that was both artistic and political. This emphasis on the freedom to think and the freedom to imagine the world differently can, in part, be explained by Mary Shelley's family background and more broadly by the wider political dramas of the age.

Mary Godwin (as she was before her marriage to Percy Shelley) was born on 30 August 1797 to Mary Wollstonecraft and William Godwin. Mary Wollstonecraft was a pioneering radical feminist and the author of the seminal *A Vindication of the Rights of Woman* (1792) which attributed gender inequality to the different forms of education received by boys and girls (an issue also addressed in *Frankenstein*), and she was the author of important works of political philosophy and fiction.[2] Mary Godwin's father was William Godwin, the radical political philosopher and novelist. His

Enquiry Concerning Political Justice (1793) examines the sources of social and economic inequality that are also explored through the theme of injustice in *Frankenstein*. Godwin sought to popularize his ideas by writing a Gothic novel, *Caleb Williams* (1794), which further addressed ideas about injustice and inequality. In Godwin's novel the central tensions between Caleb and his employer, Falkland, would become echoed in the relationship between Victor and his creature in Mary's novel – and Godwin's influence on her is indicated in *Frankenstein*'s dedication to him. Mary Wollstonecraft's influence was less direct (although no less important) as she died 11 days after Mary was born due to complications with the birth. William Godwin subsequently married his neighbour, Mary Jane Clairmont, in 1801 which was not a particularly happy experience for Mary Godwin. Mary Godwin probably first met Percy Shelley (who was estranged from his wife Harriet, who would commit suicide in December 1816) in 1812 and again in May 1814 and eloped with him to Europe in July of that year, which resulted in her first publication *History of a Six Weeks' Tour through a part of France, Switzerland, Germany, and Holland; with Letters Descriptive of a Sail Round the Lake of Geneva and of the Glaciers of Chamouni* (1817).[3]

Mary and Percy married in December 1816 (after Harriet's death). They had a son, William, born in January 1816 and a daughter, Clara, born in September 1817. In February 1815 a prematurely born daughter had died and the trauma of this is often cited as an influence on the desire to raise the dead (as Victor gives 'birth' to the creature) in *Frankenstein*. Further tragedy struck when Clara died in 1818 and William in 1819. A son, Percy, was born in November 1819 (who lived into adulthood and died in 1889). The poet Percy Shelley died in a boating accident in 1822 and Byron died in 1824. Dr John Polidori, author of 'The Vampyre: A Tale' (1819), died in 1821. Mary Shelley would write six more novels and in 1839 provided the prefatory comments to a four-volume edition of Percy Shelley's poems, as well as another travelogue, *Rambles in Germany and Italy* (1844).[4] She died on 1 February 1851 of a suspected brain tumour.

This brief biography indicates both her extraordinary radical connections and the rather tragic life that she led from her mid 20s onwards which is characterized by the deaths of those she was closest to. Death may seem to be a dominant theme in *Frankenstein* and certainly from the vantage point of 1831 Mary reflects, in her new Introduction to the novel, on both the inspiration for *Frankenstein* and her encounters with figures (most notably Percy Shelley and Byron), who have now died. It should be noted that the focus in this volume is on the 1818 edition which is read as a product of its time.[5] Many of the contributors also discuss the significance of these amendments as in several respects they represent a shift in political vision. Indeed what type of politics are involved when reading *Frankenstein* has been a concern for critics who have often been struck by the extraordinary ambivalence which the novel appears to express towards radical thought. In order to appreciate this we also need to understand the period in which the text was written.

This Introduction began by suggesting that Mary's account of the inspiration behind the novel comes out of an ambivalent attitude towards Romantic creativity. More broadly we might say that the novel as a whole represents an ambivalence towards the Romantic project and the type of artistic and political idealism with which Romanticism was associated. Victor Frankenstein should be seen as a thwarted idealist who searches for a way of overcoming death, only to create a creature that kills. He also emphasizes that he had selected the creature's 'features as beautiful' but creates monstrosity (p. 39). In other words the idealism generates the very thing that it is meant to overcome. This is a theme which recurs repeatedly in the novel in references to paradise in which Milton's *Paradise Lost* (1674) plays a crucial role in emphasizing that all of the principal protagonists (Victor, Robert Walton and the creature) inhabit a post-lapsarian and dystopian world. The question is why would someone with such ostensibly radical connections (and therefore credentials) as Mary Shelley want to emphasize the failure of idealism? It is tempting to attribute much of this to the post-Napoleonic Europe in which the novel is set. The defeat of Napoleon in 1815 effectively marked the end of the French Revolutionary politics that had been, initially, much admired by both of Mary's parents and the Romantic poets. In the end political idealism had not transformed the world and a figure such as Byron would need to find his causes elsewhere in Europe (in his case in support of Greek independence against the Ottoman Empire). However, to impose such a reading on the novel is to lose sight of the fact that its elegiac tone can be interpreted as a radical lament for this lost idealism – a theme which is addressed in her novel *The Last Man* (1826) which focuses on the last man left alive after a plague has devastated the world (a novel which includes thinly veiled portraits of the now deceased Percy Shelley and Byron).

The ambivalence in the novel can in part be attributed to this complex response towards Romantic idealism in which Victor's narrative might seem to function as a precautionary warning to Robert Walton about the dangers of surrendering to the egotism which appears to tarnish idealism. On his deathbed, however, Victor says to Walton:

'Farewell, Walton! Seek happiness in tranquillity, and avoid ambition, even if it be only the apparently innocent one of distinguishing yourself in science and discoveries. Yet why do I say this? I have myself been blasted in these hopes, yet another may succeed.' (p. 186)

Failure may only be temporary and this suggests the possible future resurrection of Romantic idealism and the radical politics with which it was associated. This is an issue that I will touch upon further in Chapter 5 in a discussion of the scientific contexts of the novel.

It is also important to acknowledge that what we are looking at is a Gothic novel and, as David Punter has argued, the Gothic is a form which is founded upon ambivalence.[6] In a novel like *Frankenstein* we witness not just ambivalence about Romanticism but also an undermining of any clearly defined concept of 'evil'. The key question is whether Victor is responsible for the creature's killings, because they are a consequence of his abandonment of the creature. If we agree, then it is still difficult to ascribe 'evil' to Victor's negligence. The creature might seem to be the more obvious 'monster' in the text, but his violent actions can be attributed to a reaction to the injustice to which he has been repeatedly subjected. The novel, in its psychological intensity, looks back towards *Caleb Williams* and anticipates Robert Louis Stevenson's *Strange Case of Dr Jekyll and Mr Hyde* (1886), which gives full treatment to the type of divided self and psychological projections which are implicit in the relationship between Victor and his creature. *Frankenstein* also represents the end of the first golden heyday of the Gothic which was broadly between 1780 and 1820, a period dominated by social, economic and political change, the upheavals of which were, at different levels of explicitness, explored by writers of the Gothic at the time. The Gothic from the late eighteenth and early nineteenth centuries can be read as responding to the revolutionary turmoil in Europe during this period, whereas later nineteenth-century Gothic narratives (as in the writing of Stevenson, Stoker and H. G. Wells, for example), engaged with issues of science, technology and urbanization. Throughout the nineteenth century the ambivalent attitude towards the French Revolution is effectively supplanted by concerns about the consequences of the Industrial Revolution and the technocratic changes with which it was associated.

There are also differences within the period between the 1818 edition and the 1831 version which are important for us to consider and consequently many of the chapters in this study address them. However, the 1831 edition is not the second edition of the novel and it is important to note that the novel was republished in 1823 following the popular success of Richard

Brinsley Peake's stage adaptation earlier that year. The 1823 edition incorporated a number of changes which were made by William Godwin as he helped to prepare the novel for republication. It was this 1823 edition that Mary subsequently revised in 1831 and it therefore includes Godwin's amendments.

The history of these editorial changes is discussed in the first section of this volume which addresses the 'Historical and Literary Contexts' of the novel and provides an important discussion of the range of different contexts which we need to consider when trying to relate *Frankenstein* to the culture that produced it. Charles E. Robinson in a chapter on '*Frankenstein*: Its Composition and Publication' explores the important differences between the 1818, 1823 and 1831 editions as well as outlining the novel's critical reception, circulation and readership. In 'Contextualizing Sources' Lisa Vargo explores the literary and non-literary textual sources cited in *Frankenstein*. To that end she examines, amongst other texts, how Volney's *Ruin of Empires* (1791), Plutarch's *Parallel Lives* (c. 120), Goethe's *The Sorrows of Young Werther* (1774), Milton's *Paradise Lost* (1674), Coleridge's *The Rime of the Ancient Mariner* (1798) and Godwin's novels and political writings were reworked by Mary to shape the main themes of her novel. Vargo also outlines how scientific ideas of the period were explored, a theme which is given more sustained treatment later in this section. Jerrold E. Hogle in 'Romantic Contexts' examines *Frankenstein*'s place within a Romantic literary culture defined by Mary's contemporaries such as Percy Shelley and Byron, but also earlier Romantics such as Wordsworth and Coleridge. Hogle also explores the important influence of Rousseau's *Confessions* (1782) which shaped Romantic models of autobiography that *Frankenstein* is also indebted to. The emphasis in some of these early chapters is on the influence of poetry over Mary's novel, but Catherine Lanone in 'The Context of the Novel' examines the culture of the novel that generated *Frankenstein* and the influence that the novel had on subsequent novelists in the nineteenth century. She explores *Frankenstein*'s indebtedness to *Caleb Williams* and its role in shaping a language of psychology, male authority and monstrosity in Brontë's *Wuthering Heights* (1847). She also examines how the psychological tensions in *Frankenstein* were developed in Wilkie Collins's *Basil* (1852) which also focuses on psychological strains and images of physical deformity which owes much to Mary's novel. Dickens's *Great Expectations* (1861) makes a direct allusion to *Frankenstein* when Pip likens himself to a creature that has been made by others, such as Magwich, which also introduces a theme of injustice that is addressed by Dickens. In the following chapter on 'Scientific Contexts' I explore how the novel draws upon the work of the chemist, Sir Humphry Davy, for its model of the scientist as an heroic Romantic adventurer. The chapter also explores how the writings of Erasmus Darwin, Charles Darwin's grandfather, influenced the novel. *Frankenstein* is also discussed in relation to contemporary debates about galvanism and some of the scientific controversies of the time. Science during this period has a clear political dimension to it as its discoveries seemed to be ungodly to many (and Victor appears to usurp the role of God in creating life), and suggested a link between scientific and political revolutions. In the following chapter Adriana Craciun argues that *Frankenstein* can not only be related to a number of contemporary political contexts, it can also be read as producing a particular type of political vision. The novel can be read as a critique of the polar explorations that became popular at the time – explorations which seemed to provide an alternative outlet for masculine adventure that had until recently been consumed by the Napoleonic wars. However, it is Safie's narrative which, whilst seemingly working within a conventional orientalist account about Turkey, indicates that a discourse of rebellion and political radicalism has not been defeated in a post-Napoleonic Europe but rather reappears within a gendered narrative which asserts the continuing need for emancipation.

The second section of this book focuses on 'Theories and Forms' and explores how a number of theoretical viewpoints can be productively applied to the novel. The first chapter in this section, by Angela Wright, on 'The Female Gothic', explores how the model of the female Gothic novel, which has been associated with the popular late eighteenth century writings of Ann Radcliffe, shaped *Frankenstein*. The 1831 Introduction, which emphasizes the subtlety of 'Terror' (as something implicit) over 'Horror' (as represented by sustained explicit violence), demonstrates that Mary was self-consciously reflecting on Radcliffe's posthumously published essay 'The Supernatural in Poetry' (1826) (in which Radcliffe discriminated between 'Terror' and 'Horror'), and so seeking to align the 1831 edition of the novel with a Radcliffean vision – an alignment which is made clear in the treatment of Safie and the resistance to power that she represents. How the novel can be read via queer theory is explored in the following chapter by George E. Haggerty. The fraught relationship between Victor and his creature and their feverish bonding can be helpfully explained by the application of queer theory which explores how the novel articulates a covert homosocial narrative which aligns it with queer politics. Patrick Brantlinger in the following chapter on 'Race and *Frankenstein*' explores how the creature's 'otherness' (his apparent 'monstrosity'), can be read in relation to racial categories in the period. The novel also makes repeated references to slavery which can also be read within the context of race. The battle between Victor and his creature is ultimately one about mastery and this conflict can be read through the racial tensions of the time. In 'Frankenstein and Ecocriticism' Timothy Morton explores how Frankenstein raises a number of questions about what we mean by nature. The creature is both seemingly 'natural' (a subject with recognizable thoughts and feelings) and completely 'unnatural' (constructed by science). Morton explores how the novel challenges the idea of nature as something which we can either possess or belong to and his chapter provides a counterpoint to Romantic conceptions of nature which had suggested that it conceals a hidden metaphysical truth, one that the knowing subject can read and so decode. Morton's ecocritical approach suggests that a more complex model of reading nature in Frankenstein helps us to understand why so many of the protagonists are in search of an idea of belonging to nature. The issue of the creature's construction is explored further by Andy Mousley in a chapter on 'The Posthuman' which examines in depth how the novel addresses what we mean by the 'human' and whether the construction of the creature points towards an emerging culture of the posthuman which is implicated in the novel's repeated questioning of what being a person might mean. The theoretical approaches in this section thus provide new and challenging ways in which we might read the novel and they also demonstrate how Frankenstein's representational complexity can be helpfully made sense of by contemporary theory.

The final section on 'Adaptations' explores how Frankenstein has gained a cultural life that transcends the form of the novel and the period which produced it. Diane Long Hoeveler explores the numerous stage productions of the play throughout the nineteenth century and discusses their variations to the original novel as well as relating them more widely to the theatrical culture of the period. In the following chapter Mark Jancovich outlines the film (and television) history of Frankenstein from the Edison Studio 1910 adaptation to the present day. He explores how these films reflect changes in the history of film production and examines the various ways that films reworked the original tale and earlier theatrical and film versions of it. The novel also gained an afterlife in science fiction and other horror writings of the twentieth century and David Punter examines their significance in a chapter which discusses, amongst others, Brian Aldiss's Frankenstein Unbound (1973), and Dean Koontz's series of five co-authored novels on Frankenstein from Prodigal Son (2004) to The Dead Town (2011). In 'Frankenstein in Comics and Graphic Novels' Christopher Murray explores how early comics drew upon the 1930s films for their aesthetic inspiration. Later comics worked at adapting Mary's novel, until in the 1990s we witness the emergence of the graphic novel which exists alongside, rather than replaces, a continuingly evolving culture of Frankenstein comics. Murray relates these adaptations to the comic industry which produced them and explores how these comics reflected some of the political concerns of their day. The final chapter by Karen Coats and Farran Norris Sands explores how *Frankenstein* has been adapted for young readers, which includes the picture book market aimed at young children consisting of texts such as *Frankenstein Makes a Sandwich* (2006) to young adult novels including Mackenzi Lee's *This Monstrous Thing* (2015). The chapter discusses how *Frankenstein* seems an appropriate text to rewrite for this younger market because at one level the original novel explores the creature's anxiety about growing up. These types of growing pains and the types of family tensions within which they may take place thus rework *Frankenstein*'s concern about childhood, parenthood and what is expected of adult life.

The continuing popularity of *Frankenstein* is clear from its many adaptations, adaptations which provide ways of reading the novel. Nick Dear's popular theatrical production (directed by Danny Boyle in 2011), for example, switched the actors playing Victor Frankenstein and the creature (Benedict Cumberbatch and Jonny Lee Miller) on alternate nights which emphasized the doubling that is implicit to the novel. In addition, Liam Scarlett's ballet of *Frankenstein*, which premiered at the Royal Opera House in May 2016, bears witness to the ever evolving form of Mary Shelley's tale.

This volume consists of chapters which are all written by experts in their field which explore how *Frankenstein* can be related to the period which produced it, to contemporary critical theories which bear testimony to its representational complexity, and to the novel's adaptations, which indicates just how deeply *Frankenstein* has penetrated the culture. This book is both a guide to the novel and an act of cultural analysis which is a starting point for students wishing to explore the novel further. At the end there is a Guide to Further Reading which relates to the sections of this book and which outlines ways in which further lines of enquiry can be pursued.

NOTES

1 Mary Shelley, *Frankenstein*, ed. and Intro., Marilyn Butler (Oxford University Press, 1998), p. 196. Future references will be made parenthetically.

2 See also her *Vindications of the Rights of Men* (1790) where she critiques Edmund Burke's view of the French Revolution and novels such as *Mary: A Fiction* (1788) and the unfinished posthumously published novel *The Wrongs of Woman, or Maria* (1798).

3 Mary Wollstonecraft had also written a travelogue, *Letters Written during a Short Residence in Sweden, Norway and Denmark* (1796).

4 Her other novels were *Valperga* (1823), *The Last Man* (1826), *Perkin Warbeck* (1830), *Lodore* (1835), *Falkner* (1837). *Matilda* was completed in 1819, but the theme of incest meant that it was not published until 1959. She also edited Percy Shelley's *Posthumous Poems* in 1824.

5 The 1831 edition contains amendments which are republished in the appendices of the 1818 text edited by Marilyn Butler. Mary Shelley, *Frankenstein*, ed. and Intro., Marilyn Butler (Oxford University Press, 1998), see Appendix B, pp. 198–228.

6 See David Punter, *The Literature of Terror*, 2 vols. (London and New York: Longman, 1996), Vol. II, pp. 181–216 on 'Mutations of terror: theory and the Gothic'.

PART I

Historical and Literary Contexts

I

CHARLES E. ROBINSON

Frankenstein

Its Composition and Publication

The stemma of *Frankenstein*, its genealogical progression from Mary Shelley's original conception in June 1816 through the first and later editions to the paperback editions of today, can help us to understand and appreciate the artistry of the novel's structure and themes. No novel is born directly from the brain of its author; and Mary Shelley's original dream was modified not only by the intricacies of her own creative process but also by the collaborative and editorial and publishing and commercial processes that ultimately led to the production and advertising and reviewing and reading of her novel. That is to say, Mary Shelley's monster was shaped and reshaped through various textual incarnations, from an hypothesized ur-text (the first and now missing manuscript version of the story) that was then transformed by a number of minds and hands into the various texts that are now denominated by the formal title of *Frankenstein; or, The Modern Prometheus.*

No history of the production of *Frankenstein* (first published on 1 January 1818) would be complete without reference to Mary Shelley's own narrative of the novel's conception in her Introduction to the third edition of 1831, in which she recalled the telling of ghost stories during that cold and rainy Geneva summer in June 1816 when gathered at Byron's Villa Diodati were the 28-year-old poet Lord Byron; his 18-year-old pregnant mistress Claire Clairmont (Mary Godwin's slightly younger step-sister); his 21-year-old doctor John William Polidori; the 23-year-old poet Percy Shelley; and the 18-year-old Mary Godwin, who by marriage would become Mary Wollstonecraft Shelley on 30 December 1816. Mary notes that, after a group reading of tales from J.-B. B. Eyriès's *Fantasmagoriana* (1812):

> I busied myself *to think of a story* . . . One which would speak to the mysterious fears of our nature, and awaken thrilling horror – one to make the reader dread to look round, to curdle the blood, and quicken the beatings of the heart. If I did not accomplish these things, my ghost story would be unworthy of its

name. I thought and pondered . . . 'Have you thought of a story?' I was asked each morning, and each morning I was forced to reply with a mortifying negative.[1]

Eventually, sometime between 16 and 18 June, Mary Shelley had the past-midnight dream by which she conceived her story. As she recalled the events of that summer:

> My imagination, unbidden, possessed and guided me, gifting the successive images that arose in my mind . . . I saw the pale student of unhallowed arts kneeling beside the thing he had put together. I saw the hideous phantasm of a man stretched out, and then, on the working of some powerful engine, show signs of life, and stir with an uneasy, half vital motion . . . On the morrow [?17 June] I announced that I had *thought of a story*. I began that day with the words, 'It was on a dreary night of November,' making only a transcript of the grim terrors of my waking dream. (pp. 196–7)

The one constant in all the versions of *Frankenstein* is the initiating sentence, 'It was on a dreary night of November', which began the first 'transcript' of the novel and was retained, perhaps as the first sentence, in what I have termed a novella-length and shorter ur-text of the novel that may have lacked both the Walton frame tale (in which the novel becomes a series of letters sent by Robert Walton to his sister, Margaret Saville) and the innermost Safie tale (which relates to the family circumstances of the De Laceys); it became the first sentence of Chapter 7A of Volume I of the two-volume Intermediate Draft; and then became the first sentence of Chapter 4 of Volume I of the differently structured 3-volume Fair Copy; and then became the first sentence of Chapter 4 of Volume I of the three-volume 1818 first edition; and then became the first sentence of Chapter 4 of Volume I of the two-volume 1823 second edition; and then became the first sentence of Chapter 5 of the one-volume third and revised edition of 1831. This sequence just outlined is best understood visually by means of the facing stemma of the novel on p. 15.

The reader interested in a more detailed history of Mary Shelley writing her novel may consult my '*Frankenstein* Chronology' that records the day-to-day facts as they are recoverable from contemporary documents.[2] I argue, for example, that Mary Shelley in Geneva from June to August 1816 wrote a shorter version of her novel; that she and 'Shelley [did] talk about my story' on 21 August, probably deciding to expand her 'short tale' into the surviving Draft of the novel; that back in England she began, most likely by mid-September and no later than mid-October, to draft the chapters of the first volume of her novel into the hard-cover Notebook A; that by early December, still in Notebook A, she finished what she conceived of as Volume I

The Eleven Texts of FRANKENSTEIN

Ur-text: Draft(s) of a 'story' written between [?17] June and [?August] 1816 – not extant, but most likely lacking the outermost and innermost tales of Walton and Safie – in the 'story' proper Victor Frankenstein grew up with Myrtella and Carignan rather than Elizabeth and Clerval.

↓

***1816–1817* MWS Draft:** 2-volume novel (in 33 chapters) in two hard-cover notebooks ([?August] 1816–17 April 1817) – hypothetically reconstructed by eliminating the PBS interventions and restoring Mary Shelley's original text – printed as the second text in *The Original Frankenstein* (2008).

↓

***1816–1817* MWS/PBS Draft:** 2-volume novel (in 33 chapters) in two hard-cover notebooks ([?August] 1816–17 April 1817) – most of these two Notebooks ('A' & 'B') survive – printed in *Frankenstein Notebooks* (1996) and as the first text in *The Original Frankenstein* (2008), both using italics for PBS text.

↓

***1817* Fair Copy:** 3-volume novel (in 23 chapters) in [?eleven] soft-cover notebooks (18 April–13 May 1817) – parts of Notebooks 'C1' and 'C2' survive – printed in *Frankenstein Notebooks* (1996).

↓

Proofs: ([?23] September–[?3] November 1817) – not extant.

↓

Revises: ([?23] September–[?20] November 1817) – not extant, but parts of these revised proofs can be determined.

↓

***1818*:** 1st edition (1 January 1818) in 3 vols. (23 chapters) – published anonymously by Lackington et al. in 500 copies – sold for 16s.6d. in boards – Mary Shelley earned £41.13s.10d. (paid to PBS).

↓

↓ ***1818 Thomas*:** 'Thomas' copy of 1st edition, corrected by Mary Shelley and preserved at
↓ Pierpont Morgan Library (corrections made before July 1823 – possibly as early as 20 December
↓ 1818, when she recorded 'Correct Frankenstein' in her Naples Journal[3] – corrections reproduced
↓ in *1818 Rieger*[4]).

↓

***1823*:** 2nd edition (11 August 1823) in 2 vols. (23 chapters), by Mary Wollstonecraft Shelley – published by G. and W. B. Whittaker (but not set from *1818 Thomas*) in 500 copies – sold for 14s. in boards (William Godwin apparently saw through the press, making 123 substantive changes[5] to the text of *1818*).

↓

↓ **[*1826*]:** [?Re-issued 2nd edition] (4 April 1826) – apparently issued by Henry Colburn.

↓

***1831*:** Revised or 3rd edition (31 October 1831) in 1 vol. (24 chapters), by Mary W. Shelley (name on engraved title page) – published by Henry Colburn and Richard Bentley in 4,020 stereotyped copies – sold for 6s., 'neatly bound' – Mary Shelley earned £30 for the copyright (and used *1823* as her copy text, thereby incorporating most of her father's 123 substantive changes).

of her novel (with Victor Frankenstein sitting with his monster before the fire and waiting to hear his narrative); that by early December, still in Notebook A, she began what she titled Volume II of the novel (the monster's narrative with its dramatic beginning, 'It is with difficulty that I remember the æra of my being'); that by January 1817 she started hard-cover Notebook B to continue drafting Volume II of her novel, which she concluded by early April, at which point she corrected her novel for a period of eight days. By this time (and most likely at intervals since September 1816), Percy Shelley also edited his wife's novel, ultimately being responsible for at least 5,000 of the approximately 72,000 words of the novel.[6] Also, by this time, in the margins of these two hard-cover Notebooks, the Shelleys mathematically calculated how they might restructure the Draft of a two-volume novel in 33 chapters into what became a Fair Copy (possibly in 11 soft-cover notebooks) of a three-volume novel in 23 chapters. These changes aesthetically altered the structure of some of Mary Shelley's chapters, essentially reducing the opportunities for emphasis at the beginning and end of chapters – in one crucial place, the monster's threatening 'I shall be with you on your marriage night' at the end of Chapter 12 of Volume II of the Draft was moved to the middle of Chapter 3 of Volume III of the Fair Copy.[7] Mary Shelley made all of these changes as she fair copied her novel between 18 April and 10–13 May, in most cases transcribing the text of the Draft word-for-word into the Fair Copy. It is noteworthy, however, that Percy Shelley undertook writing the last 12¾ pages of the Fair Copy and that he significantly altered the Draft text of Walton's description of Victor's and the monster's final words.[8]

Once the Fair Copy (which served as the printer's copy) was prepared, the Shelleys almost immediately sought a publisher, perhaps with the assistance of William Godwin. Having left their Albion House in Marlow to visit Godwin on 23 May 1817, the Shelleys most likely brought the Fair Copy Notebooks with them to submit to Byron's publisher, John Murray. As when he later negotiated with the publishers Ollier and Lackington, Percy Shelley as his wife's 'agent' would not have revealed to Murray the name of his 'friend' who had written *Frankenstein*. By 26 May, one of the Shelleys was informed directly or indirectly that 'Murray likes F'.[9] Within three more days, however, Mary Shelley in London wrote to Percy Shelley (who had returned to their house in Marlow) that 'Of course [William] Gifford[10] did not allow this courtly bookseller [Murray] to purchase F.'[11] Whether Murray returned the Fair Copy at that time or retained it for further consideration is not known, but we do know that either Murray or another publisher formally rejected the novel by 18 June, when Mary Shelley recorded in her journal that 'Frank. sent back – send it to G[odwin]'.[12]

The Fair Copy disappears for the next six weeks, perhaps because Godwin attempted during that time to find a publisher for his daughter's novel. By some means, the Fair Copy was returned to Marlow, from which Percy Shelley on 3 August wrote to his publisher Charles Ollier:

I send you with this letter a manuscript which has been consigned to my care by a friend in whom I feel considerable interest. – I do not know how far it consists with your plan of business to purchase the copyrights, or a certain interest in the copyrights of any works which should appear to promise success. I should certainly prefer that some such arrangement as this should be made if on consideration you could make any offer which I should feel justified to my friend in accepting. How far that can be you will be the better able to judge after a perusal of the Mss. – Perhaps you will do me the favour of communicating your decision to me as early as you conveniently can.[13]

Ollier obliged to the extent of an early decision, but he rejected the novel that might have helped his career as a publisher. According to Percy Shelley's postscript to Mary Shelley's 6 August letter to Marianne Hunt:

Poor Mary's book came back with a refusal, which has put me rather in ill spirits. Does any kind friend of yours Marianne know any bookseller or has any influence with one? Any of those good tempered Robinsons? All these things are affairs of interest & preconception.[14]

Two days later, Percy Shelley in a separate letter to Ollier hoped that *Frankenstein* 'did not give you bad dreams'.[15]

Acting as Mary Shelley's agent, Percy Shelley was more successful in his next dealings with the publisher Lackington and Co., which previously had acted as his bookseller and which had a backlist of titles that suggested Lackington's possible interest in the bizarre tale of *Frankenstein*. Sometime between 7 and 22 August Percy Shelley submitted the Fair Copy Notebooks to Lackington; sometime between 18 and 22 August Mary Shelley recorded that they had received a letter from Lackington.[16] On 22 August Percy Shelley sent the following reply addressed to 'Messrs. Lackington, Allen & Co., Finsbury Square, London', requesting that the contract be for half-profits:

I ought to have mentioned that the novel which I sent you is not my own production, but that of a friend who not being at present in England cannot make the correction you suggest. As to any mere inaccuracies of language I should feel myself authorized to amend them when revising proofs. With respect to the terms of publication, my first wish certainly was to receive on my friend's behalf an adequate price for the copyright of the MS. As it is, however, I beg to submit the following proposal, which I hope you will think fair, particularly as I understand it is an arrangement frequently made by Booksellers with Authors who are new to the world. – It is that you should take the risk of printing, advertising, etc., entirely on yourselves and, after full deduction being made from the profits of the work to cover these expenses that the clear produce, both of the first edition and of every succeeding edition should be divided between you and the author. I cannot in [on] the author's part disclaim all interest in the first edition, because it is possible that there may be no demand for another, and then the profits, however small, will be all that accrue.

I hope on consideration that you will not think such an arrangement as this unreasonable, or one to which you will refuse your assent.[17]

Sometime between 2 September (when Mary Shelley gave birth to her daughter Clara) and 19 September, Percy Shelley did 'Bargain with Lackington concerning Frankenstein',[18] presumably at this time settling on the one-third profits the Shelleys would eventually earn for the novel.

At least the first sheet or gathering of proofs in twelves ('B': pp. 1–24) from Lackington arrived at Albion House in Marlow by 23 September, the day that Percy Shelley with Claire Clairmont went up to London to arrange for the publication of his epic, *Laon and Cythna*; on the evening of 24 September, Mary Shelley received and sent Percy Shelley additional proofs of Volume I (probably including pp. 50–1 from the third sheet or gathering of 'D') that she judged needed alteration to fix some 'abruptnesses', giving him 'carte blanche to make what alterations you please'. At this time, Percy Shelley probably added to the proofs the long transitional paragraph in the first chapter of Volume I (p. 22):

I feel pleasure in dwelling on the recollections of childhood . . . But, in drawing the picture of my early days, I must not omit to record those events which led, by insensible steps to my after tale of misery: for when I would account to myself for the birth of that passion, which afterwards ruled my destiny, I find it arise, like a mountain river, from ignoble and almost forgotten sources; but, swelling as it proceeded, it became the torrent which, in its course, has swept away all my hopes and joys.

Natural philosophy is the genius that has regulated my fate; I desire therefore, in this narration, to state those facts which led to my predilection for that science.

The transition was less necessary in the original Draft, where a chapter break disguised one of the 'abruptnesses'. Although this permission apparently applied only to this set of proofs, Percy Shelley was clearly in charge of correcting additional gatherings, for he wrote to Lackington on the 24th and asked the publisher to send additional proofs directly to him at Leigh Hunt's at 13 Lisson Grove North where he would be for the most part of the next four weeks.[19]

On 24 or 25 September, Percy Shelley again wrote to Lackington, remarking on the accuracy of the printing and urging that proofs be expedited, and it appears that by 13 October Percy Shelley had received all of the proofs of Volume I, which he gave to Godwin to read by that date. By 23 October the proofs of Volume II were completed; and by 28 October two major alterations were made in proofs in gatherings 'B' (pp. 1–24) and 'C' (pp. 25–48) of Volume III. The first alteration, which would have appeared as printed text in the corrected proofs, was most likely authored by Percy Shelley who replaced Draft text on Holland and the Dutch with new and important material on Henry Clerval that also included quotations from Leigh Hunt's *Story of Rimini* (1816) and Wordsworth's 'Tintern Abbey' (1798). The second alteration resulted from Mary Shelley's excursion on 20 October to the monument of John Hampden (the seventeenth-century Parliamentarian leader) near Oxford, her experiences reflected in the substitutions that were made in the proofs. A month later, by 22 November, Godwin was reading a proof copy of the final volume; and, by 28 November, Percy Shelley requested proofs of the title page and of the preface that he had authored earlier in September. It is possible that Percy Shelley also wrote his review of his wife's novel in that same September, although that review was not published until a year after the third edition of 1831 was published.[20]

Pre-publication activities and advertisements culminated on 1 January 1818, when *Frankenstein; or, The Modern Prometheus* was published by Lackington, Hughes, Harding, Mavor, & Jones in three volumes in 500 copies, selling retail in paper boards for 16s.6d. and eventually earning the Shelleys one-third profits of £41.13s.10d.[21] Percy Shelley, as his wife's advocate, sent a copy of the novel to Walter Scott on 2 January, and the Shelleys learned by late February that what was to be Scott's review would appear in the March issue of *Blackwood's Edinburgh Magazine*; two other reviews appeared in March; and three more (two of which were very short) in April. Because the Shelleys had departed England for Italy on 12 March, they did not enjoy the attention these periodicals were giving them, 'them' because Scott in *Blackwood's* suggested that the novel had been written by Percy Shelley rather than Mary Shelley. Two more reviews followed in June. All told, *Frankenstein* received eight reviews, a very respectable number for a novel published anonymously in only 500 copies, only 16 of which were sent to reviewers.[22]

Despite the critical attention from major reviews and magazines, some of which praised the novel and its author, *Frankenstein* did not go into a second edition in 1818, and its print run of 500 copies pales in comparison to the sales of novels by Scott and poems by Byron. It is likely that had the Shelleys been in London rather than Italy they would have generated more interest for the reading public and the press. Without their presence, however, it appears that copies were still available for sale eight months after *Frankenstein* was published, a far cry from Byron's *Corsair* selling 10,000 copies in one day in 1814. Nevertheless, on 30 August 1818, Thomas Love Peacock from England claimed in a letter to Percy Shelley in Italy that *Frankenstein* 'seems to be universally known and read'.[23]

Godwin on 18 February 1823 similarly wrote to Mary Shelley that *Frankenstein* 'is universally known, and . . . everywhere respected', by which time a French translation had been published in Paris. And 1823 marked the first adaptation of *Frankenstein* with the 28 July opening of Richard Brinsley Peake's *Presumption; or, The Fate of Frankenstein* at the Lyceum Theatre. Godwin, sensing a commercial opportunity here, wrote to Mary Shelley on 29 July indicating that he would have 500 copies of *Frankenstein* published. Two weeks later, on 11 August, 'A New Edition' of the novel was published in two volumes by G. and W. B. Whittaker, with 'Mary Wollstonecraft Shelley' acknowledged for the first time as the author on the title page of her novel.[24] By 11 August, Mary Shelley had also been celebrated in at least two theatrical reviews of *Presumption* as the author of *Frankenstein* (written 'about five years ago from the pen of the then celebrated Miss Godwin, and since not less celebrated Mrs. Shelley'[25]). Mary Shelley herself wrote to Leigh Hunt on 9 September about having seen Peake's play (with T. P. Cooke playing '– – – –' or the unnamed monster) on Friday evening, 29 August: 'lo & behold! I found myself famous! Frankenstein had prodigious success as a drama & was about to be repeated for the 23rd night at the English opera house'.[26] Although the readers of the total 1,000 copies of the 1818 and 1823 editions (many sold to circulating libraries) accounted in part for Mary Shelley's growing reputation, her fame was also increased by the more than dozen other theatrical productions of *Frankenstein* acted between 1823 and 1826.[27]

Also in 1826, a 'puff' in the *Morning Post* for 7 January announced Henry Colburn's heavily advertised and forthcoming publication of *The Last Man* 'by the Author of that singularly bold and original work "Frankenstein"'; and it appears that in conjunction with this new novel Colburn by 4 April 1826 purchased and sold some of the unsold stock of Whittaker's 1823 edition, although without printing a new title page.[28] In each of the next five years, the newspapers increasingly referred to *Frankenstein* – and by 1831 there were frequent references to 'Frankenstein' as a racehorse, a brown colt sired by 'Manfred' (named after Byron's dramatic hero) out of General Mina's dam ('Mina', incidentally, the name later used for the heroine of *Dracula* (1897)); as a metaphor for political miscreation (unions were sometimes called Frankensteins); and as a frequently acted drama (Cooke was still performing the monster's part in *Presumption*) – and after 3 September 1831 the press somewhere in England almost daily announced the forthcoming third or revised edition of *Frankenstein* that would become No. IX of Bentley and Colburn's Standard Novels containing 'Mrs. Shelley's celebrated Romance'.

This 'revised, corrected, and illustrated [two engravings]' edition of *Frankenstein* (with a new Introduction) was published on 31 October 1831 in a one-volume small 8vo by Henry Colburn and Richard Bentley (and by Bell and Bradfute in Edinburgh; and by Cumming in Dublin) in 4,020 stereotyped copies, each 'neatly bound' and priced at 6s. The novel sold well in this format at less than half the price of a copy of the 1818 or 1823 editions, more than tripling the number of copies before the reading public within less than a year. As early as 24 November 1831, a Literary Notice in the *Bath Chronicle and Weekly Gazette* nicely summed up Mary Shelley's new won fame: '*Frankenstein* is too well known (or rather too well *talked about*) to need any remark of ours'.[29] According to the 'Estimate of Profit & Loss on Standard Novels to 31stAugst 1832', of the printed 4,020 copies, 107 copies had been given gratis (to booksellers, to reviewers and to Mary Shelley), 3,170 had been sold, 743 had not been sold (520 were still in quires and 223 were bound ready for sale).[30] The novel continued to sell at least modestly, for the stereotyped 1831 edition was reprinted with a new title page in 1832 – and, again, in 1836, 1839 and 1849.

Many of the Literary Notices on the 1831 edition mentioned or quoted in full or in part Mary Shelley's new Introduction, which was actually 'pre-published' in Colburn's *Court Journal* for 22 October 1831 (p. 724). In addition to explaining the origin of her novel in 1816, Mary Shelley explained the differences between the 1818 and 1831 editions:

> I will add but one word as to the alterations I have made. They are principally those of style. I have changed no portion of the story nor introduced any new ideas or circumstances. I have mended the language where it was so bald as to interfere with the interest of the narrative; and these changes occur almost exclusively in the beginning of the first volume. Throughout they are entirely confined to such parts as are mere adjuncts to the story, leaving the core and substance of it untouched. (p. 197)

Mary Shelley is correct in her statements, but they do not adequately represent some important changes: Elizabeth's transformation from a cousin to a foundling having no blood relation to Victor; alterations in the names and circumstances of other characters; a new chapter to accommodate a much longer exposition about Victor's childhood; and a more explicit and earlier introduction of the doppelgänger theme in Victor's allusion to Aristophanes' myth of the circular and then divided primal human beings in Plato's *Symposium*:

"I agree with you [Walton]," replied the stranger [Victor]; "we are unfashioned creatures, but half made up, if one wiser, better, dearer than ourselves – such a friend ought to be – do not lend his aid to perfectionate our weak and faulty natures. I once had a friend [Clerval], the most noble of human creatures, and am entitled, therefore, to judge respecting friendship." (pp. 202–3)[31]

As the stemma of *Frankenstein* reveals, Mary Shelley, like her protagonist Victor, made changes to her own creation as she revised her novel (adding and deleting parts) between 1816 and 1831. But she finally had to let go: on 31 October 1831 she 'bid [her] hideous progeny go forth and prosper' on its own (Introduction to the 1831 edition, p. 197). Given the numerous and different stagings of her novel since 1823, she certainly anticipated future theatrical adaptations of her novel; but she certainly could not have anticipated the various critical debates privileging one *Frankenstein* text over another in the last 50 years.[32] And she certainly did not guess at the more than 100 'moving pictures' of the twentieth and twenty-first centuries that have made the name 'Frankenstein' universally known.

Rather than conclude this chapter with a catalogue of the most famous 'Frankenstein' film adaptations and argue whether James Whale's 1931 *Frankenstein* or his 1935 *Bride of Frankenstein* was superior, I choose to bring out of the shadows an electrifying movie not often listed in a genealogy of *Frankenstein*, namely James Cameron's homage to the novel in *Terminator 2: Judgment Day* (1991). In that movie:

> Arnold Schwarzenegger comes back from the future, destroys a computer chip, and conveniently saves Los Angeles and the world from thermonuclear destruction that had occurred on 29 August, 1997, the day before Mary Shelley's two hundredth birthday – so that we could celebrate her bicentennial without holding her responsible for starting the scientific revolution that eventually led to the computer chip that led to the microprocessor that led to Skynet that led to the destruction of billions of lives.[33]

Mary Shelley would have been pleased by Cameron's tribute to her legacy that allows generations after 1997 to continue reading *Frankenstein*.

NOTES

1 Mary Shelley, *Frankenstein*, ed. and Intro. Marilyn Butler (Oxford University Press, 1998), p. 195. Future references will be made parenthetically.
2 See '*Frankenstein* Chronology' in Charles E. Robinson, *The Frankenstein Notebooks: A Facsimile Edition of Mary Shelley's Manuscript Novel, 1816–17 (with alterations in the hand of Percy Bysshe Shelley) as it survives in Draft and Fair Copy deposited by Lord Abinger in the Bodleian Library, Oxford (Dep. c. 477/1 and Dep. c. 534/1–2)*, 2 vols. (New York: Garland Publishing, Inc.,

1996), pp. lxxvi–cx. This 'Chronology' is also available on The Shelley-Godwin Archive website at: http://shelleygodwinarchive.org/contents/frankenstein, last accessed 12 April 2016.

3 See *The Journals of Mary Shelley: 1814–1844*, ed. Paula R. Feldman and Diana Scott-Kilvert, 2 vols. (Oxford: At the Clarendon Press, 1987), Vol. I, p. 245.

4 That is, *Frankenstein or The Modern Prometheus: The 1818 Text (with Variant Readings, an Introduction, and Notes)*, ed. James Rieger (The University of Chicago Press (Phoenix Edition), 1982).

5 Most of these are listed in E. B. Murray, 'Changes in the 1823 Edition of *Frankenstein*', *The Library*, 6th Series, 3 (1981), 320–7.

6 For a convenient representation (in italics) of Percy Shelley's words in Draft, see the first text of the novel in *Frankenstein; or, The Modern Prometheus: The Original Two-Volume Novel of 1816–1817 from the Bodleian Library Manuscripts, by Mary Wollstonecraft Shelley (with Percy Bysshe Shelley)* ed. Charles E. Robinson (Oxford: Bodleian Library, 2008; reprint: New York: Vintage Books, 2009) – hereafter cited by the cover title, *The Original Frankenstein*; for his words added at the end of the Fair Copy and his additions to the proofs of the novel, see Robinson, *Frankenstein Notebooks* and discussions later in this chapter.

7 For an outline of the chapter restructuring that slowed the reading experience (the shorter 33 chapters of the Draft read more quickly than the longer 23 chapters of the Fair Copy and the 1818 first edition) and also altered the reading experience (sometimes two chapters were combined into one; at other times, chapters were divided down the middle), see Robinson, *The Original Frankenstein*, p. 30.

8 For parallel texts providing a visual collation of Mary Shelley's Draft and Percy Shelley's Fair Copy of the concluding section of the novel, see *Frankenstein Notebooks*, pp. 810–17.

9 Feldman and Scott-Kilvert, *Journals of Mary Shelley*, Vol. I, p. 171.

10 Adviser to John Murray and editor of the conservative *Quarterly Review*, in which John Wilson Croker reviewed *Frankenstein* in 1818 as 'a tissue of horrible and disgusting absurdity' (18 [January 1818]): 379–85), the January issue not published until 12 June.

11 *The Letters of Mary Wollstonecraft Shelley*, ed. Betty T. Bennett, 3 vols. (Baltimore, MD: Johns Hopkins University Press, 1980–1988), Vol. I, p. 36.

12 Feldman and Scott-Kilvert, *Journals of Mary Shelley*, Vol. I, p. 174.

13 Percy Bysshe Shelley, *The Letters of Percy Bysshe Shelley*, ed. Frederick L. Jones, 2 vols. (Oxford: Clarendon Press, 1964), Vol. I, p. 549.

14 Bennett, *Letters of Mary Wollstonecraft Shelley*, Vol. I, p. 40.

15 Jones, *Letters of Percy Bysshe Shelley*, Vol. I, p. 552.

16 Feldman and Scott-Kilvert, *Journals of Mary Shelley*, Vol. I, p. 178.

17 Jones, *The Letters of Percy Bysshe Shelley*, Vol. I, p. 553.

18 Feldman and Scott-Kilvert, *Journals of Mary Shelley*, Vol. I, p. 180.

19 For Percy Shelley adding to the proofs and for his letter to Lackington, see the entry for 24 September 1817 in '*Frankenstein* Chronology'.

20 See *The Athenæum*, 10 November 1832, p. 730. For the scholarly edition of this review, see *The Prose Works of Percy Bysshe Shelley*, ed. E. B. Murray (Oxford: Clarendon Press, 1993), Vol. I, pp. 282–4, 489–92, 533, 565. For evidence and dates of the events in this paragraph, see '*Frankenstein* Chronology'.

21 For a breakdown of the expenses charged against the publisher's income, see the entry for 1 January 1818 in 'Frankenstein Chronology'.

22 For information on each of these reviews, see 'Frankenstein Chronology', pp. xciv–xcv, ci, civ–cv; for a text of these reviews, see Romantic Circles at www.rc.umd.edu/reference/chronologies/mschronology/reviews.html, last accessed 12 April 2016.

23 The Letters of Thomas Love Peacock, ed. Nicholas A. Joukovsky, 2 vols. (Oxford: Clarendon Press, 2001), Vol. I, p. 147.

24 Whittaker had recently published Mary Shelley's Valperga (February 1823), with her authorship designated 'By the Author of "Frankenstein"' on that title page, the designation on all of her subsequent novels. Although the text of the 1823 second edition was set directly from the 1818 first edition, Godwin (and possibly also the printers) made 123 substantive changes to the text of the first edition, the changes made either in the copy text or in proofs. Moreover, for an unknown reason, the 1823 second edition did not include on the title page the three-line epigraph from Milton's Paradise Lost ('Did I request thee, Maker, from my clay / To mould me man? Did I solicit thee / From darkness to promote me?').

25 From a review of Peake's Presumption in The Public Ledger, and Daily Advertiser, 29 July 1823, p. 3, col. 3; in the other theatrical review, 'It would... be presumption in us to suppose that our Readers are not acquainted with... "Frankenstein," written by Mrs. Byshe [sic] Shelley' (Bell's Life in London, and Sporting Chronicle, 3 August 1823, p. 597).

26 Bennett, Letters of Mary Wollstonecraft Shelley, Vol. I, p. 378.

27 See Steven Earl Forry (ed.), Hideous Progenies: Dramatizations of Frankenstein from Mary Shelley to the Present (Philadelphia, PA: University of Pennsylvania Press, 1990); and his earlier 'Dramatizations of Frankenstein, 1821–1986: A Comprehensive List', English Language Notes, 25(2) (December 1987) 63–79 – accessible at http://knarf.english.upenn.edu/Articles/forry2.html, last accessed 12 April 2016.

28 Morning Post, 7 January 1826, p. 3, col. 4. For evidence of this 1826 'edition', see 'Frankenstein Chronology' for 4 April 1826.

29 24 November 1831, Bath Chronicle and Weekly Gazette, p. 4, col. 1.

30 For this information, see handwritten Colburn list in Bentley Archives, University of Illinois Library (reel #10 in the Chadwyck-Healey microfilms of the Archives of Richard Bentley & Son).

31 For the most comprehensive collation that shows the differences between the 1818 first edition on the one hand and the 1823 and 1831 editions on the other, see Nora Crook (ed.), 'Endnotes: Textual Variants', Frankenstein or The Modern Prometheus in The Novels and Selected Works of Mary Shelley, 8 vols. (London: William Pickering, 1996), Vol. I, pp. 182–227. Crook also collates the first edition with Mary Shelley's manuscript changes in the so-called 'Thomas' copy of the first edition that is listed in the stemma at the beginning of this essay.

32 For an important essay on this matter, see Nora Crook, 'In Defence of the 1831 Frankenstein', the lead essay in Michael Eberle-Sinatra (ed.), Mary Shelley's Fictions: From Frankenstein to Falkner (London: Macmillan Press, 2000), pp. 3–21.

33 I quote from the introductory remarks to my detailed '*Frankenstein* Filmography' of 21 movies to be found in *Frankenstein or The Modern Prometheus [by] Mary Shelley*, Penguin Horror Edition (series ed. Guillermo del Toro). Appendices, Chronology, Filmography and Suggested Further Reading by Charles E. Robinson (New York: Penguin Books, 2013), pp. 307–30. For other lists of *Frankenstein* films, see http://knarf.english.upenn.edu/Pop/filmlist.html, last accessed 12 April 2016, and Glut.

2

LISA VARGO

Contextualizing Sources

A point of departure for a consideration of *Frankenstein*'s many sources is offered by Theodore von Holst's frontispiece to the 1831 Standard Authors Edition, which depicts the moment Victor rejects his creation and runs from his solitary chamber (see Figure 2.1). This image conveys the importance of how texts create contexts – not only with respect to the work's rich texture of sources, but for an accompanying theme that reading contextualizes how we understand the world. There is a bookcase full of volumes against one wall, and next to the creature lies the lab manual Victor leaves behind, and through which the creature later discovers his origins. Like the creature, who is the product of gathered materials, the novel itself is a palimpsest of Mary Shelley's own reading, though one can argue it is a happier assemblage than what Victor Frankenstein creates. This chapter explores many of the pre-Romantic sources that are drawn upon in *Frankenstein*, with some brief discussion of the Romantic context.

More than simply mimicking the production of the creature, the assemblage of textual sources employed by Mary Shelley provides a testament to the importance of reading, a key aspect of a programme of personal and social improvement she shared with her father William Godwin and practised throughout her life. By the time that she composed *Frankenstein*, Mary Shelley was, at 19, extremely well read, having had access to her father's library and having learnt to read before the age of 4.[1] She adopts her father's prescription in his *Enquiry Concerning Political Justice* (1793):

> It follows, that the promoting the best interests of mankind, eminently depends upon the freedom of social communication. Let us figure to ourselves a number of individuals, who, having first stored their minds with reading and reflection, are accustomed, in candid and unreserved conversation, to compare their ideas, suggest their doubts, examine their mutual difficulties, and cultivate a perspicuous and animated manner of delivering their sentiments. Let us suppose, that their intercourse is not confined to the society of each other, but they are desirous extensively to communicate the truths with which they are

Figure 2.1 Theodore von Holst, frontispiece 1831 Standard Authors Edition of *Frankenstein*.

acquainted. Let us suppose their illustrations to be not more distinguished by impartiality and demonstrative clearness, than by mildness of their temper, and a spirit of comprehensive benevolence. We shall then have an idea of knowledge as perpetually gaining ground, unaccompanied with peril in the means of its diffusion.[2]

Her dedication of the novel to the author of *Political Justice* and *Caleb Williams* (1794) suggests that in its most ideal form, reading is for Mary Shelley a communal activity, and reminds us that our own engagements with reading, such as in classes and book clubs, are models of sociability that are deeply important.

The list of the Shelleys' reading that Paula Feldman offers in her edition of Mary Shelley's journals (included in the *Romantic Circles* electronic edition of *Frankenstein*) is an invaluable help to verifying sources. While it is by no means comprehensive, it gives an excellent idea of the scope of her reading.[3] The novel too provides a working list of Mary Shelley's reading up to the age of 19, along with the sense that reading involves a sense of dialogue with individuals and with one's society. Nora Crook defines three patterns of reading documented in Mary Shelley's journals: reading silently, reading aloud (often while Mary was sewing and Percy Shelley doing the reading), and sewing and reading together.[4] When she returned to England in 1823 following the death of Percy Shelley, Mary was anxious about how she would support herself and her young son. Her father offered a comforting view in a letter: 'most fortunately you have pursued a course of reading, and cultivated your mind, in a manner the most admirably adapted to make you a great and successful author. If you cannot be independent, who should be?'[5] Independence as it relates to the pursuit of reading is a touchstone in the novel, suggesting how difficult and problematic independence can be and how it must be tempered with conversation. This has a bearing on the discussion of reading in the novel. While early on in the novel she depicts a moment of harmony when Victor, Elizabeth and Clerval read their separate books in a communal manner, the novel's three major characters misread in isolation with tragic consequences. Two sets of contexts will be explored in this chapter.

Walton and Frankenstein: Prometheus, *Rime of the Ancient Mariner*, Polar Print Culture, the Alchemists, Galvani, Darwin and Davy

The very contexts of a work subtitled 'The Modern Prometheus' date from Mary Shelley's childhood. Her father and his second wife established a publishing house, the Juvenile Library, producing books for children. A 9-year-old Mary Shelley would have read (or have had read to her) her father's account of the story of Prometheus in his volume *The Pantheon: or Ancient History of the Gods of Greece and Rome. Intended to Facilitate the Understanding of the Classical Authors, and of the Poets in General* (1806).[6] During 1816 both Percy Shelley and Byron were also fascinated by the story of Prometheus; Byron published his lyric on the Titan in 1816, and

Percy read Aeschylus' *Prometheus Bound* in 1817. A related context of a forbidden act that leads to punishment is found in Coleridge. If the story is true that when she was a child Mary Shelley hid behind a sofa to hear her father's friend recite *Rime of the Ancient Mariner* (1798), then the ballad offers another of the earliest sources for her novel.[7] Allusion to the *Rime* occurs in Robert Walton's letters to his sister Margaret Saville (the frame to the novel) where he suggests that although he is going 'to the land of mist and snow', he will kill no albatross, a reference that is expanded in the 1831 edition and includes a note identifying the quotation as being from Coleridge.[8]

A link between the situations of Walton and Frankenstein is established when Victor quotes lines 446–51 from the poem as he wanders through Ingolstadt following his creation of the being (p. 41). And later he views the prospect of marrying Elizabeth as impossible when he has the creature's request for a mate, a 'deadly weight yet hanging round my neck and bowing me to the ground' (p. 126). These references are extended in their significance through shared themes of the violation of nature, isolation and suffering, frame narratives with multiple tellers, as well as Gothic elements, while both works share an intertext with Milton's *Paradise Lost* (1674). These connections might lead one in many directions, but a clue is provided by Mary Shelley's 1831 addition to Walton's attribution of his 'passionate enthusiasm for, the dangerous mysteries of the ocean, to that production of the most imaginative of modern poets' (p. 201). Mary Shelley is validating poetry's power to inspire, and this particular poem's ability to do so, but at the same time creates characters unable to comprehend what the poem might teach them. Walton rejects the idea that he will be an Ancient Mariner figure, but he does become a Wedding Guest to Victor's telling of his tale. Yet he does not recognize his potential to gain a different sort of discovery than polar exploration. Victor seems to believe that if he fulfils his promise to the creature he can marry Elizabeth and free himself of the weight around his neck, but his identification with the Mariner suggests that this is impossible. In avoiding being a Mariner, Walton may save his crew but he fails in his quest, and yet his own familial ties might also be seen as a kind of albatross that pulls against ambition, reflected in Victor's ambivalent final words to Walton that others might succeed where he has failed. Both men act through their reading of the poem, but seem to fall short of comprehending its full imaginative power.

The allusion to the 'land of mist and snow' evokes the novel's frame setting in the Arctic. It has been a standard critical assumption that the polar setting serves as a transplanted version of the Alps and shorthand to convey the sublime. More recently questions have been raised about the extent to which Mary Shelley might disapprove of Walton's project as a form of masculinist imperialism.[9] It is important to recognize that the frame was an addition to the first draft of the work. Charles E. Robinson's study of the composition of the novel suggests that the frame dates from the autumn of 1816.[10] This timing is significant and connects the novel to a contemporary conversation of national import: discussion of a body of writings termed 'polar print culture', a public debate largely controlled by Byron's publisher John Murray.[11] The composition of the novel dates from a period of 'Arctic Fever', during which Shelley would have read John Barrow's 'On the Polar Ice and Northern Passage into the Pacific' and other articles in Murray's *Quarterly Review*, which generated national interest in polar exploration and played a role in the expeditions of John Franklin to Canada in search of the North-West Passage. It is ironic that Murray declined to publish Mary Shelley's novel when it was submitted to him, given how connected it is with his publishing interests. Mary Shelley's contemporaries certainly recognized her use of these sources. When the novel came under attack by John Wilson Croker in *The Quarterly Review* the 'absurdity' of its plot is connected with polar print culture:

> The monster, finding himself hard pressed, resolves to fly to the most inaccessible point of the earth; and, as our Review had not yet enlightened mankind on the real state of the North Pole, he directs his course thither as a sure place of solitude and security; but Frankenstein, who probably had read Mr. Daines Barrington and Colonel Beaufoy on the subject, was not discouraged, and follows him with redoubled vigour, the monster flying on a sledge drawn by dogs, according to the Colonel's proposition.[12]

At the same time Walter Scott referenced John Ross and William Edward Parry's 1818 voyage in his review for *Blackwood's Edinburgh Magazine*, suggesting they might clear up the question of the creature's disappearance at the end of the novel.[13] While neither Croker nor Scott is in sympathy with the novel, they connect Mary Shelley with other writings about polar exploration. And this might offer some clues about Mary Shelley's perspective. The writings by Barrow and others that spurred public interest were accounts of failed attempts.[14] One source that is suggestive of a mixed perspective leads once again to Coleridge. Among the collection of books left behind in their house in Marlow was a copy of Coleridge and Robert Southey's *Omniana* (1812), whose entry titled 'Labrador' (written by Southey) has clear echoes in *Frankenstein*.[15] Descriptions of the cracking of ice as a result of a ground-swell of sea, which Mary Shelley calls a 'ground sea' and a description of Eskimo dog sleds are echoed in Mary's. The account of survival and deliverance, taken from a Moravian missionary text, is noted by Southey as containing 'some of the most impressive description I ever remember to have read'.[16] Polar print culture in the early nineteenth century was noted for its debates, sense of the unknown and a confidence that present failures might lead to discovery. Her reviewers' identification of her novel with this body of writing suggests that her perspective contains positives rather than being merely critical.

With respect to their own use of reading, parallels can be drawn between the way Walton reads unnamed narratives of the polar regions as a Hyperborean paradise and Victor's own reading of the alchemists, which form the catalysts for their actions. Walton observes to his sister:

> I have read with ardour the accounts of the various voyages which have been made in the prospect of arriving at the North Pacific Ocean through the seas which surround the pole. You may remember, that a history of all the voyages made for purposes of discovery composed the whole of our good uncle Thomas's library. My education was neglected, yet I was passionately fond of reading. These volumes were my study day and night, and my familiarity with them increased that regret which I had felt, as a child, on learning that my father's dying injunction had forbidden my uncle to allow me to embark in a sea-faring life. (p. 6)

A neglected and selective education is shared by Frankenstein. One of the main sources for Victor's own inspiration is reading the works of the alchemist Cornelius Agrippa. His father tells him that the book is 'sad trash', but in leaving it at that he only makes his son more eager to read that trash, which is balanced with his reflection that if his father had corrected him then he might not have pursued creating life (p. 23). The mention of Agrippa alludes to books Percy Shelley admired as an adolescent. There is nothing intrinsically wrong with reading alchemists or old travel narratives; like reading poetry, they can be positives that inspire the imagination.[17] But both men read without connection with others and the ability to gain correction through conversation.

Shelley's own inspiration, which came to her in a dream, was suggested through conversation concerning contemporary scientific contexts like Luigi Galvani, Erasmus Darwin and Sir Humphry Davy. These sources are alluded to in her 1831 Preface to *Frankenstein*:

> Many and long were the conversations between Lord Byron and Shelley, to which I was a devout but nearly silent listener. During one of these, various philosophical doctrines were discussed, and among others the nature of the principle of life, and whether there was any probability of its ever being discovered and communicated. (p. 195)

Her experience may be contrasted with the solitary situations she creates for her characters. When Walton writes to his sister, 'I have no friend', one might think of Wordsworth's address of his sister Dorothy as a friend at the end of 'Tintern Abbey' (1798; a poem quoted by Victor to describe his friend Clerval in *Frankenstein* (p. 130)) as well as Coleridge's journal *The Friend*, which the Shelleys read between 1814 and 1816.[18] 'Friend' speaks to a sense of mutuality and connection that needs correct and supplementary reading.

Accordingly, juxtaposed with the works that inspire Walton and Victor, Mary Shelley was conversant, at least in general terms, with contemporary perspectives on chemistry and natural science. She seems to have familiarity with the writings of Erasmus Darwin and in 1816 she read what she called the 'The Introduction to Davy's Chemistry' (Davy was a friend of Godwin). Yet these contexts mix the scientific with more imaginative contexts, including Godwin's novel of guilt and pursuit *Caleb Williams*, and *St. Leon* (1799) whose protagonist suffers the consequences of receiving the 'Philosopher's Stone', the elixir of life.[19] If Godwin's novels parallel the plot and psychological aspects of her tale, reference to optimism about the possibilities of scientific discovery offers a sense of credibility that what Victor has achieved might indeed be possible, in the manner that her use of partial dates suggests the tale is a true one. An interplay of quotations from Darwin and Davy is woven into the discussions Frankenstein has with M. Krempe and M. Waldman at Ingolstadt before he isolates himself in his 'workshop of filthy creation'.[20] Of particular significance is reference to the optimism voiced by Davy and his references to galvanism, which Shelley hints at in her 1831 Preface as the spark that animates the creature. Davy's confidence in the power of science is echoed in the speeches of M. Waldman and by Victor, where Mary Shelley focuses on the irony that Victor is successful but that a necessary sense of connection to 'the public mind' and new investigations is lacking.

Contexts for the Creature: Volney, Plutarch, *Werter* and *Paradise Lost*

The novel's most notable reader is the creature. In his isolated position he learns about the world through reading. He gains language and literacy by eavesdropping on the De Lacey family, whose cottage has an attached shed in which the creature has taken refuge. Felix, the son, is teaching his Turkish fiancée Safie to read and speak French, and the creature takes benefit of these lessons by looking through a chink in the wall and hearing Felix read Volney's *Ruins of Empire* (1791), a favourite work of Percy Shelley who drew upon the work for his philosophical poem *Queen Mab* (1813) and his retelling of the French Revolution in *The Revolt of Islam* (1818).

Volney offers a critique of all theological and political ideologies, suggesting that equality is the proper 'origin of all justice and all right'. While the work seems a curious choice for Safie (Felix suggests it is chosen for its style being similar to eastern authors), it offers a view of history that leads the creature to wonder how man can be 'at once so powerful, so virtuous, and magnificent, yet so vicious and base' (p. 95). A consideration of how the creature is constructed from human ruins writes ruin into his destiny; he lacks equality or the ability to connect with others given his unique and solitary state.[21] His experience of Volney's work raises a desire for the virtue and happiness he is denied. It is significant that it is the one work that the creature witnesses in conversation, and in hearing the work read aloud, the De Lacey's family circle becomes an ideal that is balanced against Volney's account of the inevitable ruins of empires through folly and ambition. The creature's description of his earliest memories echoes Volney's 'Found naked in body and in mind, man at first found himself . . . an orphan, abandoned by the unknown power which had produced him' (p. 253). The creature cannot escape this parallel, and when he is rejected by the De Laceys he unites Milton and Volney to describe himself as an 'arch fiend' who 'bore a hell within me' and 'enjoyed the ruin' (p. 111). He burns down the cottage and the repetition of the word 'ruin' suggests how Volney's thought is repeated in the progress of his downfall during his meeting with Victor, whom he threatens as the author of his 'own speedy ruin' (p. 79). The dying Victor is described by Walton as 'godlike in ruin' (p. 179) and Walton reproaches the creature for lamenting the ruins he has caused (p. 188). But ruin is the inevitable result of his building out of the ruins of decayed bodies. His career echoes Volney's title in the destructive course he comes to adopt and his reading of Volney parallels Victor and Walton's partial understanding of *Rime of the Ancient Mariner*.

Volney provides but one example of how through reading the creature interprets his origins and creates his aspirations. One night, while collecting wood and food, he finds a leather portmanteau containing clothing and three books: John Milton's epic poem about the fall of man, *Paradise Lost*, Plutarch's *Parallel Lives* (c. 120), and a key work of sentimentality and thwarted love, Goethe's novel *The Sorrows of Young Werther* (1774). The books offer the isolated and untaught creature mental enlightenment and nourishment, or as he terms it, belong to 'the progress of my intellect'. Reading *Paradise Lost*, *Plutarch's Lives* and the *Sorrows of Werther*, he suggests, 'gave me extreme delight; I now continually studied and exercised my mind upon these histories' and he offers some deeply felt reader response: 'I can hardly describe to you the effect of these books. They produced in me an infinity of new images and feelings that sometimes raised me to ecstasy, but more frequently sunk me into the lowest dejection' (p. 103). In Goethe's novel he finds 'a never-ending source of speculation and astonishment' for the 'gentle and domestic manners it described' and sorrow over the suicide of its hero. *Plutarch's Lives* 'taught me high thoughts; he elevated me above the wretched sphere of my own reflections to admire and love the heroes of past ages' (p. 104), while Milton's epic poem *Paradise Lost* offers a meditation on his own situation as he wonders if he is Adam or the fallen angel and later demands that his creator make him an Eve. These texts offer a kind of short course in the history of Western civilization, ranging from the politics of classical heroism, to the theology of Christianity, to the virtues of feeling and the domestic of eighteenth-century sensibility.

With this curriculum the creature's experiences are tested against what he reads. He embodies the importance of reading in shaping our experience of the world as well as offering a means to help us imagine what we might have the world be even as he is the most isolated and therefore most misguided reader. The creature does not seem able to separate fiction from reality. He calls the works he reads 'histories', as he does the life of the De Lacey family (pp. 97, 103, 104). Here William Godwin's thoughts on the difference between history and romance are useful. While Godwin suggests that 'Romance, then, strictly considered, may be pronounced to be one of the species of history', their difference is that romance can generalize and combine events to create what is best for an author to 'improve the faculties of his reader' and it is necessary to discriminate between the two genres.[22] The creature's conflation of the two leads to his confusion, but more importantly his own matter of species leads him to misread, as the works he reads are not applicable to his own situation. He suggests to Frankenstein:

> 'As I read, however, I applied much personally to my own feelings and condition. I found myself similar, yet at the same time strangely unlike the beings concerning whom I read, and to whose conversation I was a listener. I sympathized with, and partly understood them, but I was unformed in mind; I was dependent on none and related to none. "The path of my departure was free"; and there was none to lament my annihilation. My person was hideous and my stature gigantic: what did this mean? Who was I? What was I? Whence did I come? What was my destination? These questions continually recurred, but I was unable to solve them.'
> (pp. 103–4)[23]

The texts he reads reflect the irony about his own situation, and suggest his tragic monstrousness. In this respect he ends up misreading, but has no one to correct his misapprehensions. It is only in reading Frankenstein's lab journal that he finds out about his creation and his response is communicated through reference to Milton:

'I sickened as I read. "Hateful day when I received life!" I exclaimed in agony. "Cursed creator! Why did you form a monster so hideous that even you turned from me in disgust? God in pity made man beautiful and alluring, after his own image; but my form is a filthy type of your's, more horrid from its very resemblance. Satan had his companions, fellow-devils, to admire and encourage him; but I am solitary and detested".'   (p. 105)

Not only is the creature denied an Eve, he is also prevented from being corrected when he misreads and misunderstands.

It is worth enquiring how the works speak to Mary Shelley's own experiences as a reader. Mary Shelley's reading list indicates that she read Plutarch in 1815 and that Percy read the work (with or without her) in 1816, 1817 and 1819. Plutarch's republican heroism and its parallel structure of lives that illustrate virtues and vices reinforce the idea of independence with the emphasis that the work places upon the individual. Shelley returned to the *Lives* again and again in her writings, and in so doing she echoes the importance her father placed on the work. She probably first encountered Plutarch in her father's library and Godwin's 'Of History and Romance' (written in 1797) recommends classical writers like Plutarch for their ability to offer lives of individuals to serve as models for readers. Plutarch is certainly a model for Shelley's own writings. She mentions Plutarch as suggesting how 'our souls have a natural inclination to love' in her novel *The Last Man* (1826) and the *Lives* served as a model for her own writing of five volumes of biographies for Lardner's *Cabinet Cyclopedia* (1829–1846).[24] In her final novel *Falkner* (1837), she seems to allude to Plutarch in the description of the heroine Elizabeth Raby who:

> Like all young and ardent minds, which are capable of enthusiasm, she found infinite delight in the pages of ancient history: she read biography, and speedily found models for herself, whereby she measured her own thoughts and conduct, rectifying her defects, and aiming at that honour and generosity which made her heart beat.[25]

Plutarch represents one of the key texts in Mary Shelley's own education by her father.

Although it seems to play little role beyond the creature's immediate response, *The Sorrows of Werther* connects Shelley with her mother Mary Wollstonecraft. It is a logical choice for its status as a key text of sensibility for Romantic readers, and another text that Percy and Mary Shelley read together in 1815. Both works incorporate an epistolary format, but there are deeper personal links with her mother, who died a few days after she was born, and whom Mary could only know through reading her writings and her father's *Memoirs of the Author of the Vindication of the Rights of Woman* (1798) which reads his wife's life through allusions to *Werther*. Accordingly, Wollstonecraft becomes a kind of 'female Werther' whose letters are, Godwin believes, superior to those of Goethe's hero.[26] Werther teaches the creature, like many of its readers, about 'despondency and gloom', but makes clear that while he weeps for its hero without quite understanding his opinions, he does 'not pretend to enter into the merits of the case' (p. 104). This ambivalence might well touch upon Mary Shelley's own private feelings about her mother's mixture of intellect and sensibility and her puzzlement about the balance between her independence as a thinker and her vulnerability and attempted suicide over her failed love affair with Gilbert Imlay. It can be argued that the work is tied up with her very being in that Godwin and Wollstonecraft were reading *Werther* as her mother went into labour.[27] While it is a book she read with Shelley, it is not one she can read with her mother and this reference to *Werther* signifies a private meditation about her mother and the pull of thought and feeling.

How Mary Shelley employs her most important source, *Paradise Lost*, touches on a number of suggestions about the nature of her sustained critique of Milton's epic. The Shelleys read *Paradise Lost* in 1815 and 1816, and for many Romantic writers it was a key text. Of the three books that the creature reads, as has already been suggested, it is *Paradise Lost* that has the most profound effect on how he reads his situation:

> 'Like Adam, I was apparently united by no link to any other being in existence; but his state was far different from mine in every other respect. He had come forth from the hands of God a perfect creature, happy and prosperous, guarded by the especial care of his Creator; he was allowed to converse with, and acquire knowledge from beings of a superior nature: but I was wretched, helpless, and alone. Many times I considered Satan as the fitter emblem of my condition; for often, like him, when I viewed the bliss of my protectors, the bitter gall of envy rose within me.' (p. 105)

Notably a quotation from Book X, 743–5 forms the epigraph to the novel and the mention of 'clay' and 'darkness' joins Milton's epic to the story of Prometheus. Parallels with Milton's work are sustained through the text in its tale of creation and disobedience and fall and unites the creature to Victor as both characters move from innocence to a fall and play varying roles from Creator to Adam to Satan. If the creature measures himself against whether he is Adam or Satan, Victor moves from being a kind of Adam in Eden to God and to a fallen figure.[28]

There are a number of suggestions as to how Mary re-reads *Paradise Lost* and she follows what is seen as the Romantic view of Satan as a flawed rebel against tyranny that Percy Shelley explores in his preface to *Prometheus*

Unbound (1820). Following the interests of her parents and Percy Shelley, reference to Milton suggests a means to create a critique of religion as being responsible for tyranny in contrast to human accountability. Such Romantic readings uncover alternative perspectives to the one offered by Milton. In so doing she follows her father's *Caleb Williams* and Coleridge's *Rime* as well as joining Blake and Shelley as revisionary readers of *Paradise Lost*.[29] Both of her parents found Milton's perspective one with which they were at odds. In his *Political Justice* Godwin reads *Paradise Lost* as a political parable:

> poetical readers have commonly remarked Milton's devil to be a being of considerable virtue. It must be admitted that his energies centred too much in personal regards. But why did he rebel against his maker? It was, as he himself informs us, because he saw no sufficient reason, for that extreme inequality of rank and power, which the creator assumed.[30]

At the same time, the contexts provided by Milton are viewed as central to a feminist critique of patriarchy.[31] In this view Mary Shelley is seen to rewrite *Paradise Lost* to portray female experience as well as a means to convey the frustrations of female experience in the world of patriarchy in an encoded manner. This is demonstrated by the scene in which the creature looks at his reflection in a pool, an allusion to Eve's own introduction to her reflection in *Paradise Lost*, Book IV, 465–8. One further contribution to these contexts is to consider the sustained critique of Milton that Mary Wollstonecraft offers in her *A Vindication of the Rights of Woman* (1792). Wollstonecraft's reading is largely centred on the matter of Eve and her unequal status, which Wollstonecraft refutes. Susan Wolfson reminds us that one particular aspect of this critique is Adam's request for an equal with whom he can have 'fellowship', and instead he receives a companion who is not his equal.[32] There is an echo here in the creature's demand that Victor create a mate in contrast to Victor's own Miltonic assumptions about the female companion. The creature sees the female as an equal while Victor in the end destroys her as he imagines her as potentially disobedient and self-willed. This complicates how one might read the creature's request as he reads like Adam (and for that matter Wollstonecraft), while Victor seems unable to free himself from Milton's perspective.

Further Contexts

Readers will continue to locate and ponder the rich contexts of Shelley's novel. Sources by her contemporaries include Shelley's poems, including 'Mutability' (1816), 'Hymn to Intellectual Beauty' (1817), 'Alastor' (1816), Byron's *Childe Harold's Pilgrimage*, Canto III (1816), and Wordsworth's poetry, as well as other sources including the Bible and Shakespeare's *King Lear* (1605). D. S. Neff suggests Robert Paltock's *The Life and Adventures of Peter Wilkins, a Cornish Man* (1750, 1751), a work admired by Percy and read by both Shelleys in 1815, is likely to have inspired the phrase 'invisible hand', signifying the idea of Providence which is later undermined through the creature's experiences.[33] The romances Clerval reads (p. 21) can be considered for their significance, along with Elizabeth's reading. These sources remind us that literary works are ever in dialogue with one another even as writers seek their own independent views. Near the end of her 1831 Preface Mary Shelley calls her work:

> the offspring of happy days, when death and grief were but words, which found no true echo in my heart. Its several pages speak of many a walk, many a drive, and many a conversation, when I was not alone; and my companion was one who, in this world, I shall never see more. But this is for myself; my readers have nothing to do with these associations.   (p. 197)

However personal the contexts for the work might be, the independence of the reader also has a role to play in *Frankenstein* as Mary Shelley makes her case for the importance of reading and of connecting with others, as the Shelleys, Byron and Polidori did that stormy night in Geneva in 1816.

NOTES

1 Emily Sunstein, *Mary Shelley: Romance and Reality* (Boston, MA: Little Brown, 1989), p. 26.
2 William Godwin, *Enquiry Concerning Political Justice*, 2 vols. (London: Robinson, 1793), Vol. I, p. 214. Hereafter PJ.
3 'The Shelleys' Reading List', *The Journals of Mary Shelley*, ed. Paula R. Feldman and Diana Scott-Kilvert (Baltimore, MD: Johns Hopkins University Press, 1987), pp. 631–84. 'Mary Shelley's Reading List', *Frankenstein: A Romantic Circles Edition*, ed. Stuart Curran www.rc.umd.edu/editions/frankenstein/MShelley/reading, last accessed 12 April 2016.
4 Nora Crook, 'Work in Mary Shelley's Journals', *Keats–Shelley Review*, 18 (2004), 123–37.
5 Mrs Julian Marshall, *The Life and Letters of Mary Wollstonecraft Shelley*, 2 vols. (London: Richard Bentley and Sons, 1889), Vol. I, p. 69.
6 See Pamela Clemit, 'William Godwin's Juvenile Library', *Charles Lamb Bulletin*, 147 (2009), 90–99 and 'Philosophical Anarchism in the Schoolroom: William Godwin's Juvenile Library, 1805–25', *Biblion: The Bulletin of The New York Public Library*, 9.1–2 (2000–2001), 44–70.
7 Chris Baldick, *In Frankenstein's Shadow: Myth, Monstrosity, and Nineteenth-century Writing* (Oxford: Clarendon Press, 1987), p. 39.
8 Mary Shelley, *Frankenstein*, ed. and Intro. Marilyn Butler (Oxford University Press, 1998), p. 10. Future references will be made parenthetically. Added in 1831: 'if I should come back to you as worn and woful as the "Ancient Mariner?"

You will smile at my allusion; but I will disclose a secret. I have often attributed my attachment to, my passionate enthusiasm for, the dangerous mysteries of the ocean, to that production of the most imaginative of modern poets' (p. 201). This deepens the tribute to Coleridge and the sense that his verse inspired her own enthusiasm for writing.

9 See Jessica Richard, '"A Paradise of My Own Creation": *Frankenstein* and the Improbable Romance of Polar Exploration', *Nineteenth-Century Contexts*, 25(4) (2003): 295–314 and Jen Hill, *White Horizon: The Arctic in the Nineteenth-Century Imagination* (Albany, NY: State University Press of New York, 2008).

10 *The Frankenstein Notebooks. A Facsimile Edition*, ed. Charles E. Robinson (New York and London: Garland, 1996), Part One, pp. lx, lxxxv.

11 Adriana Craciun, 'Writing the Disaster: Franklin and *Frankenstein*', *Nineteenth-Century Literature* 65(4) (March 2011), 433–80, 440.

12 John Wilson Croker, *Quarterly Review* 18 (1817–18), 379–85.

13 Walter Scott, 'Remarks on *Frankenstein, or the Modern Prometheus*; a Novel', *Blackwood's Edinburgh Magazine*, 2 (1818), 613–20.

14 See Jessica Richard, 'A Paradise of My Own Creation':

> Drawing on the practice of earlier polar enthusiasts, empiricists for whom the failure of expeditions proved nothing but that further expeditions were necessary, Barrow gained public support for the 1818 voyages by recounting the history of unsuccessful polar exploration as a narrative of progress and promise. (297)

15 Pointed out by Nora Crook in an email.

16 Samuel Taylor Coleridge and Robert Southey, 'Labrador', *Omniana, or Horae Otiosiores* (London: Longman, Hurst, Rees, Green, and Brown, 1812), pp. 164–87.

17 See Irving H. Buchen, '*Frankenstein* and the Alchemy of Creation and Evolution', *The Wordsworth Circle* 8 (1977), 103–12.

18 Charles E. Robinson, 'The Shelley Circle and Coleridge's *The Friend*', *English Language Notes* 8 (1971), 269–74.

19 The definitive study of Godwin's influence is Pamela Clemit's *The Godwinian Novel: The Rational Fictions of Godwin, Brockden Brown, Mary Shelley* (Oxford: Clarendon Press, 1993).

20 Macdonald and Scherf trace this in Mary Wollstonecraft, *The Vindications*, ed. D. L. Macdonald and Kathleen Scherf (Peterborough, Ontario: Broadview Press, 1997).

21 Johanne Lamoureux. '*Frankenstein* et *Les Ruines* de Volney: l'Éducation littéraire de la Créature', *Protée* 35(2) (2007), 65–73.

22 William Godwin, 'Of History and Romance 1797', *Caleb Williams*, ed. Gary Handwerk and A. A. Markley (Peterborough, Ontario: Broadview Press, 2000), p. 464.

23 The quotation is from Percy Shelley's lyric 'Mutability' (line 14).

24 Mary Shelley, *The Last Man*, ed. Jane Blumberg with Nora Crook, *The Novels and Selected Works of Mary Shelley*, ed. Nora Crook with Pamela Clemit, 8 vols. (London: Pickering & Chatto, 1996), Vol. IV, p. 75.

25 Mary Shelley, *Falkner: A Novel*, ed. Pamela Clemit, *The Novels and Selected Works of Mary Shelley*, ed. Nora Crook with Pamela Clemit, 8 vols. (London: Pickering & Chatto, 1996), Vol. VII, p. 39.

26 Roswitha Burwick, 'Goethe's *Werther* and Mary Shelley's *Frankenstein*', *The Wordsworth Circle* 24(1) (1993), 47–52.

27 Noted by Burwick, 48.

28 John B. Lamb, 'Mary Shelley's *Frankenstein* and Milton's Monstrous Myth', *Nineteenth-Century Literature* 47(3) (1992), 303–19.

29 See Lucy Newlyn, *Paradise Lost and the Romantic Reader* (Oxford: Clarendon Press, 1993).

30 Godwin, *Political Justice*, Vol. I, p. 261.

31 Sandra M. Gilbert and Susan Gubar, *The Madwoman in the Attic: The Woman Writer and the Nineteenth-Century Literary Imagination* (New Haven, CT: Yale University Press, 1979), pp. 213–47. They argue that Victor and the creature move from being Adams to Satans and therefore are Eve-like in their disobedience, representing projections of Mary Shelley's own 'fantasies of equality that occasionally erupt in monstrous images of rage' (p. 220).

32 Susan J. Wolfson, 'Mary Wollstonecraft and the Poets', in Claudia L. Johnson (ed.), *The Cambridge Companion to Mary Wollstonecraft* (Cambridge University Press, 2002) pp. 167–77.

33 D. S. Neff. '"Invisible Hands": Paltock, Milton, and the Critique of Providence in *Frankenstein*', *ANQ: A Quarterly Journal of Short Articles, Notes, and Reviews*, 25(2) (2012), 103–8.

3

JERROLD E. HOGLE

Romantic Contexts

As the previous chapter and other accounts have shown, Mary Shelley's original *Frankenstein* 'distilled' an astonishing range of 'European history (intellectual and political)' and controversies about many dimensions of culture from science to education to human rights articulated by 'the poets and the philosophical debates of her day'.[1] In particular, it conflated many visions and figures from the still-developing Romantic movement in literature (then classed under several different labels) across Western Europe. These came both from what we now see as English Romanticism's first generation that began publishing in the 1780s–90s, such as William Wordsworth and Samuel Taylor Coleridge, and from the second generation that included Mary Shelley herself, as well as Lord Byron and Percy Shelley (her husband by 1817, hereafter 'Shelley', while the author of *Frankenstein* is 'Mary', just as she referred to them in her journals and letters). In *Frankenstein*, she further interweaves these voices with the texts left her by her parents, William Godwin, still very much alive in 1818, and Mary Wollstonecraft, dead since 1797 from giving birth to Mary, as a result of which the latter never stopped feeling guilty and was always trying symbolically to recover the buried source of her being. *Frankenstein* thus manifests a facet of Romanticism that has too often been obscured by this movement's emphasis on individual imagination: the proclivity all its writers had, even in single-authored pieces, to dialogue with and incorporate several other voices in a kind of 'multiple authorship'.[2] This was never more apparent than in the gathering at the Villa Diodati near Geneva, Switzerland, during the summer of 1816, when Byron, as host, proposed that everyone present write a ghost story and from which emerged *Frankenstein* and John Polidori's novella *The Vampyre* (1819), as well as major poems by Byron and Shelley published between 1816 and late 1817, in all of which each author echoes all the others.

We are, however, still debating what is symbolized in Mary's now-classic Gothic novel because of its convergence of voices and controversies prior to many of these being suppressed by the adaptations that have oversimplified it since. *Frankenstein* makes Victor, its title character, 'fundamentally a Romantic in his faith in the power of imagination to shape a world in accord with [human] dreams and visions' only to create a monster and bring 'disaster and destruction down upon' himself and those around him. Is *this* Mary's way of exposing 'the tragedy of Romanticism itself' in a Gothic critique of that whole movement, an attack, some say, on Shelley himself (for many the primary model for Victor) as much as on Wordsworth, Coleridge and even earlier voices that Mary saw as speaking through them?[3] Such arguments, in effect, claim that she reworks the Gothic tradition that had descended from Horace Walpole's *The Castle of Otranto: A Gothic Story* (1764–65), but was also disparaged by Wordsworth and Coleridge as a lurid 'mass' of 'low and vulgar taste',[4] in order to expose the 'imaginative self-assertion' of much Romantic discourse as 'antisocial ambition' destructive of 'social relationships'.[5] But I want to argue here that the original *Frankenstein*, while indeed symbolizing several causes of tragedy in the emergence of modernity, is really more collaborative with its Romantic contexts, more a participant in a sort of 'joint authorship', than such views acknowledge. At their most suggestive and, as it happens, Gothic moments – the ones Mary Shelley most alludes to in *Frankenstein*, as I will show in what follows – the Romantic voices among whom she writes expose *their own* underlying contradictions as she channels and reconstitutes them. *Frankenstein*, in other words, by alluding to a wide range of other Romantic works, enables the contexts it recalls both to act their visions out and to intimate the unresolved hesitations between conflicted and conflicting beliefs that underlie those same visions, the tensions between opposites inherent in the assumptions most central to Romanticism that enable its imaginative aspirations and put them in question at the same time.

A case in point is what Mary's novel does with her husband as one (but, I would argue, not the only) model for her title character. Victor's rifling through cemeteries and slaughterhouses to create artificial life alludes to Shelley's 'Alastor; or, the Spirit of Solitude', the central text in a collection of his poems published in February 1816. There we find a Narrator who often echoes the early Wordsworth and who seeks to re-contact the deeply sequestered 'Mother of this unfathomable world' (line 18), like Wordsworth's 'I' in 'Tintern Abbey' (1798) and Mary Shelley seeking to revive or rejoin Mary Wollstonecraft. To reach that daunting goal, this Narrator pores over 'charnels' and 'coffins' in hopes of hearing 'a lone ghost' tell 'the tale' of our origins (lines 24–7), what Shelley himself admitted to doing 'in his youth' before writing his early Gothic novels (*Zastrozzi* and *St. Irvyne*, 1810–11) and why Frankenstein spends 'nights in vaults and charnel houses' to find fragments of death from which he can craft his demonstration of the 'causes of life'.[6] The Narrator of 'Alastor' even furthers his quest by turning to an analogue of himself, a version of the adolescent Shelley who often read ancient and Eastern lore instead of Wordsworth, in a tale-within-the-Narrator's-tale that begins 'There was a Poet' (line 50) reminiscent of the 'There was a boy' which starts the Boy of Winander episode in Wordsworth's *Prelude* (a segment published separately in 1800). This Poet searches world-wide, particularly in 'awful ruins of the days of old' in Africa and the Middle East (line 107), on his way to the 'vale of Cashmire', a large quasi-vagina mythically associated with the oldest human community, to find his own substitute for maternal origins (line 145). There he composes out of such Gothic ingredients a dream-vision of a 'veiled maid' (line 151) who murmurs back the 'Thoughts most dear to him' (line 160) from what is only a 'web' in his 'inmost sense... Of many-coloured woof and shifting hues' (lines 156–7), a miasma that makes her ghost-like visage a precursor of the multi-coloured face ('yellow skin', 'dun white sockets', 'black lips') that Victor beholds when his creation comes to life (p. 39).

In search of some external referent who might ground this spectre, the 'Alastor' Poet then quests upstream towards the primal waters of life *north* of Cashmire ultimately to die in his obsession, forecasting Victor's wasting away in pursuing his creature to the northern ice of Coleridge's *The Rime of the Ancient Mariner* (1798). The Poet thereby confirms the prose Preface to 'Alastor' (written with a voice clearly distinct from the Narrator's) in which his extremity of 'self-centred seclusion', which Shelley is admitting to at least in his younger self, turns out to be rightly 'avenged by the furies of an irresistible passion [the Spirit of Solitude named by the word "Alastor"] pursuing him to a speedy ruin', a spectre that foretells the creature, as the Poet cuts himself off from natural human contact in his quest for the feminine Other of his dreams.[7] If Mary Shelley is alluding to her spouse by making him a model for Victor, she is also bringing forward Shelley's critique of himself – and of Wordsworth and Coleridge intimating their own solipsistic inclinations within their imaginative outpourings of sympathy with nature and other human beings – precisely by channelling the most Gothic moments from 'Alastor' into her novel. To the extent that her Victor Frankenstein and his self-generated Other reflect a problematic imagination, it may really be that of at least *three* Romantic poets and their own fears about the self-centred underpinnings of their poetic calls for transformations of the whole known world by the power of imagination.

The dark undercurrents suggested in *Frankenstein* by way of these allusions, consequently, are actually extensions of the fundamental conflicts that 'Alastor' and the voices it channels have begun to reveal already. Frankenstein's creature as an externalized version of the multi-coloured 'veiled maid' conceived as partly 'Eastern', for instance, is one means by which Mary's novel suggests that white European imaginings of a greater and more unified humanity in the future must confront the multi-racial nature of that possibility and therefore the racist fear of cross-breeding in the belief-systems of Anglo-Europeans. It is this repulsion, among others, that ultimately leads Victor to stop putting together the *female* creature, another created 'maid', because he worries that a 'race of devils' too different might be 'propagated' by his creations and eventually threaten the dominant 'species' (p. 138).[8] In addition, the ways in which Victor's male creature echo the maid in 'Alastor' points, as that poem does, to several other sublimated impulses that drive the Romantic 'creator': (a) 'his desire is for his own envisionings rather than for somebody else'; (b) 'the romantic object of desire' is 'invented to replace' the lost 'mother', especially in the case of Victor, the death of whose mother is so devastating that he cannot face it consciously again, even as he fears reabsorption into her;[9] (c) 'romantic desire' thus 'seeks to do away, not only with the mother' now inadmissible to consciousness, 'but also with all [independent] females so as to live finally in a world of mirrors', such as the imaginary woman of Shelley's Poet whose 'voice is like the voice of his own soul' ('Alastor', line 153); (d) a creator with such a desire, then, 'does not so much appropriate the maternal as bypass it' – as the Poet creates his maid and Victor his creature without a biological woman – leaving 'creation entirely in control of the son'; and (e) what Victor, like the 'Alastor' Poet, is really striving for can only be found where the mother is (as Mary Shelley knew more than most), in the realm of death that finally claims the Poet.[10] Frankenstein's use of dead materials to avoid *any* mother remains a displacement of his true longing for *the* mother, which he cannot admit to consciousness because he recoils with horror at the death-wish of wanting to dissolve back into her. That is his reason for avoiding sex with, and later the creation of, any woman's body.

Hence Victor's dream right after he first sees his finished creature, which has never been duplicated in any adaptation of *Frankenstein* and forcefully echoes the 'Alastor' dream of the veiled maid, while it intensifies the suggestions that accompany that vision. Falling asleep from exhaustion, Victor imagines he sees his fiancée, Elizabeth Lavenza, in the streets of Ingolstadt only to have this spectre turn, as he embraces her, into the ghost of his dead mother. She/it then reveals the 'grave-worms' crawling in its/her 'shroud' (p. 39) before the whole image condenses into what now looms over Victor as he wakes: the face of the creature, openly displaying in its pieces of bodies the very drive towards death in his creator suggested by the shrouded ghostliness of the veiled maid, which Frankenstein has produced without a woman to be (unconsciously) a substitute for the ultimate Feminine level. The creature therefore clearly incarnates all that the dream and the 'Alastor' logic behind it have revealed as the deeper motives for a Romantic self-projection that are only half-hidden inside its process. This moment is indeed an early nineteenth-century suggestion of the longing for the mother and the drive toward death that Sigmund Freud would later find in the unconscious as it manifests itself in dreams, even as the face of the creature it explains adds the *cultural* unconscious of the fear of non-Anglo races underlying Romantic visions of human perfectibility. Yet Frankenstein's dream would not prefigure Freud as it does were it not incipient in Shelley's 'Alastor' and what it carries forward from Wordsworth, Coleridge and the younger Shelley: the haunting of visionary Romanticism by its subliminal inconsistencies, including each psyche's pre-conscious drives towards an erotic re-union with the mother and death.

Frankenstein, meanwhile, also draws its narrative structure from the way Shelley's 'Alastor' is arranged, but only as it modifies that structure by joining it to a different Romantic context, the mostly first-person and highly confessional novels of Mary's parents and the author *they* saw as an earlier model for this type of writing. 'Alastor' is composed of three nested tales: that of the Poet within the Narrator's, that of the Narrator's account of himself, and that of the Preface which frames the other two with a style different from the Narrator's. *Frankenstein* matches that pattern, with the creature's tale to Victor at the book's centre being re-told within Frankenstein's narrative that is itself transcribed in and surrounded by Captain Walton's letters to his sister from the Arctic circle. Yet this concentric scheme has Mary's narrators, clearly doubles of each other in their ego-driven quests for ultimate understanding, admit their misjudgments as well as lament the calumnies thrust upon them, each by speaking as a self-justifying 'I', which the 'Alastor' Poet and Preface do not do. This recurrent stance resembles the one in the life-history told by the oppressed and ostracized 'Jemima', very much a precursor for the tale of *Frankenstein*'s persecuted creature, in Mary Wollstonecraft's *The Wrongs of Woman* (published posthumously by Godwin in 1798) and the guilt-ridden narrator-hero of Godwin's own *Caleb Williams* (1794) as well as his *St. Leon* (1799) and all of his subsequent, equally confessional novels prior to *Frankenstein*. As we consider texts behind texts, moreover, we should recall that Godwin and Wollstonecraft admit their indebtedness for this approach, while also critiquing some of his ideas, to Jean-Jacques Rousseau, by now famous for the example of self-presentation he set, justifying himself while admitting to many sins, in his posthumously published *Confessions* (Part I in 1782, Part II in 1789). Mary Shelley, it turns out, read those very volumes repeatedly between 1815 and 1817 along with its author's fictive educational treatise *Emile* (1762), his epistolary novel

Julie; or the New Eloise (1761) and his *Essay on the Origin of Languages* (1781), among other works, several of them while staying with Shelley and Byron near Geneva, Rousseau's home city as well as the central setting of both *Julie* and *Frankenstein*.[11]

As a result of this chain of texts, some also echoed in the best-known early lyrics of Wordsworth and Coleridge, the confessions of *Frankenstein*'s hero-narrators draw the schemes and tensions in 'Alastor', including its echoes of these poets, back through the self-justifications mixed with self-doubt in the novels of Godwin and Wollstonecraft and then further back to this very tangle of motives in texts by Rousseau. He was the author whom Mary saw to be, as she says in her own later essay about him, the most 'eloquent in paradox', often by his own admission, although she, like many others, equally acknowledged him to be the forefather who most helped create a model of modern individuality further developed in Romantic writing through the innovation of the narrative modes employed by novelists and autobiographers, which helps explain the echoes of him *and* his paradoxes in the three concentric confessions that make up *Frankenstein*.[12]

The paradoxes Mary sees in Rousseau and those he has influenced, therefore, reappear, albeit differently each time, in Walton, the creature and Victor, always as foundational to, while also a threatening undercurrent within, how they behave and articulate themselves. Captain Walton, by confessing that he voyages toward an imagined 'region of beauty and delight' beyond and through the Arctic while leaving his sister far behind and overriding the concerns of his crew (p. 5), recalls, as Victor does too by fleeing from the 'child' he has made, something like the duplicity of a Rousseau who (again, in Mary's later words) can epitomize 'the elevation and intensity of delicate and exalted passion' while also 'neglect[ing] the first duty of man by abandoning' his family, as in the five children Rousseau admits to fobbing off in his *Confessions* even though he also wrote *Emile* about the hands-on education of a young boy.[13] The creature, in his turn, tells his creator the story of his solitary development as he remembers it, from his initial, chaotic understanding of sensations to his eventual learning of language and reading as the De Laceys teach their French version of both to Felix De Lacey's betrothed, Safie (another Eastern maid), while the creature himself eavesdrops unseen just outside their woodland cottage (pp. 92–7). This progression echoes a sequence in Rousseau's *Emile* itself where the reader is asked to 'suppose that a child had at its birth the stature and strength of a grown man'; such a hypothetical being for Rousseau would be unable to 'perceive' distinct 'objects' nor which 'sense organ' perceives which object at first, however big he is, until he/it can begin to formulate an 'I' as the receiver of the sensations and the observer of objects.[14] This last step becomes fully possible, as Rousseau's *Origin of Languages* elaborates, only with 'the institution of sensible signs to express thought', the means by which an 'I' can be established as a subject over against objects of any kind.[15] At the same time, this entire logic is coloured for Mary Shelley by the sharp critique of *Emile* in her mother's *A Vindication of the Rights of Woman* (1792). There, noting that *Emile* proposes a separate and lesser kind of education for the title character's love-object, 'Sophie' (undoubtedly parodied in *Frankenstein*'s 'Safie'), Wollstonecraft points out how much women in Rousseau's eyes 'are at once sentimentalized and viewed, anxiously, as deformed or monstrous' and hence in need of educational restraints on those potentials 'in comparison with an explicitly male norm', even if the prose in *Emile* uses less pejorative words.[16]

In sum, then, the creature occupies the place for Victor of the 'Alastor' Eastern 'maid' echoed also by 'Safie'; Safie echoes Rousseau's 'Sophie' while also being offered a better education than she gets (though Safie is also potentially a 'monstrous' foreign threat who needs acculturation to the West); Sophie (and, by extension, Safie) channels Western civilization's monster-izing of women compared to men (which means the creature, being analogous to Safie, feels consigned to the cultural position of females and foreigners, among other 'lesser' beings); and the resulting 'monster' of *Frankenstein*, with all these associations conflated in him, is exiled from much of the learning provided by the De Laceys, even though he has already laboured for them as an unpaid servant (and thus a slave) while he proves capable of imbibing every word put before Safie herself. The Anglo-European work of visionary art, *Frankenstein* is suggesting, now epitomized by a creature who echoes Rousseau as well as multiple Romantic poets (including their fears about their own dark sides), can appear as a symbol for a greater humanity that may fulfil imaginative longing and yet return to what is most basically human at the same time – Rousseau's famous dream of reviving 'natural man' – *only* if it assumes and yet sequesters (indeed, throws off as monstrous and *not* essentially human) two levels of culture in the development of the fabricated creature: (1) the ongoing divorce of that vision, including the science, industry, exploration and political hopes it encompasses, from the domestic relations of men with friends, women and biological children; and (2) the emergence of such a vision from the ingredients of an education that, by the very definition of it offered by Rousseau, assumes that it should keep education's highest levels distant from women, really young children, non-Anglo-Europeans, the working class, and the enslaved, all of which are suggested by the creature's mixture of incongruous parts from different classes of beings. For Mary Shelley as well as Wollstonecraft, it is not that readers of Rousseau should be forced to see how such an understanding

47

differs from his and from that of those Romantics who have followed in his wake. It is that Rousseau's writings, and later those that have carried them forward, have really been saying as much all along, which can be exposed in a novel written from 1816–18 just by its intensification of the child given the stature of a grown man proposed by Rousseau himself.

It is Victor Frankenstein, however, who replays Rousseau the most, particularly the episode in the *Confessions* for which its author feels most guilty, and that allusion ends up revealing even more inconsistencies at the root of Romantic aspirations. After Victor learns that his little brother, William, has been murdered and inwardly knows that his creature did it as soon as he views that figure looming in the distance near Geneva, he discovers that he both cannot and will not prevent the blame falling on Justine Moritz, William's lower-class *au pair*. She has been found with the locket that had been attached to William's breast, which contains a portrait of his and Victor's dead mother, and been rushed to a conviction because public prejudices about people of her gender and class make her guilt believable. 'A thousand times', Victor laments in his narrative, 'I would have confessed myself guilty of the crime ascribed to Justine; but I was absent when it was committed' – though we already know from Victor's dream that the creature is carrying out his maker's unconscious drives – so Frankenstein decides against *that* confession because 'it would have been considered the ravings of a madman' and instead accepts the perpetual guilt of his silence, part of his confession to Walton, haunting him as much as his creature, the indirect actor of his hidden motivations (p. 61). As others have seen, this sequence recalls Rousseau's memory in his *Confessions* of his theft of a ribbon in a household where he worked at the age of 16, for which he transferred the guilt to the kitchen-maid Marion, on whom, he admits, he had an unrequited crush.[17] Part of his motive, however, may have been his resentment at not receiving a legacy from his recently dead employer because he was not *official* staff like Marion (anticipating the motive of greed ascribed to Justine by the public).

The *Confessions* also claims, as though Rousseau's younger self had higher reasons (like some Victor offers for his creation), that 'she was present in my thoughts, and I threw the blame on the first person who occurred to me', assuming the association of ideas more and more accepted as the mechanism of thought since John Locke's *Essay Concerning Human Understanding* (1690), and 'I said that she had given the ribbon to me because I meant to give it to her', confessing now to a motive based more on love than on envy or greed.[18] This last slippage among adjacent thoughts, as it happens, forecasts the creature's expressed reasons, in his confession to Victor, for placing the locket taken from the strangled William onto Justine: *his* resentment that the 'smiles' of this 'blooming' woman and the maternal face in the locket (Victor's and thus the creature's ultimate object of desire), to which he feels attracted, might be 'bestowed on all but me'. Based on this non-response by others, he transfers the social guilt for the prejudice against all the 'otherness' in the world (including Justine's and his) onto Justine alone – deciding 'she shall not escape' (p. 118) – even while she is both another substitute for the lost mother and a scapegoat for the age-old patriarchal attitude that women ('monstrous' as far back as Eve) are fundamentally to blame for the ills of fallen humanity.

On one level, this transfer of Rousseau's confessed transference to Victor, Justine and the creature reveals deep, pervasive injustices against women and the underclasses, hidden, as *Frankenstein's* Elizabeth is allowed to say, by 'shews and mockeries', such as those that would find Victor 'mad' if he were to speak what he knows, that mask actual inequities and the attitudes behind them (p. 67), ones that have been exposed already by Mary's parents but have become either assumed or de-emphasized by some Romantic writers as far back as Rousseau himself. On a deeper level, though, this allusion to the Marion episode points, by its being repeated with differences in *Frankenstein*, to an unsettling undercurrent inherent in the whole Romantic enterprise, partly inaugurated by Rousseau. This paradox appears within the formation of mental visions through transfers from thoughts to analogous thoughts and from those thoughts to words interacting with other words. The words, in turn (including 'Marion' and 'the ribbon'), can even change some of the earlier thoughts in naming them, with this whole succession usually ending in publically exhibited symbolic creations, like Rousseau's *Confessions*, that propose new visions of the world not all that different from Frankenstein's creature, himself an expression of his author in a combination of different figures (signs even of races and species) transferred towards each other.

What the *Confessions* remembers its 'I' doing with Marion, and hence what Victor does with his creature and the creature does with Justine, after all, is enabled by what Rousseau writes in his *Origin of Languages* when he claims, at the point of language's invention at the time of natural man, that 'the figurative word arises before the proper [or literal] word does' based on the fact that 'words are transposed only because ideas also are'.[19] His example of such a 'Trope' preceding literal meaning, moreover, seems prophetic of what appears in *Frankenstein*: the very first human others encountered by a primal person, Rousseau writes, were called '*Giants*', even though their size was not much greater on closer observation, and that word was later seen as 'metaphorical, when the [more experienced] mind recognized its original error' and changed 'Giant' to '*man*'. Victor,

49

accordingly, can re-define what is human with a Rousseauistic 'primal man' (his creature) only if the latter is a figurative trope, albeit an 'error', where the supposed essence of humanity is manifested by a transference of it into a gigantic combination of dead bodies, and this process is really the same as what permits the creature to transfer his frustrated desire onto Justine and Rousseau to transfer a similar impulse onto Marion. True, an obvious problem here is that a possibly selfish, self-protective, sexist or racist motive can be concealed by a transference that covers it beneath a figure which can keep it hidden. But in taking that possibility back to Rousseau, who has influenced so many other Romantics, *Frankenstein* exposes how much the figurative movement which permits such 'shews and mockeries' is prior to and makes possible all constructions of meaning in thought or language, just as Rousseau says and this novel reveals in instance after instance. Whenever a Romantic construct, such as the creature, is proposed to leap beyond such displacements of meaning, it will turn out to be Gothically haunted by the primal un-truth of the figurative – and what that process can obscure (as in young Rousseau's lie) – which is what allows such fabrications, from poems to confessions to avatars, to be created in the first place.

Still, this taking of *Frankenstein* back to unresolved quandaries in Rousseau was not enough by itself to establish its creature as an alter ego for Victor or for Western society's darkest hidden assumptions. Mary needed the example of a singular *doppelgänger* into whom a large complex of these could be 'abjected', in Julia Kristeva's sense of that word, which, rooted in *ject* plus *ab*, points both to the 'throwing off' of anomalies in the self, psychological and cultural, that prevent it from crafting an illusion of coherent identity and to the 'throwing' of those projected inconsistencies 'under' the gaze of a sanctioned social authority, the hegemonic public eye, that will find them 'monstrous' within ideological standards that define 'normal' humanity.[20] She found such a figure for the 'abject' in other writings by prominent Romantics, one from the first and one from the second generation. The first of these is Coleridge's Gothic poem 'Christabel', written between 1797 and 1800 but not printed until 1816, the year of the gathering at Diodati, where Byron read it aloud to the group even as they all perused J.-B. B. Eyriès's *Fantasmagoriana* (1812), a French collection of German Gothic tales imitative of Walpole's *Castle of Otranto*.[21] In 'Christabel', the virginal medieval heroine of the title, wandering outside while longing for both a distant lover and a dead mother (as Victor Frankenstein does), confronts a tall 'lovely lady', 'Geraldine', who suddenly 'leaps up' like a spectre and whom Christabel sneaks into her father's castle to 'sleep with me' (lines 40, 117).[22] The next morning, after having dimly observed a reptilian 'sight to dream of, not to tell' on Geraldine's 'bosom', an enervated Christabel finds that her companion now has engorged 'heaving breasts' from having 'drunken deep' during the night (lines 246–7, 357, 362), as though Geraldine had fed on the life-blood of her hostess to enlarge her own female monstrosity rather than Christabel feeding on the breasts of her mother-substitute.

Geraldine is an Amazonian vampire who echoes other early-Romantic female vampires such as the man-hungry apparition of the hero's dead wife in Robert Southey's Orientalist epic *Thalaba the Destroyer* (1797–1800).[23] As such, she doubles Christabel in that she both draws living energy from her, thereby concealing her own reptilian deathliness, and proceeds to enact the self-empowerment to seduce and dominate both men and women that Christabel might attempt if she were not striving to be her father's good girl. It is therefore right to see Geraldine as 'the embodiment of Christabel's abjection' onto her, indeed as a *doppelgänger* that has risen up as a spectral answer to the title character's desire and now incarnates 'all that [Christabel] had thrown down in disgust' in order to seem a proper young lady: the potentials in women for independence, dominance, unbridled (even lesbian) sexuality and crossings of class (here species) boundaries that were feared by many during the debates about the status of women in the 1790s that Mary Wollstonecraft addressed so forcefully.[24] There could hardly be a more definite anticipation of Frankenstein's creature, so similar to Geraldine in being large and a mixture of species, as being the site for the abjection of all the anomalies and drives, including the racism and unconscious desire for his mother (like Christabel's), that Victor wants to dissociate from himself. 'Christabel', then, to a considerable degree, is why Victor in Mary's novel sees his creature, right after the murder of William, as 'my own vampire, my own spirit let loose from the grave, and forced to destroy all that was dear to me' (p. 57). Mary has built on a figure from the *Fantasmagoriana*, the dead 'sinful founder of his race' who walks out of his portrait in a 'gigantic, shadowy form' (a composite of images from Walpole) and kisses the 'foreheads' of his descendants as they sleep, 'who from that hour withered', and combined it with suggestions built by Coleridge into Geraldine to achieve one more step in the movement of the vampire into Gothic and Romantic writing.[25]

At the same time, Coleridge, Eyriès and Southey are not the only Romantics from which *Frankenstein* draws the figure of the vampire and much of what is already associated with it. The author at Diodati most associated with the vampire-figure by 1816, well before Polidori's novella, was far more Byron than it was Coleridge. Those whom Byron hosted were aware that, in his poem *The Giaour* (1813, another collation of nested narratives), he has one of his most self-tortured self-projections, a Westerner fighting in Greece against the invading Turks, be cursed by the most Turkish voice among this poem's narrators to rise from the grave 'as Vampire sent' to 'suck the blood of all thy race' (lines 755–8).[26] This curse may not come true literally in *The Gaiour*, but the title character, when he provides his own confessional narration (which often sounds like Victor's and the creature's), finally sees himself as a vampire-like 'thing that crawls/ Most noxious o'er a dungeon's walls' (lines 990–1). By this point, he bears 'of Cain the curse and crime . . . written on my brow' at least since he motivated, without himself enacting, the killing of his beloved by the Turkish chieftain *he* has since killed – 'Not mine the act, though I the cause' (lines 1056–61), a cry prophetic of the relationship between Frankenstein and the deeds of his creation. The meaning of the vampire stated in *The Giaour*, doomed to cause the destruction of those he/it loves most (like Mary's sense of Eyriès's 'sinful founder'), ultimately becomes the life-pattern of its author's principal self-projection of 1813, a vampire-monster in the eyes of several *Giaour* narrators including himself, that is then attached to the Byronic hero – and consequently to Byron himself (a link that Polidori later exploited) – by 1816.

It is therefore hardly surprising that Canto the Third of *Childe Harold's Pilgrimage*, which Byron, as Mary knew, was composing during the Diodati summer for publication later in 1816, is unusually direct about its author's projection of himself into his work by linking that process to suggestions of vampirism and to the contradictory Gothic thinker (a vestige of old aristocracy that has also outlived it) who Byron saw himself to be. Though he admits in this Canto that he 'endow[s]/ With form our fancy' in order to 'live/ A being more intense' in his poetry (lines 46–8), another moment prophetic of Victor and his creation, Byron connects that transference with what must be carried over to 'the life we image' in the new work from all the memories in the personal and the cultural unconscious that remain in his 'lone caves', the place where the vampire hordes what it has ingested and hence the locus of 'shapes which dwell/ Still unimpaired, though old, in the soul's haunted cell' (lines 43–9).[27] All the life Byron has imbibed vampirically from recent history, including the 'curses and crimes' for which he feels remorse and the 'wounds which kill not, but never heal' left from his extensive travels (l. 68), is stored as spectres in the same Gothic repository where Victor's desire for his dead mother and other abjected anomalies reside. That repository, in fact, now includes ghosts of all he has seen and considered since the first two *Harold* Cantos (1812–13): from a temporarily Wordsworthian 'companionship' with nature (line 114) to a refusal to 'yield dominion', as the later conservative Wordsworth had done, 'To spirits against whom his own rebelled' (lines 105–6) to an admiration for the 'eagle' (Napoleon, line 158) turned to repulsion in the face of that figure's eventual tyranny and its horrific result, the 'place of skulls . . . the deadly Waterloo' of 1815 (lines 145,

154–5). This itinerary climaxes in a Geneva now coloured by recollections of 'the self-torturing sophist, wild Rousseau' (line 725), whose early-Romantic visions of 'ideal beauty', still quite desirable (line 740), were 'phrensied' beneath their surface 'by disease or woe' (line 759) and so inspired a French Revolution where the 'wreck of old opinions' led to the overthrow of 'good with ill . . . / Leaving but ruins, wherewith to rebuild/ Upon the same foundations' (lines 771–6), the contradictory point of departure that currently faces Byron in the guise of an 1816 Childe Harold almost as self-torturing as Rousseau once was. Byron's production of his poetic 'being more intense', by unfolding this entire vampiric repository and thus being *his* vampire let loose, mirrors back to him, in a mottled miasma of beauty and ugliness (again prophetic of the creature's), the unresolved hesitations between conflicting and conflicted beliefs in his own mind and across the whole Romantic era since Rousseau.

Another of Mary Shelley's models, then, not so much for Victor but for the Victor–creature relationship, is surely the Byron–Harold interface at its most Gothic moments in *Childe Harold* Canto III. Here is perhaps the most conclusive instance of 'joint authorship' that explains why Mary Shelley's *Frankenstein* keeps revealing the tensions between opposites underlying Romanticism. Of all of the voices Mary echoes in her most famous novel, Byron's was the one most unashamed to reveal the irony of seeking for Romantic unities out of a collective psyche and a history that remained at odds with itself in 1816–18 – another underlying reality that the creature, like Childe Harold, ends up symbolizing, among many others.

By distilling all of these (and more) Romantic contexts in *Frankenstein*, I would also add, Mary Shelley indeed haunts Romanticism with the Gothic that Wordsworth and Coleridge sought to repress as 'low' culture, but she does so in a provocative way that reveals a truly foundational crux in Romantic writing and its ongoing legacy. As instigated by Walpole, according to the Preface to his Second Edition of *Otranto* in 1765, the 'Gothic Story' is designed 'to blend the two kinds of romance, the ancient [medieval, Catholic, aristocratic, supernatural] and the modern [Enlightenment, protestant, middle-class, realistic]'.[28] Consequently, it has always been about forcing different visions of the world based on different belief-systems into a tug-of-war with each other, pulling in retrograde and progressive directions at the same time. This very paradox, we now see in retrospect, is one of the roots of Romantic writing, which seeks to develop from empirical observations, usually of nature, a reimagined view of the world reminiscent of, but not the same as, the one in old romance. In trying to repress a mode that points so blatantly to continued conflicts between older and newer ideas, 'high' Romanticism strives to throw off an underlying awareness of deep conflict basic to itself. *Frankenstein*, by finding this awareness in the precursors and contemporary writers it draws on, as though it were reviving P. B. Shelley's early Gothic novels along with several by her parents, returns the tug-of-war in the Gothic, with great power, to Romantic writing. She thereby recalls from repression, especially in its vampiric creature, what some Romantic authors try to abject into the Gothic as 'monstrously other' even while they still use it: the quarrels between conflicting beliefs most essential to, yet still unresolved in, the Romantic movement in the Western world.

NOTES

1 Susan J. Wolfson and Ronald L. Levao, (eds.), 'Introduction', in Mary Wollstonecraft Shelley, *The Annotated Frankenstein* (Cambridge, MA: Harvard University Press, 2012), p. 19.
2 Marilyn Butler, 'Shelley and the Question of Joint Authorship', in Timothy Clark and Jerrold E. Hogle (eds.), *Evaluating Shelley* (Edinburgh University Press, 1996), pp. 42–7, p. 42.
3 Paul Cantor, *Creature and Creator: Myth-making and English Romanticism* (Cambridge University Press, 1984), pp. 114, 103, 132.
4 Coleridge's words in his 'Review of *The Monk* (1797)', in E. J. Clery and Robert Miles (eds.), *Gothic Documents: A Sourcebook, 1700–1820* (Manchester University Press, 2000), pp. 186–7.
5 Mary Poovey, *The Proper Lady and the Woman Writer: Ideology as Style in the Works of Mary Wollstonecraft, Mary Shelley, and Jane Austen* (University of Chicago Press, 1984), pp. 122–33.
6 See the introduction and notes to, as well as the text of, 'Alastor' in *Shelley's Poetry and Prose*, 2nd edn., ed. Donald H. Reiman and Neil Fraistat (New York: Norton, 202), pp. 71–90, the edition from which I quote this poem in my chapter. See also Mary Shelley, *Frankenstein*, ed. and Intro. Marilyn Butler (Oxford University Press, 1998), p. 33. Future references will be made parenthetically.
7 *Shelley's Poetry*, p. 73.
8 The wider reference points of this racism in *Frankenstein* have been treated by several scholars, starting with H. L. Malchow, 'Frankenstein's Monster and Images of Race in Nineteenth-Century Britain', *Past and Present*, 139 (1993), 90–130.
9 See *Frankenstein*, p. 39.
10 Except for those that come from 'Alastor', the words quoted here are those of Margaret Homans in *Bearing the Word: Language and Female Experience in Nineteenth-Century Women's Writing* (University of Chicago Press, 1986), pp. 100–11.
11 See the 'Reading List' in *The Journals of Mary Shelley, Volume I: 1814–1822*, ed. Paula R. Feldman and Diana Scott-Kilvert (Oxford: Clarendon, 1987), pp. 88–101.
12 Mary Shelley, 'Rousseau', in *Lives of the Most Eminent Literary and Scientific Men of France* (London: Longman, Orme, Brown, 1839), p. 174.

13 Mary Shelley, 'Rousseau', pp. 172–4.

14 Jean-Jacques Rousseau, *Emile, or On Education*, trans. Allan Bloom (New York: Basic Books, 1979), p. 61.

15 Jean-Jacques Rousseau, *The First and Second Discourses and Essay on the Origin of Languages*, ed. and trans. Victor Gourevitch (New York: Harper and Row, 1986), p. 240.

16 Alan Richardson, 'From *Emile* to *Frankenstein*: The Education of Monsters', *European Romantic Review*, 1 (1991), 147–62, 151.

17 See especially James O' Rourke, '"Nothing More Unnatural": Mary Shelley's Revision of Rousseau', *ELH*, 56 (1989), 543–69.

18 Jean-Jacques Rousseau, *The Confessions*, trans. J. M. Cohen (Middlesex: Penguin, 1953), p. 88.

19 The quoted words in this and the following sentence are from Rousseau, *The First and Second Discourses and Essay on the Origin of Languages*, pp. 246–7.

20 See Julia Kristeva, *Powers of Horror: An Essay on Abjection*, trans. Leon S. Roudiez (New York: Columbia University Press, 1982), pp. 1–11.

21 See Jerrold E. Hogle, 'The Rise of the Gothic Vampire: Disfiguration and Cathexis from Coleridge's "Christabel" to Nodier's *Smarra*', in *Gothic N.E.W.S., Volume I: Literature*, ed. Max Duperray (Paris: Michel Houdiard Editeur, 2004), pp. 50–3.

22 I cite this poem from its first printing, reproduced in Samuel Taylor Coleridge, *Christabel 1816*, intro. Jonathan Wordsworth (Oxford: Woodstock Books, 1991).

23 Hogle, 'The Rise', p. 50.

24 Robert Miles, 'Abjection, Nationalism and the Gothic', in Fred Botting (ed.), *Essays and Studies 2001: The Gothic* (Cambridge: D.S. Brewer, 2001), pp. 47–70, p. 65.

25 Mary's own words as she remembers what she drew on from Eyriès in her introduction to the 1831 re-publication of her novel (*Frankenstein*, p. 194).

26 *Byron's Poetry and Prose*, ed. Alice Levine (New York: Norton, 2010), pp. 142–3. All my citations from *The Gaiour* come from this edition.

27 *Byron's Poetry*, p. 197, the source for all my quotations from *Childe Harold* Canto III.

28 Horace Walpole, *The Castle of Otranto*, ed. W. S. Lewis and E. J. Clery (Oxford University Press, 1996), p. 9.

4

CATHERINE LANONE

The Context of the Novel

This chapter maps the influence of Mary Shelley on later nineteenth-century fiction by Emily Brontë, Charles Dickens and Wilkie Collins. It traces how questions of education, class, and psychology were inherited from *Franken-stein*. However, before exploring these matters of influence it is also important to acknowledge that *Frankenstein* was shaped by an earlier tradition of the novel associated with Mary Shelley's parents: William Godwin and Mary Wollstonecraft.

Both Mary Wollstonecraft and William Godwin turned to fiction as an area of experimentation, meant to illustrate and test the arguments discussed in their groundbreaking works, *A Vindication of the Rights of Woman* (1792) and *An Enquiry Concerning Political Justice* (1793). Conceived during a bleak summer overcast by the distant eruption of Mount Tambora, by a young woman travelling to a continent tangled in the aftermath of the French Revolution and the Napoleonic wars, *Frankenstein* also uses fiction as a means of engaging with theoretical debate.[1] Significantly enough, Mary and the poet she had eloped with felt compelled to read her parents' works together between 1814 and 1816. Within those books themselves, the discovery of books offers resistance and empowerment, as when, for instance, the eponymous Maria, in *Maria: or, The Wrongs of Woman* (1798), is sent to a lunatic asylum by her husband, and manages to keep her sanity and identity thanks to the books she is allowed to borrow. From *Maria* to Mary Shelley to the creature (who teaches himself to read Goethe and Milton), books are a source of strength, of quintessential transmission and resilience in troubled times. In the wake of the French Revolution, Wollstonecraft's and Godwin's own books were the offspring of heated intellectual debate. With *Political Justice*, Godwin seeks to cast off Government and vindicate personal responsibility; Mary Wollstonecraft's *Vindication of the Rights of Woman* calls for equal education for equally reasonable girls. Their novels implement, probe, challenge and use fiction as a test case and as a weapon. They force their readers to enter a labyrinth of oppression. In Wollstonecraft's

56

novels, marriage is a jail. In Godwin's *Caleb Williams* (1794), there is no escape from the squire's power; Falkland is a fallen man, a would-be hero turned murderer, but he holds power in his hand and turns the eponymous Caleb into an outcast, who must worm his way through prison walls, dwell with thieves or hide in disguise for dear life. In this study of social pressure and manipulation, Justice itself is on trial. In *Caleb Williams*, the law is blind, easily deceived and ruthless; because they are poor, the helpless Hawkinses, rather than Falkland, are easily convicted for the murder of the evil Tyrrel, just as the innocent Justine is hanged for the murder of little William in Mary Shelley's novel. In Godwin's *St. Leon* (1799), Hector, the faithful black man, is tortured to death and the black dog Charon shot by superstitious peasants. Godwin challenges boundaries between 'human nature and the brutes', the distinction made by 'civilized men', as the dog is deemed an almost human companion, while the mob delights in violence.[2] In the alchemical or Promethean fire of her own fiction, Mary Shelley melts those models of racial, social and patriarchal oppression into the ultimate Other struggling on the margins, without even a name to call his own.

Godwin too had, rhetorically speaking, dabbled in alchemy with his ill-named St Leon, doomed by a Faustian bargain with a mysterious old man, who grants him gold and youth but cuts him off from his wife, his children and his modest but happy domestic life.[3] Walter Scott noted the kinship between the two novels; but Mary Shelley grafts modern science onto the tale.[4] Shelley senses the potential of the new electrical spark; she reaches beyond galvanic stimulation and Erasmus Darwin's spontaneous generation of matter, to foresee and question modern achievements and problematic engagement with the ethics of responsibility. The De Lacey episode transposes the episode of the kind old man who rejects Caleb Williams, but in this case blindness is used as an ironic warning: as Gloucester has it in *King Lear*, *mutatis mutandis*, those who see are blind, and Victor, the over-reacher, is the blindest of all.

Ultimately, *Frankenstein* comes closest to Godwin in its use of kinetic suspense. Godwin invented the chase, locking Caleb and Falkland in deadly pursuit, as Caleb fails to escape from his antagonist and his emissaries. Similarly, the creature keeps reappearing, invisibly shadowing his maker: 'Yes, he had followed me in my travels; he had loitered in forests, hid himself in caves, or taken refuge in wide and desert heaths; and he now came to mark my progress, and claim the fulfilment of my promise.'[5] With the journey to the North and the sublime waste of ice, Shelley heightens tension. She also picks up the final twist that Godwin gave to the mad chase in his revised ending: the homosocial tension collapsed into illogical regret, as Caleb suddenly eulogized Falkland, trapped by 'the poison of chivalry' and his 'miserable project of imposture', yet still noble and 'sublime', cleansed by death.[6] Mary Shelley explores this matrix of reversibility and makes it the very hinge of her tale; she blurs the boundaries between creature and creator from the start, reversing posture and gaze in the laboratory and the bedroom. The creature is the Gothic Doppelgänger, but he is also the discarded son and self. For Pamela Clemit, 'Mary Shelley builds on Godwin's use of the pursuit motif to destabilize conventional moral values'.[7] In the end, the elegiac grief in Walton's cabin proves the monster's essential humanity. Revenge proves useless, but in a way which shatters Victor's moral superiority and calls for the ethics of care.

The epigraph of *Frankenstein* binds father and daughter: 'To William Godwin, *Author of Political Justice, Caleb Williams, &tc. These volumes are respectfully inscribed by THE AUTHOR.*' Muriel Spark's landmark biography has retrieved the figure of Mary Shelley from the shadows of her formidable parents, keeping the legendary contest of Villa Diodati but also casting light on Mary's pregnancies and loss, on her troubled relationship with a father who had once condemned the institution of marriage, yet never forgave his daughter's elopement.[8] In the play *Blood and Ice* (1982), Liz Lochhead's Byron mocks her troubled allegiance: 'Poor Mary – Mary. Wearing her mother round her neck and her father on her sleeve.'[9] But Mary Shelley both draws upon and revises her parents' work, to open a new world of speculative fiction. And the web of intertextual echoes shows that later fiction had to engage with Shelley's own myth, but could do so in a creative rather than monolithic way.

In 1848, Mrs Gaskell in her first novel *Mary Barton* made a brief allusion to Frankenstein (meaning, interestingly enough, the creature, not the scientist) to trope Chartism as the frightening rebellion of inarticulate people made monstrous by the powerful and indifferent middle class. But other Victorian writers, such as Emily Brontë, Charles Dickens and Wilkie Collins, probe more deeply into the politics of education and explore the making of monsters by revisiting the tropes used in *Frankenstein*, implicitly or explicitly.

The imprint of Mary Shelley's novel on *Wuthering Heights* (1847) can be clearly seen. Like *Frankenstein*, *Wuthering Heights* uses a frame narrative, although not in letters but in the form of a diary of a would-be explorer who stumbles across the swells and falls of a dangerous snow-covered landscape, 'for the whole hill-back was one billowy, white ocean'.[10] This image, however, echoes Walton's quest and Brontë's fascination with the Arctic explorer William Parry in which, for the critic Hillis Miller, the blank map that baffles Lockwood functions as a metatextual metaphor for the reader's own sense of disorientation, when entering a novel from which all the familiar landmarks are missing.[11] But (more so than the bland, unsuccessful Walton) Lockwood is an effete, helpless traveller. With Brontë the Gothic is brought home: the story dwindles to a wind-swept microcosm. Lockwood is a Londoner, a mere tourist setting out to discover the wild recesses of Yorkshire, rushing in where he should fear to tread, misreading signs: his sole function is to listen to and collect the dark tale of the Grange and the Heights in an echo of Walton's record of Victor's narrative.

The story is gradually pieced together, composed of various textual body-parts: embedded within Lockwood's diary, Nelly's tale revives the characters and events of the past and gradually leads to the present, recording entire dialogues; but the most vivid impression of childhood comes from Catherine's diary, scribbled in the margins of the *Old Testament*, turning it indeed into 'Catherine Earnshaw, her book' (p. 16).[12] This is the equivalent of the monster's tale, reduced to a fragment, a broken metonymy: the hovel at the back of the De Laceys' house is replaced by the snug shelter under the table protected by the tied pinafores, from which the children peep at Hindley and his wife holding each other by the fire; after a brief spell of parodic education (Joseph's Bible-mongering), comes the attempt at revolution ('H. and I are going to rebel' (p. 16)) and the outburst of violence and expulsion: Hindley forbids Heathcliff to eat and sit with the family or to play with Cathy, denying his status as sibling (calling him a 'vagabond' (p. 18) and claiming social (and white) supremacy, a process of interpellation which excludes him).

Never given a full identity, Heathcliff remains a misbegotten, estranged Other. He is first sprung upon the family as a fully grown child, though an 'it' rather than a 'he', as if not quite human; with his dark skin and his strange language which for Nelly is mere 'gibberish' (p. 31), he is bundled out of the father's greatcoat, in a parody of female delivery. For Terry Eagleton, '[a]s a waif and orphan, Heathcliff is introduced in the close-knit family structure as an alien; he emerges from that ambivalent domain of darkness which is the "outside" of the tightly defined domestic system.'[13] Heathcliff is given the name of a dead child, as if, like Mary Shelley's monster, he came to imperfectly resurrect the dead. After Mr Earnshaw's death, he is beaten, given no education, treated as the lowest kind of servant, enslaved. He is thus denied all hopes of ever becoming Cathy's social equal. In *Frankenstein*, Victor tears to pieces the mate he had begun to create, and looks up to find the monster glaring at him at the window. In *Wuthering Heights*, Heathcliff and Cathy make faces at the window of the Grange, sneering at Linton and Isabella who seem about to pull apart a little dog they are fighting for; Cathy's ankle is caught by the watch dog, and she is taken into the glittering world of the house, while Heathcliff is denied access, doomed to lurk outside. Catherine goes through the looking glass, recovering to identify with the Linton's upper-class manners, shunning her former companion. By degrading Heathcliff, by bringing him so low (to borrow Cathy's words), Hindley turns him into a beggar whom Cathy can never marry, but also into a monster (even Nelly confesses that such treatment is enough to turn a saint into a fiend). It is these degradations which generate the revenge plot in *Wuthering Heights*, a plot which is formed out the type of social and emotional exclusions which have their roots in *Frankenstein*.

Denied his mate, Victor's creature begins to dismember his family, killing William and Elizabeth, and indirectly Justine, the faithful servant blamed for William's death, and the father who dies of grief – not to mention Victor's best friend, Clerval. Having lost Cathy, his surrogate sister/beloved, Heathcliff also strives to shatter the family issue of his enemies. He vanishes for a while and returns, having turned himself into a gentleman of some means, or, as Terry Eagleton puts it, 'Heathcliff moves from being natural in the sense of an anarchic outsider to adopting the behaviour natural to an insider in a viciously competitive society.'[14] If the creature stood for disruptive revolutionary energy, Heathcliff is the underdog who uses the law to achieve revenge, in a parody of capitalistic logic. In *Frankenstein* the shift in power relations is demonstrated by the reversal of the master and slave narrative which the creature so clearly feels ties him to Victor. This volatile relationship is played out through a restless territorial pursuit which is different in kind to *Wuthering Heights* where hatred becomes static. There is no wild pursuit towards remote shores and harbours; yet the constant travelling to and fro between the Heights and the Grange creates a riveting polarity. Heathcliff tears the family members limb from limb; he wrenches the Heights from Hindley (who drinks himself to death), and secures his son Hareton, deliberately thwarting his good qualities to reproduce his own plight: '"Now, my bonny lad, you are *mine*! And we'll see if one tree won't grow as crooked as another, with the same wind to twist it!"' (p. 165). He marries Isabella and hastens both her death and that of his own son, used as bait to attract Cathy. Heathcliff snaps that he longs to crush their entrails, and indulge in vivisection. After the death of weak Linton Heathcliff and of Edgar Linton, Heathcliff becomes the master of both houses. He thus absorbs the abode and the offspring of his enemies, and is constantly depicted as a 'fiend' with his 'sharp cannibal teeth' gleaming in the dark (p. 156). Isabella's letter to Nelly begins by asking 'Is Mr Heathcliff a man?' (p. 120). Deemed not quite human, Heathcliff is turned into a monster by oppression; but revenge ultimately backfires: 'In oppressing others the exploiter imprisons himself'.[15] Just as the monster expresses sorrow before Victor's body, Heathcliff ultimately feels unable to destroy

Cathy and Hareton. Just as the creature and Victor are caught in a self-destructive relationship, so Heathcliff destroys himself in an inner struggle which represents, in introjected form, the destructive psychological tensions found in *Frankenstein*.

The romance of the second-generation Cathy and Hareton, however, is less powerful than the intrusion of the waif with its little icy hand, soaking with blood the broken window-pane, an image of fractured boundaries. Brontë's world, like Mary Shelley's, is stamped by motherlessness. Cathy dies when giving birth and may only return to the Heights as a ghost. Thus Brontë revisits the scenario of child abuse with a twist. The first Catherine is for Nelly a selfish wretch, who brings upon herself her own madness and death with her 'senseless, wicked rages' (p. 108): except for the brief fragment in the margins, her tale always comes at one remove, screened by a woman who fails to understand her passion for Heathcliff: the tale itself is always alienated. Nelly's narrative ultimately gives the impression that the monster is twofold, a double entity composed of Catherine and Heathcliff. Passion makes Cathy and Heathcliff each other's half, through emotional and ontological identification; division turns them into monsters, a cleft that death seems to heal only through ghostly visitation.

Charles Dickens' 1861 novel *Great Expectations* also explores the themes of warped education and the impossible shift from orphan to gentleman. As in *Caleb Williams* and *Frankenstein*, the retrospective narration traces the fall into error, the golden chain of cause and effect, with the bleak benefit of hindsight. Pip believes that Miss Havisham is acting as his fairy Godmother, a benefactor granting him the education and means of a gentleman, so that he may marry the princess of Satis House, Estella; but the masculine transposition of the Cinderella scenario is undercut by ironic references to Mary Shelley's novel. In the course of transformation, Pip loses his surname to become Mr Pip (like Heathcliff, like Victor's creature, he can never acquire a full name and identity), and his adult self is not composed of body parts but of borrowed garments: Trabbs's boy mimics awe (he feigns a 'paroxysm of terror' as he circles Pip in his splendid clothes) mocking his selfishness, while Pip dresses his valet with the 'refuse of the washerwoman's family' in waistcoat, cravat and breeches, turning him into a 'monster' and 'avenging phantom', since he does not know how to direct him.[16] Doubling is a comedic sign of imposture, and the fairy-tale scenario collapses during the great recognition scene, when the coarse grey man, cut and stung and ravenous in the opening scene, reappears on a stormy night. The parts are reversed, and blurred: Magwitch may look like the monster, but he is the creator, whereas Pip, the gentleman, turns out to be only his artificial creature, as signalled by the allusion to Victor Frankenstein:

> The imaginary student pursued by the misshapen creature he had impiously
> made, was not more wretched than I, pursued by the creature who had made
> me, and recoiling from him with a stronger repulsion, the more he admired
> me, and the fonder he was of me. (p. 335)

For Chris Baldick, this achieves a 'doubly equivocal inversion of the Frankenstein myth'.[17] Kind at heart, Magwitch is a failed creator, and so is the
real experimenter of the novel. Miss Havisham, denied a mate, jilted on her
wedding-day, seeks revenge in the Gothic laboratory of her candle-lit rooms,
by the relics of the corrupted cake and yellowing dusty dresses. Estella is the
product of the experiment, her creature raised to have no emotions, in order
to break men's hearts: '"I am what you have made me. Take all the praise,
take all the blame; take all the success, take all the failure; in short, take
me"' (p. 300). Ultimately, Miss Havisham finds no relish in revenge; Estella
is cold towards her benefactress, and Miss Havisham seems to share Pip's
pain, rather than rejoice, when he begs Estella one last time. Duplicating
and redistributing the parts of monster and creator, Dickens uses the myth
to mingle the coldness of Estella and the coldness of a society which, like
Jaggers, washes its hands of all responsibility, and simply will not allow the
transformation of orphan into gentleman. A variation on this is the fear of
the rise of the middle classes, as embodied by the *femme fatale* of sensation
fiction.

Sensation fiction offers a further line of descent for Mary Shelley's novel,
as proclaimed by an 1866 disparaging critique of Wilkie Collins's novel
Basil (1852) in the *Saturday Review*:

> The end of literature is to create what is beautiful and good, not what is hideous
> and revolting; and the man who begets murderesses and villains wholesale in
> a three volume novel is as completely a literary monster as the man who
> deliberately created a Frankenstein would be a social pest.[18]

The 'literary monster', here, is both Wilkie Collins and the eponymous Basil,
who reinvents himself as a writer when his angry father strikes his name from
the family book. For Tamar Heller, this *mise en abyme* connects the novel
with the female Gothic: 'As Basil enters the marketplace, he writes a feminine language, which Collins describes, in the image of the pen trembling in
Basil's hand, as a lack of linguistic authority'.[19] Basil's writing also turns out
to be the tale we are reading, in which the long letter of his enemy Mannion
is embedded, a Chinese-box structure that descends from the complex narrative structure of *Frankenstein*, which also includes the monster's own
tale embedded within Frankenstein's confession to Walton. Like *Frankenstein*, the novel revolves around the fall into error, and Basil's wish to piece

together the tale recalls the monster's desire that Walton should keep a correct record, not a mutilated tale.[20]

The scientist's mad pursuit and nine months' labour and toil leading to the creation scene is replaced by a year-long period of probation, which precedes physical transmutation of man into monster. The danger, here, no longer consists in crossing the boundary between life and death, but in social contamination through improper encounter. It is the social chemical reaction that is feared, the impure mix of heterogeneous flesh. For Basil falls in love with the flickering image of a woman on an omnibus, a public contact zone emblematic of modern speed. Though Basil is scarcely acquainted with the object of his fascination, Sherwin, a shrewd businessman and the father of the dark-haired beauty, agrees to give his daughter's hand, but forces Basil to wait for a year *after* the ceremony. The odd contract suggests that Basil's love is a fantasy, precluding close contact with reality. Sherwin means to give Basil a year to convince his own father – to no avail, as Basil is disowned and disinherited when the secret match is finally confessed. A parody of courtly love, the year-long paradoxical (post-marriage) courtship resembles Frankenstein's quest, in so far as it becomes an ardent pursuit far exceeding moderation, denying consummation and distancing Basil from his family, as exemplified by Clara's cheerful but pained letters, the replica of Elizabeth's. As Heller points out: 'Not only is Margaret a quotation from the female Gothic, but so is Clara, who as sister and intellectual companion plays Elizabeth Lavenza to Basil's Frankenstein.'[21]

The probation year is enough to turn Margaret, the frustrated wife, and Mannion, her tutor and father's secretary, into villains, or rather, as suggested by Basil's significant dream, into hybrid non-human 'fiends' with claws or talons (systematic repetitions hammer home haunting anamorphosis: 'the monstrous iniquities incarnate in monstrous forms; the fiend-souls made visible in fiend-shapes'[22]). The vision revives *Frankenstein*'s monster as a trope for social unrest in a post-revolutionary consumerist world. As Heller puts it, Mannion, 'a clerk who is a figure for the rebellious class subordinate' embodies class resentment.[23] Collins reads the scenario backwards, conflating the creation of the monster and the grotesquely inverted wedding night. Ironically, when on his wedding anniversary Basil believes he may now claim his wife, he eavesdrops on Margaret and Mannion's love-making, a parodic primal scene in a shady hotel. Mannion is with Basil on his wedding-night, but this also marks the end of his perfect face (just as Victor chose the limbs and features, the luscious dark hair, to achieve symmetry and proportion, Mannion's face initially achieves perfect proportion). Before the fateful night, his handsome face remains a beautiful blind disclosing no human emotion, except when a Gothic flash of lightning acts as a photographic negative, revealing the Other lurking within the patient servant: 'It gave such a hideously livid hue, such a spectral look of ghastliness and distortion to his features, that he absolutely seemed to be glaring and grinning on me like a fiend, in the one instant of its duration' (p. 106). The moment echoes Victor's glimpse of the monster, as a flash of lightning illuminates 'the deformity of its aspect, more hideous than belongs to humanity' (p. 56). The proleptic optical illusion also connects Mannion with the stormy metaphors of the French Revolution, which pervade Carlyle's *The French Revolution: A History* (1837) and Charles Dickens's *A Tale of Two Cities* (1859). In the homoerotic struggle that locks Mannion and Basil in murderous embrace outside the hotel, a scene of violence that blends creation and destruction, Mannion loses an eye. He has become a monster, his face hammered out of recognition, smashed and scarred beyond repair. Basil uses the tropes of blindness and gradual return to light, to convey the shock of error, and the swift re-reading of the scenario of courtship as deceit, a violent physical sensation.

The dark-haired *femme fatale* is swiftly disposed of, killed by a disease that tropes a fitting retribution for the promiscuous woman (she catches typhus in the hospital, failing to identify Mannion's deformed face, bending over another man's bed, an ironic displacement of the shift from Basil to Mannion; the contagious fever is a metaphor for, and an outcome of, the woman's sexual pathology). The device paves the way for the chase, a theme Mary Shelley inherited from her father's *Caleb Williams*. Like the monster, Mannion tells his own tale, and threatens Basil's closest family (though in this case the father dies of shame and both sister and brother remain unscathed). Basil runs away, offering himself as a decoy, aware that his enemy will not leave him alone and may materialize anywhere, an eerie, ruthless follower. Like the monster, like Falkland's emissary, Mannion will not leave Basil alone; he vindicates pursuit in terms reminiscent of the monster's Miltonic way of formulating his own anger and plight: '"Do you know me for Robert Mannion?" he repeated. "Do you know the work of your own hands, now you see it?"' (p. 240). As Mariaconcetta Costantini puts it, 'Mannion bears a grudge against the man who shaped his destiny of deprivation, and hatches a plot of persecution intended to compensate for his sufferings.'[24]

With the monomaniacal pursuit, the map both expands and shrinks. Wandering is a claustrophobic trap in *Caleb Williams* and *Frankenstein*. Caleb, attempting to escape from Falkland, is unable to catch a boat to escape to Ireland; however far and wide he may roam, he must remain in England. In *Frankenstein*, Victor feels elated by the snow-capped, sublime mountains, and looks with awe at the towering Montanvert and Mont Blanc; in a Romantic Shelleyan impulse, he calls out to the spirits of the mountains, only to be ironically answered by the sudden apparition of the misshaped outcome of his own creation, springing among the rocks, the return of the repressed.[25] Later on, the pattern is reversed, the pursuer becomes the object of pursuit as Victor ventures farthest north, braving the icy wastes of the Arctic, strangely helped by the monster who means to destroy him, but who leaves cached food for his creator to eat. On a lesser scale, Mannion wreaks havoc, turning Basil into an outcast by poisoning the villagers' minds against him. This time, the tale is brought home, Basil travels inward, as he withdraws to Cornwall, and the final confrontation takes place, rather than in the Arctic desert of snow, on the very edge of land and sea. Laurence Talairach-Vielmas points to the allegorical dimension of the landscape and the chasms which 'figure Basil's mental recesses and haunting secrets', as much as Mannion's obsession.[26] As in *Frankenstein*, the landscape plays a key symbolic role. The cliff is a maze, shrouded in a mist which signals confusion. The vertical dimension of Mont Blanc is inverted as the cliff is carved into a vertiginous hollow void:

> Beyond the spot where I stood, the rocks descended suddenly, and almost perpendicularly, to the range below them. In one of the highest parts of the wall-side of granite thus formed, there opened a black, yawning hole that slanted nearly straight downwards, like a tunnel, to unknown and unfathomable depths below, into which the waves found entrance through some subterranean channel. (p. 235)

The cliff turns into a Gothic dungeon, where invisible waves spell torment, mirroring the theme of imprisonment:

> The wild waves boiled and thundered in their imprisonment, till they seemed to convulse the solid cliff about them, like an earthquake. But, high as they leapt up in the rocky walls of the chasm, they never leapt into sight from above. Nothing but clouds of spray indicated to the eye, what must be the horrible tumult of the raging waters below. (p. 235)

The howling waves drown the shrill cries of sea-birds, troping the place as hell, simmering with the undecipherable cries of the damned. The 'mouth' of the vortex of invisible waters seems ready to swallow Basil, with its ungainly connotations of female sexual organs, a 'great hole' with folds of rock and 'patches of long, lank, sea-weed waving slowly' (p. 235). Mannion suddenly springs among the rocks, shouting to recall him from the brink of suicide, claiming him as his own. Here too the wretch is both ruthless pursuer and helper. The pathology of obsession is 'resonant with tones of eroticized hatred'.[27] A dark shadow, Mannion vows that they are linked for life; shaking his fist to threaten Basil, he loses his balance, is briefly raised by spray, then plunges into the abyss, 'The spray fell. For one instant, I saw two livid and bloody hands tossed up against the black walls of the hole, as he dropped into it' (p. 258). Reduced to metonymic severed limbs, helpless white and crimson hands, the monstrous body is swallowed by the chasm, a kind of inverted birth. Basil is free to resume a quiet, asexual existence with his devoted sister (a positioning that seemingly echoes Walton's in *Frankenstein*), a sexless, vaguely incestuous match which, paradoxically, preserves propriety.

Thus, to conclude, Mary Shelley's novel revisited the ethical points raised by her parents in their novels and essays. The novel's early descent latched on to the philosophical debate which concerned them, engaging with the construction of self and other, probing into education, gendered constraints and social struggle as the making and unmaking of identity. *Frankenstein* gives shape to a covert Gothic presence in the later nineteenth century. *Wuthering Heights*, *Great Expectations* and *Basil* explore issues about social exclusion, revenge and cultural legitimacy that have their roots in Shelley's novel. They are not, however, clearly defined Gothic novels. The Gothic impulses in Shelley's novel become transformed and transferred to this mid-nineteenth-century tradition of the novel, which bears testimony to just how far *Frankenstein* was subjected to a process of cultural assimilation during the period. Ultimately, with its textual body parts, the creature monster may be seen as a metaphor for intertextuality and literary filiation, elusive and strong, constantly reinventing itself:

> You sliced me loose,
> And said it was
> Creation. I could feel the knife.
> Now you would like to heal
> That chasm in your side,
> But I recede. I prowl.
> I will not come when you call.[28]

NOTES

1 Mary Wollstonecraft famously stayed in Paris during the French Revolution.
2 William Godwin, *St. Leon*, http://gutenberg.net.au/ebooks06/0605711.txt, last accessed 10 July 2015.
3 William Godwin, *St. Leon: A Tale of the Sixteenth Century* (London: G.C. and J. Robinson, 1799).

4 Walter Scott, 'Remarks on *Frankenstein, Or The Modern Prometheus; A Novel*', *Blackwood's Edinburgh Magazine*, 2 (20 March/1 April 1818), 613–20. For Scott see I. Bour, 'Sensibility as Epistemology in *Caleb Williams, Waverley* and *Frankenstein*', *Studies in English Literature 1500–1900*, 45(4) (Autumn 2005), 813–27.

5 Mary Shelley, *Frankenstein*, ed. and Intro., Marilyn Butler (Oxford University Press, 1998), pp. 138–39. Future references will be made parenthetically.

6 William Godwin, *Caleb Williams* [1794], ed. Pamela Clemit (Oxford University Press, 2009), p. 303.

7 Pamela Clemit, '*Frankenstein, Matilda*, and the Legacies of Godwin and Wollstonecraft', in Esther Schor (ed.), *The Cambridge Companion to Mary Shelley* (Cambridge University Press, 2003), p. 32.

8 Muriel Spark, *Child of Light: A Reassessment of Mary Wollstonecraft Shelley* (Hadleigh: Tower Bridge Publications, 1951).

9 Liz Lochhead, *Blood and Ice* [1982] (London: Nick Hern Books, 2009), p. 21.

10 Emily Brontë, *Wuthering Heights* [1847] (Oxford World's Classics, Oxford University Press, 2009), p. 26. Future references will be made parenthetically.

11 J. Hillis Miller, *Fiction and Repetition: Seven English Novels* (Cambridge, MA: Harvard University Press, 1982).

12 See Gilbert and Gubar's discussion of Emily Brontë's Bible of Hell in *The Madwoman in the Attic*. Margaret Homans draws attention to the episode's metatextual dimension: 'In juxtaposing the language use of an uncivilized girl to that of an overcivilized man, the novel traces Brontë's own problem as a woman writer.' Margaret Homans, 'The Name of the Mother in *Wuthering Heights*', in Linda H. Peterson (ed.), *Wuthering Heights* (Boston, MA: Bedford Books of St Martin's Press, 1992), pp. 341–58, p. 350.

13 Terry Eagleton, 'Myths of Power: a Marxist Study on *Wuthering Heights*', in Peterson (ed.), *Wuthering Heights*, pp. 394–410, p. 401.

14 Terry Eagleton, 'Myths of Power', p. 406.

15 Terry Eagleton, 'Myths of Power', p. 404.

16 Charles Dickens, *Great Expectations* [1861] (Oxford World's Classics, Oxford University Press, 1994), p. 242. Future references will be made parenthetically.

17 Chris Baldick, *In Frankenstein's Shadow* (Oxford: Clarendon Press, 1987), p. 119.

18 'Clap-Trap Morality', *Saturday Review* (1866) http://trove.nla.gov.au/ndp/del/article/20310841, last accessed 12 August 2015.

19 Tamar Heller, *Dead Secrets: Wilkie Collins and the Female Gothic* (New Haven, CT: Yale University Press), p. 71.

20 This also echoes the last sentences of *Caleb Williams*, openly depicting the truth, so that 'the world may at least not hear and repeat a half-told and mangled tale.' William Godwin, *Caleb Williams*, p. 303.

21 Tamar Heller, *Dead Secrets*, p. 63.

22 Wilkie Collins, *Basil* [1852], ed. Dorothy Goldman (Oxford University Press, 2000), p. 140. Future references will be made parenthetically.

23 Tamar Heller, *Dead Secrets*, p. 59.

24 Mariaconcetta Costantini, 'Wilkie Collins and the Anatomy of Hatred', *LISA*, Vol. VII n° 3 (2009), https://lisa.revues.org/147, last accessed 10 August 2015.

25 Though the diegesis is supposed to take place before Romanticism, Shelley's 'Mutability', for instance, is quoted.

26 Laurence Talairach-Vielmas, '"On the Very Brink of a Precipice": Landscapes of the Mind in Wilkie Collins's *Basil* (1852)', in Françoise Besson, Philippe Birgy and Catherine Lanone (eds.), 'La Montagne: entre image et langage dans les territoires anglophones/Mountains in Image and Word in the English-Speaking World', *Anglophonia*, 23 (2008), 183–90, 187.

27 Mariaconcetta Costantini, 'Wilkie Collins and the Anatomy of Hatred', *LISA*, Vol. VII n° 3 (2009), https://lisa.revues.org/147, last accessed 10 August 2015.

28 Margaret Atwood, *Speeches for Doctor Frankenstein*, in *Selected Poems*, 1965–1975 (Boston, MA: Houghton Mifflins, 1976), p. 69.

5

ANDREW SMITH

Scientific Contexts

To explore science in *Frankenstein* (1818) begs the question of what type of scientist is Victor Frankenstein? Firstly it is important to note that Frankenstein would not have referred to himself as a scientist as the term was not coined until 1834. He regards himself as a disciple of Natural Philosophy which would have included the mastery of a number of disciplines, including physics and chemistry, which constituted core elements of the physical sciences of the time. The type of science that he undertakes is initially informed by his engagement with the occult philosophies of Cornelius Agrippa, Paracelsus and Albertus Magnus. These early mystics contributed to sixteenth-century alchemy and sought to discover the elixir of life which would lead to its prolongation.[1] The alchemist's task of turning base metal into gold prefigures Frankenstein's attempt to create life out of death (with the pursuit of the elixir of life playing an obvious role in this context). His early scientific interest in these mystics is mocked both by his father, who refers to Agrippa's writings as '"sad trash"' and by M. Krempe, Frankenstein's tutor at the University of Ingolstadt, who tells him '"You have burdened your memory with exploded systems, and useless names . . . you must begin your studies entirely anew."'[2] Frankenstein responds more positively to his other tutor, M. Waldeman, who places the alchemists in context and acknowledges that their work led to many discoveries (relating to oxygen and the circulation of the blood), and claims that their model of scientific discovery has much to recommend it as '"They penetrate[d] into the recesses of nature, and shew how she works in her hiding places"' (p. 30). The gender implications of this penetrated nature will be discussed later in this chapter, but it is this approach to science which Frankenstein follows and it is in keeping with a particular version of scientific practice that was available at the time.

Waldeman encourages Frankenstein to read widely in the natural sciences and to include mathematics in his studies. Waldeman also claims that '"Chemistry is that branch of natural philosophy in which the greatest improvements have been made and may be made"' (p. 31), and this reference to chemistry suggests the influence of Humphry Davy (1778–1829) on the novel. In a distinguished scientific career Davy discovered new elements such as sodium and potassium, and was famous for discovering chlorine. He was interested in the role that electricity could play in science and delivered lectures on galvanism at the Royal Institution in 1801. Maurice Hindle has noted that Davy's *A Discourse, Introduction to a Course of Lectures on Chemistry* (1802) incorporates a Romantic manifesto for science which emphasized the creative aspects of discovery.[3] According to Davy:

> Science has given to him [i.e. the investigator] an acquaintance with the different relations of the parts of the external world; and more than that, it has bestowed upon him powers which may be almost called creative; which have enabled him, by his experiments to interrogate nature with power, not simply as a scholar, passive and seeking only to understand her operations, but rather as a master, active with his own instruments.[4]

Here the scientist is figured as an adventurer rather than as someone who simply catalogues discoveries. This is a quite different type of science than that championed by Sir Isaac Newton. His work on optics in 1672 was mocked by Keats in *Lamia* (1820), who points to the imaginative limitations of considering a rainbow as a type of prism:

> There was an awful rainbow once in heaven:
> We know her woof, her texture: she is given
> In the dull catalogue of common things.
> Philosophy will clip an Angel's wings,
> Conquer all mysteries by rule and line,
> Empty the haunted air, and gnomed mine –
> Unweave a rainbow[5]

Newtonian science provides explanations which leave the world, according to Keats, a duller place. Davy's type of scientist is of a different order as they seek to illuminate the mysteries of the natural world and in doing so enable us to see the world differently, as its occulted wonders become exposed (rather than obscured through dry analytical description).[6] Frankenstein, in highly egotistical terms, reflects some of this spirit when he tells Walton of his early scientific ambitions that:

> Life and death appeared to me ideal bounds, which I should first break through, and pour a torrent of light into our dark world. A new species would bless me as its creator and source; many happy and excellent natures would owe their being to me.　　　　　　　　　　　　　　　　　　　　　　　(p. 36)

Davy's application of electricity in his experiments enabled him to demonstrate 'that chemical affinities were related to electrical powers and that elements could be identified in electrochemical terms'.[7] This might seem to be tangential to the type of science conducted by Frankenstein, but we should note that he too has an interest in electricity. Mary Shelley would have had Davy's experiments in mind; her journal entry of 28 October 1816 indicates that she had just started reading Davy's *Elements of Chemical Philosophy* (1812) that included his electrochemical papers, which she read until 4 November whilst she was working on the novel. The journal also records that she spent much of November reading, amongst literary narratives by Richardson, Swift and Edgeworth, Locke's *An Essay Concerning Human Understanding* (1690) which would play an important role in establishing how Frankenstein's creature develops a sense of self through experiences which imprint themselves on the *tabula rasa* (blank slate) of the mind.[8]

The young Frankenstein attempts to cast off the influence of the mystics when he is introduced to electricity by his father who explains that lightning is a form of natural electricity that one can, to some degree, harness. Indeed his father appears to be familiar with the effects of electricity, with Frankenstein noting that 'He constructed a small electrical machine, and exhibited a few experiments; he made also a kite, with a wire and string, which drew down that fluid from the clouds' (p. 24). The experiment with the kite recalls Benjamin Franklin's claim in 1752 that he used a kite to conduct lightning and so proved that lightning was a form of electricity. However, the claim that electricity was a 'fluid' would prove scientifically contentious, while the contextual associations of electricity with America (a country which, like the French republic, was characterized by a spirit of open enquiry and democratic freedom) would prove, post-independence, politically controversial. First, it is necessary to consider the scientific context of electricity, although in practice this is difficult to disentangle from the wider political dramas of the time.

Mary Shelley would have been aware of the links made between electricity and ideas of life as these formed part of the discussion at the infamous ghost story competition at the Villa Diodati in June 1816, with Mary Shelley recalling in her 1831 Introduction to *Frankenstein* that:

> Many and long were the conversations between Lord Byron and Shelley, to which I was a devout but nearly silent listener. During one of these, various philosophical doctrines were discussed, and among others the nature of the principle of life, and whether there was any probability of its ever being discovered and communicated. (p. 195)[9]

The idea that electricity represented a potential life force was elaborated in the experiments of Giovanni Aldini (1762–1834) who, following the work of his uncle, Luigi Galvani (1737–1798), had demonstrated how the application of electricity to frogs' legs, bulls' heads and recently executed criminals could induce physical reflexes that appeared to restore mobility to the dead. Aldini's experiments in London in 1803, when he induced spasms in the body of the recently executed murderer, George Forster, received widespread media coverage. The followers of galvanism believed in the presence of animal electricity which lurked within the body and which could be stimulated by contact with an external electrical force. Such a view implied that if the conditions were right then it should be possible to reanimate the dead with a jolt of electricity which would re-activate the body's dormant animal electricity. A contrary view was taken by Alessandro Volta (1745–1827), who claimed that animal electricity did not exist independently of metallic electricity and 'Volta took pains to insist that animal electricity was metallic electricity and not some internal force of the animal'.[10] Ultimately it would be proved that the nerves of the body were not hollow tubes that could, as Galvani had argued, be hydraulically reanimated when the fluid within them became recharged.[11] The idea that electricity was a fluid was alluded to in Frankenstein's account of the kite experiment and electricity appears as the 'spark of being' (p. 38) that Frankenstein refers to as bringing the creature to life. This position appears to reflect Aldini's view that animal electricity can be reanimated by metallic electricity. The creature's animation is seemingly the consequence of a reactivated life force which exists within the materiality of the body parts from which he is assembled. Life is therefore not found outside the body, or separate from it, because electricity is simply the agent that is employed to bring to life what is already there to be reanimated. Such a position can helpfully be related to discussions about vitalism in the period which in turn led to a scientific (and indeed political) controversy in which Shelley's novel was to find itself implicated.

Vitalism was a theory which maintained that a life force ran through all living things including plants, animals and people. Erasmus Darwin (1731–1802), Charles Darwin's grandfather, believed that it was possible to discern patterns of inheritance in plants that could also be applied to humans. Learning from one type of life could provide the key to other forms of life. Darwin's writing blurred any easy generic distinctions between literature and science, and long poems such as The Botanic Garden (1791) and The Temple of Nature (1803) developed ideas about evolution that he had mapped in the more scientifically conventional discourse of Zoonomia (1794–1796). Darwin was also a great believer in the positive attributes of electricity and is referred to as a possible influence on Frankenstein in both the opening lines of

Percy Shelley's Preface to the 1818 edition and Mary Shelley's Introduction to the 1831 edition. Darwin attributed much of evolution to a God-like Creator. However, the idea of where 'life' might come from (from within the body, or granted to it) underpinned a scientific controversy bearing directly on Shelley's novel that took place as a series of debates in 1814–1819 between two professors from the Royal College of Surgeons: John Abernethy (1764–1831) and William Lawrence (1783–1867).

Abernethy argued for the presence of a life force which was independent of the body and this challenged a purely materialist account of physiology. For materialists, such as Lawrence, life was merely the consequence of a healthily functioning organic unity which would cease once a vital organ had become terminally diseased. Life, for Lawrence, was therefore a matter of bodily function. Mary and Percy Shelley were familiar with his views because Lawrence became Percy Shelley's physician in the period prior to the writing of *Frankenstein*. This debate can be read as reflecting the different positions on animal and metallic electricity held by Aldini and Volta earlier in the century (about whether electrical energy was located within or outside of the body). For Abernethy electricity was an outside agent which analogously suggested the presence of the soul.[12] The use of electricity in *Frankenstein*, however, is ambivalent because it does not constitute an independent life force, but rather functions as an agent of physical reanimation with the novel reflecting the material, biological organicism of Lawrence in which Frankenstein's pursuits take place 'among the unhallowed damps of the grave' in which Frankenstein 'seemed to have lost all soul or sensation' (p. 36). Abernethy's position suggests the possible presence of a soul that animates the body and which departs it on death, whereas the experiment with electricity in *Frankenstein* is a specifically secular affair (even if the novel does raise questions about whether Frankenstein has usurped the authority of God in creating life).

The public disagreement between Abernethy and Lawrence was seemingly won by Lawrence, a persuasive and charismatic public speaker whose position appeared to have more scientific coherence than that of Abernethy who, according to Marilyn Butler in her critically important account of this conflict, was searching for a compromise that could 'unite religious and secular opinion with a formula acceptable to both'.[13] This was important because in the post-French Revolutionary era there emerged a politically reactionary scepticism about the apparent atheistic radicalism of new scientific thinking. Lawrence was also aware of these contexts and had made some efforts to distance himself from earlier models of human evolutionary perfectibility that had been linked to revolutionary ideas about social and political progress mapped by Mary Shelley's father, William Godwin, in his *Enquiry*

Concerning Political Justice and its Influence on Morals and Happiness (1793), to whom *Frankenstein* was dedicated. Butler argues that *Frankenstein* can be read as a composite of Lawrence and Abernethy's views in which the assembling of the creature reworks Lawrence's materialism, whereas the notion that 'life' can be added to an organism reflects that of Abernethy.[14] However, *Frankenstein* more clearly reflects a secular view and it is not clear that there is a God in the text who has been profaned. The emphasis on the psychodrama played out between Frankenstein and his creature complicates any theologically understood notion of 'evil', while the discourses of retribution which permeate the novel can be more credibly assigned to personal rather than religiously formed grievances.

This debate is important for us to consider because it demonstrates the political context of scientific discussion and indicates how ideas about materialism shaped the construction of the creature in *Frankenstein*. This debate also explains why in the 1831 edition of the novel Shelley made Frankenstein a more ethically anxious and theologically sensitive figure. Lawrence's views might have seemed to have scientifically won the day, but the publication of his *Natural History of Man* (1819) was condemned by reactionary elements of the press who saw it as promoting atheism, and in 1822 the Lord Chancellor ruled that Lawrence's lectures were blasphemous, which led Lawrence to repudiate his book when his position at the Royal College of Surgeons became threatened. Butler argues that Mary Shelley was mindful of the hostile reception that Lawrence's views had received and moved the 1831 edition away from the stark materialism of the 1818 edition.[15]

Frankenstein attends the University of Ingolstadt which was associated with the Illuminati, a group formed in the late eighteenth century who believed in the supernatural. Crucially, they were also, in the main, supporters of the French Revolution, which means that Frankenstein, who attends university just after the Revolution (Walton's narrative fits a time frame which suggests 1799 for his letters), is positioned at the centre of political and epistemological radicalism. The alignment of science with radicalism is clear from the treatment of Joseph Priestley (who contributed to the discovery of the properties of oxygen in 1774), a supporter of the Revolution whose laboratory was burned down by an anti-Jacobin mob in 1791. This was because his scientific beliefs and political leanings were seen as mutually supportive, leading Edmund Burke to claim that (and he has Priestley explicitly in mind here), 'These philosophers are fanatics . . . they are carried with such an headlong rage towards every desperate trial, that they would sacrifice the whole human race to the slightest of their experiments'.[16] Electricity had, in a revolutionary context, seemed to symbolize the destructive capacity of revolutionary energy. As the Revolution had indicated that social progress was possible, so discoveries in electricity had suggested scientific progress.

As noted earlier, both the preface to the 1818 edition by Percy Shelley and Mary Shelley's 1831 Introduction make reference to the work of Erasmus Darwin, who had modelled an early theory of evolutionary development which suggested the interconnectedness of all life forms. Phillip Armstrong has noted that *Frankenstein* 'draws heavily on the Romantic proto-evolutionism' of Darwin's work, which suggested that death provides the context out of which new life can be formed.[17] Frankenstein recounts that he discovered the means by which life could be created by looking at death, because 'To examine the causes of life, we must first have recourse to death' (p. 33), however 'the science of anatomy...was not sufficient; I must also observe the natural decay and corruption of the human body' (p. 33). To that end he visits a churchyard in order to observe the process of organic decay in which he notes 'the change from life to death, and death to life' until 'from the midst of the darkness a sudden light broke in upon me' (p. 34). This moment of proto-Enlightenment revelation accords, as Armstrong notes, with Darwin who stated in an essay published in 1803 that 'the most simple animals and vegetables may be produced by the congress of the parts of decomposing organic matter'.[18] This was a position that Darwin would pursue in his long poem *The Temple of Nature*, which records how life is generated out of death. Indeed Darwin would go so far as to assert in *Phytologia; or, The Philosophy of Agriculture and Gardening* (1800), in an extended account of composting, that human remains could enrich the soil from which plants could be grown.[19] Darwin also had interests in electricity and, as Tim Fulford, Debbie Less and Peter J. Kitson have noted in *The Botanic Garden*, Darwin accords electricity a vibratory power which could control and subdue the minds and bodies of others:

> Starts the quick Ether through the fibre-trains
> Of dancing arteries, and of tingling veins,
> Goads each fine nerve, with new sensation thrill'd,
> Bends the reluctant limbs with power unwill'd.[20]

These models of life generated out of older, dead forms in which electricity shapes mental processes can be read as analogies about the generation of revolutionary ideas. This is a view confirmed by Darwin's enthusiastic endorsement of the destruction of the Bastille, which he also refers to in *The Botanic Garden*. Miranda Burgess has noted that conceits about electrical influence also appeared in reactionary descriptions of how the National Assembly in France had supposedly manipulated the media in order, according to one political pamphleteer, to 'direct...the electrical fluid of...popular phrenzy against the ancient fabric' of monarchical rule.[21] Political freedoms and scientific discoveries were thus analogously aligned as Darwin argues that a revolution in science, as in politics, would set the populace free. The energy of a revolutionary mob thus resembles the transformative power of electricity. What is noteworthy about these connections between progressive science and radical politics is how self-conscious they are. The attempt to discredit a certain type of science because of these links gained currency in the late eighteenth century and explains why Davy was, by 1812, keen to distance himself from this earlier tradition even though he had some links to it, having worked with the radical scientist Thomas Beddoes in the late 1790s.

By the time we get to the genesis of *Frankenstein* it is important to note that the French Revolution was a dead letter. Bonaparte had been defeated at Waterloo in 1815 and the type of geographical journeying around mainland Europe that *Frankenstein* represents was only possible once the restrictions on movement imposed by war were removed. As we have seen in the instance of Lawrence, however, the cultural policing of science was still ongoing. These contexts are important because they indicate where Mary Shelley's political enthusiasms lay.

At one level the novel can be read as a critique of idealism. The novel makes frequent reference to models of paradise from which the chief characters (Frankenstein, the creature and Robert Walton) are estranged. The repeated references to Milton's *Paradise Lost* (1674) indicate that the world of *Frankenstein* is a post-lapsarian, post-idealistic one, and given Mary Shelley's associations with a radical circle of poets and philosophers it is tempting to read the novel as a lament for a now lost idealistic discourse of scientific and political radicalism. This disjunction between idealism and reality is graphically captured in Frankenstein's account of the creature's construction. The passage is worth quoting in full:

> How can I describe my emotions at this catastrophe, or how delineate the wretch whom with such infinite pains and care I had endeavoured to form? His limbs were in proportion, and I had selected his features as beautiful. Beautiful! – Great God! His yellow skin scarcely covered the work of muscles and arteries beneath; his hair was of a lustrous black, and flowing; his teeth of a pearly whiteness; but these luxuriances only formed a more horrid contrast with his watery eyes, that seemed almost of the same colour as the dun white sockets in which they were set, his shrivelled complexion, and straight black lips. (p. 39)

The disjunction between conception and reality is stark. The pursuit of beauty has generated ugliness. The creature is a mixture of parts, some of which are more aesthetically pleasing than others. Overall, however, there is a sense that the experiment has been botched in part because the creature with his 'dun white sockets...shrivelled complexion, and straight black lips' resembles a corpse rather than a living person. The creature is an aesthetic failure as, although he does represent the triumph of a certain scientific process, Frankenstein at this point is unable to think scientifically because he is looking aesthetically (as will all the characters who encounter the creature). It is important to read this moment figuratively because Mary Shelley wants to stress the failure of an idealistic vision and this can be read in scientific and political terms despite the ostensible focus on the 'beautiful'.

Given the clear cultural links which existed at the time between science and politics, we can read this loss of idealism as representing a loss of faith in the radical models of social progress that the French Revolution had seemingly engendered. Idealism leads to murder, terror and death and suggests that what works in theory might not work so well in practice. The novel is, however, equivocal about such matters and the psychologically complex relationship between Frankenstein and the creature makes it difficult to apportion blame in any easy way. At one level Frankenstein will take responsibility, eventually, for having created a creature which has killed his brother William, the family servant Justine Moritz and his friend Henry Clerval. Nevertheless Frankenstein remains a tragic figure who invites a certain amount of sympathy for his failed ambitions. The creature can also, to some degree, be excused for his behaviour because as he tells Frankenstein '"I am malicious because I am miserable; am I not shunned and hated by all mankind?"' (p. 119). Frankenstein tells his story to Walton because he sees in Walton an earlier version of himself. At the end, as he lies dying, Frankenstein says to Walton:

'Farewell, Walton! Seek happiness in tranquillity, and avoid ambition, even if it be only the apparently innocent one of distinguishing yourself in science and discoveries. Yet why do I say this? I have myself been blasted in these hopes, yet another may succeed.'   (p. 186)

The failure of idealism may be only partial and this is in keeping with an ambivalent response to the radicalism which underpins the science of the time. However, when we consider some of the gendered aspects of science a different narrative emerges.

A key critical intervention in debates about gender in *Frankenstein* was made by Anne K. Mellor in '*Frankenstein*: A Feminist Critique of Science' (1987) where she argues that Shelley produces a feminist reading of the gendered metaphors which pervaded the science of the time.[22] Mellor notes that scientists such as Davy represented nature as female and that science functioned as a masculine assertion of mastery over this feminized nature. These gendered roles are also registered in the different types of education followed by the young Frankenstein and Elizabeth, with Frankenstein recalling that:

> I delighted in investigating the facts relative to the actual world; she busied herself in following the aerial creations of the poets. The world was to me a secret, which I desired to discover; to her it was a vacancy, which she sought to people with imaginations of her own.　　　　　　　　　　(p. 21)

Waldman had, as we saw earlier, endorsed the practices of the mystics because '"They penetrate[d] into the recesses of nature, and shew how she works in her hiding places"' (p. 30), and later Frankenstein recounts that 'with unrelaxed and breathless eagerness, I pursued nature to her hiding places' (p. 36). Education is gendered, but so is a scientific conception of nature. The pursuit of science is an exclusively masculine one and the difference and distance between male and female worlds is dramatized in Walton's sending of letters from the North Pole to his sister, Margaret Saville, who represents a model of domesticity that he has left behind. Mellor argues that this triumph over a feminized nature is also implied by how Frankenstein, in creating life, has eradicated the role of women in giving birth which in turn explains why the women in the novel seem so sexless (and why he wishes to destroy the potential mate he is making for the creature).[23] Read in this way, science appears to be individualistic, egotistical and opposed to the feminine.

We have noted how Frankenstein indicates that in order to understand life we need to have recourse to death and the points of contact that this had with Erasmus Darwin. Frankenstein also indicates a further development which would become highly controversial in the nineteenth century when he recounts that he 'tortured the living animal' as part of his experiments. Anita Guerrini has noted that the creature is assembled from human and animal parts and so 'inhabits that liminal area between human and animal'.[24] The issue of vivisection was less contentious in 1818 than it was by the time of the 1831 edition. In 1824 the French physiologist François Magendie (1783–1855) conducted a series of experiments in London in which he vivisected several animals. Whilst at the time this was not seen as morally questionable, the media returned to these experiments in early 1825 when a bill to abolish bear-baiting was being discussed in Parliament and Magendie's animal cruelty was used as a context for these debates.[25] The Society for the Prevention of Cruelty to Animals was established in 1824 (becoming the RSPCA in 1840), and the growing public mood against vivisection was clear. To some degree anatomists, who had complained for some time about the difficulty of gaining access to the recently deceased (which had in turn led to bodysnatching and the infamous murders committed by Burke and Hare in Edinburgh in 1828), were able to move from live animals to dead humans after the passing of the 1832 Anatomy Act. The Act gave physicians access to unclaimed corpses and this often meant that those dying in penury, such as in workhouses, could often find themselves on the anatomist's slab. Whilst there would be public concern about such treatment of the poor (and vivisection would be pursued with varying degrees of scientific enthusiasm until the passing of the Cruelty to Animals Act of 1876 placed firm limits on animal experimentation), it is important to note the context in which Frankenstein worked. As Guerrini argues, the composite creature is part animal and part human and so 'offers himself as an object of experimenta-tion in terms' of both vivisection and human anatomy, which demonstrates Shelley's awareness of the contexts in which anatomical investigations took place.[26]

So far we have considered the type of science and scientific practice pur-sued by Frankenstein, but his is not the only scientific narrative in the novel and we also need to account for how Walton's ambitions are also staged within the context of polar explorations of the time. Walton indicates that he had renounced his early interests in poetry due to his failure to become a writer and embraced the more masculine (so the novel suggests) endeav-ours of working on the North Sea whaling ships when he 'devoted . . . nights to the study of mathematics, the theory of medicine, and those branches of physical science from which a naval adventurer might derive the greatest practical advantage' (p. 7). Walton's science might be less metaphysical than that of Frankenstein but the sense of egotistical ambition is similar. Walton, like Frankenstein, is an idealist who believes that he may discover a tropical paradise at the North Pole – which develops the theme of paradise which runs throughout the novel.

Jessica Richard has noted that in the immediate post-Napoleonic era 'both the history and the future of polar exploration were subject to increasingly fervent discussion in scientific circles and popular journals in England'.[27] Walton's frame narrative was added to the novel at some point in late 1816 (after Shelley had begun work on the novel over the summer) and coincides with these debates. Richard has argued that Mellor's claim that the novel represents a feminist critique of science can be extended to Walton because his endeavours are also an attempt to master nature, at a time when there was much discussion concerning the heroism of those who could discover the North-West Passage, find a true bearing for magnetic north and locate the temperate polar sea that many saw as characterizing the terrain at the North Pole. Walton sets out his various ambitions to his sister. He claims:

> you cannot contest the inestimable benefit which I shall confer on all mankind
> to the last generation, by discovering a passage near the pole to those countries,
> to reach which at present so many months are requisite; or by ascertaining the
> secret of the magnet, which, if at all possible, can only be effected by an
> undertaking such as mine.
> (p. 6)

Walton's ambitions are both scientific and commercial. The 'secret of the magnet' at this time had much in common with ideas about electricity. Both electrical and magnetic forces were controlled through polarities (negative and positive – electricity; attraction and repulsion – magnetism), which has led to the view that 'Walton's magnetic science is shown as being...analogous to Frankenstein's electro-chemistry'.[28] These models of energy, which suggested the power of the relationship between polarities, can also be more widely applied to Romanticism as evidenced by Blake's claim in 'The Marriage of Heaven and Hell' (1790) that 'Without contraries there is no progression. Attraction and repulsion, reason and energy, love and hate, are necessary to human existence.'[29] These scientific discoveries were thus reworked as analogies about dialectics which in political terms emphasized the necessity of conflict as a means of enabling progress. Ideas, and societies, can thus be overthrown by opposition to the ruling conventions. This also indicates just how far science at the time was understood as providing metaphors for social and political change.

Tellingly, Walton refers to Coleridge's *The Rime of the Ancient Mariner* (1798) when writing to his sister 'I am going to unexplored regions, to "the land of mist and snow;" but I shall kill no albatross' (p. 10). Walton is clear that he intends not to make the same mistakes as the ancient mariner, and so avoid the type of destruction faced by the mariner's crew which occurs when Walton, reluctantly, agrees to turn the ship towards home once it has become free of its frozen moorings. Walton's ambitions are not just scientific, they are also commercial because the discovery of a North-West Passage through the ice cap would have made European trading with the East more lucrative as it would have eliminated the need to sail around the landmass of America.[30]

Jessica Richard has noted that Walton's ambitions appear to be the product of romance rather than science because they seem to extend his earlier poetic fancies. The great adventure of discovery accorded to polar investigation was granted an heroic status in the period which contrasts somewhat with Frankenstein's secretive scientific explorations which take place in his 'workshop of filthy creation' (p. 36). There is an argument therefore that these scientific investigations function as metaphors about creativity and the imagination. Frankenstein focalizes a language of creativity which makes him resemble the Romantic writer who celebrates the power of the imagination, and who strives after beauty even whilst in this instance it leads to the creation of ugliness because the imagination is diseased and feverish – he tells Walton that as he worked on the creature 'Every night I was oppressed by a slow fever, and I became nervous to a most painful degree; a disease that I regretted' (p. 38). The creature can therefore be seen as a product, not just of science, but also of a disorientated imagination. Christa Knellwolf has also argued that scientific explorations, like that of Walton's, also blurred the distinction between inner and outer worlds. For Knellwolf, 'The attempt to map inner geography was a new approach to the understanding of human nature. It modelled itself on the real experience of the world's geography made available by contemporary journeys of exploration'.[31] The way out was also the way in and this demonstrates the highly mobile metaphors around science which existed at the time.

Reading *Frankenstein* within its various scientific contexts reveals not just how aware Mary Shelley was about scientific debates (and her journal indicates quite extensive reading in areas of science), but also the political flavour of science at the time. Images of scientific progress were echoed in ideas of social and political progress, which unsettled many who were opposed to the radical ideas which had shaped the French Revolution. Writing from the vantage point of 1818, in a novel begun the year after Napoleon's defeat at Waterloo, this radicalism seems to have lost its way. However, as *Frankenstein* illustrates, the picture is much more complex than that and the novel's refusal to either fully endorse or extol radical views should be seen as part of the political ambiguities of the time in which radicals, such as Mary Shelley and her milieu, were unclear about where to go next. Science both reflected and fed these ambiguities and provides a context through which we can, retrospectively, make sense of them.

NOTES

1 For a tale in which Mary Shelley explores ideas about the elixir of life see her 'The Mortal: Immortal: A Tale' in *Mary Shelley: Collected Tales and Stories*, ed. Charles E. Robinson (Baltimore, MD: Johns Hopkins University Press, 1976), pp. 219–30.

2 Mary Shelley, *Frankenstein*, ed. and Intro. Marilyn Butler (Oxford University Press, 1998), pp. 23, 29. Future references will be made parenthetically.

3 Maurice Hindle, 'Introduction' to *Frankenstein*, ed. and Intro. Maurice Hindle (Harmondsworth: Penguin, 1985), pp. 7–42, p. 25.

4 Humphry Davy, 'A Discourse, Introduction to a Course of Lectures on Chemistry', in *The Collected Works of Sir Humphry Davy*, 9 vols., ed. John Davy (London: Smith, Elder and Co, 1839), Vol. II, pp. 307–26, p. 319.

5 John Keats, *Lamia* in *Keats: Poetical Works*, ed. H. W. Gorrod (Oxford University Press), pp. 161–79, lines 231–7. The reference to Newton is to his essay 'New Theory about Light and Colours' in *Philosophical Transactions*, 80 (1672), pp. 3086–7.

6 See Richard Holmes's *The Age of Wonder: How the Romantic Generation Discovered the Beauty and Terror of Science* (New York: Harper Collins, 2009).

7 Tim Fulford, Debbie Lee and Peter J. Kitson, *Literature, Science and Exploration in the Romantic Era* (Cambridge University Press, 2004), p. 194.

8 See *The Journals of Mary Shelley Vol 1: 1814–1822*, eds., Paula R. Feldman and Diana Scott-Kilvert (Oxford: Clarendon, 1987), pp. 142–8.

9 The 1831 Introduction can be found as Appendix A in *Frankenstein*, ed. and Intro. Marilyn Butler (Oxford University Press, 1993), pp. 192–7, p. 195.

10 Richard C. Sha, 'Volta's Battery, Animal Electricity, and *Frankenstein*' in *European Review*, 23(1), (2012), 21–41, 22.

11 See ibid., 29.

12 Abernathy set out his views in *An Enquiry into the Probability and Rationality of Mr Hunter's Theory of Life* (London: Longman, 1814).

13 Marilyn Butler, '*Frankenstein* and Radical Science', in *Frankenstein*, ed., J. Paul Hunter (London: Norton, 2012), pp. 404–16, p. 406. The article was originally published in the *Times Literary Supplement*, 9 April 1993.

14 Ibid., p. 409.

15 Ibid., p. 415.

16 Edmund Burke, *A Letter from the Right Honourable Edmund Burke to a Noble Lord* (London, 1796), p. 26.

17 Philip Armstrong, *What Animals Mean in the Fiction of Modernity* (London and New York: Routledge, 2008), p. 73.

18 Erasmus Darwin, 'Spontaneous Vitality of Microscopic Animals' in *The Golden Age: The Temple of Nature, or, the Origin of Society* (New York and London: Garland, 1978), p. 8.

19 Erasmus Darwin, *Phytologia; or, The Philosophy of Agriculture and Gardening* (London: John Johnson, 1800).

20 Erasmus Darwin, *The Botanic Garden: A Poem in Two Parts. I, The Economy of Vegetation* (London, 1791), p. 35.

21 Quote from *The Antigallican: or, Strictures on the Present Form of Government Established in France* (London: Faulder, 1793), p. 19. See Miranda Burgess 'Transporting Frankenstein: Mary Shelley's Mobile Figures', *European Romantic Review*, 25(3) (2014), 247–65.

22 Anne K. Mellor, '*Frankenstein*: A Feminist Critique of Science' in *One Culture: Essays in Science and Literature*, ed. George Levine (University of Wisconsin Press, 1987), pp. 287–312.

23 Ibid., p. 308.

24 Anita Guerrini, 'Animal Experiments and Antivivisection Debates in the 1820s' in Christa Knellwolf and Jane Goodall (eds.), *Frankenstein's Science: Experimentation and Discovery in Romantic Culture, 1780–1830* (Aldershot: Ashgate, 2008), pp. 71–85, p. 71.

25 Ibid., p. 78.

26 Ibid., p. 73. For a full account of the 1832 Anatomy Act and how it relates to *Frankenstein* see Tim Marshall's *Murdering to Dissect: Grave-Robbing, Frankenstein, and the Anatomy Literature* (Manchester University Press, 1995).

27 Jessica Richard, '"A Paradise of My Own Creation": *Frankenstein* and the Improbable Romance of Polar Exploration' in *Nineteenth-Century Contexts: An Interdisciplinary Journal*, 25(4) (2003), 295–314, 296.

28 Fulford et al., *Literature, Science and Exploration*, p. 170.

29 William Blake, 'The Marriage of Heaven and Hell' in *William Blake, Selected Poetry*, ed. and Intro, Michael Mason (Oxford University Press, 1998), pp. 74–86, p. 74.

30 See Fulford et al., *Literature, Science and Exploration*, p. 159.

31 Christa Knellwolf, 'Geographic Boundaries and Inner Space: *Frankenstein*, Scientific Explorations and the Quest for the Absolute' in Christa Knellwolf and Jane Goodall (eds.), *Frankenstein's Science: Experimentation and Discovery in Romantic Culture, 1780–1830* (Aldershot: Ashgate, 2008), pp. 49–69, p. 49.

6

ADRIANA CRACIUN

Frankenstein's Politics

Frankenstein's approach to the revolutionary politics of the early nineteenth century was complex and ambivalent, making this novel a powerful touchstone for subsequent eras. Mary Shelley crafted *Frankenstein* using a nested set of narrative frames so that each frame's protagonist – Walton, Victor, the creature, and (via the creature) Safie – refracts the novel's politics through a different contemporary debate. The result is a kaleidoscopic political imaginary that has helped regenerate the novel's iconic status for new generations. The political dimensions of *Frankenstein* were immediately apparent to its original readers and reviewers, and have continued to evolve as new media returned to Shelley's iconic monster in particular, and his protean ability to voice and embody a remarkable range of later political crises – from revolutionary Marxism, Irish independence, abolition and slave rebellions, to animal rights, human cloning and genetic research. This chapter focuses on the original political concerns of the 1818 novel in Shelley's day, as channelled through its distinct frame narrators.

As the daughter of Britain's leading radical writers of the 1790s – William Godwin and Mary Wollstonecraft – Mary Shelley inherited a radical political legacy difficult to sustain, and one that overshadowed her writing throughout her career. By dedicating the anonymously published *Frankenstein* to 'William Godwin, author of *Political Justice* [and] *Caleb Williams*', Shelley situated the novel deliberately in this radical legacy of Godwinian radical idealism and his novel of persecution and paranoia. In the 1790s, Godwin's *Enquiry Concerning Political Justice* (1793) had become the incendiary text most identified with British radicalism – its combination of commitment to austere justice, passionate denunciation of economic inequality and idealist faith in the withering away of unjust institutions through rational enlightenment, permeated public debates in the revolutionary decades and made Godwin's name notorious.

Godwin's philosophy of perfectibility envisioned doing away not only with the state but with sexual reproduction, perhaps even all sexuality and mortality, as he described in the famous section on 'Of Health, and the Prolongation of Human Life':

> The men... who exist when the earth shall refuse itself to a more extended population, will cease to propagate, for they will no longer have any motive, either of error or duty, to induce them. In addition to this they will perhaps be immortal. The whole will be a race of men, and not of children. Generation will not succeed generation, nor will truth have in a certain degree to recommence her career at the end of every thirty years. There will be no war, no crimes, no administration of justice as it is called, and no government... Beside this, there will be neither disease, anguish, melancholy, nor resentment.[1]

By taking to the (il)logical extreme Godwin's faith in the potential for human immortality through reason, Shelley uses Victor's obsession with creation without sexual reproduction to recast Godwin's utopian vision as a dystopian 'usurpation of the female'.[2] Had Shelley simply thus caricatured Godwin and his utopian project, *Frankenstein* would have been a forgettable anti-Jacobin screed, one of many. But instead, Shelley ingeniously imbricated the novel's inflammatory politics in a series of concentric narratives, so that narrative authority is notoriously difficult to assign, making for a nuanced and ambivalent political vision.

Shelley's approach to Godwin's political philosophy is thus extremely complex. While Godwin's philosophical radicalism was associated by counter-revolutionary writers with French revolutionary agitation and English Jacobinism, Godwin himself had remained opposed to putting democratic reforms in practice, taking issue with associations like the London Corresponding Society because he feared their populist appeals would unleash 'disorder and tumult' and drown out the sober reasoning of 'persons of distinction'.[3] Godwin preferred that political change happen through rational contemplation and 'universal benevolence' on the part of educated philosophers like himself. This fundamental tension between Godwinian idealism ('metaphysics', to use the language of his day) and its material and social practice is central to *Frankenstein*'s politics – central to the novel's critique of radical philosophy and revolutionary change, and to the novel's, and especially the creature's, two centuries of permutations as icon of revolutionary philosophy gone horribly wrong.

From his inception in Ingolstadt, the legendary origin of the Illuminati order, to his surreptitious education via the works of Volney, Goethe and Plutarch, *Frankenstein*'s creature embodied revolution. But Shelley's genius was in elevating her revolutionary creature above the polarized visions of the pro-revolutionary and anti-Jacobin writings on which she drew. Edmund Burke's *Reflections on the Revolution in France* (1790) had been the central counter-revolutionary text of the 1790s, popularizing a highly charged language of monstrosity, parricide and cannibalism when speaking of the French Revolution. For Burke, the Revolution was 'a species of political monster, which has always ended by devouring those who have produced it.'[4] An even more sensationalized political inspiration was Abbé Barruel's *Memoirs Illustrating the History of Jacobinism* (1797), a vast conspiracy theory that located the philosophical origins of the 1789 Revolution in the secretive Illuminati order founded in Ingolstadt, which 'engendered that disastrous monster called Jacobin, raging uncontrolled, and almost unopposed, in these days of horror.'[5]

A favourite book of Percy Shelley's, and one read by Mary Shelley in 1814, Barruel's *Memoirs* along with Burke's *Reflections* provided the counter-revolutionary landscape of paranoia and unnatural revolt that has long associated Shelley's romance with counter-revolutionary reaction against her radical parentage. As Lee Sterrenburg showed in a groundbreaking essay, Burke's demonization of the Revolution as a monster saturated counter-revolutionary narratives and became attached to William Godwin. For Sterrenburg, Shelley 'has appropriated the standard conservative portrayal of Godwinism' as monstrous, 'but purges it of virtually all reference to collective movements', transforming it from political melodrama to 'domestic tragedy'.[6] The result is that this domesticization and internalization effectively depoliticizes the creature's eloquent protests against class privilege and inequality. But simultaneously, Shelley's internalization of political debates creates an original and more complex political dynamic, in which the monstrous Jacobins imagined by Burke and Barruel are entangled with their monstrous progenitors, the men of privilege like Victor, whose egocentric rants against the creature's demands for equality appear as diabolical as the creature's rationalization of violence.

In fact the language of monstrosity was used widely by counter-revolutionaries and pro-revolutionaries alike throughout the 1790s. Godwin had described the feudal system as a devouring 'ferocious monster', and Thomas Paine in *Rights of Man* (1791) wrote of 'exterminat[ing] the monster Aristocracy'.[7] Mary Wollstonecraft, Shelley's mother, whom she reread closely throughout her life, voiced in 1794 a sentiment that may as well have been spoken by the creature himself: 'People are rendered ferocious by misery; and misanthropy is ever the offspring of discontent.'[8] As Chris Baldick shows in *In Frankenstein's Shadow* (1987), though it was Burke who 'first recognized and named the great political "monster" of the modern age', the language of monstrosity saturated the full spectrum of political discourse in the revolutionary decades.[9]

Ingolstadt, where Victor creates the creature and the epicentre of Illuminati conspiracy according to Barruel, and Geneva, Victor's and Rousseau's birthplace, anchor the political geography of the novel within this polarized debate on the French Revolution. The creature's origins in Ingolstadt and Geneva fit well with the revolutionary questions he asks about privilege, property and equality, as he gives voice to the Rousseauvian and Jacobin critiques of his imagined birthplaces.

Educated by overhearing the lessons of the De Lacey family taken from the works of Plutarch and Volney, two revolutionary favourites, the creature learns of class inequality:

> I heard of the division of property, of immense wealth and squalid poverty; of rank, descent, and noble blood.
>
>   The words induced me to turn towards myself. I learned that the possessions most esteemed by your fellow-creatures were, high and unsullied descent united with riches. A man might be respected with only one of these acquisitions; but without either he was considered, except in very rare instances, as a vagabond and a slave, doomed to waste his powers for the profit of the chosen few.[10]

Seeking sympathy and equality, Shelley's creature here also echoes Rousseau, who like him had famously lamented in *The Reveries of a Solitary Walker* (1782):

> Here I am then, alone on the earth, having neither brother, neighbour, friend, or society but myself. The most sociable and the most friendly of mankind is proscribed from the rest by universal consent. They have sought in the refinements of their malice to find out that torment which could most afflict my tender heart; they have violently broken every tie which held me to them: I had loved mankind in spite of themselves.[11]

The Shelleys were 'immersed in both the literary as well as the literal landscapes of Rousseau's life and work' in the summer of 1816, visiting Lake Geneva and rereading *La Nouvelle Héloïse* (1761).[12] The renowned Genevan philosopher of sentiment, liberty, exile and education was at one point described by Wollstonecraft as the 'true Prometheus of sentiment',[13] and his influence is visible in Shelley's characters' intense experience of Alpine nature and the creature's development in solitude.

But Rousseau was also an infamous figure in counter-revolutionary circles for his abandonment of his five children to a foundling hospital, seen as a failure of revolutionary philosophy (and sympathy) that outdid Godwin's. By ingeniously overlaying this series of flawed father figures who neglected their children (Victor, Godwin, Rousseau, God), Shelley is able to both evoke their most powerful political claims while holding them subject to the critique of the 'domestic affections' and of gender, which their consistently masculinist political liberties denied.

Of all the voices in Shelley's polyvocal text, it is the creature's that captivates us the most. The creature's political education generates the novel's most radical provocations linking the oppression of gender, class, race and empire together in such a way as to resonate with new audiences across two centuries on a scale unknown with other Romantic-era works. Thus the creature learns of the link between class inequality, racism and empire: 'I heard of the discovery of the American hemisphere, and wept with Safie over the hapless fate of its original inhabitants' (p. 95). His own experience is distinctly racialized and deliberately compared to that of African slaves:

> I knew that I possessed no money, no friends, no kind of property. I was, besides, endowed with a figure hideously deformed and loathsome; I was not even of the same nature as man. I was more agile than they, and could subsist upon coarser diet; I bore the extremes of heat and cold with less injury to my frame; my stature far exceeded theirs. When I looked around, I saw and heard of none like me. Was I then a monster, a blot upon the earth, from which all men fled, and whom all men disowned? (p. 96)[14]

Burke had famously compared French revolutionaries to rebelling slaves 'suddenly broke loose from the house of bondage'[15] and unfit to rule themselves, and as Malchow has shown, Shelley's descriptions of the creature's size, strength and implied sexual threat would have been suggestive of African racial difference to her British readers. The threat the creature embodies thus included 'the threat of non-white races' claiming equality, at a time when slavery continued in the British colonies.[16]

Frankenstein as a novel of racial panic was most famously evoked by the foreign secretary George Canning in an 1824 parliamentary debate about whether the children of West Indian slaves should be freed:

> In dealing with the negro, Sir, we must remember that we are dealing with a being possessing the form and strength of a man, but the intellect only of a child. To turn the negro loose in the manhood of his physical strength, in the maturity of his physical passions, but in the infancy of his uninstructed reason, would be to raise up a creature resembling the splendid fiction of a recent romance; the hero of which constructs a human form, with all the . . . sinews of a giant; but being unable to impart to the work of his hands a perception of right and wrong, he finds too late that he has created a more than mortal power of doing mischief and himself recoils from the monster which he has made.[17]

Shelley had invoked slavery in the literal sense when contemplating the creature's abject disenfranchisement, as we see here in this 1824 political representation, despite the stage version (*Presumption*) having already begun the novel's transformation into a narrower concern with an out-of-control science. In subsequent decades, the monster's racial otherness would resonate more closely with the Irish working classes than with African slaves, in further permutations throughout nineteenth-century popular culture in Britain, Ireland and the US.[18]

If we start to look beyond the creature/Victor dyad discussed above (and its Geneva/Ingolstadt geography) as the key to *Frankenstein*'s politics, we see further signs of Shelley's political complexity. As Fred Randel has shown, readings of *Frankenstein* as broadly conservative tend to neglect the nuances that Shelley suggests through the more diverse settings in which she situated Victor's travels and later his quest to create a second monster. Victor escapes from the continent to Britain, echoing the earlier flights of Rousseau and Voltaire to Britain in the eighteenth century, part of the 'Anglomanie' in which the Britain of Newton, Locke and Hume was the beacon of enlightened freethinking for continentals. In Victor's sojourns in England, Scotland and Ireland, Shelley contemplates the radical legacies of the British Isles, before and beyond the French Revolutionary crises.

It was while travelling through Oxford with Clerval that Victor contemplated 'the most animating epoch of English history', the civil war, and its greatest revolutionary hero according to the Shelleys, John Hampden:

> We visited the tomb of the illustrious Hampden, and the field on which that patriot fell. For a moment my soul was elevated from its debasing and miserable fears, to contemplate the divine ideas of liberty and self-sacrifice, of which these sights were the monuments and the remembrancers. For an instant I dared to shake off my chains, and look around me with a free and lofty spirit; but the iron had eaten into my flesh, and I sank again, trembling and hopeless, into my miserable self.
> (pp. 133–4)

Doubling the creature's similar evocations of the language of enslavement (here, in a psychological sense, compared to the creature's more profound experience of physical and psychological enslavement), Victor briefly reconnects to the spirit of political radicalism indigenous to England. Hampden was arguably 'the ideal male revolutionary' for both Godwin and Percy Shelley, and in 1817 Mary Shelley and Godwin had visited together Hampden's monument.[19] In 1817 radical Hampden Clubs, a legacy of the disbanded 1790s societies like the London Corresponding Society, gathered hundreds of thousands of signatures advocating universal male suffrage and annual parliaments, prompting a serious governmental crackdown on reform, including the suspension of *Habeas Corpus*.[20] A year after the publication of *Frankenstein*, Percy Shelley wrote of the Hampden Clubs in 'A Philosophical View of Reform', that 'the petitions of a million of men [were] rejected with disdain. Now they are more miserable, more hopeless, more impatient of their misery.'[21] Victor's admiration of Hampden is thus one of the many shared affinities between him, his creature and 'the divine ideas of liberty' that initially inspired all of them. Visiting Hampden's tomb fails to reawaken in Victor 'the free and lofty spirit' of liberty, but Shelley's highlighting of this English revolutionary tradition in 1817 is 'a political act implying just the reverse of the conservatism now sometimes attributed to *Frankenstein*.'[22]

While the creature's and Victor's narratives have enjoyed the most attention, they are framed from without and within by those of Walton and Safie, which as we shall see significantly shape how we read them. Because 'Walton both begins the story and ends it', his narrative provides 'The broadest, most comprehensive, most universal narrative viewpoint' according to Franco Moretti.[23] For Moretti, Walton's narrative frame subordinates those of Victor and the creature, and effectively erases the political conflict embodied in Victor's and the creature's dialectic of mutual pursuit and class antagonism. Lee Sterrenburg had made the most powerful case for the impact of Shelley's device of psychologically internalizing politics, as we saw earlier. But Walton's narrative does not remove the novel's politics from a collective to a psychological setting – it extends them to a newly contentious collective context, that of geographical exploration.

Walton's narrative on board a voyage to the North Pole is often seen in largely symbolic terms, as a high Romantic fantastic voyage that parallels Victor's Promethean quest for discovery in science. Traditionally, Walton's Arctic voyage has been read by literary scholars through the lens of literary influence; namely, Walton's early interest in poetry and specifically in *The Rime of the Ancient Mariner* (1798) and its 'land of mist and snow'. Seen this way, Walton's pursuit of a 'paradise of my own creation' remains primarily a mythic and literary pursuit, one that ties his idealism closely to Victor's, Godwin's and Percy Shelley's, but largely through an apolitical and internalized poetic frame.

But readers of *Frankenstein* and of contemporary periodicals would have seen Walton's expedition not as a throwback to Coleridgean or Miltonic symbolism, but as a companion voyage to the two Admiralty voyages that in 1818 set off for the North Pole and North-West Passage. In four ships that departed with much fanfare in the popular press, the 1818 Arctic naval expeditions promised much and ultimately delivered nothing. Walton's private voyage in search of the North Pole and open polar sea, while set in the

1790s like the rest of the novel, sought a similar geographical discovery but by a different route than did the 1818 British voyages (through the Russian Arctic, less familiar and thus probably more intriguing to Shelley's readers). Shelley had begun writing *Frankenstein* in 1816, and added Walton's Arctic frame around 1817, after she had begun reading the *Quarterly Review*'s accounts of Arctic exploration written by contributor and Second Secretary to the Admiralty John Barrow.

Writing in the October 1816 *Quarterly Review* (actually published in 1817), Barrow provided a detailed history of British attempts to locate the North-West Passage and North Pole, arguing that 'the polar regions of the globe within the arctic circle offer a wide field for the researches of a philosophic mind.'[24] Barrow described the voyages of famous explorers like the Elizabethan John Davis, who named southern Greenland the Land of Desolation but also waxed lyrical about the extraordinary sights awaiting Englishmen who dared to reach those latitudes. The most 'sanguine' seeker of the North-West Passage according to Barrow was Charles Duncan in the early 1790s, one of the inspirations for Walton, whose crew were 'terrified at the idea of going on discovery' and mutinied, precipitating the captain's mental breakdown.[25] Duncan's was the last Arctic expedition before the outbreak of war in 1793, meaning that the governmental reward of £20,000 for traversing the Passage, and £5,000 for reaching within 1 degree of the North Pole, remained unclaimed when Shelley's imaginary voyage and the naval voyages set out in 1818.

Walton's speculations about the Arctic are wholly in keeping with the voyage literature that Shelley would have read in periodicals and compilations like John Pinkerton's fourteen-volume *General Collection of the Best and Most Interesting Voyages and Travels* (1813).[26] As Walton writes to his sister:

> I try in vain to be persuaded that the pole is the seat of frost and desolation; it ever presents itself to my imagination as the region of beauty and delight. There, Margaret, the sun is forever visible; its broad disk just skirting the horizon, and diffusing a perpetual splendour. There – for with your leave, my sister, I will put some trust in preceding navigators – there snow and frost are banished; and, sailing over a calm sea, we may be wafted to a land surpassing in wonders and in beauty every region hitherto discovered on the habitable globe. Its productions and features may be without example, as the phænomena of the heavenly bodies undoubtedly are in those undiscovered solitudes. What may not be expected in a country of eternal light? (pp. 5–6)

Walton describes his Arctic speculations originating in his reading 'with ardour the accounts of the various voyages which have been made in the prospect of arriving at the North Pacific Ocean through the seas which surround the pole' (p. 6). His language reflects experienced Arctic voyagers like John Davis, who sailed three times in search of the North-West Passage, and made repeated visits to Greenland. Noting the profusion of animal life and human occupancy that challenged his expectations of the Arctic as a desolate environment, Davis imagined that Greenlanders even farther north would enjoy 'a wonderfull difference from al the rest of the world', experiencing:

> life, light, and comfort of nature in a higher measure then all the nations of the earth. How blessed then may we thinke this nation to be: for they are in perpetualle light, and never knowe what darknesse meaneth, by the benefit of twylight and full moones.[27]

Walton's first love may have been poetry, but his fascination with the Arctic as a wondrous place of perpetual light and vibrant life is drawn from this long history of Arctic exploration and science. Thus Walton's confidence that the North Pole is habitable and a land of perpetual enlightenment is resonant with Romantic idealism and literature, but it is not derived from it. Shelley's originality is in forging this new connection (between the long history of exploration and the recent history of literature) through the three male narrators' interleaved quests, through which we are invited to see Britain's Arctic fever in 1818 as part of the modern landscape of utopian thought.

More naval Arctic voyages followed in quick succession in 1819, 1821 and 1824, led by William Parry, John Franklin and others. While *Frankenstein* began its new life on stage in 1823 in Peake's *Presumption* without Walton's Arctic frame, the connections Shelley had forged between Walton's and Victor's projects remained intact in the popular imagination. In *The Spirit of the Age* (1825), William Hazlitt had connected the Admiralty voyages of Arctic discovery to Godwin's exploration of ideal reason in *Political Justice*:

> Captain Parry would be thought to have rendered a service to navigation and his country, no less by proving that there is no North-West Passage, than if he had ascertained that there is one: so Mr. Godwin has rendered an essential service to moral science, by attempting (in vain) to pass the Arctic Circle and Frozen Regions, where the understanding is no longer warmed by the affections, nor fanned by the breeze of fancy! This is the effect of all bold, original, and powerful thinking, that it either discovers the truth or detects where error lies.[28]

For Hazlitt, Godwin's and Parry's voyages are valuable as *negative* discoveries – in Godwin's case, of the undesirability of reason 'no longer warmed by the affections' as a foundation for political justice. *Frankenstein* had first made this now commonplace 'use of polar cold as a metaphor for emotional coldness.'[29] Thanks to Hazlitt we can see that Shelley's brilliant, implicitly feminist critique of the denial of the 'domestic affections' in Godwinian radicalism was inseparable from the debates surrounding the high-profile but repeatedly unsuccessful attempts in Arctic discovery promoted by Britain's Tory government and press.

Central to *Frankenstein*'s political charge was its intervention into the polar politics and print culture of its day. The naval voyages were combined with a robust publication programme that together portrayed the Arctic as a new potential imperial front extending British national interests north from its existing British North American colonies. Shelley's first choice publisher for *Frankenstein* had been John Murray, who held the legal rights to publishing all official Arctic exploration accounts and also published the *Quarterly Review*, but he had turned the manuscript down.

On the disastrous 1819 Franklin overland expedition to the Arctic Ocean, Franklin's naturalist Dr John Richardson had imagined one of their indigenous female guides as 'a fit companion for Frankenstein's chef d'oeuvre', having crossed out 'monster' in his letter.[30] He could imagine Frankenstein's creature at home in the Arctic because Shelley had already imagined him promising 'to leave Europe, and inhabit the deserts of the new world' with his female companion, before Victor reneged on his promise to create her, fearing they would propagate a new 'race of devils' (p. 138). *Frankenstein*'s racial politics emerged even more provocatively later in the nineteenth century, as its creature was taken up in popular political commentary as an avatar of Britain's racialized others like the Irish and Africans, as we have seen. But the creature's racial otherness was clearly visible in 1819 to this naturalist, who imagined the monster as a version of the ignoble savage in the North American Arctic, with an imperial politics at odds with Shelley's critical version. Shelley's creature had 'wept with Safie over the hapless fate' of the 'original inhabitants' of the Americas, and imagined an alternative history in which they could 'have been discovered more gradually' (p. 95). Typically we have read this imperial dimension of *Frankenstein* solely through its later evocations in abolitionist and Irish colonial debates, or through Henry Clerval's commitment to Orientalist study, which Shelley upholds as a preferable (commercial) alternative to the violence of Victor's egotistical pursuit of scientific knowledge. But in 1819 the creature's racial difference was fully visible in the Arctic of Shelley's narrative setting and the Admiralty's theatre of exploration. Walton's Arctic frame thus provides much more than a cultural or symbolic imaginary of ice or the Arctic sublime. Even though Shelley is clearly not interested in the specifics of any Arctic places or people, she is deliberately setting the novel within the contentious political dimensions of Arctic exploration in her day.

Frankenstein's innermost narrative frame is that of Safie, which many scholars identify as the feminist core of Shelley's novel. The daughter of a 'Christian Arab' mother and Muslim merchant father, Safie has fled her father's control and taken refuge with the De Laceys. It is her radical education via the works of Milton, Volney and Plutarch that the creature overhears and shares, aligning his rebellion with her own. Mellor argues that 'Safie, whose Christian mother instructed her "to aspire to higher powers of intellect, and an independence of spirit, forbidden to the female followers of Mahomet," ... is the incarnation of Mary Wollstonecraft.'[31] In the highly gendered world of *Frankenstein*, Shelley had already shown how the doctrine of the separate spheres destroys the women – Elizabeth, Justine, Caroline Lavenza – who rely upon it. But Safie is different because, as Wollstonecraft had advocated in *A Vindication of the Rights of Woman* (1792) and in the example of her own extraordinary life, Safie pursues physical, intellectual, romantic and spiritual liberty outside the literally patriarchal limits set by her father and his culture.[32] Like Wollstonecraft herself had done in her voyage to Scandinavia (secretly pursuing her lover Gilbert Imlay's business interests), Safie travels unchaperoned to Switzerland in order to reunite with her beloved Felix De Lacey, whom her father has forbidden her to marry because of his religion. 'Mahometanism', the code word for the nadir of women's oppression throughout British eighteenth-century writing, including that of Wollstonecraft, is incorporated by Shelley in Safie's narrative in order to explore through a safely distanced context her own culture's sequestration of women in the so-called private sphere. Thus, like Wollstonecraft, Safie was accustomed to 'grand ideas and a noble emulation for virtue', not the 'puerile amusements' reserved for women of her class (p. 99). In educating Safie and enabling her flight from her father and his religion, the unconventional De Lacey family put into practice Wollstonecraft's radical ideas about the rights of woman to education and public agency, making this central narrative of *Frankenstein* one that works against the male narrators (Walton, Victor, creature) and their disastrous separation from the women in their lives.

As a racial and religious outsider, Safie is embraced by the De Laceys in a way that gives the creature hope that he too may find acceptance at last, as he does at first with the blind grandfather. But Shelley denies the creature a lengthy stay in this utopian vision of an egalitarian society and unconventional family. As Kate Ferguson Ellis argues:

Shelley seems to be suggesting that, if the family is to be a viable institution for the transmission of domestic affection from one generation to the next, it must redefine that precious commodity in such a way that it can extend to 'outsiders', while at the same time proving hardy enough to survive in the world outside the home.[33]

For Mellor, Shelley's revision of the egalitarian family does not go far enough politically because it upholds the private/public dichotomy in order to maintain 'domestic affection' as a class privilege: 'Mary Shelley grounded her alternative political ideology on the metaphor of the peaceful, loving, bourgeois family' and 'therefore implicitly endorsed a conservative vision of gradual evolutionary reform, a position articulated most forcefully during her times by Edmund Burke.'[34] But the egalitarian, feminist (and arguably Orientalist) idyll at the heart of *Frankenstein*'s works is designed as an ephemeral counterpoise working against the other concentric narratives, not a utopian synthesis meant to sustain Shelley's final vision.

In the shared desires and similar barriers to belonging of Safie and the creature, Shelley connects political claims across racial, sexual and class differences that the novel explores, in ways inconceivable to followers of Burke, who had literally demonized political radicals. The Orientalism of Safie's plight, her dread of 'being immured within the walls of a haram' (p. 99), like that of Clerval's fascination with Eastern knowledge, is highly conventional, unlike the striking originality of Shelley's imagination in linking medical and geographical discovery. But in placing this dramatic example of feminist cultural rebellion at the heart of this novel littered with the bodies of ineffectual, passive or self-sacrificing women, Shelley expands the revolutionary political critique of her time, reviving a radical case for the rights of woman that had been vilified along with Wollstonecraft's reputation. 'Conservative' remains an anachronism in Romantic-era political discourse, and counter-revolutionary or reactionary likewise do not serve *Frankenstein*'s politics well. Mary Shelley is, rather, 'an informed, critical observer and liberal sympathizer who wishes to prevent both continued injustice and revolutionary violence.'[35] As such, she fashioned an intricate and deliberately fugitive political imaginary in *Frankenstein*, one that continues to inspire new possibilities in radically different times and places.

NOTES

1 William Godwin, *Enquiry Concerning Political Justice*, 2 vols. (London: Robinson, 1793), Vol. II, pp. 872–3.
2 See Chapter 6 in Anne Mellor, *Mary Shelley: Her Life, Her Fiction, Her Monsters* (New York: Methuen, 1988), pp. 115–26.

3 William Godwin, *Political Justice*, p. 288. On Godwin's resistance to politics in practice, see Kramnick's Introduction to *Political Justice*, pp. 32–50.

4 Edmund Burke, *Reflections on the Revolution in France*, ed. Frank Turner (New Haven, CT: Yale University Press, 2003), p. 179.

5 Abbé Barruel, *Memoirs Illustrating the History of Jacobinism* (London, 1798) 3:414.

6 Lee Sterrenburg, 'Mary Shelley's Monster: Politics and Psyche in *Frankenstein*', in George Levine and U. C. Knoepflmacher (eds.), *The Endurance of Frankenstein* (Berkeley, CA: University of California Press, 1979), pp. 143–71, pp. 148, 157. Sterrenburg's brilliant essay appears to have introduced the widely repeated error that Walpole called Godwin 'one of the greatest monsters exhibited by history', when in fact Walpole was referring to Condorcet (letter to Hannah More, Jan. 1795, in *Private Correspondence of Horace Walpole*, 4 vols. (London: Rodwell and Martin, 1820), Vol. IV, p. 545; see Sterrenburg, p. 146. Sterrenburg seems to have misread Ford Brown's *Life of William Godwin* (London: J.M. Dent & Sons, 1926), p. 154n.

7 Godwin, *Political Justice*, Vol. II, p. 475; Tom Paine, *Rights of Man* (Dublin, 1791), p. 34.

8 Mary Wollstonecraft, *An Historical and Moral View of the Origin and Progress of the French Revolution* (London: Joseph Johnson, 1794), p. 71.

9 Chris Baldick, *In Frankenstein's Shadow: Myth, Monstrosity, and Nineteenth-Century Writing* (Oxford: Clarendon Press, 1987), p. 20.

10 Mary Shelley, *Frankenstein*, ed. and Intro. Marilyn Butler (Oxford University Press, 1998), 96. Future references will be made parenthetically.

11 Jean-Jacques Rousseau, *The Confessions of J.J. Rousseau with The Reveries of a Solitary Walker* (London: J. Bew, 1783) Vol. II, 1.

12 David Marshall, Chap. 6 in *The Surprising Effects of Sympathy: Marivaux, Diderot, Rousseau, and Mary Shelley* (University of Chicago Press, 1988), pp. 178–227; 183. Mary Shelley wrote a lengthy essay on Rousseau in her *Lives of the Most Eminent Literary and Scientific Men of France* (1838–9).

13 Mary Wollstonecraft's Romantic hero Darnford writes this in *The Wrongs of Woman* (1798) from Michelle Faubert (ed.), *Mary, A Fiction and The Wrongs of Woman, or Maria* (Peterborough: Broadview, 2012), p. 177. Wollstonecraft's relationship to Rousseau's diverse writings was famously conflicted, and she issued a blistering critique of his gendered educational theories in *A Vindication of the Rights of Woman*.

14 On race and slavery in *Frankenstein*, see Howard Malchow, 'Frankenstein's Monster and Images of Race in Nineteenth-Century Britain', *Past and Present*, 139 (1993) 90–130; Anne Mellor, 'Frankenstein, Racial Science, and the Yellow Peril', *Nineteenth Century Contexts*, 23(1) (2001) 1–28; Elizabeth Young, *Black Frankenstein: The Making of an American Metaphor* (New York University Press, 2008).

15 Burke, *Reflections*, p. 31.

16 Malchow, 'Frankenstein's Monster', p. 127.

17 George Canning, March 1824, as quoted in Malchow, 'Frankenstein's Monster', p. 122. The British slave trade had ended in 1807 but slavery in its colonies was permitted to continue until 1833.

18 On Frankenstein's creature as Irish, see Baldick, *In Frankenstein's Shadow*, pp. 90–91; Fred Randel 'The Political Geography of Horror in Mary Shelley's Frankenstein', *ELH*, 70(2) (2003), 465–491, 482–3.

19 Randel, 'Political Geography', 479.

20 Ibid., 479.

21 Percy Bysshe Shelley, 'A Philosophical View of Reform', *Shelley's Prose*, ed. David Lee Clark (Albuquerque, NM: University of New Mexico Press, 1954), pp. 229–60, p. 255.

22 Randel, 'Political Geography', 478. For a more ambivalent reading of Hampden's role, see Iain Crawford, 'Wading Through Slaughter: John Hampden, Thomas Gray, and Shelley's *Frankenstein*', Studies in the Novel, 20(3) (1988) 249–61.

23 Franco Moretti, 'Dialectic of Fear', *Signs Taken for Wonders* (London: Verso, 1983), pp. 83–108.

24 John Barrow, rev. of Thomas Selkirk's *Sketch of the British Fur Trade* and *Voyage de la Mer Atlantique à l'Océan Pacifique*, Quarterly Review, 16 (1816), 129–72; 170. The *Quarterly Review* was typically published late – the October 1816 issue appeared in February 1817.

25 Barrow, ibid., 166. On Duncan and Walton, see Adriana Craciun, Introduction to *Writing Arctic Disaster: Authorship and Exploration* (Cambridge University Press, 2016).

26 John Pinkerton, *General Collection of the Best and Most Interesting Voyages and Travels* (London: Longman, Hurst, Rees, Orme and Brown, 1813).

27 John Davis, *The Worldes Hydrographical Description* (1595) in *The Voyages and Works of John Davis*, ed. Albert Hastings Markham (London: Hakluyt Soc., 1880), pp. 191–228, p. 223. Davis had been reprinted in Pinkerton.

28 William Hazlitt, *The Spirit of the Age* (London: Henry Colburn, 1825), pp. 47–48.

29 Francis Spufford, *I May Be Some Time: Ice and the English Imagination* (London: Faber and Faber, 1996), p. 87.

30 Richardson, unpublished letter, as qtd. in Adriana Craciun, 'Writing the Disaster: Franklin and *Frankenstein*', Nineteenth-Century Literature 65.4 (2011), pp. 433–80, p. 452. Richardson's extensive reference to *Frankenstein* is the only known one in contemporary Arctic exploration texts, and was censored by Richardson's Victorian editor when his correspondence was eventually published, which is why it has only surfaced recently (see Craciun, 'Writing the Disaster', 452–6).

31 Mellor, *Mary Shelley*, p. 118.

32 Shelley was rereading *Rights of Woman* while writing *Frankenstein*; *The Journals of Mary Shelley 1814–1844*, 2 vols., eds. Paula R. Feldman and Diana Scott-Kilvert (Oxford: The Clarendon Press. 1987), Vol. I, p. 97.

33 Kate Ferguson Ellis, 'Monsters in the Garden: Mary Shelley and the Bourgeois Family', in *The Endurance of Frankenstein*, pp. 123–42, p. 140.

34 Mellor, *Mary Shelley*, p. 86.

35 Randel, 'Political Geography', 488.

PART II

Theories and Forms

7

ANGELA WRIGHT

The Female Gothic

Just as the parts of the creature at the heart of *Frankenstein* do not, in the eyes of their beholder, make up a pleasing and coherent whole, so too the novel's categorization as an exemplar of female Gothic is at first glance somewhat ungainly. Dedicated to Mary Wollstonecraft, Shelley's father 'William Godwin, author of *Political Justice, Caleb Williams, etc*', inaugurated with an epigraph from Book X of Milton's *Paradise Lost* (1674), and with a reading list within its pages that lists only works authored by men, *Frankenstein* bears none of the hallmarks of what we might recognize as female Gothic writing as it was composed, published and critically derided during the decade in which it was written. Derided because, by the 1810s, satirization and scorn of the increasingly commercial and formulaic nature of women's Gothic writing had become commonplace.

In part, criticisms aimed at women's Gothic writing helped to define the contours of this particular form by focusing upon the stable set of tropes which this fiction offered. Mysterious monks, tyrannical Catholic abbesses and sexually licentious villains stalked the pages of romances in the circulating libraries of the 1790s, 1800s and 1810s, haunting the dreams of a readership that many critics imagined (falsely) to be largely female. Critical articles such as 'Terrorist Novel Writing' (1798), 'The Terrorist System of Novel Writing' (1797) and many others provided satirical recipes where a combination of draughty castles, scared heroines, dark, silent villains and evil monks was prescribed to would-be authors who were in desperate need of an income.[1] During the 1790s, this parodied set of tropes was ascribed quite particularly to women authors who were accused of 'unsexing' their female characters. 'Is the corporeal frame of the female sex so masculine and hardy', the author of the satirical 'Terrorist Novel Writing' asked, 'that it must be softened down by the touch of dead bodies, clay-cold hands and damp sweats?'[2] This question articulated a fascinating logic; only fear, transmitted through contact with 'dead bodies, clay-cold hands and damp sweats' could halt the masculinization of the female body. Fear was the ingredient that would make women faint, swoon and render them helplessly feminine.

Such performative anxiety about the blurring of proscribed gender roles spoke to anxieties about female authorship. Ann Radcliffe was not just the most commercially and critically successful female Gothic novelist of the 1790s; she was *the* most commercially successful novelist of that decade. Critics and fans sought to account for her success, however, by maintaining a careful balance between her femininity and her claims to masculine genius. In the anti-Jacobin poem *The Pursuits of Literature* that the Reverend Thomas Mathias composed between 1793 and 1797, for example, Radcliffe's contemporaries Charlotte Smith, Mary Robinson and Elizabeth Inchbald were lambasted as 'unsexed female writers' while Radcliffe's fictional practice rather questionably remained remote from their more politically subversive art: 'Not so the mighty magician of THE MYSTERIES OF UDOLPHO, bred and nourished by the Florentine Muses in their sacred solitary caverns, amid the paler shrines of Gothic superstition and in all the dreariness of Inchantment [*sic*]'.[3] 'Magician' was on occasion invoked negatively by anti-Jacobins in relation to women who spoke with authority and power; but Mathias here counterpoised his image of Radcliffe as 'mighty magician' with an infantine image of her being 'nourished by the Florentine Muses'.[4] Mathias's exemption of Radcliffe from the charge list of female subversives was followed quickly by that of Richard Polwhele in his satirical anti-Jacobin poem *The Unsex'd Females* (1798).[5] In spite of, or perhaps because of, receiving such equivocal praise at the expense of her fellow female authors, after the publication of her fifth novel *The Italian, or the Confessional of the Black Penitents* in 1796/7, Ann Radcliffe withdrew from the republic of letters, creating a void that was all too readily filled with a host of imitative works that drew heavily and unimaginatively upon the names, locations and fictional tropes of her most successful Gothic novels *The Romance of the Forest* (1791), *The Mysteries of Udolpho* (1794) and *The Italian*. Imitations of Radcliffe and her fellow authors also gave rise to the spate of parodies of Gothic fiction in the 1810s, including Eaton Stannard Barrett's *The Heroine* (1813), Jane Austen's *Northanger Abbey* (1818) and Thomas Love Peacock's *Nightmare Abbey* (1818).

When Ellen Moers first defined the contours of her definition of 'female Gothic' in the *New York Review of Books* in 1974, she placed Ann Radcliffe at the heart of her definition of female Gothic as 'the work that women writers have done in the literary mode that, since the eighteenth century, we have called the Gothic.'[6] Only after Radcliffe did Moers cite Mary Shelley's *Frankenstein*, and in arguing for the centrality of fear to the experience of women's Gothic, Moers had to resort to Mary Shelley's Preface to the 1831 edition of her novel in order to argue for its inclusion in the aesthetics of a women's Gothic: 'Mary Shelley said she intended *Frankenstein* to be the kind of ghost story that would "curdle the blood, and quicken the beatings of the heart."'[7] Although Moers did not acknowledge that this was from the later 1831 edition in the *New York Review of Books* article, her subsequent book *Literary Women* (1976) separates the strands of Radcliffe's earlier form of female Gothic. This earlier form was characterized for Moers by a 'travelling heroinism' which differs from Mary Shelley's *Frankenstein*, which Moers acknowledges to be closer to a 'male Gothic' with its focus upon the Promethean over-reacher.[8] At the same time, Moers, and later Anne K. Mellor, have argued that the female author's self-effacement, her later frank account of the 'blank incapability of invention' that confronted her at the Villa Diodati when she was challenged to write a ghost story, speaks to the 'birth myth', or, as Mary Shelley herself owned it, her 'hideous progeny'.[9] The novel's genesis became closely associated with procreation and gestation in that later account of Mary Shelley, and spoke to her anxieties concerning her parentage, and her own parenting. There is, as I will demonstrate, a certain amount of inadequacy on display in *Frankenstein*, but whether this can be accounted for by a female Gothic remains open to question. The still hesitant inclusion of *Frankenstein* in a tradition of female Gothic writing is important, for it speaks to a broader anxiety about how to account for this novel in any gendered account of Gothic literature.

Despite the treatment of *Frankenstein* in the sterling works of feminist criticism offered by Sandra M. Gilbert and Susan Gubar, Mary Poovey, Margaret Homans, Anne K. Mellor, Diane Long Hoeveler and E. J. Clery, it is quite remarkable to note just how seldom Shelley's *Frankenstein* is discussed at any length in critical essay collections upon 'Female Gothic'.[10] A special issue of the journal *Women's Writing* dedicated to 'Female Gothic', edited by Robert Miles and published in 1994 contained five insightful essays which mentioned Ann Radcliffe in their title, but none which mentioned Mary Shelley or *Frankenstein*.[11] Two subsequent essay collections upon the Female Gothic edited by Andrew Smith and Diana Wallace in 2004 and 2009 successfully extended the chronological and thematic scope of female Gothic, but still *Frankenstein* eluded any sustained treatment in these strong essays.[12] Perhaps this is not surprising; a novel whose sole female authorship has been questioned, and which contains no central female characters will of course not sit easily within the parameters of any account of female Gothic either from the point of view of female authorship or characterization, the two key things which Moers set out to define as 'female Gothic' in her pioneering work. What's more, Mary Shelley and *Frankenstein* have been the beneficiaries of so many single-author studies that there is less of an urgency in reintroducing her works to the attention of the scholarly community than there is with authors such as Ann Radcliffe, Maria Regina Roche and Eleanor Sleath, to name but a few Gothic novelists from the 1790s that still suffer from neglect in the form of being out of print, and being under-recognized. In critical accounts of the Gothic, there is instead a tendency to discuss *Frankenstein* alongside the male pursuit narratives offered in William Godwin's *Caleb Williams* (1794) and the later examples of Charles Robert Maturin's *Melmoth the Wanderer* (1820) and James Hogg's *The Private Memoirs and Confessions of a Justified Sinner* (1824).[13] As I shall argue in the remainder of this chapter, however, such annexations of *Frankenstein* towards the male pursuit Promethean narrative are equally uncomfortable, and especially so when one considers the silences of the female author and characters in the 1818 edition, and how some of them are redressed in the later, considerably altered 1831 edition.

The Preface to the 1818 edition of *Frankenstein*, which Mary Shelley later acknowledged that Percy Bysshe Shelley wrote, situates the novel to follow within an explicitly male canon of literature. Citing '*The Iliad*, the tragic poetry of Greece, – Shakespeare... and most especially Milton', it apologetically relegates the attempts of 'the humble novelist' to a position considerably below these 'highest specimens of poetry'.[14] While Percy Shelley persists in the abasement of prose fiction, however, he seeks to elevate *Frankenstein* above the other novelistic products on offer at the time:

> I am by no means indifferent to the manner in which whatever moral tendencies exist in the sentiments or characters it contains shall affect the reader; yet my chief concern in this respect has been limited to the avoiding the enervating effects of the novels of the present day, and to the exhibition of the amiableness of domestic affection, and the excellence of universal virtue.   (pp. 3–4)

The allusion to the 'enervating effects of the novels of the present day' brings to mind William Wordsworth's earlier implicit denigration of the Gothic in the Preface to *Lyrical Ballads* (1800) where he complained of the 'frantic novels, sickly and stupid German tragedies and deluges of idle and extravagant stories in verse' that he perceived to be contaminating literary taste in Britain.[15] *Frankenstein*'s 1818 Preface takes considerable care to distance itself from the Gothic form, only admitting its inspiration from the collection of German ghost stories *Fantasmagoriana* in the famous ghost story competition of the Villa Diodati in the most coyly apologetic terms with the comment that 'These tales excited in us a playful desire of imitation' (p. 4). The Preface concludes by moving away from this carefully encoded reference to the ghost story competition: 'The weather, however, suddenly became serene; and my two friends left me on a journey among the Alps, and lost, in the magnificent scenes which they present, all memory of their ghostly visions' (p. 4). Nature, in this Preface, trumps the light amusement of fictional creation, exorcizing the 'ghostly visions' that the male friends in the group only entertained when they were in need of indoors diversion. This Preface, then, offers an extraordinarily modest account of the genesis and significance of *Frankenstein*, speaking more to Percy Bysshe Shelley's anxieties about exorcizing his own fascination with the supernatural and Gothic, nurtured in his earlier Gothic works *Zastrozzi* (1810) and *St Irvyne* (1811), from his later poetic creations. Here, fear is conspicuous by its absence. The privileging of poetry over prose; of nature over 'playful' ghost stories: if we did not have that later admission from Mary Shelley that Percy Shelley wrote this Preface, we may well have been able to guess at the truth, for the Preface's laboured humility about the playful contexts in which *Frankenstein* was conceived speaks to anxieties about what Michael Gamer and others have argued for as the arbitrary divide between 'high and low Romanticism', or Romanticism and the Gothic.[16]

The silence of the female author of *Frankenstein* in the 1818 Preface is echoed uncannily in the very framework of the tale. It begins with a series of four letters, addressed from the explorer Robert Walton to the silent addressee Mrs Saville. We learn in the second sentence of the novel, and of Letter I, that Mrs Saville is Walton's 'dear sister' but only after Walton has mentioned in his opening sentence that this addressee has regarded his enterprise 'with such evil forebodings'. This is in fact the only thing that we learn of Mrs Saville's feelings. Walton's letters continually emphasize feeling and want, but the question that he poses to his sister Margaret in that very first letter, 'Do you not understand this feeling?' is swiftly supplanted by assertions of what Walton wills her to feel and think: 'you cannot contest the inestimable benefit which I shall confer on all mankind to the last generation', Walton pleads at one point; further on in Letter I, he tries to convince himself of the merit of his enterprise with 'And now, dear Margaret, do I not deserve to accomplish some great purpose' (p. 5). More statements than questions, Walton tries to convince himself that he has convinced his sister of the merit of his voyage. Mrs Saville remains silent throughout *Frankenstein*; never responding, we learn of no other emotion felt by her other than the 'evil forebodings' that are mentioned in the very first sentence. Irrational, prophetic, they seem to construct her as a character who relies upon instinctual feeling. As the opening letters unfold, however, we learn from Walton's self-corrections that it is his own irrationality that he fears: he 'greatly' needs a friend to help to 'regulate' his mind, he informs Margaret in Letter II, and in Letter III he tries to convince her that he 'will be cool, persevering, and prudent' (p. 5). Walton's expositional letters demonstrate that he is not fixed in his purpose; he reminds Margaret of his earlier ambitions to create poetry, and how they have now transformed into greater quests for glory in the sea-faring life that his father explicitly denied him upon his deathbed. As Anne K. Mellor has observed, like Victor Frankenstein himself, 'Walton is thus another Promethean poet, seeking to create a more perfect humanity by revealing a new land of fire and light to man.'[17] Walton provides a shadowy double of Victor Frankenstein in his Promethean quest, ambition and inattention to the safety of those around him. This double of Frankenstein, if we accept this reading, only becomes interesting in his exchanges with the silent Mrs Saville.

Anne K. Mellor was the first critic to identify the link between the initials of Mrs Saville (MWS for Margaret Walton Saville) with the initials of the author herself.[18] Although when Mary Shelley wrote the novel she was not yet married to Percy Bysshe Shelley, the use of those initials is in part a tribute to her mother, Mary Wollstonecraft.[19] Wollstonecraft, whose works were avidly absorbed by the young Mary Godwin in the shadow of her grave, haunts this novel at every level of interpretation; thematically, she is the absent mother who Victor Frankenstein seeks to replace with his assumption of the procreative function; philosophically, she is the conduit for the feminist critique that lurks in the silences at the heart of *Frankenstein*. In a section entitled 'Parental Affection' of her 1792 work *A Vindication of the Rights of Woman*, Mary Wollstonecraft argued that 'To be a good mother a woman must have sense, and that independence of mind which few women possess who are taught to depend on their husbands.'[20] Walton's pleading to his silent sister, Margaret Walton Saville, indicates that this silent addressee has that 'independence of mind' that Wollstonecraft advocated in mothers, an independence that, the novel implies, has led this sister to entertain and articulate 'evil forebodings' concerning her brother's expedition. U. C. Knoepflmacher reads Mrs Saville as the 'female ego-ideal of Walton' that his friend Victor Frankenstein rejects in the character of Elizabeth Lavenza.[21] Walton's dependence upon the 'civilizing and restraining' opinions of his sister is clear in these opening letters.

The name Mrs Saville aurally bears a close resemblance in the French language (which will be the language spoken by the De Lacey family in the cottage) to another silent female character in the novel, that of Safie, whose letters are collected by the creature at the very heart of the novel, and which are then presumably transmitted to Victor Frankenstein, Walton, and then collated and curated by Mrs Saville. Safie, the daughter of a Turkish merchant who betrays Felix, explicitly rejects the oppression of women offered by the religion that her father follows. She flees the patriarchal home in Turkey to seek Felix and his family in Switzerland. As a traveller who rejects her father's injunctions, Safie is for Anne K. Mellor the 'incarnation of Mary Wollstonecraft in the novel'.[22] Providing strong testimonies of a woman being able to choose and judge for herself, Safie's letters offer the traces of a strong female role model that is otherwise lacking within the novel. The creature relates the genesis of Safie's letters:

> 'During the ensuing days...the zeal of Felix was warmed by several letters that he received from this lovely girl, who found means to express her thoughts in the language of her lover by the aid of an old man; a servant of her father's, who understood French. She thanked him in the most ardent terms for his intended services towards her father; and at the same time she gently deplored her own fate.
>
> 'I have copies of these letters; for I found means, during my residence in the hovel, to produce the implements of writing; and the letters were often in the hands of Felix or Agatha. Before I depart, I will give them to you, they will prove the truth of my tale;'   (p. 99)

Frankenstein's creature is only able to produce visual evidence of the truth of his tale from the pen of Safie, who labours to produce those letters that relate her mother's independence, and her father's tyranny in using his daughter as a marriageable commodity. She becomes the active narrator of her own tale, and those letters are 'often in the hands of Felix or Agatha'. Safie's story is attended to and read many times, both in the De Lacey's cottage, and by the creature and his creator Victor Frankenstein. Providing the only strong visual testimony in the novel, her story of fleeing patriarchal oppression to join a more structured community where she can learn and express opinions is placed at the structural and thematic centre of the novel.

Gothic literature frequently concerns itself with silence, with inarticulacy, with the moments when manuscripts and letters become unreadable, effaced by time, or when heroines are silenced by imprisonment, enforced marriage or death. This is certainly the fate of the majority of female characters in the 1818 edition of *Frankenstein*. Their stories are all narrated through the lens of the male narrators. Thus we discover that Caroline Beaufort (later to become Frankenstein's mother) as a young woman confronted with family impoverishment, works for a living, plaiting straw, while tending her sick father. When her father dies, she is left 'an orphan and a beggar' who is only rescued by the 'protecting spirit' of her father's friend, who first takes care of her financially, before marrying her two years later. Her fate is retold by her son, Victor Frankenstein, and so the contradiction in her narrative, that while she on the one hand tends her father and provides financially for them both, but then is left 'an orphan *and* a beggar' upon his death is never resolved. Prior to her marriage, one can almost compare her industry and determination to make a living to sustain herself and her father, to the industry of another heroine, Ann Radcliffe's Ellena di Rosalba from *The Italian*, who maintains herself and her aunt by embroidery. Caroline's death, after contracting scarlet fever from Elizabeth Lavenza, is recounted as sacrifice; having jeopardized her own health by tending to Elizabeth, her final breaths are expended in imploring Elizabeth to 'supply my place to your younger cousins', and to unite her to her son, Victor. Elizabeth Lavenza, the orphaned cousin of Victor Frankenstein, thus becomes the silent, acquiescent replacement for Victor Frankenstein's mother, revealed only through the letters that Frankenstein chooses to share, letters through which we gain a glimpse of a rational, if superhumanly patient female character. Elizabeth swiftly supplants Caroline as the sacrificial victim; there to service the needs of others' illness and afflictions, but never of sufficient significance to be protected fully.

Female community in the world of Victor Frankenstein almost always exists only as women service the needs of others; besides the sacrifices of Caroline and Elizabeth, the image of Justine Moritz taking the death penalty in place of the creature for the murder of Frankenstein's younger brother William is another such instance. When Justine is first convicted, Elizabeth immediately believes her to be guilty, crying '"how shall I ever again believe in human benevolence?"' (p. 65). It is only when she speaks with Justine herself, her 'sister', that Victor reports that Elizabeth's faith in Justine's innocence is restored. At this point in the narrative, Elizabeth utters a declamatory speech, which closely echoes one uttered by the victim Caleb Williams in Mary Shelley's father's novel from 1794: '"They call this *retribution*. Hateful name!"' (p. 67). That sole speech by Elizabeth cuts through to challenge the patriarchal tyrannical version of justice that is being served to Justine, and by implication, it challenges the silences of Victor Frankenstein upon the guilt of his creation.

If we read the first 1818 edition of *Frankenstein* through the lens of a female Gothic narrative, then the survival of Safie's direct testimonial is remarkable, a clear articulation of a proto-feminist message that pulses to the surface of this complexly structured novel. All other female characters are muted, redefined by the male characters who narrate them. If Mrs Saville, that opening, silent addressee seems at first to conform to this pattern, however, then one must bear in mind her silent editorship of the entire text. At one point, one imagines that it is she who notes 'Walton, in continuation', a gesture that places her close to the authorship and source of the novel, the real MWS. Walton, the would-be explorer who is on a similar trajectory to Victor Frankenstein in his misguided quest for glory, pleads with his sister to approve of his quest, but she remains silent, refusing to grant approval, one imagines, to an expedition that she regards in the words of Walton with 'evil foreboding'.

Frankenstein, or the Modern Prometheus thus succeeds in resolving the contending hermeneutics of the 'female gothic'. At the level of authorship, although the 1818 Preface seems to over-write the female authorship of the novel, the framework's silent addressee determines which testimonies survive and are transmitted unmutilated. Walton pleads with that silent sister to award him some form of approbation, but crucially, this is withheld from him, and the judgement upon his actions, and those of Victor Frankenstein, remain unarticulated. At the level of thematics, there is a clear attention to the tale of a female, Safie, who challenges patriarchal dictates of marriage and authority, and flees from those dictates. This corresponds to the 'travelling heroinism' that Ellen Moers first defined in relation to the fictional examples of Ann Radcliffe, the idea of the heroine who flees from the male tyrant across countries.

Even more crucially, *Frankenstein* participates in the culture of a female Gothic tradition through what remains silent in the novel. Whereas a Radcliffean heroine such as *The Mysteries of Udolpho*'s Emily St Aubert swoons in order to avoid overt confrontation with her worst fears, the equivalent of the female Gothic swoon in *Frankenstein* erupts through the novel's layers, forcing its readership throughout the ages to make the connections between male solitude, the disposability of the female and the novel's very repression of sexual desire. Anne K. Mellor reads this in relation to the very disposability of all the female characters in the novel, arguing that:

> The death of Elizabeth Lavenza Frankenstein on her wedding night draws our attention to the fact that female sexuality is at issue here. The denial of all overt sexuality in the surface texture of the novel – Walton is alone, writing to his beloved . . . sister; Victor's mother marries her father's best friend, to whom she becomes a devoted and dutiful daughter/wife; even Felix and Safie meet only in an entirely public, chaster, domesticated space – forces the more powerful erotic desires in the novel to erupt as violence. The repression of sexual desire, in the male as well as the female, generates monstrous fantasies.[23]

The silences on these issues, particularly in the 1818 edition, conjure up the possibilities of those feelings that 'Mrs Saville' experiences as she reads the letters; Walton indeed, as I have already mentioned, constantly tries to gauge and check his sister's feelings, but her fear, to him, is ultimately unreadable, unknowable. In relation to the weather, for example, Walton recounts to his sister his feeling of delight in the 'cold northern breeze' that plays upon his cheeks. He asks of her 'Do you understand this feeling?'; the lack of response, perhaps, indicates that whereas he professes to feel delight, his silent sister experiences a fear, a terror, which refuses to be articulated, and which corresponds to our definitions of the sublime.

Mary Shelley's extensive revisions to her novel *Frankenstein* for the ninth volume of Colburn and Bentley's Standard Novels Series in 1831 have already been well documented, but her Preface to that particular edition nonetheless merits attention due to the ways in which it sharpens the Gothic themes of the novel to follow. Whereas Percy Bysshe Shelley's Preface to the first edition sought to distance *Frankenstein* from the Gothic tradition, the 1831 Introduction by Mary Shelley capitalized upon terror, and it did so by drawing upon the posthumous work of Ann Radcliffe, the author most explicitly associated with the female Gothic. Radcliffe's theorization of terror and horror had been published after her death as 'On the Supernatural in Poetry' in *The New Monthly Magazine* in 1826. There, drawing upon Edmund Burke's theories of the sublime from *A Philosophical Enquiry into the Origin of our Ideas of the Sublime and Beautiful* (1757), Radcliffe had argued for the superiority of terror over horror, arguing that 'the first expands the soul, and awakens the faculties to a high degree of life' while the other, horror, 'contracts, freezes and nearly annihilates them'.[24] Radcliffe presents the appearance of the ghost in Shakespeare's *Hamlet* as a model of skilfully managed terror, arguing that:

> Above every ideal being is the ghost of Hamlet, with all its attendant incidents of time and place. The dark watch upon the remote platform, the dreary aspect of the night, the very expression of the officer on guard, 'the air bites shrewdly; it is very cold;' the recollection of a star, an unknown world, are all circumstances which excite forlorn, melancholy, and solemn feelings, and dispose us to welcome, with trembling curiosity, the awful being that draws near; and to indulge in that strange mixture of horror, pity, and indignation, produced by the tale it reveals.[25]

The 'incidents of time and place' only serve to complement the 'tale' that the ghost reveals, but they are crucial, in Radcliffe's view, to the indulgence of the 'strange mixture of horror, pity and indignation' that the readers experience. Mary Shelley's own technique in the 1831 Introduction to *Frankenstein* draws upon Radcliffe's theorization of terror. There, she reveals the minute circumstances of the 'wet, ungenial summer, and incessant rain' that confined herself, Shelley, Byron, Polidori and Claire Clairmont to the Villa Diodati. She further explicitly links the tale that they were reading from *Fantasmagoriana* to *Hamlet* (1603) through its similar use of attendant incidents of time and place:

> There was the *History of the Inconstant Lover*, who, when he thought to clasp the bride to whom he had pledged his vows, found himself in the arms

of the pale ghost of her whom he had deserted. There was the tale of the sinful founder of his race whose miserable doom it was to bestow the kiss of death on all the younger sons of his fatal house, just when they reached the age of promise. His gigantic, shadowy form, clothed like the ghost in *Hamlet*, in complete armour, but with the beaver up, was seen at midnight, by the moon's fitful beams, to advance slowly along the gloomy avenue. The shape was lost beneath the castle walls, but soon a gate swung back, a step was heard, the door of the chamber opened, and he advanced to the couch of the blooming youths, cradled in healthy sleep. (p. 094)

The level of detail awarded to the attendant incidents of time and place, and its comparison with the same scene from *Hamlet*, force one to conclude that Mary Shelley was drawing upon the same lexicon and theorization of terror that had been articulated in Radcliffe's 'On the Supernatural in Poetry'. Mary Shelley creates terror by recounting the story in such close detail as a *prelude* to describing what she sets as the preconditions for the ghost story that she seeks to invent as part of the competition, 'One which would speak to the mysterious fears of our nature and awaken thrilling horror – one to make the reader dread to look round, to curdle the blood, and quicken the beatings of the heart' (p. 195). The emphasis upon physical sensation, fear and terror serve to galvanize the 'evil forebodings' in the reader that Walton ascribes to his sister Mrs Saville in the first letter. But Mary Shelley does not stop there in the Introduction; when she does finally come up with the idea for her ghost story 'with shut eyes, but acute mental vision' she takes her readership slowly over the contours of the story before admitting to being overcome by its terrors herself:

> I opened [my eyes] in terror. The idea so possessed my mind that a thrill of fear ran through me, and I wished to exchange the ghastly image of my fancy for the realities around. I see them still; the very room, the dark parquet, the closed shutters with the moonlight struggling through. (p. 196)

This is a skilful Introduction to the novel, and one that aligns it far more closely with the aims of female Gothic: through recounting the genesis of her tale in such minute circumstances, paying attention to space, fitful sleep and a feeble moonlight, Mary Shelley creates an external scene of terror that unites both her and the readership more explicitly in a shared language of terror. The silences of Mrs Saville become less important, for the feelings of terror already provoked in this Introduction's multi-layered tale align both author and reader more explicitly with that silent addressee.

The changes made by Mary Shelley to the 1831 edition of *Frankenstein* testify to the author's increasing ease with the tradition of female Gothic that her own mother, Mary Wollstonecraft, reviewed and read extensively.

This is not only evident in the ease with which Mary Shelley practises an aesthetics of terror praised by Ann Radcliffe; it is also there in the changes that she made to the novel itself. Her claim that these were merely 'stylistic' in the Introduction to this edition do not hold water. Elizabeth Lavenza's transformation from cousin of Victor Frankenstein to orphan fostered by his mother recalls the plot of many a female Gothic novel, and most particularly Eleanor Sleath's *The Orphan of the Rhine* (1798).[26] A peasant woman, who has raised Elizabeth when Frankenstein's mother first comes across her, states that she is the 'daughter of a Milanese nobleman. Her mother was a German and had died on giving her birth' (p. 206). Elizabeth's lineage recalls very closely that of Sleath's orphan heroine, but the textual change goes beyond mere tribute towards her Gothic predecessors. If the female Gothic illustrates the terrors of the disposability of the female, then this transformation underscores that concern. Victor Frankenstein's mother playfully presents the orphaned Elizabeth to Victor as a gift:

> On the evening previous to her being brought to my home, my mother had said playfully, 'I have a pretty present for my Victor – tomorrow he shall have it.' And when, on the morrow, she presented Elizabeth to me as her promised gift, I, with childish seriousness, interpreted her words literally and looked upon Elizabeth as mine – mine to protect, love and cherish. All praises bestowed on her I received as made to a possession of my own. We called each other familiarly by the name of cousin. No word, no expression could body forth the kind of relation in which she stood to me – my more than sister, since till death she was to be mine only.   (p. 207)

Frankenstein's arrogant certainty of his possession of Elizabeth 'till death', encouraged by his mother's own casual, thoughtless approach to the disposal of Elizabeth, anticipates the bloody demise of Elizabeth at the hands of his creature. From the moment that she enters into the sphere of his life as 'a child fairer than a pictured cherub' so she becomes his to dispose of as he wishes. In Chapter 2 of the 1831 edition, Elizabeth continues to be moulded more closely in the conventions of the Gothic heroine, for here, Mary Shelley extemporizes further upon Elizabeth's love of sublime nature. She 'following the aerial creations of the poets' is supplemented by her 'admiration and delight' in 'the sublime shapes of the mountains, the changes of the seasons, tempest and calm, the silence of winter, and the life and turbulence of our Alpine summers' (p. 207). Her careful appreciation of the changing seasons, the 'silence of winter' is diminished in Victor's account to her appreciating 'the magnificent appearances of things', taking a poor second place to his superior investigation of 'their causes'. But his superior arrogation of divine, Promethean power leads only to death and destruction, pulling Elizabeth Lavenza in its wake. Her careful attention to seasons and her delight in sublime shapes in the landscape, so closely connected to the landscape appreciation characteristic of the Radcliffean Gothic heroine, is a more sensitive, less destructive, approach to nature.

Elizabeth Lavenza's rapprochement to the Gothic heroine in the 1831 edition, both in terms of her orphaned status, her immediate possession by the male usurper and her appreciation of landscape lend the 1831 edition of *Frankenstein* a sharper edge of critique, one that is more explicitly moulded through the female Gothic tradition. Yet still it speaks to the silences within the novel; Elizabeth's responses to sublime nature never get to be spontaneously expressed in the mode of Ellena di Rosalba, the heroine of Radcliffe's *The Italian*. Her voice remains stifled in the paratextual layers, her letters are possibly mutilated by Victor Frankenstein as he recounts them to Walton. Her own story is never revealed, but in its fragmented, partial retelling through the mouthpiece of Victor Frankenstein; the details of her story, narrated at such an early juncture in the novel, become a crucial incident in Mary Shelley's carefully constructed story of terror. The female Gothic tradition was always lurking in the shadows of the 1818 edition of *Frankenstein*, as I hope to have demonstrated, but Mrs Saville's 'evil forebodings' are more fully anticipated and realized in both the Introduction and transformations to the later 1831 edition. *Frankenstein* in 1818 revealed the young female author's anxieties about her literary relationships with her mother, father and soon-to-be husband in her abrogation of authorial intent to Percy Bysshe Shelley. These anxieties may persist into the later 1831 edition, but the author who comes to embrace the terror of a particularly female strain of Gothic literature in the Introduction is more confident and comfortable in her own experience and mediation of that self-same blood-curdling terror.

NOTES

1 [Anon.] 'Terrorist Novel Writing', *The Spirit of the Public Journals for 1797* (London: Richardson, Symonds, Clarke, Harding, 1798); 'The Terrorist System of Novel Writing', *Monthly Magazine* (August 1797).
2 'Terrorist Novel Writing', ibid., pp. 224–5.
3 Thomas Mathias, *The Pursuits of Literature: A Satirical Poem in Four Dialogues. With Notes*. 8th edn. (Dublin: J. Milliken), pp. 238 and 258.
4 See, for example, Laura Brown's essay 'The Feminization of Ideology: Form and the Female in the Long Eighteenth Century' for an analysis of the posthumous anti-Jacobin attacks upon Mary Wollstonecraft, which often represented Wollstonecraft as magician, in David Richter (ed.), *Ideology and Form in Eighteenth-*

Century Literature (Lubbock, TX: Texas Tech University Press, 1999), pp. 223–40, p. 237.

5 Richard Polwhele, *The Unsex'd Females: A Poem Addressed to the Author of the Pursuits of Literature* [1798] (New York: William Cobbett, 1800). For further discussion of Radcliffe's critical exoneration by anti-Jacobin authors, see Dale Townshend and Angela Wright, 'Gothic and Romantic Engagements: The Critical Reception of Ann Radcliffe, 1789–1850' in Townshend and Wright (eds.), *Ann Radcliffe, Romanticism and the Gothic* (Cambridge University Press, 2014), pp. 3–32.

6 Ellen Moers, 'Female Gothic: The Monster's Mother', *New York Review of Books*, 21 March 1974.

7 Ibid.

8 See in particular Chapters 5 and 7 of Ellen Moers, *Literary Women* (Garden City, NY: Doubleday, 1976).

9 See Ellen Moers, *Literary Women*, Chapter 5, and Anne K. Mellor, *Mary Shelley: Her Life, Her Fiction, Her Monsters* (London and New York: Routledge, 1988), Chapter 2 'Making a Monster'.

10 Sandra Gilbert and Susan Gubar, *The Madwoman in the Attic* (New Haven, CT: Yale University Press, 1979); Mary Poovey, *The Proper Lady and the Woman Writer – Ideology as Style in the Works of Mary Wollstonecraft, Mary Shelley and Jane Austen* (Chicago University Press, 1984); Margaret Homans, *Bearing the Word – Language and Female Experience in Nineteenth-Century Women's Writing* (Chicago University Press, 1986); Anne K. Mellor, *Mary Shelley: Her Life, Her Fiction, Her Monsters*; Diane Long Hoeveler, *Gothic Feminism: The Professionalization of Gender from Charlotte Smith to the Brontës* (Pennsylvania State University Press, 1998); E. J. Clery, *Women's Gothic: From Clara Reeve to Mary Shelley* (Tavistock: Northcote, 2000).

11 Robert Miles (ed.), 'Female Gothic', a special issue of *Women's Writing* 1(2) (1994).

12 Andrew Smith and Diana Wallace (eds.), 'Female Gothic', a special issue of *Gothic Studies* 6(1) (May, 2004); Diana Wallace and Andrew Smith (eds.), *The Female Gothic: New Directions* (Basingstoke: Palgrave, 2009).

13 See, for example, David Punter's chapter 'Gothic and Romanticism' in Vol. I of *The Literature of Terror* (Longman and New York: 1996), pp. 87–113, and Benjamin Eric Daffron's *Romantic Doubles: Sex and Sympathy in British Gothic Literature, 1790–1830* (New York: AMS Press, 2002).

14 Percy Shelley, Preface to the 1818 edition of *Frankenstein* by Mary Shelley, ed. and Intro. Marilyn Butler (Oxford University Press, 1998), p. 3. As Marilyn Butler notes, 'The unsigned Preface was written by Percy Shelley, as though author of the novel. See MWS, Introduction to 3rd edition, Appendix A: 'As far as I can recollect, it was entirely written by him' (p. 252). Future references will be made parenthetically.

15 William Wordsworth, Preface to the second edition of *Lyrical Ballads* (London: 1800), p. vi.

16 Michael Gamer, *Romanticism and the Gothic* (Cambridge University Press, 1999). See also Angela Wright and Dale Townshend (eds.), *Romantic Gothic: An Edinburgh Companion* (Edinburgh University Press, 2015).

17 Anne K. Mellor, *Mary Shelley: Her Life, Her Fiction, Her Monsters* (London and New York: Routledge, 1988), p. 77.

18 Mellor, *Mary Shelley*, Chapter 3 'My Hideous Progeny', pp. 52–69.

19 Mary and Percy married in December 1816. There has been some critical discussion (most notably by Charles E. Robinson, see his chapter 'Frankenstein: Its Composition and Publication', Chapter 1 in this volume), which has argued that the frame narrative relating to Walton may have been added somewhere between late 1816 and early 1817, so it is possible that the initials could refer to Mary Wollstonecraft Shelley.

20 Mary Wollstonecraft, *A Vindication of the Rights of Woman*, ed. Miriam Kramnick (Harmondsworth: Penguin, 1978), p. 266.

21 U. C. Knoepflmacher, 'Thoughts on the Aggression of Daughters' in George Levine and U. C. Knoepflmacher (eds.), *The Endurance of Frankenstein* (Berkeley and Los Angeles, CA, and London: University of California Press, 1979), pp. 88–119, p. 107.

22 Mellor, *Mary Shelley*, p. 118.

23 Ibid., p. 56.

24 Ann Radcliffe, 'On the Supernatural in Poetry', *The New Monthly Magazine and Literary Journal*, 16(1) (1826), 145–52, p. 149.

25 Radcliffe, 'On the Supernatural in Poetry', pp. 147–8.

26 Eleanor Sleath, *The Orphan of the Rhine* (London: William Lane, 1798).

8

GEORGE E. HAGGERTY

What is Queer about *Frankenstein*?

A more reasonable question would surely be 'what is not queer about *Frankenstein*?' After all, an obsessive scientist crawls around graves and into charnel houses and drags variously corrupted body parts back to his laboratory; out of these decomposing parts he constructs a hideous male monster. After the monster is created the scientist flees, but he does not do so before falling asleep and dreaming that he is carrying the corpse of his dead lover in his arms, and as he looks at her, she transforms herself into the dead body of his mother, now corrupted and crawling with worms. Later he meets his monster, who pleads with him to create another of his kind. He gives in to these demands and begins to create another monster, this time a female. Again he isolates himself, this time in the northern islands of Scotland. As the monster comes to gaze at him working, he loses heart and destroys the creature he is creating: he mangles her parts and strews them around his laboratory. After this, the scientist and his creature are locked in a dance of death: the monster kills the scientist's best friend and later his fiancée. Before the novel ends, they are pursuing each other into the northern climes of the Atlantic Ocean. The scientist dies on a passing ship of exploration, and the monster disappears into the frozen north.

This bald version of the plot of the novel shows how very queer it can seem: masculine birth, lurid devotion between males, sexual aggression, and finally a completely obsessive relation between a scientist and the violent other he has created. There is nothing normative about the relation between Frankenstein and his creature: the almost-by-definition dysfunctional family relations are transgressive from the start; and as various feminist critics have argued, Frankenstein sacrifices the domestic in an egotistical urge toward creativity: he gives birth to the monster as a mockery of motherhood and the pain associated with giving birth.[1] This urge, this need to centre all creative activity in himself and to sacrifice everything to the power of his own imagination, would be queer enough in itself, but as it is played out in the novel, with all of Frankenstein's family being sacrificed to the horror of his creativity, the creative imagination is isolating and debilitating in a way that sexual dysfunction closely approximates.

Queer Theorists offer various ways to make sense of this bizarre configuration. In her chapter on Gothic fiction in *Between Men* (1985), Eve Kosofsky Sedgwick argues that many of these novels locked two men, or a man and a supernatural power, in a paranoid relation reminiscent of the Freudian case of Dr Schreber.[2] This case, as Sedgwick describes it, suggests that one man made himself victim to and penetrable by another. When ascribed to male novelists such as Walpole, Beckford and Lewis, this configuration can perhaps be marshalled to suggest something about authorial sexuality; but in the case of Mary Shelley, it is equally possible that the author is using a proto-Freudian configuration in order to diagnose what she experienced as a form of male aggression. Shut out, that is, from intimate relations between men, as Shelley recounts in her introduction to the 1831 (third) edition of the novel, the author goes on to show how her masculine figures, obsessed only with each other, destroy the female in their quest for masculinized mutuality.[3] The implicit uncanniness of the action that results registers as queer precisely to the degree that normative sexual and domestic relations between man and woman are blasted by imaginative creativity and the quest for intimate and almost obsessive relations with the demonic. The demon that haunts Frankenstein throughout this novel is a demon of his own creation, and the ruthless pursuit of this creature that the novel dramatizes is, in one sense, a debilitating and self-destructive form of narcissism.

As feminist critics and others have often observed, Shelley seems to offer an alternative to this seething self-obsession. This she does by outlining in the creature's interpolated tale the story of the De Lacey family. There a devoted group of cottagers – an elderly father and his two children – form a melancholy but moving picture of domestic life. When later an exotic looking young woman arrives at their home, the mood brightens and we come to learn of the love between Felix, the son, and Safie, the Turkish girl, and also the tale of friendship and betrayal between Felix and Safie's father that has led her finally to seek refuge in the younger man's arms. This scene of celebrated domesticity, however, from which the agonizing lonely creature learns about family and amorous devotion, ultimately depends upon another level of male–male devotion, deceit and cruelty: Felix has befriended and helped Safie's father escape from prison, only to be betrayed and exposed, with the result that his family has had to go into hiding and live in penury. Domestic happiness, such as it is, is brutalized by and through a masculinist configuration of social relations, and if this family does survive, it does so only as a debilitated and ineffectual version of its previously well-established and fully respected self. What the creature sees in the cottage is

the failed remains of domesticity that cannot offer him a home because the
De Laceys are already paranoid and defensive about what they represent.
The De Laceys do not so much represent an ideal as they do the failure of an
ideal. And as if to underline this fact, the creature dances around the cottage
and sets it afire:

> 'I lighted the dry branch of a tree, and danced with fury around the devoted
> cottage, my eyes still fixed on the western horizon, the edge of which the moon
> nearly touched. A part of its orb was at length hid, and I waved my brand;
> it sunk, and, with a loud scream, I fired the straw, and heath, and bushes,
> which I had collected. The wind fanned the fire, and the cottage was quickly
> enveloped by the flames, which clung to it, and licked it with their forked and
> destroying tongues.'[4]

This nocturnal scene of almost ritualistic destruction has the quality of a
purging or purification: as if the creature must destroy the vestiges of the
family life to which he became 'devoted'. His disillusionment with the family
is measured in this violent scene. His actions reflect the violence with which
they threatened him.

Another queer theorist whose work could help explain some of the more
lurid features of *Frankenstein* is Carla Freccero. Her essay, 'Queer Spectrality: Haunting the Past' which appeared in the *Blackwell Companion to
Lesbian, Gay, Bisexual, Transgender, and Queer Studies* (2007), explores
how queer behaviours in historical materials can come to haunt those of us
working in the present, who recognize ourselves in those past events even as
we acknowledge historical difference.[5] There is a quality akin to that queer
spectrality when a reader encounters *Frankenstein*. This lost figure of the
creature howling in the night-time, when he realizes that he has no friends
and that even the family is not the answer: how familiar a configuration
is that? Even more, this creature given life by the mad scientist that then
disowns him: this calls to mind the struggles a young gay man, monstrous to
himself in so many ways, confronting the man who has perhaps first seduced
him but now refuses to support or even acknowledge him. *Frankenstein*, in
other words, goes to the heart of queer relations in explaining the contempt
one man can feel for another who was closest to him and has in fact been
his 'creator.' Mary Shelley may not have had such a configuration in mind,
but given the curious relations among her closest friends, it is not at all clear
that she was not caught up in the intrigues of contemptuous intimacies.

Frankenstein exerts this queer spectrality because it haunts us with its
familiarity. I am not saying we all create monsters, but we do create ourselves, and in doing that we sometimes destroy those we love whether we

want to or not. Mary Shelley makes clear in her 1831 Introduction that she herself identified with the mad scientist, and she places herself in the bed in which her hero confronts the creature for the first time: 'He sleeps; but he is awakened; he opens his eyes; behold the horrid thing stands at his bedside, opening his curtains, and looking on him with yellow, watery, but speculative eyes. I opened mine in terror' (p. 196). Shelley confronts the horror of a creation – '"How [did] I, then a young girl . . . think of and dilate upon, so very hideous an idea?"' – by explaining that the very same creature haunted her dreams (p. 192). Every queer reader knows that her or his or their own dreams are deeply threatening, first to themselves and then to everyone around them. This is queer spectrality at its most trenchant: even those dreams are damning and debilitating, and the fondest hopes become acts of treachery.

Queer theory allows us to speculate about more than what happens in a novel like *Frankenstein*, and it asks us to speculate how it achieves the effects that it does. How, that is, can the eccentric obsessions of a mad scientist begin to have such monumental significance that they begin to shape the very culture we are trying to understand? No fiction of the nineteenth century, that is, resonates with such deeply haunting presence as *Frankenstein* does. Why is this novel nearly canonical in course outlines from high school to graduate school? And why are there novels, films, operas and musicals all devoted to the story of the obsessive creator and his monstrous creation? Why, that is, does this story obsess us all so very much? Queer theory can explain that the Promethean myth that it embodies does nothing less than explain what it is to be a human being. To be a breathing, desiring, needing, feeling creature, that is, can only be measured in levels of monstrosity. If Shelley understood that instinctively, then her novel makes it available as a shibboleth to us all. In her landmark essay, 'My Monster/ My Self' (1992) Barbara Johnson says as much:

> *Frankenstein* . . . combines a monstrous answer to two of the most fundamental questions one can ask: Where do babies come from? And Where do stories come from? . . . Mary's book would suggest that a woman's desire to write and a man's desire to give birth would both be capable only of producing monsters.[6]

If we were to think of this 'monstrous' answer as a queer answer, then we might begin to understand why this novel is so haunting. How are queer subjects formed? This is how.

Bette London, in her proto queer reading of the novel, makes this provocative argument:

> This vision of authorship as self-contained and self-continuous – as a coherent extension of the self into an extracorporeal existence – turns out to be *Franken-stein*'s informing fiction . . . This contradiction, predicated on the simultaneous avowal and disavowal of difference – between the literal and figurative, the unique and reproducible, and the bodily and textual – marks the productions of masculinity as fetishistic. And it is precisely this fetishistic structure that *Frankenstein* both illuminates and experiments with, in its intertextual networks, as well as in its intratextual thematics.[7]

What London argues here – about the fetishistic representation of masculinity – can tell us even more about how this novel continues to command our almost subconscious engagement. After describing various nineteenth-century memorials to a fallen Percy Shelley, London argues: 'If *Frankenstein* recalls what is monstrous, what lurks beneath the surface, in this memorial imagery – the displayed male body, the "hideous phantasm stretched out" – the memorials reactivate *Frankenstein*'s own iconography, opening the novel to new interpretive possibilities.'[8] What is monstrous and beneath the surface is what makes this novel as compelling as it is. The new interpretations that London mentions are those that see into the hideous phantasms that are inscribed onto or indeed into the male body.

Recent collections on queering the nineteenth-century canon have included discussion of *Frankenstein*. In Mair Rigby's '"Do you Share my Madness": *Frankenstein*'s Queer Gothic' (2009), for instance, we learn that '*Frankenstein*'s "queer" and "Gothic" textuality has something further to reveal about the relationship between the language of Gothic fiction and the language of sexual "deviance"'.[9] I make a similar argument in my own *Queer Gothic* (2006), where I ask:

> What does it mean to call gothic fiction 'queer'? It is no mere coincidence that the cult of gothic fiction reached its apex at the very moment when gender and sexuality were beginning to be codified for modern culture. In fact, gothic fiction offered a testing ground for many unauthorized genders and sexualities, including sodomy, tribadism, romantic friendship (male and female), incest, pedophilia, sadism, masochism, necrophilia, cannibalism, masculinized females, feminized males, miscegenation, and so on. In this sense, it offers a historical model of queer theory and politics: transgressive, sexually coded, and resistant to dominant ideology.[10]

If we apply these concerns to *Frankenstein*, there is no end to the directions in which this novel could lead us. In the first place, consider the situation in the Frankenstein home. Victor's mother introduces him to a cousin (in the 1818 edition), and in her attempt 'to bind as closely as possible the ties of domestic love', she is determined 'to consider Elizabeth as my future wife; a design which she never found reason to repent' (p. 20). Later, after Victor has been successful in giving life to the body parts he had assembled and flees the scene, he throws himself onto the bed and tries to sleep:

> But it was in vain: I slept indeed, but I was disturbed by the wildest dreams. I thought I saw Elizabeth, in the bloom of health, walking in the streets of Ingolstadt. Delighted and surprised, I embraced her; but as I imprinted the first kiss on her lips, they became livid with the hue of death; her features appeared to change, and I thought that I held the corpse of my dead mother in my arms; a shroud enveloped her form, and I saw the grave-worms crawling in the folds of the flannel.   (p. 39)

When Victor recounts this horrifying image, we are reminded of his mother's enthusiasm for Elizabeth, and we must assume that in some way his mind has connected the two female forms. If Victor were not already guilty of searching for bodies in graves and charnel houses, we might say that he has an incestuous desire for his mother through the woman she provided as his wife. Instead, as feminists have argued, he has supplanted his mother in his lurid creation and carries her as a sacrifice to his own creative genius.[11] Queer Theory would go one step further, and begin to see this aberrant maternity as the kind of gender inversion in which this novel of horror regularly deals. It would also point to the implicit incest: it is there vaguely in his being promised to his cousin, but it is there even more vividly when his sweetheart transforms into this mother, dead and corrupted, in his arms.

Since *Frankenstein* is so much about life and death – or death from life – this image at the moment of Frankenstein's brilliant creation reminds him of how anti-normative his act of creation has been. I mentioned above the graveyards and charnel houses. In Victor Frankenstein's own words:

> These thoughts supported my spirits, while I pursued my undertaking with unremitting ardour. My cheek had grown pale with study, and my person had become emaciated with confinement. Sometimes, on the very brink of certainty, I failed; yet still I clung to the hope which the next day or the next hour might realize... I pursued nature to her hiding-places. Who shall conceive the horrors of my secret toil, as I dabbled among the unhallowed damps of the grave, or tortured the living animal to animate the lifeless clay? My limbs now tremble, and my eyes swim with the remembrance; but then a resistless, and almost frantic, impulse urged me forward: I seem to have lost all soul or sensation but for this one pursuit.   (p. 36)

In this passage Victor sounds like some kind of maniac, lost in a compulsion that is driving him beyond the normative. Indeed, this near-madness could almost be mistaken for a sexual compulsion or an obsession with a form of necrophilia that could hardly be imagined. Victor shuts himself up with the dead – pale and emaciated – as he struggles to find life in the very materials of death. This is a queer enough pursuit, and it is no wonder that when he succeeds, he is both horrified and disgusted.

In his book *No Future: Queer Theory and the Death Drive* (2004), Lee Edelman posits the queer as an isolated figure, what he calls the sinthomo-sexual in the Lacanian terms of his study. For Lacan, symptoms, or sinthomes, are those fissures in the symbolic where its very structure is revealed. These fissures are like the dark holes in cultural coherence: if you look into them, the entire rationale of the symbolic is revealed. The figure that Edelman calls the sinthomosexual performs this revelation of every-thing that the culture would like to hide. In that sense, this figure is the very mark of culture's undoing, and as such he is labelled as anti-life or as indeed death-obsessed. The following quotation from Edelman's book both gives a précis of his concerns and suggests some of the ways in which his thesis is vividly identified in this novel:

> Abjuring fidelity to a futurism that's always purchased at our expense . . . we might rather, figuratively, cast our vote for . . . the primacy of a constant *no* in response to the law of the Symbolic, which would echo that law's foundational act, its self-constituting negation.[12]

Edelman's argument centres on a queer rejection of what he calls 'repro-ductive futurity'. For Edelman, 'The Child . . . marks the fetishistic fixation of heteronormativity: an erotically charged investment in the rigid sameness of identity that is central to the compulsory narrative of reproductive futur-ism.'[13] Edelman's queer, the sinthomosexual, is in his very commitment to the death drive of desire, placed in opposition to the future that childhood represents. His '*no* in response to the law of the symbolic' is a queer rejection of this commitment to the future.

When Victor Frankenstein's creature goes on the rampage, the first char-acter he murders is Victor's youngest brother William – the boy is Elizabeth's darling and she speaks of him almost like a son – almost answering the wildly incestuous and necrophiliac image that he dreams after the act of creation. Victor also answers 'no in response to the law of the Symbolic, which would echo that law's foundational act, its self-constituting negation'. In pursuing a creative drive of his own, he negates the symbolic law of futurism; or, rather, he so radically rewrites it that he ends up destroying all those he loves, in a queerly motivated bloodbath that isolates him from family, friendship and love.

'Queerness embodies this death drive', Edelman says, 'this intransigent jouissance, by figuring sexuality's implication in the senseless pulsations of that drive. De-idealizing the metaphorics of meaning on which heteroreproduction takes its stand, queerness exposes sexuality's inevitable coloration by the drive.'[14] Sexuality, in these terms, does not have meaning in the ways that family and home do. It is almost the negation of meaning. If Frankenstein has done anything in this novel, it has been to de-idealize 'the metaphorics of meaning'. He insists on making his own meanings, and instead all he does is destroy all that he pretended to love.

After the creature has met Victor in the Alps and pleaded with him to make him a mate – a female creature like himself whom he can love and nurture as a companion – Victor almost relents. Before marrying Elizabeth, who now feels that marriage would be best for his health as well as their joint happiness, he says he has to travel in order to 'restore my tranquillity' (p. 127). He travels north with his friend Clerval, and then finds his way to the Orkney Islands of Scotland, where he will finally honour his pledge and create a second creature. As he sets to work here, he finds that he cannot complete this task:

> I grew restless and nervous. Every moment I feared to meet my persecutor. Sometimes I sat with my eyes fixed on the ground, fearing to raise them lest they should encounter the object which I so much dreaded to behold. I feared to wander from the sight of my fellow-creatures, lest when alone he should come to claim his companion. (p. 137)

Victor continues this act of creation while looking over his shoulder and fearing to see the creature he calls his 'persecutor', and in a sense almost expecting him to appear 'to claim his companion'. When he does appear, Frankenstein cannot complete his second creation, and he destroys the new life even before he finishes creating it:

> I sat one evening in my laboratory; the sun had set, and the moon was just rising from the sea; I had not sufficient light for my employment, and I remained idle, in pause of consideration of whether I should leave my labour for the night, or hasten to its conclusion by an unremitting attention to it. As I sat, a train of reflection occurred to me, which led me to consider the effects of what I was now doing...I had before been moved by the *sophisms* of the being I had created; I had been struck senseless by his fiendish threats; but now, for the first time, the wickedness of my promise burst upon me; I shuddered to think that future ages might curse me as their pest, whose selfishness had not hesitated to buy its own peace at the price perhaps of the existence of the whole human race. (pp. 137–8)

In this change of heart, Victor uses his own sophisms to talk himself out of the creation he had promised, and before he can even think beyond these first reactions:

> I trembled, and my heart failed within me; when, on looking up, I saw, by the light of the moon, the dæmon at the casement. A ghastly grin wrinkled his lips as he gazed on me, where I sat fulfilling the task which he had allotted to me...As I looked on him, his countenance expressed the utmost extent of malice and treachery. I thought with a sensation of madness on my promise of creating another like to him, and, trembling with passion, tore to pieces the thing on which I was engaged. The wretch saw me destroy the creature on whose future existence he depended for happiness, and, with a howl of devilish despair and revenge, withdrew. (pp. 138–9)

Almost as if he had decided to subscribe to Edelman's notion of *No Future*, Frankenstein deprives his creature of a future and in a single act also destroys his own. Victor was formerly a creator, but in this scene he does nothing but destroy. If he can destroy 'the creature on whose future existence he [the creature] depended for happiness'; then he rejects any future in favour of a present that is both unthreatening and resistant to the demands of procreation. If that earns the despair and revenge of the creature, Victor is willing to face that as long as he can avoid giving life to the creature he detests. That creature threatens him with a resounding, '"I go; but remember, I will be with you on your wedding-night"' (p. 140). Victor takes this as a direct threat to himself, never even imagining that the creature will destroy both Elizabeth and Clerval.

When Victor realizes that the creature has murdered Clerval, which happens almost immediately after the scene quoted above, he lapses into a heartfelt lament that spells out the terms of his transgression:

> I entered the room where the corpse lay, and was led up to the coffin. How can I describe my sensations on beholding it? I feel yet parched with horror, nor can I reflect on that terrible moment without shuddering and agony, that faintly reminds me of the anguish of the recognition...I saw the lifeless form of Henry Clerval stretched before me. I gasped for breath; and, throwing myself on the body, I explained, 'Have my murderous machinations deprived you also, my dearest Henry, of life? Two I have already destroyed; other victims await their destiny: but you, Clerval, my friend, my benefactor-'. (p. 148)

Victor's sensations here – the sense of loss coupled with responsibility – unmans him (he is 'carried out of the room in strong convulsions' (p. 148)) and it also reminds him what his act of creation has really meant. Not only his almost non-existent love-life with Elizabeth, but also the world of masculine privilege that he shared with Clerval is now blasted. If Bette London talks about the world of masculine privilege in *Frankenstein*, a scene like this reminds us how truly fragile that world is. London argues that feminist readings of the novel 'cover over *Frankenstein's* investment in male exhibitionism'; and this scene of Henry Clerval's demise would more than support London's argument.[15] Victor laments this loss so bitterly because he knows that his refusal to create a second dæmon has broken the bond of friendship that has allowed him to flourish as he has. If, in other words, what Sedgwick called the homosocial is exploded in this novel, then it becomes even queerer than the Gothic works that surround it. Victor's masculine other is gargantuan and overpowering, as this murder suggests, and he knows that destroying friendship will hit Victor at his core. It is significant that most film versions of the novel leave Clerval alive or neglect to tell the final story. His loss in the novel is almost more devastating to Victor than his loss of Elizabeth. It is queer because, as Edelman reminds us, 'the death drive names what the queer, in the order of the social, is called forth to figure: the negativity opposed to every form of social viability.'[16] Edelman's queer embraces the death drive because he needs to resist the overwhelming cultural force of reproductive futurism; being true to ourselves, that is, means accepting the symptom (sinthome) of this future-obsessed cultural moment, confronting death and what it tells us about our lives. This is what happens to Victor, and it seems to be the lesson that he learns after his long and debilitating encounter with the creature.

After Elizabeth dies and Victor finds himself pursuing the creature and being pursued to the frozen north, he laments to Walton:

> My imagination was vivid, yet my powers of analysis and application were intense; by the union of these qualities I conceived the idea, and executed the creation of a man. Even now I cannot recollect, without passion, my reveries while the work was incomplete. I trod heaven in my thoughts, now exulting in my powers, now burning with the idea of their effects. From my infancy I was imbued with high hopes and a lofty ambition; but how am I sunk!
> (p. 180)

Victor knows his defeat and he also knows that he must depart without a resolution of any kind. Victor is not allowed to claim his creation or to position himself as the creative genius that the story has celebrated. Instead, he is broken and frustrated, 'how am I sunk!' Edelman reminds us that 'queerness can never define an identity, it can only disturb one';[17] and *Frankenstein* ends with a similar reminder: the creator has really created nothing but he has disturbed the very nature of creation. He has queered the very notion of God, and in doing so, he has deprived himself of all satisfaction, love or friendship.

The surprising feature of the novel's closing pages is the creature's own sense of loss and the sudden and urgent meaninglessness of his own position:

'After the murder of Clerval, I returned to Switzerland, heartbroken and overcome. I pitied Frankenstein; my pity amounted to horror. I abhorred myself... Evil thenceforth became my good. Urged thus far, I had no choice but to adapt my nature to an element which I had willingly chosen. The completion of my demoniacal design became an insatiable passion. And now it is ended; there [pointing at Frankenstein's body] is my last victim!'   (p. 188)

The creature, like the queer subject, is driven to destroy because he is not allowed the solace of any real companionship. He mimics Milton's Satan because he is shut out from the pleasures of sociability. The creature is that negativity that Edelman describes, that death drive; and as such his misery is but the measure of all that he would destroy. Edelman calls this the 'unthinkable jouissance that would put an end to fantasy', and Frankenstein's creature does just that. As he is 'lost in darkness and distance' at the end of the novel, we are forced to acknowledge that there is absolutely nothing else he could have done.

Frankenstein is queer, then, in its very conception. The isolation of the scientist, the un-sexual creativity, the solitude and misery all create a queer uncanny out of which the queer construction of the malevolent creature assumes all the contours of the abject and isolated queer subject, who although the victim of society and public ridicule, is really in the end his own worst enemy. As Edelman reminds us, the queer undoes all sociability, and for that he must be isolated and expunged.

NOTES

1 See, for instance, Mary Poovey, who, in *The Proper Lady and the Woman Writer*, argues that egotistical creativity is her bête-noir in the novel ('"My Hideous Progeny": The Lady and the Monster', Norton Critical Edition of *Frankenstein*, ed. Paul Hunter (New York: Norton, 2012), pp. 344–55).

2 Eve Kosofsky Sedgwick, *Between Men: English Literature and Male Homosocial Desire* (New York: Columbia, 1985), pp. 83–96.

3 See Mary Shelley, Introduction to the 1831 edition of *Frankenstein*, in *Frankenstein*, ed. and Intro. Marilyn Butler (Oxford University Press, 1998), pp. 192–7; see also Anne K. Mellor, 'Possessing Nature: The Female in *Frankenstein*', in Norton Critical Edition of *Frankenstein*, ed. Paul Hunter (New York: Norton, 2012), pp. 355–68, esp, pp. 355–58.

4 Mary Shelley, *Frankenstein*, ed. and Intro. Marilyn Butler (Oxford University Press, 1998), p. 113. Future references will be made parenthetically.

5 Carla Freccero, 'Queer Spectrality: Haunting the Past', in George E. Haggerty and Molly McGarry (eds.), *A Companion to Lesbian, Gay, Bisexual, Transgender, and Queer Studies* (Oxford: Blackwell, 2007), pp. 194–231.

6 Barbara Johnson, 'My Monster/ My Self', in Melissa Fruerstein, Bill Johnson González, Lili Porten and Keja Valens (eds.), *The Barbara Johnson Reader: The Surprise of Otherness* (Durham, NC: Duke University Press, 2014), pp. 179–90;

pp. 186–7. The article was originally published in *Diacritics*, 2 (Summer 1992), 2–10.

7 Bette London, 'Mary Shelley, *Frankenstein*, and the Spectacle of Masculinity', *PMLA*, 108(2) (March 1993), 253–65; rpr. Norton Critical Edition of *Frankenstein*, ed. Paul Hunter (New York: Norton, 2012), pp. 391–403; see pp. 400–1.

8 London, ibid., p. 393.

9 Mair Rigby, '"Do you Share my Madness": *Frankenstein*'s Queer Gothic', in William Hughes and Andrew Smith (eds.), *Queering the Gothic* (Manchester University Press, 2009), pp. 36–54, p. 37. See also Ardel Haefele-Thomas, *Queer Others in Victorian Gothic: Transgressing Monstrosity* (Cardiff: University of Wales Press, 2012).

10 George E. Haggerty, *Queer Gothic* (Urbana, IL: University of Illinois Press, 2006), p. 2.

11 See, for instance, Ellen Moers, 'Female Gothic: The Monster's Mother', Norton Critical Edition of *Frankenstein*, ed. Paul Hunter (New York: Norton, 2012), pp. 317–27, esp. pp. 320–1.

12 Lee Edelman, *No Future: Queer Theory and the Death Drive* (Durham, NC: Duke University Press, 2004), pp. 4–5.

13 Ibid., p. 21.

14 Ibid., p. 27.

15 London, 'The Spectacle of Masculinity', p. 394.

16 Edelman, *No Future*, p. 9.

17 Ibid., p. 17.

9

PATRICK BRANTLINGER

Race and *Frankenstein*

What is the race of Frankenstein's monster? Asked that question, most readers of the novel are likely to think first about the monster's physical appearance. Racial stereotypes are primarily based on physical markers such as skin colour, quality and amount of hair, beards, stature and the like. As most scientists now recognize, such markers, and also the very idea of racial differentiation based on them, are not biologically or genetically significant. From the Renaissance onwards, however, race has acquired immense and immensely damaging cultural significance.

In the late 1700s and early 1800s, what has come to be called 'race science' or 'scientific racism' was beginning to emerge as an offshoot of natural history, a vast field that consisted of everything that Victor Frankenstein studies at the University of Ingolstadt, including chemistry, physiology and anatomy. (An alternative name for natural history was 'natural philosophy', the phrase Victor and his professors use to describe their areas of study.) During the 1700s, natural history was beginning to transition into the modern disciplines that included those Victor studies but also biology, zoology and anthropology, among others.[1]

Although Carl Linnaeus was not the first natural historian to attempt to classify organisms, his *Systema Naturae* (1735) was highly influential. He was followed by several other natural historians who produced similar taxonomies. They classified organisms by orders, genera and species, including *homo sapiens*, which they further subdivided into 'races'. At first Linnaeus identified four major human races – American, European, Asian and African. In Linnaeus's scheme, these four races belonged to the order of primates. Georges Louis LeClerc, Comte de Buffon, who is mentioned in *Frankenstein*, expanded the number of 'races' in his thirty-six volume *Histoire naturelle* (1749–1788).[2] Buffon defined 'races' as varieties of the human 'species' while asserting that climate was 'the chief source of the different colours of men': a black African might gradually turn white if he lived in northern Europe.[3] For Buffon, race was not as important a variable in human populations as it was for Linnaeus; both, however, thought that the different races of humans were members of the same species.

Other natural scientists who sought to classify humans by race and who probably had some influence on Mary Shelley, and possibly on *Frankenstein*, were Johann Friedrich Blumenbach, William Lawrence and Erasmus Darwin, Charles Darwin's grandfather. Percy Bysshe Shelley mentions Erasmus Darwin in his Preface to the 1818 edition of the novel.[4] Lawrence may have been especially influential, because he was Percy's physician and friend.[5] Lawrence's *Lectures on Physiology, Zoology, and the Natural History of Man* appeared in 1819, the year after the first edition of *Frankenstein*, but some of his lectures were published earlier, and in any case Mary Shelley may have participated in conversations with Lawrence about 'the natural history of man'. Many critics who comment on the scientific ideas in *Frankenstein* mention Lawrence, ordinarily because of his debate over 'vitalism' with his former teacher, John Abernethy.[6] But Lawrence had much to say about race and also about monsters.

Many of Lawrence's lectures deal with the races of the human species. Lawrence, moreover, dedicated his 1819 book to Blumenbach. Chapter 2 in that book concerns the 'varieties of colour in man, and their causes'. Skin pigmentation was then and is still the most cited outward sign of racial difference. In regard to the monster's race, his skin is 'yellow', perhaps hinting at something Oriental in his composition. But he is stitched together from dead body parts that Frankenstein has collected from 'dissecting rooms' and 'charnel houses' in and around Ingolstadt, so if the monster has a racial or national identity, it is Germanic (in the early 1800s, the word 'race' often served as a synonym for 'nation'). It seems unlikely, however, that Mary Shelley wanted her readers to think of the Monster as somehow Oriental, and she also does not stress the fact that the various pieces of his anatomy come from German corpses.

At any rate, just as race was supposedly visible, in their oldest versions monsters were visible prodigies or aberrations from nature. The expectation is still that monsters are visible, just as freaks in a freak show are visible. It is certainly the case that everyone who looks upon Victor's monstrous creation, including Victor himself, is horrified by his 'countenance'. But does that countenance bear any racial, or racially stereotypic, features besides yellow skin? To rephrase the question, is the monster tall, dark and handsome? Tall, yes: at eight feet, he is a giant. Dark, partly: his hair and lips are black. Handsome, no: the monster is frequently described, and describes himself, as 'hideous'. Perhaps by definition, all monsters are hideous. Not always, however: if he does not bare his fangs, Count Dracula is sexually alluring, and so is Hannibal Lecter in *The Silence of the Lambs* (1988). But the repeated rejections that Frankenstein's creature experiences, starting with his creator's instantaneous fear and loathing, is caused by his 'hideous' appearance.

Victor says he intended his creature to be 'beautiful', but he is just the opposite – he is horrifically ugly. He has 'dull yellow eyes', and:

> His yellow skin scarcely covered the work of muscles and arteries beneath; his hair was of a lustrous black, and flowing; his teeth of a pearly whiteness; but these luxuriances only formed a more horrid contrast with his watery eyes, that seemed almost of the same colour as the dun white sockets in which they were set, his shrivelled complexion, and straight black lips.   (p. 39)

In her biography of Mary Shelley, Miranda Seymour speculates that the monster bears a resemblance to 'the Eastern lascars' who often served as crew members on the slave ships that came to British ports before Parliament outlawed the slave trade in 1807. Even after that, lascars and former slaves were still visible in London and in ports such as Liverpool and Bristol. 'In the nameless Creature', writes Seymour:

> whose yellow skin, black hair, and giant limbs allowed her to combine contemporary perceptions of the Eastern 'lascars' with the African and West Indian, she examined the plight of a seemingly non-human being, judged by his looks to be incapable of moral feelings or elevated sentiments.[7]

Perhaps so. Several other recent critics of the novel have also seen connections between the monster's physical appearance, the slave trade and slave rebellions, including the one in Haiti in the 1790s that turned into a full-fledged revolution.[8] In *Gothic Images of Race* (1996), Howard Malchow interprets the scene in which the monster strangles Elizabeth in her boudoir as drawing upon 'the classic threat of the black male' raping white women.[9] Malchow also asserts: 'Race itself ... is in its most emotive sense a construct of romanticism ... Prejudice, like the imperialism that was its crudest manifestation, worked to produce the abject degradation and dependency it expected to find in the Other.'[10]

The main reason race came to the fore during Mary Shelley's lifetime was not Romanticism nor even science, but the abolitionist movement. Whether or not Mary Shelley saw lascars, Africans or West Indians in Bristol, as Seymour suggests, it would have been impossible for her to overlook the propaganda and debates sparked by the abolitionist movement. Parliament abolished the slave trade in 1807 and then slavery in all British territories in 1833. Slavery and its opposite, freedom or liberty, were major themes for many Romantic writers, including Lord Byron, Percy Shelley and Mary Shelley's parents, William Godwin and Mary Wollstonecraft. In her *A Vindication of the Rights of Woman* (1792), Wollstonecraft uses 'slavery' many times over to describe the general condition of women and on one occasion explicitly compares women to African slaves in the West Indies.[11] She calls marriage a version of 'slavery' and asserts that 'women are the slaves of injustice'.[12] As for Godwin, for example, the protagonist of his novel *Caleb Williams* (1794) declares: 'I have felt the iron of slavery grating upon my soul'.[13] The terms 'slave' and 'slavery' also crop up several times in *Frankenstein*, but usually with the generic meaning that can most often be found in the writings of Godwin and Wollstonecraft.

In their confrontation in the Orkney Islands, after Victor has destroyed the female monster he has been making, the quarrel between himself and his creature is couched in terms of slave versus master:

> Slave, I before reasoned with you [says the monster], but you have proved yourself unworthy of my condescension. Remember that I have power; you believe yourself miserable, but I can make you so wretched that the light of day will be hateful to you. You are my creator, but I am your master; – obey!
>
> (p. 140)

This moment in *Frankenstein* has many resonances, from Hegel's famous master–slave dialogue in *The Phenomenology of Spirit* (1807), to much of the writing about the American and French Revolutions, to Shakespeare's *The Tempest* (1611), in which Caliban chants 'Ban, ban, Caliban! Has a new master. Get a new man' (Act II, Scene 2). In his examination of racial discourse in *Frankenstein*, Allan Lloyd Smith notes several similarities between Caliban and the monster, including the master–slave language employed by both.[14]

Although *Frankenstein* can be interpreted as allegorizing other versions of the master–slave dialectic – for example, that of class conflict between the capitalist bourgeoisie and the emerging industrial proletariat – throughout nineteenth-century discourse about slavery and abolition the monster is frequently rendered as a rebellious black slave.[15] In *Black Frankenstein* (2008), Elizabeth Young surveys much of this use of the story in the American context. Lloyd Smith emphasizes the Shelleys' familiarity with the Haitian rebellion and with abolitionism. In her journal, Mary Shelley indicates that she read Bryan Edwards' 1793 *History of the West Indies*, 'a book that discussed differences of race and colour, and the horror of the slave rebellions, and described the "Carribees" ... as unnaturally cruel and violent, however peaceful and affectionate among themselves'.[16] She and Percy read other texts that dealt with slavery and issues of race, such as Mungo Park's *Travels into the Interior Districts of Africa* (1799).

The structural similarities Lloyd Smith finds between *Frankenstein* and slave narratives, which were a staple of abolitionist propaganda, are intriguing. Even if they did not have an explicit narrative frame, slave narratives were typically first-person accounts narrated by an escaped slave to a white abolitionist. The escaped slaves were ordinarily illiterate; the white abolitionists acted as literate intermediaries. *Frankenstein*, of course, has several narrators: the monster, Victor and Captain Walton. While the frame-tale structure may have been similar to that of slave narratives, however, it was also a standard convention in Gothic fiction. The analogy between the two types of narrative is, nevertheless, suggestive, although perhaps not one that Mary Shelley had in mind.

There is, however, no direct evidence that the struggle between Victor and the monster reflects the African slave trade, Haiti and the abolitionist movement. Mary Shelley's tale of terror more directly reflects the debates over the American and French Revolutions, including the writings of her parents. As Chris Baldick remarks:

> In Britain the first decade of the French Revolution witnessed the prodigious proliferation of two bodies of writing: a boom in 'Gothic' novels led by Ann Radcliffe, and a flurry of books and pamphlets provoked by Edmund Burke's *Reflections on the Revolution in France*   (1790).[17]

The rhetoric on both sides of the debate over the French Revolution could be described as both Gothic and Burkean, including the frequent use of metaphors of demonism and monstrosity. Depending whose side a writer was on, the other side were either monsters or produced monsters. Baldick quotes a representative passage from Burke that suggests in *Frankenstein*:

> we are taught to look with horror on those children of their country who are prompt rashly to hack that aged parent in pieces, and put him in the kettle of magicians, in hopes that by their poisonous weeds, and wild incantations, they may regenerate the paternal constitution, and renovate their father's life.[18]

Burke also portrays the French revolutionaries as a 'race of monsters', to which Mary Wollstonecraft responded that this 'race of monsters in human shape' has been called into being by 'a despotism in the government, which reason is teaching us to remedy'.[19]

Slavery in *Frankenstein* may reflect the abolitionist movement, but it more explicitly refers to the French Revolution. In the Orientalist subplot concerning the De Laceys and Safie the 'Arabian', the slavery involved refers both to Safie's Turkish father (he has been wrongfully imprisoned in France) and to the Ottoman Empire. Safie's 'mother was a Christian Arab, seized and made a slave by the Turks' (p. 99). Perhaps the only clear use of a racial stereotype in *Frankenstein* is the depiction of Safie's father as a dishonest, treacherous Turk.[20] Safie's mother, however, is an Arab Christian, so perhaps her father's treachery has more to do with religion than with race. In any event, the tale of Felix and Safie has many of the characteristics of Romantic Orientalism, including Safie's fear of returning to Asia and 'being immured within the walls of a haram' (p. 99). This sentence hints at how women were portrayed in Western haram porn, a staple of Romantic poetry and art, which lasciviously depicted Turkish and other Eastern men lording it over their many wives and concubines. In contrast, the 'prospect of marrying a Christian, and remaining in a country where women were allowed to take a rank in society, was enchanting to' Safie (p. 83). There is little if anything in this Orientalist tale within the larger tale of terror that suggests 'Turks' are racially or biologically inferior to Europeans, although they are evidently culturally and religiously inferior to Christians. The emphasis on slavery in much Romantic literature, including Byron's and Percy Shelley's poetry, is often an Orientalist one, as in Byron's immensely popular oriental tales such as *Childe Harold* (1812) and *The Giaour* (1813).

As Victor describes him, the monster is a bizarre mixture of physical features, perhaps without any definitive racial markers. Precisely because he is a monster, it seems unlikely that Mary Shelley wanted her readers to identify him with lascars, African slaves or any other actually existing human group. 'Oh! No mortal could support the horror of that countenance', Victor tells Captain Walton; 'A mummy again endued with animation could not be so hideous as that wretch' (p. 40). A mummy? Is the monster's racial or national identity Egyptian? No, of course not, despite his yellow or corpse-like complexion and black lips. Even reanimated mummies, Victor says, could not be that repulsive in appearance.

The main contrast to the monster's ugly deformity comes from the emphasis on how 'beautiful' the other, non-monstrous characters are. Victor says that although 'I had selected his features as beautiful. Beautiful! – Great God!', they are just the opposite of beautiful (p. 39). According to Victor's mother, however, Elizabeth is 'the most beautiful child she had ever seen' (p. 20). Victor's youngest brother, William, is 'the most beautiful little fellow in the world' (p. 25). When the monster accosts William before killing him, he also says that he is 'a beautiful child' (p. 116). And when the monster sees the portrait of Elizabeth in the locket William is wearing, he thinks to himself: 'I was for ever deprived of the delights that such beautiful creatures could bestow' (p. 117). Even the servant Justine is described by Victor as beautiful; in court, her 'countenance . . . was rendered exquisitely beautiful' by her predicament (p. 61). And the monster says that 'God, in pity, made man beautiful and alluring, after his own image' (p. 105).

Beauty, then, is a godlike attribute of humans, but not of monsters, no matter how human they seem. Instead of indicating that the monster has a specific racial but still human identity, the text raises the question of what species he belongs to. Mary Shelley's generic use of 'beautiful', when applied to her non-monstrous characters, suggests that the 'hideous' creature Frankenstein produces is not human. This then raises the further question of what exactly it is that he has created? When he first contemplates 'bestowing animation' through his knowledge of chemistry and anatomy, he doubts his ability to create 'an animal as complex and wonderful as man'. Nevertheless, he sets about 'the creation of a human being' (p. 35). Yet in the next paragraph, he says that he hoped 'A new species would bless me as its creator and source; many happy and excellent natures would owe their being to me' (p. 36).

The monster later says that not only is he 'hideously deformed and loathsome', he is 'not even of the same nature as man' (p. 96). When he is rejected by the De Laceys, he declares 'everlasting war against the species' (p. 111) – that is, against humans. And when he pleads with Victor to create a mate for him, he says: 'My companion must be of the same species, and have the same defects' (p. 118). So is the monster human, or does he belong to 'a new species'? And if so, what is that species? Do monsters constitute a separate species?

It is also possible that, when Mary Shelley uses the word 'race' in her novel, it carries the same meaning as 'species'. In no case does 'race' in *Frankenstein* appear to designate some specific variety of human beings distinct from Europeans. Travelling through the Alps, Victor says that their 'white and shining pyramids and domes towered above all, as belonging to another earth, the habitations of another race of beings' (p. 73). Perhaps he has the angels in mind, but 'race' in this passage clearly means the same as the word 'species'.

In the Orkneys, as he is working on a mate for the monster, Victor worries that they might loathe each other because of their mutual 'deformity . . . She also might turn with disgust from him to the superior beauty of man; she might quit him, and he be again alone, exasperated by the fresh provocation of being deserted by one of his own species' (p. 138). The monster, then, according to his creator, belongs to a different species from 'man', a species characterized by hideousness and 'deformity', while 'man' is characterized by 'superior beauty'. In the next paragraph, moreover, Victor adds to his anxiety about creating a second, female monster this fearful thought:

Even if they were to leave Europe, and inhabit the deserts of the new world, yet one of the first results of those sympathies for which the daemon thirsted would be children, and a race of devils would be propagated upon the earth, who might make the very existence of the species of man a condition precarious and full of terror. (p. 138)

Within this single sentence, the words 'race' and 'species' carry the same meaning. The paragraph ends with the thought that, because of his monstrous dual creations, Victor would be endangering the very existence of 'the whole human race' – or species (p. 138).

The debate among the natural historians in the 1700s about whether the 'races' of humans constituted different 'species' continued through Charles Darwin and beyond. Although in *The Descent of Man* (1871) Darwin leaves no doubt that he believes the different 'races' constitute a single human 'species', he leaves unsettled the issue of just how sharp the dividing line is between species within the same genus. If different races can produce fertile hybrids, so perhaps can different but closely allied species. Mary Shelley, of course, has no reason to make a sharp distinction between races and species. Perhaps the blurring of the lines between the monster and humanity adds to his monstrousness. He is a monster because he is not-human *and* because he is almost human.

The non-monstrous characters in *Frankenstein* have another distinguishing feature besides their often-emphasized physical beauty. They all have specific national identities. Despite his Germanic last name, Victor tells Captain Walton that he is 'Genevese'. Captain Walton and his sister are obviously white and British; the ship's officer Walton hires is Russian; Victor's professors are Germans; Elizabeth Lavenza is Italian; the De Laceys are French; Safie is an Arabian; her father is Turkish. Of these diverse nationalities, two of them – Arabian and Turkish – could equally well, in the early 1800s and also today, serve as racial signifiers. In contrast, the homeless monster is never labelled as German or anything else referring to a particular place, nation or race.

Victor, however, frequently refers to his creature as a 'fiend' or 'daemon'. Those terms echo Milton's *Paradise Lost* (1674), a text that the monster reads and that has parallels throughout *Frankenstein*. The monster likens himself to Adam and Victor to God. Victor considers the monster to be more like Satan than like Adam. While these comparisons have no racial overtones, both Satan and 'daemons' for ages have often been depicted as black and as creatures of darkness.

Another text that the monster reads and that teaches him the most about human history, C. F. Volney's *Ruins of Empire* (1791), makes precise albeit stereotypic racial and national distinctions, while often using the terms 'race' and 'nation' interchangeably.[21] In chapter 19, entitled 'General Assembly of the Nations', Volney writes:

> A scene of a nature at once both novel and astonishing then presented itself to my view. All the people and nations of the globe, every different race from every different climate, advancing on all sides, seemed to assemble in one inclosure, and there to form an immense congress. The motly appearance of this innumerable crowd, distinguishable into groupes [sic] by their diversity of dress, of features, and of complexion, exhibited a most extraordinary and engaging spectacle.[22]

Volney continues:

> And, observing the Kachemirean with his rose-coloured cheek, beside the sunt-burnt [sic] Hindoo, and the Georgian standing by the Tartar; I reflected on the effects of hot and cold climate, of mountainous and low, marshy and dry, wooded and open grounds. I compared the dwarf of the pole with the giant of the temperate zone.[23]

Volney's stress is on the variety of the human species, but also on the beauty of the spectacle their 'assembly' represents. One phrase worth noting in this lengthy passage is 'savage nations', implying the major if stereotypic distinction between civilization and savagery. To many observers in Mary Shelley's time, that distinction often seemed as great as one between species.

So is the monster a savage? No, although his behaviour becomes stereo-typically savage. His conversion from 'benevolence' to serial killer occurs, according to himself, after he has learned to speak and read by spying on the De Laceys and Safie. In other words, when Victor confronts him in the Alps, his behaviour shows signs of his being civilized rather than savage. The monster tells Victor his story, and tells it presumably using Victor's language. Mary Shelley does not make the monster's narrative linguistically distinct from Victor's or from Captain Walton's English by using some ver-sion of monster-speak, as savage characters are sometimes made to speak in imperialist romances. This is, of course, one way in which the author under-scores the idea that the monster is his maker's alter ego or *doppelgänger* and also her own alter ego, since she is the ultimate creator of her 'hideous progeny'.

So the monster is not clearly on the wrong side of the civilized/savage divide evident in Volney's *Ruins*. Yet David Hirsch is surely right when he contends that the monster subverts the French revolutionary ideals of equal-ity and fraternity. Hirsch argues that 'Frankenstein's creature [is] described in terms . . . commonly encountered in colonial depictions of Asian, Indian, and African "savage"'.[24] Whether that is what Mary Shelley meant to do perhaps does not matter. But it is clear that the monster 'is terrifying not merely in his physical otherness but more profoundly in his call for recognition as a humane, if not also human, being'.[25] It is in this regard rather than in terms of his skin colour or his hideous mish-mash of a 'countenance' and physique that the monster most clearly draws on abolitionist iconography. The famous Wedgwood medallion, showing a black slave in chains, on his knees, pleading 'Am I not a man and a brother?' is precisely the dilemma the monster finds himself in.

When the monster accosts Victor's youngest brother, William calls him an 'ogre', a term that perhaps has a bearing on the issue of race. Besides the four main races that Linnaeus identified, in later writings he also discussed three varieties or subspecies of humans, including *homo ferus, homo troglodytes* and *homo monstrosus*.[26] The first of these varieties were 'wild men' or 'wild children', who were sometimes found living by themselves in the woods like the wild boy of Averon. The second were chimpanzees, orangutangs and the 'pongos' or giant apes supposedly inhabiting Borneo. And the third consisted of several difficult-to-categorize creatures like satyrs, based on mythological sources. So perhaps the monster belongs to one or more of these varieties, lying just outside Linnaeus's four principal races. His story of being alone in the forest is similar to that of a wild man like Peter of Hanover. He has some ape-like features – long limbs, incredible climbing skills. And he is definitely a version of an ogre, something like Homer's Cyclops. There is no indication, however, that Mary Shelley had Linnaeus in mind when she was conjuring up her 'hideous progeny'. The term 'ogre' moreover, is an old one; cannibalistic, often hideous giants occur in the mythologies of many cultures. So when William calls the monster an 'ogre' that term has no particular racial resonance.

One response to the question of the monster's race is to insist that he has no race or nationality precisely because he is a monster. By definition, a race is an entire population, and ordinarily a very large population: all Mongolians, for example, or all Caucasians. It does not make sense to refer to all monsters, or for that matter all 'ogres' as a population category; they are typically loners or monstrous singularities, solitary creatures beyond the bounds of civilization, which is exactly the situation Frankenstein's monster finds himself in after his creator abandons him. In her consideration of 'the gigantic' and of giants, Susan Stewart mentions 'the loneliness of Frankenstein outside the peasant hut', apparently forgetting that it is not the mad scientist but his creature who is alone.[27]

Monsters, however, were sometimes treated by other natural historians besides Linnaeus as a human subspecies, if not a distinct racial category.

As Melinda Cooper points out, William Lawrence discusses the work of Étienne Geoffrey Saint-Hilaire, 'who no doubt exercised the greatest influence on innovative English medical thought of the early nineteenth century'.[28] Cooper credits Saint-Hilaire with establishing the science of 'teratology' by conducting numerous 'experiments designed to produce monstrous births from animal embryos'. For Saint-Hilaire, 'the study of monstrous anatomy was integral to the project of comparative anatomy *tout court*, and both were illuminated by the experimental art of *teratogeny* (the technical reproduction of monstrosities)'.[29] For his part, Lawrence wrote on monsters in Rees's *Cyclopedia* (1819) around the time of the publication of *Frankenstein*. He also kept 'a brain-damaged child "monster" in his own home'.[30] And in his lectures, Lawrence wrote about *homo ferus* partly to debunk notions that 'wild men' or 'wild children' had been living in some sort of natural, ideal state.[31]

The large categories of races in Linnaeus or Buffon can be whittled down to smaller ones that frequently amount to nationalities: all Turks, for example, or all Norwegians, still considered as distinct 'races'. Notions of race and nation are also notions of descent: by definition, somebody from Norway has Norwegian parents and ancestors. But a monster or an 'ogre' does not fit into any standard category of race or even nation. They are not only loners like examples of *homo ferus*, they are outliers beyond most or perhaps all normal and natural categories. And in *Frankenstein*, of course, the monster has no parents or ancestors, unless one counts Victor as father or considers all the dead body parts the monster consists of as his piecemeal Bavarian ancestors.

Mary Shelley, however, was well aware that race was a factor of growing importance in the late 1700s and early 1800s. As noted earlier, in 1818 scientific racism was just coming into prominence through investigators like Erasmus Darwin and William Lawrence. The abolitionist crusade against slavery and the slave trade drew the sympathies of the Shelley circle and of Mary Shelley's radical parents, William Godwin and Mary Wollstonecraft. In his *An Enquiry Concerning Political Justice* (1793), Godwin offers his own version of the classification of human populations by race and nation, writing:

> It would be reasonable to expect that different races of men, intermixed with each other, but differently governed, would afford a strong and visible contrast. Thus the Turks are brave, open and sincere; but the modern Greeks mean, cowardly and deceitful.[32]

Here and throughout this passage, Godwin is questioning racial and national stereotypes while also employing them. He is also questioning the effects climate and other factors such as government may have in causing racial traits to develop, as when he writes:

> If... climate were principally concerned in forming the characters of nations, we might expect to find that heat and cold produc[e] an extraordinary effect upon men, as they do upon plants and inferior animals. But the reverse of this appears to be the fact.[33]

So Godwin expresses scepticism about the natural historians' various attempts to explain racial differences in any meaningful way:

> It was the opinion of the ancients that the northern nations were incapable of civilization and improvement; but the moderns have found that the English are not inferior in literary eminence to any nation in the world. Is it asserted that the northern nations are more hardy and courageous, and that conquest has usually travelled from that to the opposite quarter? It would have been truer to say that conquest is usually made by poverty upon plenty.[34]

And so on. Perhaps Mary Shelley acquired a healthy scepticism about racial distinctions from her father.

Even though the monster has no pointedly racial features and is made out of the body parts of dead Germans, the Oriental tale about Felix, Safie the 'sweet Arabian' and her Turkish father has prompted some critics to interpret *Frankenstein* from a postcolonial perspective. Captain Walton's voyage of Arctic exploration coupled with Victor's ambition to create a new 'race' or 'species' who will view him as 'children' view their 'father' (p. 36) are additional factors, as is Volney's account of the rise and fall of empires. When the monster listens to Felix reading Volney, he weeps 'with Safie over the hapless fate of [the] original inhabitants' of 'the American hemisphere' (p. 95). Still another factor concerns the imperial ambitions of Henry Clerval, with whom Victor reads 'the works of the orientalists':

> Their melancholy is soothing, and their joy elevating to a degree I never experienced in studying the authors of any other country. When you read their writings, life appears to consist in a warm sun and garden of roses... How different from the manly and heroical poetry of Greece and Rome. (p. 50)

In the 1831 edition of *Frankenstein*, moreover, Clerval's career goal is specifically imperialist:

> His design was to visit India, in the belief that he had in his knowledge of its various languages, and in the views he had taken of its society, the means of materially assisting the progress of European colonization and trade. (p. 225)

The discourse of slave and master in the novel, including its echoes of Shakespeare's *The Tempest*, further the thought that the novel has many connections to imperial themes. In *Race* (2003), Brian Niro reads *Frankenstein* in terms of 'imperial paranoia'.[35] Elizabeth Bohls also finds a 'critique of empire' in Mary Shelley's tale.[36] And Gayatri Chakravorty Spivak writes that 'the discourse of imperialism surfaces in a curiously powerful way in Shelley's novel'.[37] These aspects of *Frankenstein* that suggest reading Victor as colonizer and the monster as a figure for the colonized do not rely on specific instances of race or racism. Yet when Victor sets about creating and then destroying the female monster, he dreads that the two monsters will propagate 'a race of devils' (p. 138) threatening all of humanity. That dread seems readily translatable into the fear repeatedly expressed in the literature of Western colonization and decolonization – that is, the fear aroused in the colonizers that the colonized will turn against their would-be masters in various forms of revenge and rebellion. In this reading, the rebellious colonized could easily be rebellious slaves, as in Haiti.

In her postcolonial reading of *Frankenstein*, Spivak notes the liminal but still significant role played by Mrs Saville. She is the recipient within the novel of the various narratives of her brother Captain Walton, of Victor Frankenstein, of the monster and of the monster's Oriental tale about Felix and Safie. Her silent position is similar to that of many other women in European tales about the exploration and conquest of new colonies. Of these female figures, recipients of male stories about the far reaches and races of the world, perhaps the most notable is Kurtz's 'Intended' in Joseph Conrad's *Heart of Darkness* (1899). In that tale, Marlow returns from the Congo after listening to Kurtz's 'The horror! The horror!' and witnessing Kurtz's death, only to lie to the Intended. In *Frankenstein*, there is no evidence that Captain Walton lies to his sister. And yet the stories his letters convey to her are both horrific and incredible – stories of imperial ambition and retribution in which masculine (and white, European) dreams of the mastery of nature and of other races and species result in disaster. In conclusion, although *Frankenstein* has very little to say about racial distinctions among humans, it is nevertheless very much about races, species and the monsters we create or make out of ourselves.

NOTES

1 See Michel Foucault, *The Order of Things: An Archaeology of the Human Sciences* (New York: Vintage Books, 1970), especially p. 265.
2 Mary Shelley, *Frankenstein*, ed. and Intro. Marilyn Butler (Oxford University Press, 1998), p. 25. Future references will be made parenthetically.
3 Bruce Baum, *The Rise and Fall of the Caucasian Race: A Political History of Racial Identity* (New York University Press, 2006), p. 69.

4 Anne K. Mellor, in *Mary Shelley: Her Life, Her Fiction, Her Monsters* (New York: Methuen, 1988), provides an account of how Erasmus Darwin may have influenced Mary Shelley (pp. 95–101). She also examines the possible influence of a number of other natural historians, but not that of William Lawrence.

5 See 'Introduction', *Frankenstein*, ed. and Intro. Butler, pp. ix–li. Melinda Cooper, 'Monstrous Progeny: The Teratological Tradition in Science and Literature', in Christa Knellworth and Jane Goodall (eds.), *Frankenstein's Science: Experimentation and Discovery in Romantic Culture, 1780–1830* (Aldershot: Ashgate, 2008), pp. 87–97.

6 See, for instance, Timothy Morton, *A Routledge Literary Sourcebook on Mary Shelley's* Frankenstein (London: Routledge, 2002), pp. 17–23.

7 Miranda Seymour, *Mary Shelley* (London: John Murray, 2000), p. 139.

8 See Allan Lloyd Smith, '"This Thing of Darkness": Racial Discourse in Mary Shelley's *Frankenstein*', *Gothic Studies*, 6(2) (November 2004), 208–22.

9 Howard Malchow, *Gothic Images of Race in Nineteenth-Century Britain* (Stanford University Press, 1996), p. 23.

10 Ibid., p. 39.

11 Mary Wollstonecraft, *A Vindication of the Rights of Woman*, ed. Miriam Kramnick, (Harmondsworth: Penguin, 1978), p. 257.

12 Ibid., p. 313.

13 William Godwin, *Caleb Williams, or Things as They Are* (London: Colburn and Bentley, 1831), p. 251.

14 Allan Lloyd Smith, '"This Thing of Darkness": Racial Discourse in Mary Shelley's *Frankenstein*', *Gothic Studies*, 6(2) (November 2004), 208–222.

15 Chris Baldick provides a summary of several interpretations of the monster as the emerging, potentially revolutionary proletariat *In Frankenstein's Shadow: Myth, Monstrosity, and Nineteenth-Century Writing* (Oxford: Clarendon Press, 1987), pp. 54–5, pp. 121–40.

16 Allan Lloyd Smith, '"This Thing of Darkness"', 218.

17 Baldick, *In Frankenstein's Shadow*, p. 16.

18 Quoted in Baldick, *In Frankenstein's Shadow*, p. 17. The extract comes from Conor Cruise O'Brien (ed.), *Reflections on the Revolution in France* (Harmondsworth: Penguin, 1968), p. 194.

19 Quoted in Baldick, *In Frankenstein's Shadow*, pp. 21–22. The extract comes from Wollstonecraft's *An Historical and Moral View of the Origin and Progress of the French Revolution; and the Effect it has Produced in Europe* (London: np: 1794), p. 515. Baldick is drawing on Lee Sterrenburg, 'Mary Shelley's Monster: Politics and Psyche in *Frankenstein*' in George Levine and U. C. Knoepflmacher (eds.), *The Endurance of Frankenstein* (Berkeley and Los Angeles, CA: University of California Press, 1979), pp. 143–71.

20 For a survey of British responses to Turks and the Ottoman Empire in the nineteenth century, see my 'Terrible Turks: Xenophobia and the Ottoman Empire' in Marlene Tromp, Maria Bachman and Heidi Kaufman (eds.), *Fear, Loathing, and Victorian Xenophobia* (Columbus, OH: The Ohio State University Press, 2013), pp. 208–30.

21 Constantin-François Volney, *The Ruins: or, A Survey of the Revolutions of Empires*. New translation (Philadelphia, PA: James Lyon, 1799).

22 Ibid., pp. 186–7.

23 Ibid., pp. 188–9.

24 David A. Hedrich Hirsch, 'Liberty, Equality, Monstrosity: Revolutionizing the Family in Mary Shelley's *Frankenstein*', in Jeffrey Jerome Cohen (ed.), *Monster Theory: Reading Culture* (Minneapolis, MN: University of Minnesota Press, 1996), pp. 115–40, p. 119.

25 Hirsch, ibid., p. 119.

26 See Julia Douthwaite, 'Homo Ferus: Between Monster and Model', *Eighteenth-Century Life*, 21(2) (May 1997), 176–202; and Richard Nash, *Wild Enlightenment: The Borders of Human Identity in the Eighteenth Century* (Charlottesville, VA: University of Virginia Press, 2003).

27 Susan Stewart, *On Longing: Narratives of the Miniature, the Gigantic, the Souvenir, the Collection* (Durham, NC and London: Duke University Press, 1993), p. 71.

28 Melinda Cooper, 'Monstrous Progeny: The Teratological Tradition in Science and Literature' in Christa Knellwolf and Jane Goodall (eds.), *Frankenstein's Science: Experimentation and Discovery in Romantic Culture, 1780–1830* (Aldershot: Ashgate, 2008), pp. 87–97, p. 89.

29 Cooper, 'Monstrous Progeny', p. 95.

30 Ibid., p. 95.

31 William Lawrence, *Lectures on Physiology, Zoology, and the Natural History of Man, Delivered at the Royal College of Surgeons* (London: Callow, 1819), p. 121.

32 William Godwin, *Enquiry Concerning Political Justice*, 2 vols. (London: Robinson, 1793), Vol. I, p. 65.

33 Ibid., p. 66.

34 Ibid., p. 66.

35 Brian Niro, *Race* (Basingstoke: Palgrave Macmillan, 2003). See pp. 83–9.

36 Elizabeth A. Bohls, 'Standards of Taste, Discourses of "Race", and the Aesthetic Education of a Monster: Critique of Empire in *Frankenstein*', *Eighteenth-Century Life*, 18(3) (November 1994), 23–36.

37 Gayatri Chakravorty Spivak, *A Critique of Postcolonial Reason: Toward a History of the Vanishing Present* (Cambridge, MA: Harvard University Press, 1999), p. 133.

10

TIMOTHY MORTON

Frankenstein and Ecocriticism

Biology, Arctic ice, animal flesh, Alpine landscapes, vegetarianism, life, death, undeath: you would have thought that with juicy topics such as these, there would be hundreds of studies specifically devoted to ecological readings of Mary Shelley's novel. Yet this is not the case. If you search on a database such as ABELL (the Annual Bibliography of English Language and English Literature), you will find countless texts on *Frankenstein* – there are more than 2,500 entries for items published in the last twenty years. But only a very few of those are explicitly about ecology.[1] Indeed, only about one per cent of the 2,500 items on ABELL explicitly pertain to ecology, and many of those only tangentially. The first question we have to ask, then, is what is it about *Frankenstein* that *does not* lend itself to explicitly ecological treatment?

There seem to be two main answers. The first is about the impact of the novel; the second is about its internal dynamics. First of all, to say that the novel has been widely received, adapted, disseminated and otherwise absorbed is the slimmest of understatements. It would be hard to name another work of literature that has had the impact of *Frankenstein* since its first publication in 1818. The very 'universality' of this impact – the way in which the novel has become something like what Richard Dawkins calls a *meme* – a virus-like string of code that can easily be reproduced and circulated – mitigates against the specific, explicit study. Everyone wants to talk about *Frankenstein* – so no one talks directly about *Frankenstein*. If there ever were a candidate for a modern myth, *Frankenstein* would be it – its subtitle (*The Modern Prometheus*) throws down that gauntlet directly. Myths might be defined in part as stories whose original format is irrelevant: Hesiod, or Ovid, or Virgil do not have a monopoly on the myths they are telling. Myths are precisely stories that exceed their authors in a profound way. You do not need to quote Ovid to talk about Arachne. You do not need to read the *Theogony* to talk about Prometheus. You do not need to cite *Frankenstein* to refer to 'Frankenfoods', which is how many began to talk about genetically modified crops in the 1990s.[2]

The pervasiveness of the Frankenstein myth affects art itself. Philip K. Dick and subsequently Ridley Scott did not need to refer directly to Mary Shelley's novel in *Do Androids Dream of Electric Sheep?* (1968) and Scott's film adaptation, *Blade Runner* (1982). Yet both are profoundly allusive meditations on the Promethean theme – the human use of 'technology' to make life – and the theme of what it means to be alive, let alone the theme of what it means to be a person. With his plangent Blake quotations, his murderousness and aesthetic awe ('I've... *seen* things you people wouldn't believe...'), Roy the replicant is a twentieth-century upgrade of the creature.

When it comes to readings of *Frankenstein* that relate it to ecological themes, one might argue that the novel is a victim of its very success.

The ways Dick and Scott adapt *Frankenstein* are deeply about how the novel explores issues related to ecology, at the beginning of the Western intellectual disciplinary period of *biology* (a term coined both in Germany and in England, roughly simultaneously, about 1800). Yet another reason why ecocriticism has not done much with *Frankenstein* has to do with the *ways in which* ecological issues are presented and explored. *Frankenstein* is hardly comforting if one is interested in promulgating a traditional, normative concept of Nature (with a capital N). And the novel sits awkwardly in relation to the fields of ecology and what is now called critical animal studies. Ecology has to do with populations, systems, species – things that seem vast and abstract to many. Animal studies has to do with animal rights – how one disposes oneself towards this particular life form, right here. For this reason, there are clashes between literary criticism inflected by animal studies and criticism inflected by ecology. *Frankenstein* does not necessarily make one think about ecology, unless one is a rather odd ecological thinker (such as myself).

The novel might make one consider how we treat other life forms; about what constitutes a human as opposed to a non-human – urgently, it meditates on the uncanniness of the nearly-or-not-quite-human; the novel explicitly addresses topics in vegetarianism. None of these has an easy-to-identify, traditional 'ecological' resonance, especially if one believes that ecology is about studying and preserving something definitely non-human called Nature. The same applies when we consider the phenomenological chemicals of *Frankenstein* – the emotions and states of mind and flavours of thought in which it deals. Melancholy, horror, disgust and searing pain – and refreshing, cold, liberating reason and its sadistic shadow side – are the novel's phenomenological landscape, not the awe, wonder, reverence – and warm, familiar, unreflective or 'pre-theoretical' cosiness and its politically oppressive shadow side. Yet the latter are the cognitive chemicals that eco-criticism has often been most keen to explore and reproduce, at least in its early days.

Frankenstein seems to have been designed to slip cheekily out of the holes in standard ecocritical sieves. So we confront a paradox. In *Frankenstein* we encounter a novel whose ecological resonance is so obvious that ironically hardly anyone tackles it directly; and a novel, the very same one, whose ecological resonance is so uncanny in relation to standard beliefs about Nature that hardly anyone tackles it directly.

Yet we inhabit an era in which the cognitive chemicals of melancholy, disgust and horror are central to how we are beginning to react to the ecological era that began shortly before Mary Shelley was born, an era we now call the *Anthropocene*, marked by decisive human intervention in geophysical systems, a whole new geological period with a concomitant mass extinction of life forms, only the sixth one to have occurred on this planet. A consideration of the ways in which we might think in a critical ecological way about *Frankenstein* seems especially urgent.

Frankenstein and Nature

There are many kinds of ecological literary criticism, but this was not always the case. When it first developed in the early 1990s, ecocriticism had far more specific and unique qualities: they could be summed up as a reaction against the constructionism of the kinds of thought one encounters in (now tradi-tional) theory class, and a counter-assertion of an unconstructed Nature. (In this chapter I shall be capitalizing the term Nature to draw attention to this specific concept – which should of course be distinguished from actually existing mountains and foxes.) Then ecocriticism fanned out like an allu-vial flow of water, opening up and significantly diverging from the starting position. In a way, one might say that however surprising early ecocriticism was – it was a surprisingly conservative (small c) rearguard action against theory – it fit the same mould as the very theory it was opposing, insofar as it relied on a very familiar dichotomy between humans and Nature, just slightly reweighted. Whereas undergraduates had become used to pointing out how ideas and institutions and all kinds of things we take for granted were social constructs, ecocriticism wanted to show that many things in our world are not constructed.

But both these positions are anthropocentric: they assert that there is a sharp difference between humans and the non-human. For good or bad, it is humans who do the constructing, and everything else that gets to be constructed. This position is not all that different from the Cartesian dualism in which there is a (human) intellect and soul opposed to a (non-human) universe of matter. And it is hard to distinguish from the Kantian version of this idea, namely that things exist, but they are not 'real' until some (human) adjudicator – in Kant's case this is the transcendental subject, but later versions included Spirit (Hegel), human economic relations (Marx) and will (Nietzsche) or Dasein (Heidegger's 'being-there') – correlates with things or observes them or works with them in some way.

If ecological criticism is about critiquing and transcending anthropocentrism, it needs to get past this mode, the mode in which there is construction, and something that is constructed, and a sharp difference between those, usually in just one place in the universe – the difference between human beings and everything else. And in a way, this undoing of the sharp difference is precisely what many Romantic-period writers were up to. It was the previous period of art and culture, commonly known as the age of sensibility, which valued Nature as opposed to (human) society: just think of Jean-Jacques Rousseau and his rigid dividing lines between the artificial and the natural. Or consider the sentimental mourning for the destruction of indigenous cultures that we find in the poetry of the 'Celtic twilight'. Romantic-period authors such as Wordsworth and Shelley strove to confuse and undermine the difference between Nature and the human, the object and the subject, history and natural history, not necessarily by blowing it up completely, but by exploring its ironies and paradoxes. And William Blake found the concept Nature downright politically oppressive.

Nature is... natural: it sounds like a truism but we should think about this a little. It means that the concept Nature is *normative*, which is a philosophical term for something that establishes differences between the normal and the abnormal, often with ethical overtones. For something to be natural, it must be not unnatural. The concept *natural* implies that some things are not. If everything were natural, if everything was Nature, then the concept would lose all its teeth. Nature cannot cover everything – although some philosophers such as Spinoza use the term that way, they therefore bar themselves (whether they like it or not) from using the term Nature in the way early ecocriticism did: to draw a difference between what is natural (for instance, non-theory-influenced readings of literary texts) and what is not.

Nature is defined as 'not unnatural'. So what happens when someone writes a novel about confusing the difference between humans and nonhumans, and between the natural and the unnatural? What happens, in other words, when someone writes about something *monstrous*: something that is not only 'natural' in the sense that it is non-human, but also 'unnatural' in the sense that it defies expectations about what nature is, that it has been manufactured by a human, and so on? What happens when Shelley writes *Frankenstein*?

Frankenstein is in a way a deconstructive work of art, because it does not *get rid of* categories. Instead, it tests these categories to breaking point so that they start to speak their paradoxes and absurdities, absurdities that themselves might be seen as monstrous. Perhaps the very idea that there is a Nature and that this means 'not monstrous' is precisely the monstrous idea, responsible for all kinds of phenomena such as racism or homophobia. Perhaps trying to establish rigid and thin boundaries between Nature and non-Nature is the monstrous act – or perhaps trying to blow them up completely is monstrous, as when we reduce things to piles of atoms or other substances taken to be 'more real' than minds or pandas, eliminating the weird gaps between things and between concepts, breaking them down into something easier to manipulate in thought or in deed.

Moreover, as a Gothic horror novel, *Frankenstein* operates in a region slightly to the side of mainstream high Romantic art, shadowing the latter with something like a weird, uncanny double. This doubling is also deconstructive, in this case of official Romanticism. Imagine, for instance, a literal version of a Romantic poem – an 'organic' artwork with a life of its own – imagine it as a physical body that gets up and walks out of its creator's house to find its way in the world, whether its creator likes it or not. This would be not a bad description of Frankenstein's creature, who drastically threatens his creator simply by being autonomous, let alone murderous.

It follows from this argument – *Frankenstein* is a work that questions and undermines all kinds of differences between categories, not by completely eliminating them, but by *multiplying differences* – that it might be possible to produce a wide variety of different sorts of ecocritical readings of Mary Shelley's novel. That *Frankenstein* might spawn all kinds of 'hideous progeny' in the way of variant readings – and we know from Darwin that variance and monstrosity are very difficult to distinguish – would also explain why it was almost completely neglected in what is now known as first-wave ecocriticism.

The cyborg, the spectre, the uncanny double, the abject animated pile of flesh endowed with a razor-sharp reason and poignant emotion: none of these beings seem to fit within a paradigm that is about Nature versus the human, but all could encapsulate the creature in some way. If, however, we drop the concept Nature – has it ever truly coincided with ecological and evolutionary reality? – we find that issues concerning abjection and spectral beings whose ontological status is uncertain and uncanny, because of the fuzzy boundaries between the human and the non-human, between life and non-life, between organic and inorganic, and between conscious being and android, are precisely what ecological and evolutionary science begin to point out. *Frankenstein* is ideally suited to an ecological criticism without Nature.

Environmentality

What would an ecocriticism without Nature look like? For a start, it might begin to investigate how *Frankenstein* allows for – or does not allow for – a sense of 'being in'. We might give a name to this quality: environmentality. What kind of surroundings does *Frankenstein* offer, and what happens in them? What affordances do the worlds of the novel offer? Are the novel's surroundings simply a backdrop for human projects, or is there some sense that there are other life forms, other entities whose 'worlds' might overlap with that of humans, or not?[3] What is included, and what is excluded?

We might begin by noting that the novel takes the form of three nested sets of narratives. Evidently each narrative takes place 'in' certain specific domains: the Arctic, Geneva, university, lab, forest, cottage. All, that is, except for the ultimate frame. If we think that envrionmentality has to do with specific 'settings', we have seriously crippled the concept of environmentality. This just reinvents the wheel of 'characters' (and we have pre-formatted concepts about what a 'character' is) living 'in' a particular 'setting' (about which we also have preconceptions as to what those mean). In the end, such an analysis will be circular, as it never questions its initial assumptions. Environmentality is a rare beast one needs to sneak up on.

Let us instead proceed more carefully. The creature's narrative is 'in' Frankenstein's, and in turn Frankenstein's is 'in' Walton's. And in turn again, this set of sets is being held in the hands of Walton's addressee, Margaret Saville. This 'top level' of the narrative is significantly vague: are we in a parlour, or a study, or a garden, or are the bundled letters being read in a coach? The lack of a setting induces anxiety. Anxiety causes us to fill in the surroundings – though they are vague, they are vivid. They are *our* surroundings, because Shelley spells out no specific difference between where we are reading and where Mrs Saville is reading. We get the uncanny feeling of *being* Mrs Saville – and of not quite being her, of holding Walton's letters in our own hands – or not. Maybe they are just sitting on a desk. Maybe some have not even arrived.[4]

This kind of uncertainty is in fact a default form of envrionmentality – the feeling of being in an environment boils down to being uncertain as to whether you are in one. It is a common feeling to wonder whether we have yet entered the age of global warming. To the extent that we are unsure, we *have* entered this age. We are preoccupied with it – 'in' in the non-trivial sense, not as a pin on a Cartesian grid, not as a point in abstract Newtonian space, but 'in' as in 'into it' – we care. We have anxiety because we care.

In outlining how Mrs Saville's vague environment provides us with a default environmentality that evokes feelings of anxiety, enabled by a caring 'into it'-ness, I am simply guiding you through the main arguments in Division 1 of Martin Heidegger's masterpiece, *Being and Time* (1927).[5] It is Heidegger who enables us to think about what it means to inhabit a world in a sense that transcends simply being-located-at point *x* at time *y*. If you think about it, that kind of argument, however picturesquely dressed up, begs the question: 'What is an environment?' 'It's a space that you are in at a certain point.' 'Great. And what is a certain point?' 'It's a location in an environment.' 'And what is an environment?' (And so on.) It is a shame that we do not read enough Heidegger, mostly because he unfortunately went on to argue that Germans are the best at inhabiting worlds, an argument that is wrong by his very own logic – so we can happily ignore that part. Ecological awareness precisely means inhabiting a vague number of such worlds. Where and when are you right now? In a college room in the early twenty-first century? In the Anthropocene? In the Western world? In the biosphere? In the time of oxygen, that disastrous (for anaerobic bacteria) pollutant that flooded the biosphere several billion years ago, enabling life forms like us to evolve? We cannot point to where and when we are exactly; yet we are not living in the Renaissance and we are not on Mars.

Heidegger's whole argument is devoted to showing how *being is not presence*. An environment is precisely something one is unable to point to, yet is strangely there nonetheless. When you look for the environment, you find things that are in it: a hammer, a smartphone, some rusty nails, a shed, a spider, some grass, a tree. So there is a big difference between environmentality and Nature. Nature is definitely something you *can* point to: it is 'over yonder' in the mountains, in my DNA, under the pavement. Nature is what is constantly present despite ... (fill in the blank). But constant presence is just what environmentality is not.

Environmentality is a manifold of things and certain ways of experiencing or relating to those things. Environmentality is made of caring, of *being-into*. Being-into involves being weirdly smeared out: Heidegger calls this smearing *ekstasis*, which should not be confused with states of bliss. *Ekstasis* means standing-outside-oneself, self-transcending. We are reaching for the smartphone in-order-to ... We look out of the shed window with-a-view-to ... Another word for this smearing is *time*, again not in the trivial objectified sense of LED lights flashing 8:30 on an old alarm clock, or the vibrations of an atom, or pieces of metal going around a circular piece of metal: those are ways of measuring time, and those ways depend upon a sense of time, a *temporality* that is already in place, because we are into certain projects. We want to commemorate the English Revolutionary dead, so we make a tomb that Victor Frankenstein visits in his journey up the Thames – that tomb is a haunting place of half-forgotten revolutionary projects. We need to buy and sell shares as fast as possible, so we have clocks that time transactions in nanoseconds. Time is not an objectified box, but is precisely this smearing, the way a thing does not coincide with what appears to be present – there is a not-yet quality about existing; most Western philosophy restricts this to the human realm, although there is no particularly good reason for that. Environmentality shimmers.

Mrs Saville gets to hold at least three kinds of spacetime in her hands, three modes of being-into: Walton's, Frankenstein's, the creature's. And who knows whether she is even reading them, or whether she is reading them in sequence? Mrs Saville stress tests the you-can-point-to-it idea of what an environment is, to the point where it collapses: surely this is an important feature of *Frankenstein*, overlooked as it often is. The many environmental modes of the novel overlap and fail to overlap in all kinds of fascinating ways. Sometimes we glimpse something happening from the environmentality of Frankenstein, only to witness it differently from the environmentality of the creature. This is not just about 'point of view', because that concept depends upon environmentality, not the other way around. 'Point of view' is a way of objectifying environmentality into a concept of a physically located being with a particular attitude. But beings such as humans with attitudes such as contempt for their bioengineered creations are *produced* by certain kinds of environmentality, certain kinds of care. A different world would have produced a different Frankenstein. Frankenstein himself wonders what he would have been like if he had come of age in a different era, which again does not mean a point on a timeline but a set of projects and care formats.[6]

The minimalist vagueness of Mrs Saville's environmentality is precisely the point. *How are we to care for the story?* This question is analogous to *How is Walton to care for Frankenstein?* and more importantly, *How is Victor Frankenstein to care for the creature?* The very blankness of the environmentality awakens our anxiety, which serves two functions. First, the anxiety we lend to the text blows up the story into something like three-dimensional realism, like air in a balloon. This is a common technique in naturalist realism, which employs free indirect speech to just this end – we do not know whether the speech belongs to the narrator or to a character, and thus our slight anxiety blows air into the character in question, resulting in what some call *focalization*, where we feel as if we are telepathically inside a character's head. In this case, the epistolary and first-person-narrative driven novel admits of no substantial focalization – instead Shelley relies on the technique of dissolving the aesthetic screen, as if we were holding the letters in our own hands. In each case, the sense of reality depends upon a sense of *ambiguity*, not of something definite we can point to. And in turn this reminds us of what Heidegger says about being: being is not presence.

Secondly, the vague environmentality opens up the central problem of the novel: what are we to care for, for whom are we to care, what is care, how do we care, why care, who cares? Perhaps the pristine blankness of the Arctic landscape later in Frankenstein's narrative is an objective correlative for the blankness available at the form level in the guise of Mrs Saville and whatever space she finds herself in. The last lines of the novel are about being 'lost in darkness and distance' (p. 191), the creature blending into the Arctic just as words are lost as we finish reading and encounter a blankness at the end of a text, and start to forget. Perhaps the characters all care in all the wrong ways – too aggressively, too melancholically, too violently. Heidegger argues that even indifference is a form of care.[7] Perhaps the very indifference of Mrs Saville is pointing to a way to care for humans and non-humans in a less violent way – simply allowing them to exist, like pieces of paper in your hand, like a story you might appreciate – or not – for no reason.[8]

Perhaps care is fragile and contingent and uncertain, and trying to delete this fragility – just think of a thousand pieces of heavy-hitting environmental PR, and the idea that art should (only) be PR for a cause such as environmentalism – is part of the violence we do to ourselves and other life forms. It is Victor's obsession with being interesting and exciting and praised that causes him to invent, then abandon, his creature. He cares too much and he wants too much for people to care about him. Perhaps this is another way to read the 'watery eyes' of the creature (p. 39). They are not simply expressions of psychopathic malice or zombie animation: those might be anthropocentric, overcharged (Victor-centric) reactions to something that might seem more like the eyes of a sheep. Their blankness invites Victor's horror, whereas it might invite a caring uncertainty. The cold hostility Werner Herzog sees in the seemingly blank eyes of bears is an index of his anthropocentrism: he sees Nature red in tooth and claw, but perhaps the bears are just into something he is not into.[9]

Is it just humans we are talking about when we talk about environmentality? Are non-humans allowed to be 'into' in *Frankenstein*? We are beginning to glimpse that they are. Heidegger only allows humans to have and bestow environmentality, and German humans most of all; so it would be excellent to find Mary Shelley letting non-humans in on the fun. On the whole, the novel appears to be typically anthropocentric in this regard, typically that is as a product of Romantic-period values and concerns. But one answer to the question is surely yes. Think not only of watery eyes, but of the letters themselves: they sit there, perhaps unopened, precisely *not* waiting for a human to activate them. Rather they exceed what humans do with them (namely open and read them): they collect dust, they shelter insects, they rest for days on tables, like Mrs Saville's eyes resting on the words. Because of Mrs Saville, whenever we close the book we might notice that the pages and the words are behaving without reference to us, even if they are just inertly lying there. Language itself is a non-human being. One might even argue that language makes humans – we would not know what 'human' meant unless language told us and we could speak it.[10] In this sense, language is logically prior to humans, though it might not be chronologically prior – though this is highly debatable (do no other life forms communicate?). The creature's narrative shows us all kinds of non-humans interacting without a human in sight to give them meaning and graciously bestow reality on them. It all happens in a forest, a thickly non-human environment in which trees and mammals and birds and insects (and, we now know, bacteria and fungi) exchange more or less explicit communications without reference to humans at all. This lack of reference is noted by the creature himself as an opacity, ingeniously rendered not at total nothing, but rather as a *meaningfulness not for him* (pp. 79–81).

As we have just seen, an ecocritical approach can illuminate features of a text that no other approach has yet illuminated. There are precious few readings of the role of Mrs Saville, the silent reader – and because of her silence, she is silenced and rendered invisible in most readings of *Frankenstein*. But the fact that she is present in the text, even in this minimal way, must have some significance, which I hope I have elucidated. In the future, *all texts* will be read with regard to environmentality, just as now they are all read with regard to race, gender and sexuality, whether or not they have to do explicitly with race, or gender, or what have you. This is because, as I hope I have shown, environmentality is not about stock descriptions of bunny rabbits and mountains. Environmentality is a fundamental feature of representation, because it is a fundamental feature of being.

Non-humans

When we consider a life form, we need to consider the monstrous. The monstrous is the minimal unit of evolution. Darwin argues that sometimes monstrosities can become variations, and sometimes those variations can result in speciation – the development of a new species.[11] But the quantum of evolution is a random mutation for no reason at all: evolution is a cheapskate, without teleology. Pre-Darwinian ideas about life forms were dominated by Aristotle, whose concept of life was deeply teleological: ducks are for swimming, Greeks are for enslaving barbarians and so on.

So Frankenstein's creature weirdly *typifies* what we now consider to be a life form, rather than deviating from it. Or rather, all life forms are deviance all the way down, kluges of other life forms' parts. Our lungs evolved from the swim bladders of fish, yet there is nothing remotely like a lung-in-waiting about a swim bladder.[12] Swim bladders were 'exapted', adapted from another function.[13] The monstrosity of variation, speciation and so on is the reason why evolution works at all. Monstrosity is *functional*.[14]

Life is monstrosity, but the reaction to life need not be horror; many reactions to the monstrous are possible. Frankenstein is hamstrung by his *concept* of life, which he derives from vitalism, a view popular in Shelley's day that life is enabled by some animating spark different from matter. John Abernethy popularized this view in England with flashy experiments whose showmanship Frankenstein perhaps imitates. Opposed to this view was materialism, the idea that life could be explained simply in terms of the organization of matter itself. Shelley's doctor, William Lawrence, held the materialist view.[15]

For vitalism to work, it must view life as something absolutely different from what it sees as 'dead' matter. Thus arises a dilemma: in a sense, all life forms are zombies, because they are all mere bodies, corpses animated by an external force. When the creature is animated by the bolt of lightning, Frankenstein's fantasy becomes reality, another term for which is *nightmare*. The idea that life is merely animated meat becomes horribly real, right in front of him. On a materialist view, life is less sharply opposed to death and the inorganic: it is simply a certain configuration of matter, as Shelley's contemporaries would have put it, or (as we might say now) an emergent property of how some kinds of matter interact. On this view it is difficult to distinguish life from non-life. Indeed, life relies deeply on non-life (we are made of chemicals after all), such that as biology has continued to probe into the *logos* of *bios*, stranger and stranger forms have been discovered, such as viruses – are they alive? A virus is a protein-encapsulated string of RNA or DNA, code made of proteins. A computer virus is a piece of software made of electronic charges in silicon and other materials. If one thinks a virus is alive, one might have to concede that a computer virus is also alive. In a way, on the materialist view, all beings are alive, or rather, all beings are equally undead. Uncanny feelings pertaining to how loose this boundary is afflict Frankenstein as he tries and fails to assemble a female creature: the creature-to-be is at once a pile of dismembered limbs, and the disfigured corpse of someone who already existed: 'I almost felt as if I had mangled the living flesh of a human being' (p. 142).

I say *undead* because being alive is very difficult to find – it is hard to point to life as such. Perhaps life as such does not exist. Or perhaps it is more subtle than that. Perhaps 'life', like 'environment', is a curious being whose way of existing is different from constant presence. The more we know about life forms, the more they slip into an uncanny valley between our traditional categories of life and death. And that is no bad thing – a rigid distinction between life and death, as in vitalism, results in violence in all kinds of ways. Violence distinguishes between living and non-living things. This distinction is maintained by banishing, yet secretly admitting, a monstrous category between life and death, the category into which the creature falls.

In robotics design, the Uncanny Valley is a region in which androids that too closely resemble humans look like horrifying zombies.[16] According to the model, we 'healthy' humans live on one peak, and all the cuter robots on the other. Zombies live in the Uncanny Valley because they ironically embody Cartesian dualism: they are animated corpses. They are 'reduced' to object status – default, manipulable object status, that is – and mixed with other beings: they have been in the soil. The Uncanny Valley concept explains racism and *is itself racist*. Its decisive separation of the 'healthy human being' and the cute R2D2 type robot (not to mention Hitler's dog Blondi, of whom he was very fond) opens up a forbidden zone of uncanny beings that reside scandalously in the Excluded Middle region.

The distance between R2D2 and the healthy human seems to map quite readily onto how we feel and live the scientistic separation of subject and object, and this dualism always implies its repressed abject (that it attempts to reject or suppress) as we have just seen.[17] R2D2 and Blondi are cute because they are decisively different and less powerful. It is this hard separation of things into subjects and objects that gives rise to the uncanny, forbidden Excluded Middle zone of entities who approximate 'me' – the source of anti-Semitism to be sure, the endless policing of what counts as a human, the defence of homo sapiens from the Neanderthals whose DNA we now know is inextricable with human DNA.

The more we know about life forms, the more the Uncanny Valley actually widens, opens up and flattens into what we might call the Spectral Plain. Ecological awareness takes place on the Spectral Plain whose distortion, the Uncanny Valley, separates the human and non-human worlds in a rigid way that spawns the disavowed region of objects that are also subjects – because that is just what they are in an expanded non-biopolitical sense.

It is like animism but it would be better to write it with a line through it. A rigid and thin concept of Life is what the awareness I call *dark ecology* rejects. That concept can only mean one thing: business as usual for post-Neolithic 'civilization'. Life is the ultimate non-contradictory Easy Think Substance that we must have more and more of, for no reason. A future society in which being ecological became a mode of violence would be still more horrifying than the neoliberalism that now dominates Earth. Such a society would consist of a vigorous insistence on Life and related categories such as health. It would make the current control society (as Foucault calls it) look like an anarchist picnic.[18] If that is what future coexistence means, I would like to exit Earth. The wider view of dark ecology sees life forms as spectres in a charnel ground in which Life is a narrow metaphysical concrete pipe. Death is the fact that ecological thought must encounter to stay soft.

In ecological awareness differences between R2D2-like beings and humans become far less pronounced; everything gains a haunting, spectral quality. This is equivalent to realizing that abjection is not something you can peel off yourself. The Nazi tactic of peeling off abjection while supporting animal rights is not inconsistent at all. Consistency is its very goal. Nazis are trying to maintain the normative subject–object dualism in which I can recognize myself as decisively different from a non-human or to be more blunt a non-German, a recognition in which everything else appears as equipment for my Lebensraum project. So there is little point in denigrating ecological politics as fascist. But there is every point in naming some Nature-based politics as fascist. Here is a strong sense in which ecology is without Nature.

The creature provides those around him with lessons in abjection, and abjection is the basic feeling of ecological awareness: I find myself surrounded and penetrated by other beings that seem to be glued to me, or which are so deeply embedded in me that to get rid of them would be to kill me. Tolerance of the creature, and anything greater than tolerance, would require becoming accustomed to abjection rather than trying to get rid of it. The creature himself suffers from it. Many have found it strange that when he looks into the pool like Eve in Milton's *Paradise Lost* (1674), he finds himself terrifyingly ugly. But perhaps Shelley is making a point here, a point we can now detect because of our increasing interest in ecology. Shelley in part is insisting on an Enlightenment concept of the normative human being above and beyond appearances, a concept that Frankenstein finds it hard to rise to, and the creature too.

Or perhaps Shelley is making it clear that this pristine idea of a human unsullied by appearances depends upon this abject extra. On this view, *to be a person is to be invisible* – the creature has no idea what he looks like at this point, and in the text he is just a voice, so this provocative separation of being and appearance is profoundly part of the texture of the novel. Theories of race often remark that whiteness is that skin colour that pretends not to be one, as if white people were invisible or transparent. Ecological awareness is the drastic perception that there is no such thing, which is why staying in a state of abjection or horror is far from ecological – in the end it is merely a (probably male) white Westerner's shock at having the rest of reality included in his view. Frozen in his abjection reaction, Frankenstein simply cannot care for his own creature.

And perhaps this is a not so subtle comment on monotheism, a persistent product of the agricultural age that began in the Fertile Crescent and elsewhere about 12,000 years ago, whose inner logic resulted in industrialization and hence the Anthropocene with its global warming and mass extinction. God creates Man and is horrified by what he sees of himself in the mirror of human flesh. The logic implies that God and monotheism cannot cope with ecology at all. Shelley's point is that everyone is afflicted with this idea, not just Frankenstein. Indeed, the creature was perhaps primed for it by all those Enlightenment reading materials he finds. In so doing, Shelley is suggesting that ideas are like computer viruses – they are not just symptoms of minds (or brains for that matter), but independent entities, strings of code lying around waiting for a vector.

Perhaps Shelley is suggesting that if we are going to think and write in an ecological way, we have to confront the thought viruses that are inhibiting us from doing so. Otherwise we will end up caring for dolphins because they are cute: they do not push us into abjection. But this is not such a powerful way of being ecological. We need to care about everything, and as I argued earlier, everything, aka the environment, has an uncanny, spectral quality just like Frankenstein's creature. It is as if the creature were a full-frontal, fully visible incarnation of environmentality itself. Caring for such a being involves accepting the super-natural, that is to say, what goes beyond our concepts of Nature, perhaps in an irreducible way. The monstrous is what we cannot predict. But the shock of the unpredictable must give way to compassion and solidarity. The question is, how?

NOTES

1 Helena Feder, '"A Blot Upon the Earth": Nature's "Negative" and the Production of Monstrosity in Frankenstein', *The Journal of Ecocriticism*, 2(1) (2010), 55–66, 55–6. *Frankenstein* is also briefly discussed in Andrew Smith and William Hughes (eds.), *EcoGothic* (Manchester University Press, 2013), see 'Introduction: Defining the ecoGothic', pp. 1–14, pp. 2–3. Two exceptions are Jonathan Bate, *The Song of the Earth* (Cambridge, MA: Harvard University Press, 2000),

pp. 49–55; Timothy Morton, *Shelley and the Revolution in Taste: The Body and the Natural World* (Cambridge University Press, 1994), 47–51.

2 An exemplary instance is Anne-Lise François, '"Oh Happy Living Things": Frankenfoods and the Bounds of Wordsworthian Natural Piety', *diacritics*, 33(2) (2005), 42–70. François is a scholar of the Romantic period, and even *she* does not need to refer to *Frankenstein*, even in an essay about 'Frankenfoods'.

3 Jakob von Uexküll, *A Foray into the Worlds of Animals and Humans*; with *A Theory of Meaning*, tr. Joseph D. O'Neil, introduction by Dorion Sagan, afterword by Geoffrey Winthrop-Young (Minneapolis, MN: University of Minnesota Press, 2010).

4 Gayatri Chakravorty Spivak notes the significance of Margaret Saville as a deliberately vague cipher for the reader in *A Critique of Postcolonial Reason: Towards a Theory of the Vanishing Present* (Cambridge, MA: Harvard University Press, 1999), pp. 132–40.

5 Martin Heidegger, *Being and Time*, tr. Joan Stambaugh (Albany, NY: State University of New York Press, 1996), pp. 37–211.

6 Mary Shelley, *Frankenstein: Or the Modern Prometheus; the 1818 Text*, ed. and Intro. Marilyn Butler (Oxford and New York: Oxford University Press, 1998), p. 23. Future references will be made parenthetically.

7 Heidegger, *Being and Time*, pp. 40–1, 113–14, 115, 116, 127.

8 Some serious ecological philosophy points in this direction. See, for instance, Giorgio Agamben, *The Open: Man and Animal*, tr. Kevin Attell (Stanford University Press, 2004).

9 Werner Herzog (Dir.), *Grizzly Man* (Discovery Docs, 2005).

10 Martin Heidegger, 'Language', *Poetry, Language, Thought*, tr. Albert Hofstadter (New York: Harper and Row, 1971), pp. 187–210.

11 Charles Darwin, *The Origin of Species*, ed. Gillian Beer (Oxford and New York: Oxford University Press, 1996), pp. 63, 108–39.

12 Ibid., p. 160.

13 Daniel Dennett, *Darwin's Dangerous Idea: Evolution and the Meanings of Life* (Harmondsworth: Penguin, 1996), p. 281.

14 Darwin, *The Origin of Species*, p. 102.

15 Marilyn Butler, 'The Shelleys and Radical Science', in *Frankenstein* (ed. Butler), pp. xv–xxi.

16 Masahiro Mori, 'The Uncanny Valley' (Bukimi no tani) tr. K. F. MacDorman and T. Minato, *Energy*, 7(4) (1970), 33–5.

17 The abject is formulated by Julia Kristeva in *Powers of Horror: An Essay on Abjection*, tr. Leon S. Roudiez (New York: Columbia University Press, 1982).

18 Michel Foucault, *Society Must be Defended: Lectures at the Collège de France, 1975–1976*, tr. David Macey (New York: Picador, 2003), pp. 243–7.

11

ANDY MOUSLEY

The Posthuman

The term 'posthuman' names several striking, even sensationalizing, prospects for humanity. Apocalyptically, the term suggests the demise of the human species due to such real or imagined dangers as environmental catastrophe, global warfare or diminishing resources. Less drastically, though not by much, the posthuman signifies the passing of the human as we know it, or think we know it. There are a number of contributors to the kind of posthuman condition in which we might one day find ourselves or which might already exist. The first is that increasingly sophisticated machines may render human beings and whatever special characteristics they (think they) possess superfluous, with computers, for example, composing music, adjudicating on legal matters and predictively writing our emails and texts for us. A second scenario is that instead of being left behind by (new) technologies, humans or a privileged few of them will be enhanced by them (as they have been by past technologies), living longer, improved lives liberated from the limitations of being 'merely' human. In some of its more wildly egocentric manifestations, 'posthuman' here spells a desire for 'superhuman' existence. A third, related contributor to a posthuman condition is the morphing of the human into its often-presumed 'others': the machine, the animal, the digital, the automated. Such morphing may occur either through the *importation* into the human body of cybernetic implants, animal tissue and genetic modifications, or through increased *exportation* of mechanized processes into the human world. Such multiple, two-way hybridizations may make it difficult to distinguish the natural from the artificial, or the simulation of the human by a machine, especially given that humans, always good mimics, may come to act in increasingly mechanistic ways; already, I sometimes have difficulty when answering a cold call in differentiating straight away between a human voice and a digitized version of one.

A fourth contributor to a posthuman condition, not always observed in discussions of posthumanism, are the various de-humanizations effected by

158

contemporary capitalism, with its subordination of all putatively human needs and wants to the impersonal and largely mysterious operations of 'the market', the priority of which is reinforced by the ubiquity of the language of marketing and corporate management-speak. Where once there were human beings with rich and complex interiorities – or so we might like to think – there are now ciphers whose principal way of conceiving of themselves is either as brands or loci of consumption.

Explorations of the posthuman and posthumanism have become growth areas across a wide range of academic disciplines since the 1990s. Although the terms may be new, like many concepts they have a pre-history. In the versions of literary and critical theory that presided in the 1970s and whose influence can still be felt, the presumed integrity of the human subject was scrutinized from different directions: by poststructuralists who emphasized the role of language in the construction of subjectivity; by psychoanalytic critics who displaced the notion of entirely rational human agents; and by Marxists influenced by Louis Althusser for whom human subjectivity was an ideological illusion. These anti-humanists, as they were often termed, themselves had antecedents, not least in some aspects of the work of their primary sources (Saussure, Freud and Marx). However, it would be mis-leading to write the genealogy of posthumanist ideas solely through these thinkers or other challenges to anthropocentric thinking as posed by such figures as Friedrich Nietzsche, Charles Darwin or Galilei Galileo. That is because the posthuman is not exclusively the invention of philosophers and scientists. Nor is it solely the result of techno-scientific changes. Rather, to adopt N. Katherine Hayles' insight that 'we have always been posthuman', the posthuman names a tendency internal to the human condition itself.[1] The posthuman and its near conceptual neighbours – the inhuman, subhuman, superhuman, anti-human, trans-human and non-human – have from this perspective arguably always shadowed the human, with the idea of the intactness of the human and human subjectivity being more the stuff of myth than reality.

Given its capacity to explore all corners of human existence, often prior to their formalization as named theories or philosophies, literature is one of the places to which we might turn to witness the human condition in all its post/human variety. Depictions of hollowed-out subjectivities (conspicuous examples being T. S. Eliot's *The Waste Land* (1922) and 'The Hollow Men' (1925), and the plays of Samuel Beckett) might offer one point of entry into the posthuman. The horror provoked by co-opted or radically transformed human subjects – a staple ingredient of the Gothic – might be another. If the term posthuman, as I suggested at the outset, verges on the sensationalistic, then its natural literary ally may indeed be the Gothic, a genre dealing in extremes, and one which, like the foreboding term posthuman, incites us to ask or ask again: what is human? what do we mean by the human?

Posthuman Humans in *Frankenstein*

Frankenstein's artificially made creation may cause us to ponder the conditions for accepting him or 'it' as human. The claims that the monster himself makes upon Frankenstein, and us, to be accepted as human (in a positive sense of that term) are especially compelling in that part of the creature's autobiographical narrative where he demands that Frankenstein create a mate for him: 'I am alone, and miserable; man will not associate with me; but one as deformed and horrible as myself would not deny herself to me... This being you must create.'[2] At various moments in *Frankenstein*, one or another of its narrators implicitly or sometimes explicitly asks us to recognize a common human plight or condition. The fear of total isolation invoked here by the creature is one of them. Frankenstein's unnatural creature has 'natural' human feelings and affections, it seems, and ironically even appears more human than the human who created him. In his utopian vision of a future life with a companion, the unnatural creature's natural human compassion extends to the natural world itself, thus making him more ecologically part of nature than an aberration from it:

> My food is not that of man; I do not destroy the lamb and the kid, to glut my appetite; acorns and berries afford me sufficient nourishment. My companion will be of the same nature as myself, and will be content with the same fare. We shall make our bed of dried leaves; the sun will shine on us as on man, and will ripen our food. The picture I present to you is peaceful and human, and you must feel that you could deny it only in the wantonness of power and cruelty. Pitiless as you have been towards me, I now see compassion in your eyes. (p. 120)

'Inhuman' might easily substitute here for 'pitiless', the creature's word for his human creator. The world of *Frankenstein* is at this point a topsy-turvy one in which the human seems more monstrous than the monster, and the monster outstrips the human in its humanity. The unsettling of boundaries between human and inhuman, natural and unnatural, does not resolve itself into this simple inversion, however, for if the creature acts as a touchstone for human values (such as compassion, peaceful co-existence with nature, living within boundaries rather than in excess of them), then it is immediately necessary to say that it may be 'all too human' to betray these and all other human touchstones. We can forget ourselves. We can become 'denatured'.

We can behave inhumanly. Indeed, so routinely may we forget the 'milk of human kindness' that 'man's inhumanity to man' looks to be the more accurate proverbial encapsulation of a condition which in reality is rarely self-identical, rarely a matter of the simple recognitions that the narrators in *Frankenstein* sometimes invite.

Frankenstein himself is a prime example of a human whose humanity paradoxically consists in the simultaneous recognition and denial of human limits. As one of literature's most notorious Promethean over-reachers, he exemplifies the posthuman in the human, or at least one kind of posthumanity, bent on surpassing himself. Shelley takes pains, though, to ground Frankenstein in recognizably ordinary human feelings of which he then takes leave, as if to imply that the condition of being ordinarily human and wanting to exceed that condition are thoroughly intertwined. When he departs for the University of Ingolstadt his 'melancholy reflections' naturally turn towards the 'amiable companions' (p. 28) he will miss, but equally natural, we are encouraged to think, is his youthful desire for adventure (intellectual adventure, in his case): 'I had often, when at home, thought it hard to remain during my youth cooped up in one place, and had longed to enter the world, and take my station among other human beings' (p. 28). So far, so 'normal', we are led to believe, until the solitary pursuit of forbidden knowledge becomes obsessive, leading him to 'spend days and nights in vaults and charnel houses' (p. 34) in search of body parts for his creation. Frankenstein marks the anti-human monstrosity of his activity – 'often did my human nature turn with loathing from my occupation' – but he continues anyway, 'urged on by an eagerness which perpetually increased' (p. 37). Natural human revulsion can be overcome by a variety of countervailing compulsions: insatiable curiosity; an urge to defeat human mortality – 'I thought . . . I might in process of time . . . renew life where death had apparently devoted the body to corruption' (p. 36); and the ultimate ego gratification of securing the unalloyed devotion of the 'new species' he will bring into existence (p. 36). Yet these overriding compulsions also stem from feelings – curiosity, fear of death, a need to be loved – that are equally identifiable as 'human'. They also derive from a recognition on Frankenstein's part of the limiting conditions of human existence. His curiosity, for example, can be seen as an attempt to mitigate the wondrous as well as frightening mystery of what he calls 'our dark world' (p. 36). Death, fresh in Frankenstein's consciousness as a result of his mother's recent demise, is another obvious constraining fact of existence, as is the uncertain conditionality of love. It is against these givens of existence that Frankenstein rebels. Unlike his creature who later imagines a life modestly accepting of the limits which his extraordinary circumstances have imposed, Frankenstein seeks to transform his conditions of existence in a way that will make him impervious to them. Born as it is of a 'human' desire to overcome his humanity, Frankenstein is thus a 'posthuman human', a human who refuses to live within the boundaries of the human.

There have been times when faith in the capacity of human beings to change themselves and their environment, ostensibly for the better, has been more conspicuously evident than at other times. In a theocentric universe governed by ideas of original sin and humanity's fixed place in a God-given scheme of things, the potential for transformation is limited. The world of *Frankenstein* is otherwise, and not just because Frankenstein as a spectacular Promethean figure co-opts the role of a creator-god in a capricious act of individualistic hubris, but because as a *modern* Prometheus he inhabits a world which propels him in several different ways towards notions of transformability. Ideas of self- and world-transformation form part of the fabric of Frankenstein's day-to-day world and way of thinking, and not some aberration from them. The view that selves and worlds can be radically transformed is in other words so embedded in Frankenstein's world as to make it almost second nature to think beyond nature. The assumption, tempered to different degrees, of the radical transformability of human nature, nature and society is advanced in *Frankenstein* across a number of different discourses. As a student of modern chemistry, for example, as eulogized by one of his early teachers M. Waldman, Frankenstein hears of how the '"modern masters"' (p. 30) of chemistry have '"penetrate[d] into the recesses of nature"' and '"have acquired new and almost unlimited powers"' (p. 30). From his father and his father's secular materialism, he learns to be afraid of 'no supernatural horrors' and to view a churchyard as 'merely the receptacle of bodies deprived of life' (p. 34), an attitude which facilitates his profane treatment of corpses as manipulable objects available to him for vivisection.

As a Romantic, susceptible to the power of the imagination, and in awe of the sublime majesty of nature from which he at the same time draws inspiration, Frankenstein also privileges world-making imaginative consciousness above mere imitation of what already exists (this despite the more dialectical attitude of a Romantic poet like Wordsworth). Traumatized by the thought that he is ultimately responsible for the creature's murder of his brother William, Frankenstein travels with his family to the iconically Romantic destination of Mont Blanc. There he experiences a degree of relief from his misery, with Mont Blanc exerting some psychologically restorative influence upon him: 'These sublime and magnificent scenes afforded me the greatest consolation that I was capable of receiving. They elevated me from all littleness of feeling; and although they did not remove my grief, they subdued and tranquillized it' (p. 74). Yet it is this same feeling of elevation – this same desire for transcendence – that contributed in the first place to Frankenstein's vision of harnessing the power of nature for his own purposes. 'No one', writes Walton in an early description he gives of Frankenstein, 'can feel more deeply than he does the beauties of nature. The starry sky, the sea and every sight afforded by these wonderful regions, seems still to have the power of elevating his soul from earth' (p. 16). Sublime nature itself appears 'posthuman' because its vastness and grandeur are beyond human scale and comprehension. Elevation above the 'merely human' is what Frankenstein himself craves. He achieves an elevated, sublime state, equal to nature's, by the immensity of his own transformative vision and imagination. Nature has a humbling effect upon Frankenstein, and increasingly so, but it is also the site of projection, a vehicle for the expression of a desire for extra-ordinary powers, realized in the creature's 'superhuman speed' and stature (p. 76).

Scientific and Romantic discourses propel this modern Prometheus towards ideas and feats which refuse or radically modify the ordinary limits of human existence. So, too, do some of the libertarian principles which inspired, or were ignited by, the French Revolution. Brought up unconventionally by parents who 'never forced' particular 'studies' upon their children or 'disciplined' them 'according to the ordinary methods' (p. 21), Frankenstein's resulting free spirit of enquiry echoes the libertarian beliefs of Mary Shelley's father William Godwin. In his *An Enquiry Concerning Political Justice* of 1793, published in the year after the establishment of the French Republic, Godwin proposes that no government ought 'to set up a standard upon the various topics of human speculation, to restrain the excursions of an inventive mind'. 'It is only by giving a free scope to these excursions', he continues, 'that science, philosophy and morals have arrived at their present degree of perfection, in comparison of which all that has already done [sic] will perhaps appear childish'.[3] Godwin is also in the tradition of thinkers, stretching at least as far back as John Locke, to argue for the priority of nurture over nature in the formation of human consciousness and morality. There being 'no innate principles', argues Godwin after Locke, we are 'neither virtuous nor vicious as we first come into existence'.[4] In *Frankenstein*, the monster advances a similar understanding in his insistence that '"misery made me a fiend"' (p. 78) and that happiness can return him to the virtue he learned from the cottagers in whose house he secretly resided in one formative part of his life. Monsters are made not born. Likewise, the benevolent humanity of humans is a matter of cultivation, and not some inalienable fact of human nature.

In the 1805 (and 1850) editions of *The Prelude*, Wordsworth writes of the joyful state of the Europe he visited in 1790: "'twas a time when Europe was rejoiced/ France standing on the top of golden hours,/ And human nature seeming born again.'⁵ A born-again humanity permits a fresh start, a Lockean *tabula rasa* on which a 'posthuman' humanity may liberate itself from its own former errors and limitations. The posthumanism in question here is in many ways continuous with that form of Enlightenment humanism that invested, as did Godwin, though circumspectly, in ideas of human progress and perfectibility. 'Man is not . . . a perfect being', writes Godwin, 'but perfectible'.⁶ Uninhibited and unchecked, however, self-legislating refashioning of internal and external realities can go awry. The human nature 'born again' in the figure of Frankenstein's creature is the product of an arrogant anthropocentrism primed with the sense that no or few obstacles stand in the way of the human will. 'Standing on the top of golden hours', as Wordsworth puts it, all seems possible. Likewise, Frankenstein's 'imagination . . . too much exalted by my first success' did not allow any 'doubt of my ability to give life to an animal as complex and wonderful as man' (p. 35). If all obstacles fall away, then these include not only practical obstacles but moral ones as well, as far as Frankenstein is concerned, for in giving birth to a new order of humanity he represses that part of his humanity which nevertheless keeps on telling him that something about his ambition is morally repugnant: he has acted too much alone and on his own initiative; he has ignored friends and family; he has operated instrumentally upon nature and 'tortured the living animal to animate the lifeless clay' (p. 36); he has played God; he has appropriated female biology. Whichever way the moral perspectives play out, Frankenstein's *post*human re-creation of the human also means that he is in danger of becoming *in*human. Thus not only does the posthuman (meaning, in one of its senses, the desire to transform or transcend the human) inhabit the human, the inhuman also exists within the (post)human.

What then is left of the human as a stable ethical or epistemological category when it seems to slide so easily into its 'others'? When Frankenstein reassembles the human remains he collects from graveyards into a new creature what should we then call that creature? Human? Inhuman? Superhuman? Posthuman? Non-human? The terms that Frankenstein uses when describing the human he is intent on creating – 'animal', 'complex', 'wonderful' – themselves signal the presence within the human of hybridity and difference. Joyful wonder may have been the early response to the French Revolution's re-animation of the human, but notoriously the Revolution (as has often been the case with revolutions subsequently) also gave birth to terror. That does not mean that humans should give up on ideas of progress, but it does imply that progress is hardly ever likely to be 'pure'. Humans being, in Frankenstein's words, 'complex' as well as 'wonderful', means that our better selves are always likely to be tarnished.

Automata and Monstrous Egos

The inhuman in the (post)human is also manifest in Frankenstein's auto-maton-like behaviour. Again, though, Shelley shows how the automated stems from qualities we can recognize as human. The automated is in other words not externally imposed, but seems naturally to evolve out of such human attributes as, in this case, passion and enthusiasm. These are noted as exceptional – Frankenstein tells us that putting his 'heart and soul' into his studies at university with 'ardour' won him the 'astonishment' of his fellow-students (p. 32) – but the exceptionalism is in many ways unexceptional. He pours himself into his work as a religious devotee might give herself to her prayers, or a lover to his beloved, or a fan to her recreation. His teacher and mentor M. Waldman himself tells Frankenstein that he is happy '"to have gained a disciple"' (p. 31) and the day on which this occurs is remembered by Frankenstein as 'memorable' (p. 32), as though he has experienced a conversion or met the love of his life. Words like 'ardour' (p. 32), 'eagerness' (p. 35), 'delight' (p. 34), 'rapture' (p. 34), and 'enthusiasm' – enthusiasm of an 'almost supernatural' kind – (p. 33), are used profusely by Frankenstein. They eroticize and/or spiritualize his scientific occupation, and in many ways humanize it as well, by charging it with human emotion. However, the humanity drawn over the face of science is at the same time an inhumanity, for only a slight conceptual and emotional distance separates Frankenstein's ardour from a driving compulsion. The use of passive verb forms signals this compulsiveness: 'Now I was led to examine . . .' (p. 34), 'My attention was fixed upon . . .' (p. 34). His emotions, body and mind are not his own, it seems, as a 'resistless, and almost frantic impulse, urged me forward' (p. 35). Frankenstein, self-determining human subject that he might aspire to be, becomes mindless, like a form of automaton.

This aspect of Frankenstein persists. The object of his compulsion changes, from the need to create to the need to destroy his creature, but it is still a compulsion, as strong if not stronger than the monster's own uncontrollable drives. The human creator and his posthuman creation mirror one another in language, thought and deed. The creature's '"insatiable thirst for vengeance"' upon his creator for rejecting him is described by him as an '"impulse"' of which he is '"the slave"' and '"not the master"' (p. 188). Passions not only run high, then; they also have a life of their own, causing their slaves to become robotic. At one point Frankenstein himself uses an image of the mechanical. Describing how he sometimes fantasized about his dead loved ones being still alive, he says that at such moments 'vengeance ... died in my heart' and that 'I pursued my path towards the destruction of the daemon, more as a task enjoined by heaven, as the mechanical impulse of some power of which I was unconscious, than as the ardent desire of my soul' (p. 174). The 'ardent desire' that comes from within is distinguished here from the 'mechanical impulse' that seems to originate from without, but the majority of Frankenstein's descriptions of his actions and impulses confuse such distinctions. The mechanical in *Frankenstein* is not apart from the human, but part of it, if not as an innate principle then as an ever-present propensity.

There is something automated as well about Frankenstein's persevering determination to compete against nature – against both his own and the natural world. Penitent, worn-out and close to mental and physical collapse, Frankenstein towards the end of the book nevertheless summons the energy to rally the crew of the ship hired by Walton for his scientific expedition. The crew members should, according to Frankenstein, battle against the elements and continue on their voyage:

> 'Oh! be men, or be more than men. Be steady to your purposes, and firm as a rock. This ice is not made of such stuff as your hearts might be; it is mutable, cannot withstand you, if you say that it shall not.' (p. 183)

Defiance of limits is still his theme, even when he appears to have reached his own, because such defiance has become 'hard-wired', as we might now say using a posthuman metaphor.

Frankenstein believes that the monstrous posthuman that he has let loose in the world has a purely physical existence which he feels compelled to track down and destroy. With the creature gone, monstrosity will have been successfully cast out. Frankenstein seeks the catharsis of conventional tragedy whereby a sacrificial scapegoat becomes the tangible focus for the ills of the world. But the monstrous posthuman is not 'out there', but in him, as a potential. What is bleak, or some might say just realistic about *Frankenstein* is that several of those traits which I have so far been associating with the posthuman – automation, inhumanity, superhuman overreaching – appear to define the human more decisively than do any of the 'traditional' human virtues and verities. These are weak and unsustainable by comparison with the strength and durability of other impulses. Yes, Frankenstein is moved to compassion by the monster's story of rejection, but not for long. The same applies to Walton who, having been 'first touched by the expressions of his misery', catches sight once again of the 'lifeless form of my friend' and instantly finds his 'indignation ... re-kindled' (p. 188). 'Wretch' and 'fiend' are the terms Walton then uses to project inhumanity onto a monster which has been created and inhumanly treated by humans.

History keeps on repeating itself, with little chance of a break in the cycle, because the inhuman treatment of the creature leads it to commit further inhuman atrocities, which then generate further inhuman treatment by humans. The words 'wretch' and 'fiend', and others such as 'monster' and 'daemon' (p. 140 and *passim*), are repeatedly used in the book to describe the creature. They imply that the creature is an aberration from the ethical norms upheld by human society. But might it be more normal than abnormal for humans to act with the 'barbarity' (p. 134) attributed to the monster? Human history to date might lead us to conclude that civilized, enlightened humanity has always been more of an ideal than a reality, and even the ideal has a limited history insofar as it operated as the foundational principle of that *particular* phase of human history known as the Enlightenment. According to the influential sociologist and philosopher Jürgen Habermas, the project of modernity, by which he means the Enlightenment ideals of freedom, justice and understanding, remains incomplete.[7] Taking our cue from *Frankenstein* and the persistent power of the myth of *Frankenstein*, we might say that the project of modernity is always likely to remain incomplete. That is because, as Shelley's tale and before it the French Revolution demonstrate, progress towards enlightened humanity (or to recall the terms used earlier, towards a posthuman humanity that has shed its darker side), can all too easily be derailed.

It is the monstrous egotism of both Frankenstein and Walton that most conspicuously undermines Enlightenment principles by privatizing them. Both men appeal to Enlightenment aims. Walton, for example, writes to his sister Margaret about his scientific quest being for the 'inestimable benefit' of 'all mankind' (p. 6), yet much of what he writes is about self-fulfilment. 'This expedition', he says, 'has been the favourite dream of my early years' (p. 6). Like Frankenstein, Walton the scientist is also possessed of a (simplified) Romantic sensibility which as a youth led him to become a poet and live for one year 'in a Paradise of my own creation' (pp. 6–7). Self-fulfilment and a life lived co-operatively for the betterment of humanity in general need not be at loggerheads, but they become so in *Frankenstein*. Walton and Frankenstein may need company, but both are loners who go their own way and appropriate for their own glorification Enlightenment ideals of free enquiry and independent judgement. Ego thwarts enlightenment even as it (initially) speaks its name. As events unfold, the unleashed barbarism of the ego cannot hide behind the respectability of learning, science and free rational enquiry. A confessional Frankenstein admits that his 'selfish pursuit' had 'cramped and narrowed me' (p. 51), and rendered him 'unsocial' (p. 50). Frankenstein at least displays the virtue of calling a spade a spade here. Narcissistic extension of the boundaries of the self has all along been his real project and has outstripped by some way anything we might recognize as 'enlightened' self-interest.

Human Witnesses to the Posthuman

The 'human', then, as a term expressing value, has a torrid time in *Franken-stein*. What is left of the human as an ethical category are a few scattered moments of remorse, tenderness or compassion, all too quickly consumed by one or another alarming form of post- or in-humanity. Yet amidst the blurring of the boundaries cordoning off the human from the inhuman, posthuman, superhuman, animal, monstrous and non-human, another more welcome meaning of the posthuman can be glimpsed. To be posthuman, on this view, means not to sit comfortably in one's skin, not to take for granted one's 'human-ness', not to assume that being human guarantees morality, progress or ontological stability. It means being aware instead that we are always coming 'after' the human: not just in the sense of pursuing a cat-egory of being that remains elusive, but also in the sense that, whatever identifiable remnants of humanity may survive its deconstruction, we are forever in danger of leaving those remnants behind. This is what happens to Frankenstein and, to a lesser extent, Walton. But 'happens to' is in this instance too passive a formulation, for Frankenstein especially is painfully aware of what happens to him as it is happening to him, at least according to the retrospective autobiographical account he gives of himself. Acutely aware of being split between versions of himself, one recalling him to limits even as the other takes him beyond them, Frankenstein is constantly telling his tale only to interrupt it with reflections upon what lessons might be learned. At one point, he even stops himself, mid-reflection, as a result of thinking that he may have lost his audience, Walton, and perhaps us as well. This is the slice of moral philosophy he offers just as he is nearing the climax of the story, namely the moment of the attempted animation of his creature:

> A human being in perfection ought always to preserve a calm and peaceful mind, and never to allow passion or a transitory desire to disturb his tranquil-lity. I do not think that the pursuit of knowledge is an exception to this rule. If the study to which you apply yourself has a tendency to weaken your affec-tions, and to destroy your taste for those simple pleasures in which no alloy can possibly mix, then that study is certainly unlawful, that is to say, not befit-ting the human mind. If this rule were always observed; if no man allowed any

pursuit whatsoever to interfere with the tranquillity of his domestic affections, Greece has not been enslaved; Caesar would have spared his country; America would have been discovered more gradually; and the empires of Mexico and Peru had not been destroyed.   (pp. 37–8)

Noticing his listener Walton's apparent lack of interest in these reflections, Frankenstein then adds: 'But I forget that I am moralizing in the most interesting part of my tale; and your looks remind me to proceed' (p. 38). Two versions of the posthuman collide here. One manifests itself in what might be called the pre-reflective nature of storytelling. Walton's desire to have the tale 'proceed', uninterrupted, to its climax is a desire for a state of thoughtless captivation comparable with Frankenstein's own automated drives. The opposing version of the posthuman is represented by Frankenstein's albeit simplistic moralizing, simplistic given that the values of 'tranquillity' and 'domestic affections' were so easily abandoned by him. There is nevertheless some angst-ridden musing going on here, born of the acute sense of a crisis occurring in what it is to be human. There is 'someone' here, that someone being a human individual bearing witness to the problem of being a human individual, and what limits or 'rules' humans might impose upon themselves in order to preserve their humanity.

Tortured consciousness is built into the very structure of the text. All three first-person narrators, Walton included, worry away to varying degrees at the 'big' questions, the 'who am I?', 'who are we?' questions. Citing Percy Shelley's poem 'On Mutability' (1816), Frankenstein at one point laments the state of metaphysical homelessness and chronic instability which seems to be humanity's lot. We are 'moved', he says, 'by every wind that blows, and a chance word or scene that that word may convey to us' (p. 75). All three protagonists are by choice or obligation wanderers who, having left their homes behind them, deploy the autobiographical mode to pose fundamental questions about the nature of self and humanity. First-person narration lends itself to the monstrously inflated egoism already discussed, but it lends itself equally to introspection, self-examination and self-critique. A tussle goes on between these two 'posthuman' autobiographical possibilities, as the narrators who also listen to each other's stories question themselves and their humanity whilst struggling to keep their egos intact against the demands of the other. Focus on the 'mythic' Frankenstein, the Frankenstein who comes to be confused with the monster as a result of his own monstrosity, including his monstrous egotism, has often overshadowed the self-doubting, tortured Romantic soul, but it is this more introspective Frankenstein who regularly interrupts his own narrative to testify to his own ambivalent sense of personhood. As readers of his tale, and the tales of the other two key protagonists, we are encouraged (though not obliged) to feel the gravity and urgency of existential questions as they are 'lived out' – felt upon the pulse – by these post/human subjects. In an utterly 'post' human world, would such questions register?

Autobiography also lends itself, although not in any inevitable way, to the *construction* of psychological motivation. I stress 'construction' to indicate that motivation is not necessarily a given that invites immediate consensus, but is produced for inspection and speculation. All three narrators produce reasons for being as they are and behaving as they do, seeking by this process to explain themselves to themselves as well as to both the near and far-away listeners to their tales. 'Do you understand this feeling?' (p. 5) asks Walton early on in the letter to his sister, Margaret, which opens the text of *Frankenstein*. He is referring to the 'delight' he feels at the 'cold northern breeze' of Petersburgh playing bracingly 'upon my cheeks' (p. 5). It is a casual and innocent enough question, but it makes us aware of the distant listener, one who in some ways mirrors our own distance, albeit in time rather than imagined space, from the first of the three first-person narrators who between them compose the story of a strange, unnatural birth. Walton's question – 'Do you understand this feeling?' – may be casual, but it is not, I think, purely rhetorical, especially given Margaret's reported view of his brother's enterprise: 'You will rejoice to hear that no disaster has accompanied the commencement of an enterprise which you have regarded with such evil forebodings.' (p. 5). Does Margaret – do we – understand the feelings of this voluntary isolate? Are these feelings sufficiently 'human' for them to travel across space and time? Or is Walton illegible to us and his sister? Walton wants connection (hence the letter) as well as recognition from outside of himself of the value and psychological credibility of his enterprise. The production of autobiographical discourse goes hand in hand with the production of a plausible human psychology. 'Ardent curiosity' (p. 6) and the self-fulfilment that comes with conferring 'inestimable benefit' on 'all mankind' (p. 6) are Walton's motivations for undertaking the project to discover the Northern magnetic pole. We may speculate about other possible motivations: machismo, Oedipal rebellion against a father who did not want his son 'to embark in a sea-faring life' (p. 6) and the like. We can speculate because we are given the opportunity to do so through the autobiographical production of psychologically motivated subjects whose motivations are nevertheless open to question. So we may wonder whether the call to adventure is an adequate substitute for the 'domestic affections' (p. 38), implicitly gendered female, which he and subsequently Frankenstein leave behind on their boys' own adventures.

Letter-writing is a way of maintaining the human contact that Walton has decided to abandon. Bereft of company, Walton tells Margaret that he desires 'the company of a man who could sympathize with me' (p. 8). The discourses of sentimentalism and sensibility in Shelley's time aimed amongst other things to produce and promote sympathetic connection between individuals. In *Frankenstein*, the sympathetic soulmate craved by Walton (one who he thinks he finds in Frankenstein) compensates for the feeling that his feelings may not be 'understood' or understandable, that in his self-elected separation from the rest of his species, he may also have passed beyond the spectrum of recognizable human psychologies and identities. Thus buried inside Walton's question – 'Do you understand this feeling?' – lies an anxiety that feelings may not be transferrable from one human being to another and that one person's idea of meaningful psychological fulfilment may be another's idea of pointlessness. Nevertheless, to adapt a previous point: there is 'someone' present in this narrative, concerned to give an account of himself and make himself understood. Characters are not so 'post' human, as to be untroubled by thoughts about who they are and what makes them human.

Like his creator, Frankenstein's creature seems 'naturally' to gravitate towards reflection. The 'wonderful narrations' (p. 95) he hears being read out loud from his hideaway in the cottage cause him to ponder, Hamlet-style, the nature of humanity. 'Was man', he muses, 'at once so powerful, so virtuous, and magnificent, yet so vicious and base?', appearing 'at one time a mere scion of the evil principle, and at another as all that can be conceived of noble and godlike' (p. 95). *Frankenstein*'s continual meta-fictional emphasis upon the situation of listeners listening to stories in different ways, and with different outcomes, *might* cause us to reflect upon our own reception of the stories, as well as upon the meditations of the characters on being human. Or not. Perhaps there is nothing inevitable about reflection, just as there is no inevitability about any other trait we might want to designate as human. Trained readers, readers educated into reading 'for meaning', may read Shelley's tale for the questions it poses about our post/human condition, but such a reading is not guaranteed. The reflective consciousness which seems to be second nature to Frankenstein and his creature may be the result of a certain kind of literary education, resembling Mary Shelley's own, in which books, poems and narratives are thought to matter to us for the light they cast upon our condition. Many may still hold this view about the value of literature. However, one day, fully posthuman beings that we might become, such reflective consciousness may not seem necessary.

NOTES

1 N. Katherine Hayles, *How We Became Posthuman* (University of Chicago Press, 1999), p. 291.
2 Mary Shelley, *Frankenstein*, ed. and Intro. Marilyn Butler (Oxford University Press, 1998), p. 118. Future references will be made parenthetically.
3 William Godwin, *An Enquiry Concerning Political Justice*, 2 vols. (London: Robinson, 1793), Vol. I, p. 118.
4 Ibid., p. 12.
5 William Wordsworth, *The Prelude 1799, 1805, 1850*, ed. Jonathan Wordsworth, M. H. Abrams and Stephen Gill (New York: W. W. Norton & Company, 1979), p. 204.
6 Godwin, *Political Justice*, p. 70.
7 Jürgen Habermas, 'Modernity – an Incomplete Project', in Peter Brooker (ed.), *Modernism/Postmodernism* (London: Longman, 1992), pp. 125–38.

PART III

Adaptations

12

DIANE LONG HOEVELER

Nineteenth-Century Dramatic Adaptations of *Frankenstein*

Hence when a Monarch or a mushroom dies,
Awhile extinct the organic matter lies,
But, as a few short hours or years revolve;
Alchemic powers the changing mass dissolve...
The wrecks of Death are but a change of forms;
Emerging matter from the grave returns,
Feels new desires, with new sensations burns...
Erasmus Darwin, *The Temple of Nature* (1803)

R. B. Peake's *Presumption; or, The Fate of Frankenstein*

Mary Shelley's *Frankenstein, or the Modern Prometheus* is a novel that, from the vantage point of two centuries, seems to have captured its zeitgeist perfectly. Like Erasmus Darwin's poetry about the mysterious processes of birth and rebirth, the novel tapped into its culture's curious mix of existential anxieties and scientific aspirations. But while Darwin's poetry has never functioned as a cultural touchstone, Shelley's novel has remained front and centre in public consciousness, if not solely as a novel, then as a series of popular dramatic adaptations that changed as each era's anxieties altered. In fact, the novel has been continually reborn as a drama on stage and later in filmic adaptations over the past two centuries because of its myriad concerns with the origins of life, the fear of death and the many forms taken by thwarted human desire.[1] Within months of its publication by Lackington & Hughes on 1 January 1 1818, the novel was receiving mixed reviews at best. Styling himself as ever the bearer of good news, Thomas Love Peacock wrote to Percy Shelley toward the end of the summer of 1818 to inform him that Mary's novel was 'universally known and read'.[2] The fact was, however, that its sales were sluggish because of the negative reviews it had received and the novel was not a viable candidate for a second printing.[3]

This might have been the end of the story for *Frankenstein* had it not been for the appearance in late July of 1823 of what Steven Earl Forry has called a 'tawdry melodrama' written by Richard Brinsley Peake, one of those stage hands turned hack writers who heavily populated the London theatrical scene during the early nineteenth century.[4] Peake's *Presumption; or, The Fate of Frankenstein* was thought by many to be impious, so much so that the London Society for the Preservation of Vice picketed the play in protest and distributed leaflets against its performance.[5] Despite all of the negative publicity, or maybe because of it, the play was a success, with the *Theatrical Observer* claiming that '[t]he moral here is striking. It points out that man cannot pursue objects beyond his obviously prescribed powers, without incurring the penalty of shame and regret at his audacious folly'.[6] *Presumption; or, The Fate of Frankenstein* was performed at the English Opera House thirty-seven times during the 1823 season and its popularity caused a proliferation of other theatrical adaptations that same first season: another melodrama which has been lost – Henry M. Milner's *Frankenstein; or, The Demon of Switzerland* (Royal Coburg Theatre, 18 August 1823) – an early version of his later *The Man and the Monster*; Peake's adaptation of his own earlier adaptation, *Another Piece of Presumption* (Adelphi Theatre, 20 October 1823); and three very light burlesques.[7] It was because of the success of these various theatrical adaptations that a second edition of the novel was commissioned and published in 1823 by Whittaker. And, as William St Clair has noted, 'every single night when one of the *Frankenstein* plays was performed brought a version of the story of the manmade monster to more men and women than the book did in ten or twenty years'.[8]

Frankenstein is, along with Bram Stoker's *Dracula* (1897), one of the seminal Gothic texts of the British tradition. And like other Gothic novels by Ann Radcliffe, Horace Walpole and Matthew Lewis, among others, *Frankenstein* was seen as rich material for dramatic adaptation.[9] This chapter will discuss the major dramatic adaptations of the novel written in English between 1823 and 1887. While there were several minor and very short burlesques of the novel performed during this period, none of them is considered seminal or influential in the dramatic tradition of *Frankenstein* adaptations. The emphasis here is on the heyday of popular theatrical adaptations during the nineteenth century, before the advent of film in the twentieth century. In the original playbill, the creature is listed as ***, and described as nameless, mute and wearing a light blue body suit. The blue costuming assumed by the creature plays on, I think, the blue light that had long been associated in Gothic poetry and ballads with the supernatural (see Wordsworth's 'The Thorn', (1789) and William Taylor's 'The Parson's Daughter' (1799)). In the Larpent version of the drama, the licensing manuscript sent by the theatre to the official licensor, John Larpent, before the play was performed, the creature is listed as 'the demon'.[10] Popular anxieties about the threatening identity and attractiveness of the creature can be detected when 'John Bull' observes in the *Theatrical Observer*: 'I would not take my wife . . . to see this blue devil'.[11] Much of the success of the Peake adaptation has been attributed to the original performance of T. P. Cooke, one of the earliest stars of the London stage. In 1820 he had played the villain in James Robinson Planché's *The Vampyre; or, The Bride of the Isles*. But performing as the mute creature, he would have recalled to his audience the very popular pantomimic and mute heroes in Thomas Holcroft's *Deaf and Dumb: or, The Orphan Protected* (1801) and *A Tale of Mystery, A Melo-Drame* (1802).[12] And as such, he would have been understood by the audience, not as a villain, but as the sympathetic figure in the drama. As Emma Raub has argued, Peake's portrait of the creature as mute 'challenges that other melodramatic convention, the supposed dichotomy between clearly depicted good and evil . . . In so doing, he [Peake] fractures melodrama's framework, inviting the audience not to hiss at the villain but instead to sympathize with him.'[13] Mary Shelley herself was particularly amused by Peake's performance, writing to Leigh Hunt: 'Cooke played –'s part extremely well . . . I was much amused, & it appeared to excite a breathless eagerness in the audience.'[14] Perhaps the most effective measure of Cooke's success in portraying the creature can be found in his very longevity in the role. *The Illustrated London News* in 1853 observed that Cooke had performed the role at least 365 times.[15]

In this version of the novel, Victor has been driven to impious experiments because he has been separated from his true love, Agatha De Lacey. Whereas Shelley's Victor is depicted as a confused blend of chemist, natural philosopher and a sympathizer with alchemy, Peake's Victor is a much more primitive character, Faustian and hubristic, a dealer in the occult, the demonic and alchemical potions. In fact, Frankenstein's servant Fritz anxiously acknowledges his belief in the devil, whom he is sure is motivating Frankenstein to pursue his strange and dangerous scientific experiments: '"It's the Devil – for I'm sure *he's* at the bottom of it, and that makes me so nervous"' (I: i). Foregrounding the sacrilegious aspects of Frankenstein's pseudo-scientific experimentation would have appealed to the lower-class anxieties of the public, highlighting Victor's identity as an over-reacher, a Promethean figure who could only ultimately bring catastrophe down on those he was supposedly attempting to help.

There are other crucial differences between the novel and the play as well. All of the action of the play, which occurs over two days, takes place in Geneva. Agatha, the daughter of De Lacey, is Victor's love object; Elizabeth is now the sister of Victor and engaged to marry Clerval; Fritz, a servant to Frankenstein, is introduced for the first of what will be many later filmic appearances, along with his wife Madame Ninon. Felix, Safie and De Lacey appear in an extended series of scenes in Act II. Finally, 'gipsies'

MAT. P. COOKE,
Of the Theatre Royal Covent Garden.
In the Character of the Monster, in the Dramatic Romance of Frankenstien.

Figure 12.1 T. P. Cooke as the creature, painted by Wageman and drawn on stone by Whittock

and 'peasants' also appear in order to explore more fully the class (or anti-elitist) issues that are raised by discussions of access to knowledge and, implicitly, specialized scientific education (II: ii). Clerval sings of his love for Elizabeth (I: i) in the first of many songs and duets in the play, suggesting the long-established melodramatic tradition of interspersing music with spoken words. The creature himself is sensitive to the power of music, a trope that will continue to be emphasized in the later adaptations. Through a series of complications, Agatha finds herself suddenly confronted by the creature/demon, who at first causes her to fall into a river; he then rescues her just as Victor appears and shoots the creature in order to free Agatha from his arms (II: v). This melodramatic adaptation of the novel retains the Gothic trope of the identificatory locket, but as there is no Justine in this version, the locket is worn instead by Agatha and never given to William, although William is snatched by the creature and never seen again.

The most Gothic scene of the drama occurs in the last act of the Larpent version of the play, when the stage directions make it clear that the demon creeps into Agatha's room and strangles her:

> In a large glass – Agatha appears on her knees with a veil over her head. – The Demon with his hand on her throat – she falls – the Demon disappears – after tearing a locket from Agatha's neck.[16]

The fact that this dream-like scene is 'reflected in the glass' to audience members recalls the earlier history of Gothic drama, its tendency to obscure onstage the most violent and Gothic moments of any play, just as gauze had been used earlier to occlude the ghosts who functioned in James Boaden's *Fountainville Forest* (1794), an adaptation of Ann Radcliffe's *Romance of the Forest* (1791). In the conclusion, the creature taunts Frankenstein with his possession of Agatha's locket and Frankenstein pursues him into the Alps with two pistols and the rest of the cast. Although warned not to fire for fear of bringing down an avalanche, Frankenstein does precisely that and he and the creature disappear in an onslaught of ice (III: v). As Forry has observed, early melodramas tended to develop the most Gothic aspects of their sources. In the case of his adaptation of *Frankenstein*, Peake dropped the doppelgänger in favour of the simplified Byronic hero-villain (Frankenstein) who was set in opposition to a dumb show villain-hero (the creature). Peake removed Walton's narrative as a framing device and reduced the major characters to four stock types: the hero, the villain, the persecuted heroine, and the comical rustic. The popularity of the Peake adaptation can be seen in the fact that performances in Great Britain continued throughout the 1820s and 1830s. The first American performance was staged in 1825, and the French version, *Le monstre et la magicien*, opened in Paris in 1826. This popularity was most likely due to the play's simplicity, both in characterization and in ideology: wealthy and educated men – 'presumptious' because of their advantages – who dabble in new scientific discoveries should not be envied or admired, for they can only bring ruin down on themselves, their families and communities. The status quo is reinforced and the middle class is reassured about the value of its religious traditions and continued social conformity.

Henry M. Milner's *The Man and Monster; or, The Fate of Frankenstein* and John Kerr's *The Monster and Magician; or, The Fate of Frankenstein*

The next major British adaptations appeared just three years later, in 1826: namely, Henry M. Milner's *The Man and Monster; or, The Fate of Franken-stein* (Royal Coburg Theatre, 3 July 1826), and John Kerr's *The Monster and Magician; or, The Fate of Frankenstein* (New Royal West London Theatre, 9 October 1826).[17] Little is known about Milner, but his catalogue of plays suggests that he built his career by adapting the works of major artists of his day, also writing *Mazeppa: A Romantic Drama in Three Acts: Dramatised from Lord Byron's Poem* (1831). Milner's version bears little resemblance to Shelley's novel, being set in Italy and heavily Orientalized. In fact, the playbill states that the action occurs in a 'SICILIAN LANDSCAPE', while the play ends as the creature jumps into Mount Etna after killing Franken-stein. This time Victor is married to a Bavarian woman named Emmeline Ritzberg; some months before the action begins he has deserted her and their young son in order to pursue his scientific experiments in the household of the Prince of Piombino, his son Julio and his sister Rosaura on the edge of Mount Etna.

Milner's version of the play is famous for being the first to show the awakening of the monster on the stage, a scene that was to prove so dramatic in the earliest film versions. In Milner's play the stage directions read:

> Laboratory with bottles and chemical apparatus. First sight of the monster an indistinct form with a black cloth...music...A colossal human figure of a cadaverous livid complexion, it slowly begins to rise, gradually attaining an erect posture. When it has attained a perpendicular position, and glares its eyes upon him, he starts back with horror. (I: iii)

It is not long before Emmeline, her father and her son, in their attempts to find Frankenstein, cross paths with the monster (I: vi; II: iii–iv), who initially seeks to befriend them and later, when he learns their identities, attacks them. In this transformation of characters we can see that the Ritzbergs are standing in for the De Lacey family, while Julio takes the place of William.

It is not long before Julio is found dead in Frankenstein's scientific pavilion with the marks of strangulation on his neck (I: vii).

The next few scenes depict a flurry of activity and just as it seems that the monster will kill Frankenstein's young son, his wife Emmeline pulls out a small flute and begins playing; the effect on the monster is immediate: 'He is at once astonished and delighted – he places the Child on the ground – his feelings become more powerfully affected by the music, and his attention absorbed by it . . . he is moved to tears' (II: iv). Like Shakespeare's Caliban, when brute force could not contain him, music's mysterious power to touch his emotions brings the monster literally to his knees, allowing the Prince's soldiers to capture and pin him to a rock, thereby recalling Prometheus and switching the roles that had earlier been established in the novel of *Frankenstein* as Prometheus and the monster as a vulture (II: iv). In the pursuit that concludes the drama, the monster stabs Victor and jumps in a suicidal plunge into the crater of Etna. Apparently the special effects on stage – complete with flowing and erupting lava – were a major reason for the play's popularity, along with the acting of O. Smith as the creature. Richard John O. Smith was so successful in the role of the creature that he rivalled T. P. Cooke as a star on the British stage.

John Kerr's *The Monster and Magician; or, The Fate of Frankenstein* is a translation of the French drama *Le Monstre et le magician* by Jean Toussaint Merle and Antoine Nicolas Béraud who wrote under the pen name Béraud Antony. Originally produced in Paris at the Théâtre de la Porte Saint-Martin on 10 June 1826, the French play exported T. P. Cooke to star in its production as the creature and his performance was considered a triumph. Kerr translated the drama into English and had it ready for performance only four months later in London. Opening at the New Royal West Theatre on 9 October 1826, this translation reveals a heavy nautical influence, with the creature and Frankenstein dying on a storm-tossed boat on the Adriatic Sea instead of under a crashing avalanche or in a volcano. Reviewers of the play were also quick to equate the creature with the threat of mob violence, anarchy or any man-made catastrophe. But it is the character of Victor that is most altered. The Victor of this play is very clearly a 'magician', an alchemist who is devoted to the studies of 'Albert and Faustus' in order to pursue his 'guilty pretentions' (I: i). In a scene that recalls the conjurings of the Wandering Jew in Matthew Lewis's *The Monk* (1796), Victor calls up a 'Genie of the tomb' (I: i); who helps him create the monster out of the contents of a magical vial, the elixir of life and a ring of fire, suggestive of the electrical charges that characterized galvanism and that would later animate the creature in the earliest film adaptations. In a revealing list,

Figure 12.2 O. Smith as the monster in *Frankenstein*

Victor's servant Pietro describes Victor's laboratory as filled with 'crucibles, alembecks, and devil's kitchen utensils' (I: iii).

In this version Frankenstein's first wife has died, leaving him father to a boy named Antonio. He is now engaged to a beautiful but poor young Bohemian woman named Cecilia, for whom he has promised to give up his magical and mysterious pursuits. Cecilia's father, Holbein, is blind and they live in a humble cottage in the woods. Clearly this transformation suggests an appropriation of the De Lacey family for a lower-class agenda, sympathy for Frankenstein's love-object, who is now not a class equal but a lower-class woman who is victimized by his dealings in 'magic'. On their wedding day, Frankenstein fails to appear, but the monster does, first viewing the lovely Cecilia and then spotting himself in a mirror from which he recoils: 'he endeavours to catch his own reflection, and after some pantomime business, conceals himself' (II: ii). But the monster's envy and desire for Cecilia has been inflamed, and so he pursues her even more aggressively when he sees her in the arms of Frankenstein. Cecilia attempts to flee, Victor fires his pistol, Holbein attempts to rescue her and in the tumult the monster sets Holbein's cottage on fire and shoves the old man into the house to face a fiery death (II: ii).

The climax of this adaptation comes as Venetian soldiers – minions of the Council of Ten – attempt to arrest Victor for his unholy experiments, and in this episode we hear the echo of numerous Gothic novels, including those by Percy Shelley, in which the Inquisition played a prominent disciplinary role. The monster pursues Antonio and Cecilia, killing them both in vengeance against his creator. In the final scene, the two men go down with the ship amidst much tumult:

> The monster darts from the rock into the boat, seizes Frankenstein – a moment after a thunderbolt descends and severs the bark, the waves vomit forth a mass of fire and the Magician and his unhallowed abortion are with the boat engulphed in the waves. (III: iii)

Exploiting the popularity of the many nautical dramas that were currently playing in a variety of London theatres, this version of *Frankenstein* references the Arctic scenes in the novel and concludes in a watery inferno.

William and Robert Brough's *Frankenstein; or, The Model Man* and Richard Henry's *Frankenstein; or, The Vampire's Victim*

There were two final mid to late British Victorian adaptations of the novel: William and Robert Brough's *Frankenstein; or, The Model Man* (Adelphi Theatre, 26 December 1849) and Richard Henry's (pseud. of

Richard Butler and Henry Chance Newton) *Frankenstein; or, The Vampire's Victim* (Gaiety Theatre, 24 December 1887), both of which originated as special Christmas performances.[18] Robert Brough was considered in his own day to be a Radical and Republican who particularly despised aristocratic claims to property, governance or social status. As such, the adaptation that he penned with his son William is considered to be the first to develop the political dramas of the novel as they could be translated to the stage. As the 1832 Reform Bill made its way through Parliament a number of conservative political cartoonists began employing the Frankenstein myth for satiric commentary. For them, the liberal Scottish reformer Henry Brougham was a Frankenstein, the second Lord Grey was his crazy assistant Fritz, and the monster they were bringing to life was the new and enlarged voting public, a ragtag composite of men without sufficient property to merit the right to vote. In their adaptation the Broughs seized on this earlier tradition of conservative critique and turned it on its head. For them the danger facing England was France, not its own newly enfranchised citizens. As Frankenstein says, "'But take my defence, I'll soon be showing/ I'm not the only man who's set a going/ A horrid monster that he couldn't stop./ For precedents across the channel pop"' (VII).

This was a period that also saw the expansion of the railway system, steam power and engines, and we could expect that British popular drama would reflect its audience's concerns about the rapid growth of industrialization and a machine culture that was displacing traditional human labour. The Brough version was the first to depict the creature as a machine, 'A mechanical man with skill supreme', whose every joint 'is as strong as an iron beam/ And the springs are a compound of clock-work and steam' (I). This 'model man' can only be brought to life by an alchemical 'Elixir Vitae' mixed with a concoction of fantastical Victorian remedies: 'Slolberg's lozenge . . . Cockle's pills [and] Parr's life pills' (I). Mixing references to the alchemical with the modern would become the dominant technique in the *Frankenstein* adaptations that followed the Brough version.

This humorous and crude play is an example of what was called at the time an 'Adelphi melodrama', a mash-up of Gothic and sentimental tropes that came close to being a burlesque-extravaganza.[19] Its simple structure can be seen in the fact that it consisted of one long act divided into seven scenes. On the playbill the creature is referred to as 'The What Is It', suggesting that the blankness and muteness of the earlier stage monsters has been replaced by a puzzling creature who in this version sings a number of songs that query his origins and purpose. The true villain in this adaptation is a magical creature named Zamiel who was portrayed by the now elderly O. Smith, whom audiences would have remembered from his performance as the monster in the earlier Milner play. By bifurcating the creature in this way, the drama works to place its audience's sympathies with the singing and clownishly dancing creature and his creator, the naive Frankenstein, even while it demonizes and places the blame for his misdeeds on the influence of Zamiel, a primitive force of alchemy and magic who also would have been understood by his audience as a medical galvanist.

Following in the footsteps of Luigi Galvini, who claimed that he had found a force he called 'animal electricity' within all living creatures, medical galvanists like Giovanni Aldini attempted to apply electrical charges to the nerves of corpses. These 'scientists' were viewed as charlatans or quacks by the majority of the public, but at the same time they drew in crowds who were eager to observe their experiments with primitive batteries connected to just-dead bodies. Aldini was expelled from England in 1805 because of the general public outcry against his experiments.[20] Another showman-scientist was Andrew Crosse who synthesized crystals with electricity and then claimed that he had created life when he applied the electricity to volcanic rock.[21] Through the creation of Zamiel, the Broughs broadly gestured toward a critique for what was passing at the time as scientific advances.

There are several other differences between the novel and this adaptation: Frankenstein is now a German student who seeks to marry the wealthy heiress Agatha in order to gain access to the fortune of her father, the Baron Von Donnerund-Blitzen. Agatha, however, loves Otto of Rosenberg, who plots to elope with her from the party at which the Baron intends to announce Agatha's engagement to Frankenstein. In addition to echoing aspects of the harlequinade, references are made throughout this adaptation to the most famous German Gothic opera of the period, *Der Freichütz* (The Marksman), and to the water sprite Undine who plays a crucial role in denouncing and expelling Zamiel at the conclusion of the play: "'Sir – Hence – nor dare again be found/ Playing your wicked pranks on German ground'" (VII). When the threats in this adaptation can be referred to as 'pranks', and when Frankenstein and his Model Man can dance together at the conclusion of the work, then we know that the genre has exhausted itself and collapsed into absurdity.

Set at the University of Crackenjausen, the play begins with a heavy tone of mockery as German students drink beer, dance around in lederhosen and mock the scientific pretensions of their fellow student Frankenstein. Clearly the play is intended to spoof the popularity of *Der Freichütz* by Carl Maria von Weber (1786–1826). *The Model Man* picks up and plays with all those tropes even while it points a finger at the political unrest in France. *Der Freichütz* is based on a German folk legend about a young ranger named

Max who needs to win a shooting contest in order to claim the right to marry his beloved, Agatha. Because he has missed his last several shots, he is vulnerable to the machinations of a fellow ranger, Kaspar, who has sold his soul to the devil and is hoping to find in the lovely Agatha a sacrificial substitute to offer to the devil in his place. A folk-version of the *Faust* tale, the similarity in plot to Maturin's *Melmoth the Wanderer* (1820) is also striking. Kaspar persuades Max to go with him to the ominous wolf's den at midnight in order to cast seven magic bullets that will have the power to kill anything the shooter wants. Kaspar invokes the aid of Zamiel to guide his hand as he shoots, just as Frankenstein in *Model Man* asks Zamiel to help him brew an elixir to give his creature life.

The Germanic folk sprite Undine in this adaptation assumes the role of a sort of *deus ex machina* when she aids the elopement of Otto and Agatha by giving Otto a magic flute that has the power to tame the creature. This flute recalls a similar use of music as a humanizing force in Milner's play, although in Broughs' version the creature literally dances on stage to suggest his complete domestication.

Finally, Richard Butler, editor of *The Referee*, and Henry Chance Newton, theatrical correspondent for *The Referee*, wrote their libretto for *Frankenstein; or, The Vampire's Victim* under the name 'Richard Henry'. The music for the production was composed by William Meyer Lutz; what the playbill refers to as a 'Burlesque Melodrama' was first performed at the Gaiety Theatre, 24 December 1887, as yet another Christmas special. As Forry notes, the performance involved thirteen solos, two duets (one between the creature and Frankenstein, and the other between the creature and the vampire Visconti), one quartet, five choral pieces, three finales for each act, and nineteen musical interludes that set the tone for a character's entrance.[22] Each act ends in a musical number featuring the Gaiety Girls who came onstage to dance and sing with the main characters. One of these characters is a Sun Goddess, which causes one to think that she may have been included because a spectacular costume was at the ready. So many musical numbers produced a lengthy three-act extravaganza, complete with a creature, a terra cotta model and two vampires. This work is a confused jumble of comic and visually stunning scenes, with the creature having a vampire wife and part of Act III set in the Vampire's Club. In Act I the creature kidnaps Frankenstein in Germany, but Act II begins with Frankenstein first a prisoner and then the leader of Spanish bandits (recalling Friedrich von Schiller's robber-rescue drama, *Die Raüber* (The Robbers, 1781). In Act III the creature and the vampire Visconti are scheming against Frankenstein with the play concluding in the Arctic, complete with dancing sailors and bears, one of whom is the creature in disguise:

Don't be frightened, please – (taking off Bear's Head)
It's only me,
A poor benighted Monster here you see,
This is a neat disguise of double form
It serves to hide me, and to keep me warm,
Besides it is in the fashion in these times.[23]

Frankenstein in this version was performed as a 'breeches part' by the Gaity Girl Nellie Farren, best known for her legs and dimples, while the creature was acted by Frank Leslie, famous for his mocking portrayal of an effeminate Oscar Wilde fending off the police.[24]

There was very little of the Shelley novel by this time left on the stage, and this production, for all its outrageous parodies and sexual innuendos, suggests that the concerns that Mary Shelley explored in her novel were largely lost in a swirl of late Victorian self-consciousness. By the time the creature and the vampire emerge together on stage, we are into another cultural moment altogether. As a conjoined unit of horror and abjection, they by this time have come to represent the dominant fears of their era: scientific experimentation run amuck and primitive superstitions left to infect and fester. In such a confrontation we can see the ancient and modern worlds aligned and yet at the same time at odds with each other, while their audience looked on, sometimes laughing and oftentimes staring in mute horror.

NOTES

1 Steven Earl Forry, 'Dramatizations of *Frankenstein*, 1821–1986: A Comprehensive List', *English Language Notes*, 25 (1987), 63–79, provides publication information on all of the dramatic adaptations of the novel, a listing that runs into the hundreds.

2 *Shelley and Mary*, ed. Lady Jane Gibson Shelley and Sir Percy Florence Shelley (Privately Printed, 1882) Vol. II, p. 327.

3 William St Clair notes that the initial print run of *Frankenstein* was 500 copies and that 'for the first fourteen years of its life in print *Frankenstein* existed in about a thousand copies, fewer than most of the works of Byron and Scott sold on publication day'. See his *The Reading Nation in the Romantic Period* (Cambridge University Press, 2004), p. 365. *The Reading Nation* also provides a useful appendix on the publication history of the novel and plays, pp. 644–7.

4 The first dramatic adaptation of *Frankenstein* was written in French in 1821 but appears to have never been performed: *Frankenstein; ou, Le Promethée moderne* (Bibliothèque de l'Arsenal MS. p. folo, aoust 1821./A.T. sc Ms carton 8). According to Forry, the play consists of a fragmentary manuscript of one act (six leaves) and a single leaf of act two. In addition to the British dramatic adaptations discussed in this chapter, there are at least a dozen French adaptations that I do not have the space to analyse here. Forry, 'Dramatizations of *Frankenstein*', 63.

5 Jeffrey Cox (ed.), *Seven Gothic Dramas, 1789–1825* (Athens, OH: Ohio University Press, 1992), p. 386. Richard Brinsley Peake, *Presumption; or, The Fate of Frankenstein*, reprinted in Steven Earl Forry (ed.), *Hideous Progenies: Dramatizations of Frankenstein from Mary Shelley to the Present* (Philadelphia, PA: University of Pennsylvania Press, 1990) pp. 135–60. Further references are given in parenthesis to Acts and Scenes.

6 *Theatrical Observer*, 1 August 1823.

7 The frivolity of the 1823/24 burlesques can be seen in their titles: *Humgumption; or, Dr. Frankenstein and the Hobgoblin of Hoxton* (New Surrey Theatre, 1 September 1823); *Presumption and the Blue Demon* (Davis's Royal Amphitheatre, 1 September 1823); and *Frankin-Steam; or, The Modern Promise to Pay* (Olympic Theatre, 13 December 1824). See Forry (ed.), *Hideous Progenies*, p. 4, for a discussion of their significance.

8 William St Clair, *The Reading Nation*, p. 369.

9 A recent analysis of the *Frankenstein* adaptations within the tradition of the Gothic stage can be found in Francesca Saggini's chapter 'Uncloseting the Gothic Monster', chapter 4 in her *The Gothic Novel and the Stage: Romantic Appropriations* (London: Pickering & Chatto Publishers, 2015).

10 Forry's *Hideous Progenies* publishes the print version, published by *Dick's Standard Plays* later in the century (1865). Cox's text uses both Dick's and the Larpent version, which was the licensing manuscript sent by the theatre to licensor, John Larpent, before the play was performed. The Larpent version gives us our best idea of what was put on the stage in 1823. Dick's version reflects later changes made as the play continued to be performed over the next thirty years.

11 *Theatrical Observer*, 31 July 1823.

12 Also see my discussion of the connection between muteness and melodrama, as well as the use of deafness in Holcroft's two most famous melodramas, in my *Gothic Riffs*, pp. 136–62.

13 Emma Raub, '*Frankenstein* and the Mute Figure of Melodrama', *Modern Drama*, 55(4) (2012), 437–58, 441.

14 Mary Shelley, *The Letters of Mary Wollstonecraft Shelley*, 2 vols., ed. Betty Bennett (Baltimore, MD: Johns Hopkins University Press, 1981), Vol. I, p. 378.

15 *The Illustrated London News*, 15 October 1853.

16 Quoted in Cox, *Seven Gothic Dramas*, p. 423.

17 Henry M. Milner, *The Man and Monster; or, The Fate of Frankenstein*, reprinted in Forry, *Hideous Progenies*, pp. 187–204. John Kerr's *The Monster and Magician; or, The Fate of Frankenstein*, reprinted in Forry, *Hideous Progenies*, pp. 205–26. Further references are given in parenthesis to Acts and Scenes.

18 William and Robert Brough, *Frankenstein; or, The Model Man* and Richard Henry's *Frankenstein; or, The Vampire's Victim*, reprinted in Forry, *Hideous Progenies*, pp. 227–50. Further references are given in parenthesis to Acts and Scenes.

19 Forry, *Hideous Progenies*, p. 57.

20 See Ian Jackson, 'Science as Spectacle: Electrical Showmanship in the English Enlightenment', in Christa Knellwolf and Jane Goodall (eds.), *Frankenstein's Science: Experimentation and Discovery in Romantic Culture, 1780–1830* (Aldershot: Ashgate, 2008), pp. 151–66; and Jane Goodall, 'Electrical Romanticism', in Knellwolf and Goodall (eds.), *Frankenstein's Science*, pp. 117–32.

21 See Susan Tyler Hitchcock, *Frankenstein: A Cultural History* (New York: Norton, 2007) p. 104.
22 Forry, *Hideous Progenies*, p. 290. My discussion of this work is based on Forry. The only copy of this adaptation is a typescript in the British Library (L.C. 53392B).
23 Quoted in Forry, *Hideous Progenies*, p. 68.
24 Forry, *Hideous Progenies*, pp. 68, 57.

13

MARK JANCOVICH

Frankenstein and Film

One of the central problems with writing an account of filmed adaptations of the Frankenstein story is that the list of potential texts seems almost limitless. The term 'Frankenstein's monster' has moved into popular language, where it refers to any creation that seems to take on a life of its own, particularly a life that threatens those that have created it. For example, it is now common to talk of 'Frankenstein Foods': foods that are the product of science (usually genetically modified foods) which are supposed to be potentially dangerous. Consequently, one could talk about a vast number of films that involve those who wield powers that get out of control, films that might range from Mickey Mouse's appearance as the magician's apprentice in Disney's *Fantasia* (1940) to classic horror films such as *The Golem* (1915). Of course, these films deal with supernatural powers that may have some association with science but are not explicitly about the powers of scientific progress and modernity; but even films that are more specifically about modern science (whether or not they are scientifically accurate or plausible) would include a dizzy array of texts that might include *Metropolis* (1927), *Man Made Monster* (1941), *Colossus: the Forbin Project* (1970), *The Terminator* (1984) and many more.

One particularly interesting version (perhaps only because it is associated with a female author like Mary Shelley's original novel) is Susan Seidelman's *Making Mr. Right* (1987), which dispenses with the death and destruction to focus on the confrontation between the uncaring creator and his emotional creation. Here a woman (Frankie Stone) is hired to help a scientist with his public relations. As she discovers, the scientist has invented an android that 'has been custom-designed to withstand a long, boring trip into deep space', and particularly the rigours of loneliness and isolation associated with such a journey.[1] However, as the narrative progresses, it is revealed that the scientist is emotionally repressed and suffers from a fear of others, while his creation ('the wide-eyed Ulysses') is emotionally sensitive with a 'childlike charm'. By the end of the film, then, the scientist has rejected earth for the isolation of deep space and his creation has escaped the laboratory so that he and Frankie can live happily ever after as a romantic couple.

Even if one limits the account to explicit 'adaptations', there are still problems. Few, if any, of the films that are associated with Mary Shelley's novel were actually an adaptation of this source text. Many are actually adaptations of other sources, such as plays, other films and comic books. They are also rarely even simply adaptations of these other sources but are rather produced in relation to a range of different intertexts. Indeed, texts never have a one-to-one relationship with an original source text, but are also constructed through the hybridization of many different materials.[2] Adaptations of the Frankenstein story are inevitably a response to a range of other trends within the period within which they were made, trends that not only motivate an interest in materials culled from Mary Shelley's novel but also shape what materials are deemed to be of interest and how they are interpreted and hybridized with other elements from elsewhere. One can even see how changes in film and television production have created other trends and periods.

This chapter will therefore examine various films and use reviews of them (particularly focusing on the culturally important *New York Times* reviews) as a way of clarifying some of the ways in which these films were understood within the periods in which they were made and the ways in which these texts were seen as drawing upon other texts and production trends. It will begin with an account of the various ways in which filmmakers used Mary Shelley's novel and theatrical versions of the story to lend prestige and respectability to their projects, before moving on to examine the ways in which earlier *Frankenstein* films started to become a key reference point for later ones. In the process, this chapter also examines the ways in which television played into these developments, and the ways in which the Frankenstein story has been subject to a range of different strategies of appropriation.

From Prestige Adaption to Series Production

The silent adaptation of *Frankenstein* made by the Edison Studio in 1910 was largely a stand-alone production that, like many productions of the period, turned to classic literature. At the time, various filmmakers were using this strategy in a bid to make cinema respectable and attract affluent, middle class audiences, given that the period around 1907 had seen a series of moral campaigns around cinema, and many film companies turned to adaptations of legitimate cultural materials to escape moral censure while simultaneously targeting more affluent (and hence profitable) markets. Indeed, marketing for Edison's *Frankenstein* not only emphasized its use of classic literature but also explicitly stressed that its makers had toned-down the horror and focused instead 'upon the mystic and psychological problems that are to be found in this weird tale'.[3] Even then it turns the tale into a familiar moral drama of a young man who leaves home for college, where he commits acts that threaten his marriage night, while also featuring carefully staged sequences of trick photography that could be marketed as cinematic spectacle.

It was then about twenty years before the next significant version, Universal pictures' 1931 production of *Frankenstein* that made a star of Boris Karloff. Although this is often seen as the first in a long series of Frankenstein films, the 1931 film was not made with this intention but was a prestige production and hence a stand-alone film. Nor was it an adaptation of Mary Shelley's novel. Earlier the same year, Universal had enjoyed box office success with a film version of a theatrical hit, *Dracula*, and it was keen to cash-in on this success with another film version of another theatrical version of a weird tale, John L. Balderston's stage conception of Mary Shelley classic tale. The *New York Times* review also noted *Frankenstein*'s pedigree as a Universal production, the 'firm [that] presented Lon Chaney in "The Hunchback of Notre Dame"', even if it stressed that this earlier 'repellant sight' was 'a creature for sympathy compared to the hideous monster in this "Frankenstein."' If these features emphasized earlier Universal productions that the film sought to emulate or surpass – *Frankenstein* was supposed to make *Dracula* seem 'tame' – the review also noted that it was part of a larger production strategy that was not built around sequels but would include other weird stories based on literary works, so that, just as the studio had followed *Dracula* with *Frankenstein*, the latter film would in turn be followed by Poe's 'Murders in the Rue Morgue'.

In other words, *Frankenstein* was not conceived of as material that would form the basis of a film series and it was only right near the end of the 1930s horror cycle that Universal made another Frankenstein film, *The Bride of Frankenstein* (1935), but again this was seen as a prestigious follow-up, not the start of a film series. The same was also true of the third film, *Son of Frankenstein* (1939), which was another prestige production that was designed to cash in on the phenomenal success of a re-release of *Frankenstein* and *Dracula* as a double bill. Furthermore, it was only with the second film that the *New York Times* started to see the creature as a sympathetic figure. Its review of the first film had referred to the creature as 'the brute' and had explained that 'the reason given here for his murderous onslaughts is that Frankenstein's Man Friday stole an abnormal brain' rather than a normal one, when collecting elements for the creature. This means that the review regarded Frankenstein, and not his creature, as being the lead figure in the first film, although by the second film, this position had begun to change. According to the *New York Times*, *Bride of Frankenstein* was the next 'astonishing chapter in the career of the Monster' and it was Karloff who was the principle attraction: 'Boris Karloff comes again to terrify the children, frighten the women and play a jiggling tune upon masculine spines as the snarling, lumbering, *pitiful* Thing' (my emphasis).[4] If the review still claimed that the monster had been 'a pretty much a thorough-going brute' in the first film, it was clear that, by the second film, 'he is slightly moonstruck, hungry for kindness and even – perish the thought – for love'.

However, despite this review's suggestion that 'the lovelorn, calf-eyed Mr. Karloff' is 'a changed Monster', there is no sense that this is inappropriate. On the contrary, the review suggests that the monster had long since over-taken its creator as the focus of its audiences' affections. After all, it was Karloff who played the monster, not Colin Clive who had played his creator, who had achieved stardom as a result of the film; and while *Frankenstein* was Karloff's breakthrough role, Clive's career went into decline afterwards. The story is that of the creature, who had 'taken refuge in the tower's water-filled cellar' at the end of the last film but 'clambers out' at the start of the new film where, 'hated by man', he begs Frankenstein 'to create a mate for him'. It is also clear that the review expects us to revel in this return of the monster, and even suggests that he should 'not be permitted to pass from the screen. The Monster should become an institution, like Charlie Chan.' Consequently, while some critics have bemoaned the device by which the monster's outrages are blamed upon his 'abnormal brain', rather than his anger at an uncaring creator, the monster's deviance could still be given a sympathetic inflection and the abnormality of his brain does not necessarily make his actions illegitimate.[5]

It was therefore only once a new cycle of horror films was well established that Universal began to treat *Frankenstein* as the basis for the production of a film series, and after the studio had already had hits with *The Mummy's Hand* (1940) and *The Wolf Man* (1941). Furthermore, the series (such as it was) was not interested in Mary Shelley's original story and even re-interpreted its own earlier production within the terms of this new cycle. Many commenters from the 1940s to the present have complained that, during the period, the Frankenstein monster lost its complexity and ceased to be a sympathetic, lonely and alienated figure and became a robotic killing machine. But this was due to a larger trend in Universal monsters, in which the narratives were often about mad controlling figures who sought to dominate others; and this was not just a tendency in mad scientist films such as *Man Made Monster* so that Universal's new mummy was a killing machine sent out to do the bidding of various high priests. Even the Wolf Man was a

young man overwhelmed by urges that he cannot control and driven to per-
form acts of violence that he finds horrifying and shameful. Furthermore,
it is debatable whether we can even identify a *Frankenstein* series at all.
If the first three films were clearly intended as prestige productions rather
than part of series production, and while *The Ghost of Frankenstein* (1942)
places the Frankenstein monster within its own narrative, the following film,
Frankenstein Meets the Wolf Man (1943) is not focused on Frankenstein's
monster but was a continuation of the Wolf Man's story so that Frankenstein's monster becomes very much a subsidiary character, a trend that is
continued with both *House of Frankenstein* (1944) and *House of Dracula*
(1945).

Cinema, Television and the Gothic

By 1945, the Universal *Frankenstein* series – if that is what it was – had
ended and, although the Frankenstein monster would be disinterred briefly
in 1948, for an encounter with Abbott and Costello, there was another
lull in production for over a decade until, in 1957, Hammer released the
first film in a new series of Frankenstein films. Again, *The Curse of Frankenstein* was very much designed as a stand-alone film but would generate a
long running series of Frankenstein films that ended with *Frankenstein and
the Monster from Hell* (1974), which featured a creature very similar in
appearance to the Edison version.

Reviewers of *The Curse of Frankenstein* doubted that anyone 'outside
some very young kids' would 'not yet [be] acquainted with the monster of
Baron Frankenstein' but recommended that anyone suffering such ignorance
could 'remedy' their 'social shortcoming' by seeing the new film.[6] Unfortunately, it also thought that these might be the only people who would really
appreciate the film, which was dismissed as a 'routine horror picture', despite
being one that had shifted from the monster to its creator, a feature that continued throughout the series, in which the Baron remained the key character
while his various creations came and went. As *Variety* noted: 'The emphasis lies not so much on the controllable blood lust of the created monster
as on the gruesome, distasteful clinical details whereby the crazy scientist
accumulates the odd organs with which to assemble the creature.'[7]

Again the film was not understood as an adaptation and while it was
associated with 'Mary Shelley's 140-year-old tale', the *New York Times*
also referred to the creature as 'the most famous monster of screen fiction',
and *Variety* described the film as a '*remake* of [the] classic thriller' (my
emphasis), not an adaptation of the literary classic.[8] Indeed, while Hammer had a reputation for adaptations at this point, it was not for literary

adaptations. On the contrary, Hammer as a studio had largely specialized since the 1940s in adaptations of radio and television programming. It had made films of *Dick Barton: Secret Agent* (1948) but had enjoyed considerable success with film adaptations of the BBC *Quatermass* serials, which had been written by Nigel Kneale and were the studio's first significant forays into horror filmmaking.

Kneale also wrote *The Creature* (1955) for the BBC, which Hammer adapted for the big screen as *The Abominable Snowman* (1957), and a version of George Orwell's *1984*, which divided critics. If Kneale's adaptation of the Orwell novel was widely praised at the time, and has acquired classic status since, it also provoked a moral panic in which many critics dismissed it as sensational horror.[9] In a sense, then, the association with Kneale's television plays offered the studio a rare opportunity to develop projects that had associations with quality on the one hand and sensationalism and notoriety on the other. Furthermore, both *The Creature* and *1984* had starred Peter Cushing, whom the studio would cast in its next horror production but one that was not based on a BBC production written by Kneale.

If Cushing maintained a link with the Kneale plays, the studio's turn to the literary Gothic was a development that had other motivations. On the one hand, 1957 was the year in which Universal's horror films were sold as a package to television and, on the other, as Kevin Heffernan notes, many aspects of the *Curse of Frankenstein*, and particularly its use of colour, clearly demonstrated the company's ambition to attempt to break out of low budget production and into the 'middle bracket' of the film market.[10] If literary sources helped suggest some semblance of respectability, while Hammer also traded in sensational materials, the studio also made another strategic choice. They did not adapt *1984*, one of Kneale's most infamous scripts, and this may well have been due to competition from the American film version which was released in 1956, even if they had been able to acquire the rights. But this American adaptation also demonstrated that, in the 1950s, Hollywood productions largely located science fiction and horror materials within contemporary or even futuristic settings, and had virtually abandoned the Gothic. By returning to the Gothic, Hammer sought to clearly distinguish its product and offer something that did not compete with American companies.

In other words, one can see that Hammer was looking in various different directions, none of which were particularly directed at Mary Shelley's novel. They were not only drawing on a cinematic past associated with Universal at a time of renewed interest, and on aspects of contemporary television (while their use of colour and graphic horror also offered something that television could not deliver – as *Variety* stressed, 'As this is the first time the subject has been depicted in color, all the grim trappings are more vividly impressive').[11] But they were also looking to distinguish their films from American horror production at the time, a strategy that proved phenomenally successful. Indeed, American cinema initially sought to respond by presenting the Gothic settings of the Hammer film as anachronistic. AIP's *I was a Teenage Frankenstein* (1957) therefore restaged the story in a contemporary setting with the monster recast as an alienated teenager, and *Frankenstein 1970* (1958) contrasted Karloff's tragic scientist with a crass Hollywood production crew who are trying to film the story of his ancient ancestor, while he tries to make a creature of his own. However, despite the implicit suggestion that Gothic versions of the tale were old hat, it was Hammer's films which would prove the more commercially successful versions of the story and AIP and others were soon moving into Gothic productions of their own, even if they turned to Poe, rather than Mary Shelley for their source materials.

If Hammer's *Frankenstein* was developed through a complex relationship to television, television also produced a series of its own adaptations of the story. In 1952, *Tales of Tomorrow*, an American science fiction series dedicated a half-hour episode to the tale, and interprets the story as one of hubris that was clearly intended to articulate fears of science during the early years of the nuclear age. It also repeats Shelley's opposition between the obsession with science (which requires the male scientist to hide himself away from his loved ones) and the world of domestic affection, which is simply reduced to the nuclear family of Frankenstein's wife and child. However, after a fairly short moral preamble, in which Frankenstein's family try to discover what the scientist has been doing in his weird castle on an island surrounded by water, the story descends into a fairly standard spectacle of destruction as the monster goes on the rampage. In this way, the episode owes far less to Mary Shelley's original story than to familiar popularizations of the tale, and even pays homage to the Universal versions through the casting of Lon Chaney Jr, Universal's key horror star of the 1940s, although his make up recalls Boris Karloff's version of the creature.

In 1958, the year after its success with *The Curse of Frankenstein*, Hammer tried to move into television and made a pilot for a series that was never commissioned, *Tales of Frankenstein*. The credit sequence features a narrator who positions the programme in a very specific way:

> From the beginning of time, many men have sought the unknown, delving into the dark regions where lie those truths which are destined to destroy. Of all these eerie adventures into darkness, none was more driven by insatiable curiosity, nor went further into the unknown, than the unforgettable Baron

Frankenstein. So infamous were his exploits that his name stands forever as a symbol of all that is shocking, unspeakable, forbidden. Thus, in our day any story that chills the soul and freezes the blood is truly a tale of Frankenstein. Now join us in the mystery, the excitement and stimulation that comes when we tell you a story so weird, so dark and so harrowing that it deserves to be called one of the many Tales of Frankenstein.

In this way, the introduction not only evoked contemporary fears about the dangers of scientific progress in the nuclear age, but also enabled the series to present any horror story under its title. The series also featured a version of the Frankenstein story as its pilot episode, and its style was very different from the cinematic version of the previous year. The studio even imported Curt Siodmak as a director, the writer of many of the classic horror films of the 1940s (*The Wolf Man*, 1941; *I Walked with a Zombie*, 1943; and *The Beast with Five Fingers*, 1946) and brother of Robert Siodmak who was one of the 1940s key horror directors. The opening sequence also borrows footage from Universal's 1940s horror films, particularly the weird face in a crystal ball which operated as the host to Universal's *Inner Sanctum* series, and which *Tales of Frankenstein* reused as its own narrator.

Finally, in 1968, the British horror series, *Mystery and Imagination*, also did an adaptation of the Mary Shelley story, although this was far more strongly presented as an adaptation of the novel, rather than of other popular versions of the story, and adopted a far more serious attitude. Frankenstein and his creature are even played by the same actor, Ian Holm, as a self-conscious mirroring device. The result is a fascinating version that owes far more to the stylistic experimentation that British television was engaged in during the period than any cinematic versions of the story.

Camp, Parody and Spoof in the 1970s

Hammer's version of *Frankenstein* dominated the 1960s but by the time of their last version of the story in 1974 the situation had dramatically changed. Consequently, the early 1970s witnessed a series of different versions, which treated the Frankenstein story as camp. *Flesh for Frankenstein* (1973), for example, was explicitly sold in the US as 'Andy Warhol's Frankenstein', largely due to Paul Morrissey's involvement as writer and director, and was clearly constructed as a confrontational film that revelled in its trashy materials. If Warhol was one reference point, *The Exorcist* (1973) was another, although here *Flesh for Frankenstein* was supposed to surpass the excesses of the earlier film: 'While one suspects that the tales about upchuck at "The Exorcist" were eagerly exaggerated, "Andy Warhol's

Frankenstein" ... almost begs the gorge to rise.'[12] Its 3D effects were said to make one nostalgic for the 3D of 1950s horror, and were 'used to project the butchery. Dripping giblets on forceps are thrust into the audience'. Consequently, the film was largely dismissed on the basis that it 'drags as much as it camps: despite a few amusing moments, it fails as spoof and the result is only a coy binge in degradation.'

Again, then, the film is far less interested in adapting Mary Shelley's novel than in playing with popular materials and addressing an audience imbued with the aesthetics of 1970s camp. It dispenses with any semblance of the original story and introduces us to Frankenstein's children, who have an unhealthy fascination with his experiments, and are offspring of his incestuous relationship with his sister/wife. Both Frankenstein and his incestuous partner are presented as perverts, so that his experiments are reduced to a rather too obvious 'substitute for sex'. Furthermore, both brother and sister are 'fascistic' and view others as mere objects for their gratification, so that Frankenstein's 'plans to create and control a new master race' no longer seem to be motivated by a desire for world domination, as with earlier mad scientists, but with a perverse desire to create 'beautiful rigid zombies' that can be used as sexual playthings.

A similar theme was also explored the same year in a fascinating TV version of the story, *Frankenstein: The True Story*, written by Christopher Isherwood, and while its sets and costumes suggest that it is a more faithful version of the original novel, Isherwood actually pillages from a variety of sources. For example, James Mason makes a notable appearance as Dr Polidori and, as in James Whale's *Bride of Frankenstein*, he persuades Frankenstein to help him create a female creature as an antidote to the failures and disappointments associated with the first creature. The result is a fascinatingly odd television drama that hovers between respectable adaptation and elaborate invention. It is also awash with camp references not only to different versions of the tale, but also with coded gay subtexts. Frankenstein moves through a series of intense relationships with men (Clerval, the creature, Polidori) which promise fulfilment but end in frustration and disillusionment; and he, his collaborators and his male creature are all obsessed with beauty – in fact, the only real reason that Frankenstein seems to reject the monster is when it starts to look ugly.

The following year, yet another camp version would appear, although in this case it was an explicit spoof, Mel Brooks' *Young Frankenstein*, and this was anything but an adaption of Mary Shelley's novel, but rather an overt parody of the Universal horror films in particular and 'the clichés of horror films in the 1930s' more generally.[13] Furthermore, it did not even take the 1931 *Frankenstein* as its template but rather the third Universal film,

Son of Frankenstein. The film is also positioned by the *New York Times* as somewhere between the 'deadpan humor' of the Hammer productions and the 'all-out assault ... wild anachronism and grotesque special effects' of 'Andy Warhol's *Frankenstein*'. Here the past is recalled 'lovingly' so that *Young Frankenstein*'s targets are never 'rudely used' and the film 'has an affectionate look to it'. Again sexual subtexts become a key focus of attention and the baron's repressed fiancée 'eventually finds sexual fulfillment in the arms of the monster', while Frankenstein shares 'a keen appreciation of beautiful bosoms' with 'your average playboy reader'.

Of course, if these film and television versions literalized certain sexual elements in the original story and particularly in James Whale's films, these elements ran riot in *The Rocky Horror Picture Show*, the film version of a 1973 stage musical that appeared in cinemas in 1975. The *New York Times* does not even seem to have bothered with reviewing the film on its initial release, although the film has gone on to become a cinematic phenomenon over the years; but, according to *Variety*, the film was a 'monster film spoof', in which the Frankenstein character was now 'the bisexual Frank N Furter', whose 'bizarre appetites' have created an ideal (muscle) man, the 'synthetic' Rocky.[14] The story (such as it is) opens with the introduction of a couple of 'wholesome straights', Brad and Janet, who confess their love for each other in the aftermath of a wedding but are soon forced to seek refuge in Frank N Furter's castle. Once inside its Gothic doors, they are witness to a series of strange goings on, and Frank N Furter 'first seduces Janet and then conquers Brad'. In the process, the film 'sends up a number of Hollywood clichés' and reveal the couple's heterosexual identities to be the product of repression. In other words, the film literalizes in almost bald terms Robin Wood's claim that 'the true subject of the horror genre is the struggle for recognition of all that our civilization oppresses or represses', although this might suggest (given that he was making this claim at about the same time as the film) that this was a historically specific understanding of the horror tale, rather than its inner and inevitable essence.[15]

Monster Mash: Heterogeneity, Eclecticism and Incongruity

Of course, if these films viewed earlier versions of *Frankenstein* as anachronistic and ripe for camp appropriation, this was due to the ways in which the horror film of the 1970s had departed from the Gothic horrors of Hammer and was going in very different directions. For example, *Night of the Living Dead* (1968), *The Exorcist*, *The Omen* (1976), *Halloween* (1978) and many others placed their horrors within a contemporary landscape and, by the time of the next adaptation in the mid 1980s, the Frankenstein film was no longer the material of series production but returned to a form of production that was organized around the stand-alone prestige adaptation. Indeed, when *The Bride* was released in 1985, it was at a time when *Night of the Living Dead*, *The Omen* and *Halloween* had all become virtual franchises along with others series such as *Friday the 13ᵗʰ* (1980–2009); and the result was that the horror films of the 1970s in turn came to be seen as tired and clichéd. Kim Newman even sees the period after 1984 as one in which the genre degenerates into virtual horror parody.[16]

In contrast, *The Bride* is a lavish production with a name director (Franc Roddam) but it is hardly an adaption of Mary Shelley's novel. Indeed, the *New York Times* explicitly identifies it as 'a very loose, freewheeling remake of "Bride of Frankenstein"', and even then the film opens where the previous film had ended, with Frankenstein's attempt to create a mate for his creature.[17] However, in this film, when the creator discovers that his female creature is beautiful, he decides to keep her for himself, at which point his original monster wanders off to find himself with the circus, before returning to reclaim his bride and rescue her from Frankenstein at the precise moment that the mad scientist decides to rape her.

Despite the high production values, star names and respected director the result is a fairly risible affair. It may borrow from *Bride of Frankenstein* but is also awash with references to pop music. It stars Sting as Frankenstein, who is hardly even a mad scientist after the first sequence but 'a glowering supercilious fiend spouting philosophical gibberish'; and it also stars Jennifer Beals as the bride, the film being her first cinematic feature after her breakthrough appearance as a dancer in *Flashdance* (1983). It therefore seems to hover somewhere between the heritage cinema that would achieve critical and commercial success in the same year with Merchant and Ivory's *A Room with a View*, and the stylistic excesses of the music videos during the period. Indeed the *New York Times* complained that the film 'never makes up its mind whether it is a horror movie spoof or an earnest exploration of the genre's myth', and it is this confusion (combined with its 'funereal pace') that is ultimately supposed to sink the film:

> In its earliest sequences, the film . . . is a gothic farce full of comic book thunder and lightning and machinery gone haywire. Minutes later, it aspires to the icy historical detachment of films like 'Barry Lyndon.' In other scenes, it becomes a sentimental fairy tale spouting inspirational clichés out of a Sylvester Stallone movie.

Elsewhere it 'is structured as an allegory relating the Frankenstein myth to "Pygmalion" and "Beauty and the Beast," but the connection seems painfully forced and heavy handed.'

The film was therefore condemned for its combination of incompatible materials and the same was also true of the next significant film, nearly a decade later. The title, *Mary Shelley's Frankenstein* (1994), might explicitly present the film as an adaptation, but it is very misleading, given that even this title was a borrowing from another cinematic source, *Bram Stoker's Dracula* (1992), which it was clearly meant to emulate. Directed by and starring Kenneth Branagh, who had made his name with filmed versions of Shakespeare, the film 'will not strike anyone as chiefly Mary Shelley's invention' but was seen as an 'overheated romantic fable' by a director with 'a flair for capturing the mass appeal of familiar texts' but is hampered by material that 'is easily caricatured and dauntingly overexposed. The monstrousness of "Frankenstein" extends to nearly 30 other films, not to mention a permanent place in the pantheon of Hollywood masks and pop-cultural archetypes.'[18]

If this *Mary Shelley's Frankenstein* was clearly inspired by Francis Ford Coppola's recent hit with *Bram Stoker's Dracula* (Coppola even produced Branagh's film), it comes off second best, so that Coppola's film is described as 'a more stylish, rapturous undertaking', while Branagh's film is dismissed as a contradiction, like *The Bride*. It is 'exaggeratedly quaint', a massively overblown extravagant affair ('For a film of such lavishness and chaotic sprawl, creating-a-monster quips are obvious but inevitable') that tries to be faithful and respectable but fails to even acknowledge 'Mary Shelley's implicit prophecies' in the process.

After this it was yet another decade before Frankenstein's monster made another significant film appearance and, when it did, the cycle had come around again. In 2004, there were two appearances of the Frankenstein monster, both of which were designed to establish a series, while still featuring the wild conglomeration of different materials that had distinguished the previous two efforts. Oddly, Martin Scorsese was executive producer of a television film *Frankenstein* based on a script by Dean Koontz, which was directed by Marcus Nispel, who had directed a commercially successful and visually stylish remake of *Texas Chainsaw Massacre* the previous year. Again, this television film was not an adaptation of the novel but was set in contemporary New Orleans where Parker Posey plays a tough detective who is investigating a series of murders that appear to be the work of a serial killer. In the process, she gets caught up in a conflict between Victor Helios (supposedly the inspiration for Victor Frankenstein) and his creation, and the film simultaneously updates the story with issues of genetic experimentation while turning the monster into a kind of superhero.

The association with superheroes was even more explicit the same year, when Universal combined a variety of monsters and other elements together in *Van Helsing*, which starred Hugh Jackman, 'whose performances as the heartsick Wolverine in Bryan Singer's "X-Men" franchise has set a new standard for emotionally insightful acting in comic-book-based movies'.[19]

Clearly intended to establish its own franchise, the film centres on the character of Van Helsing who is now an action hero 'employed by a top secret multireligious task force'. In other words, he is on a mission that pits him against 'brawling ghouls, vampires and werewolves wreaking havoc in Dracula's castle under a full moon' as he tries to thwart Dracula's 'diabolical plan to harness the power of Frankenstein's monster . . . which will enable him to breed thousands of bat babies'.

If no franchise emerged from *Van Helsing* (2004), almost exactly the same 'diabolical plan' lay at the heart of another 'apparent franchise bid in "*I, Frankenstein*"'.[20] This 2014 film is another amalgam of elements which 'largely shuns Shelley's anguished creator as a character and turns his lonely monster into a football between the forces of good and evil: protective gargoyles and demons who covet his secret of immortality.' After a very brief series of striking images, in which the backstory of Mary Shelley's novel is alluded to, the film brings the action into the contemporary world, so that the film's debts are not to Shelley's novel but to other texts: the film is not only 'the brainchild of Kevin Grevioux', a comic book artist, but is produced by the makers of the *Underworld* franchise, which it clearly hopes to emulate. It even features an appearance by Bill Nighy, whose 'presence is part of a certain overlap with the "Underworld" series, in which he also appeared'. In the process, then, Frankenstein's monster is turned into a kind of supernatural superhero and it is still to be seen whether the result will be further films 'or straight-to-video-on-demand sequels'.

Conclusion

Of course, while this account of the last thirty years might look like one of degradation and decline, it is always difficult to predict where things will go next. Indeed, the latest version, *Victor Frankenstein* (2015), has been described as 'a jaunty bromance' between Victor (played by James McAvoy, or Dr X from the most recent X-Men films) and Igor (played by Harry Potter's Daniel Radcliffe).[21] Given that Igor does not even appear in Shelley's novel, the *New York Times* claimed that the film 'owes less to Shelley (or most Frankenstein flicks) than to Guy Ritchie's Sherlock diversions, which turned Holmes . . . and Watson . . . into 19th-century action heroes complete with cheerfully deployed violence and self-regarding smiles.' The review also points out that *Victor Frankenstein* is indebted to yet another version of the

Holmes stories, given that its director, Paul McGuigan, has 'directed episodes of the BBC show "Sherlock"'. However, for all its supposed failings – it is claimed to be 'thin as a halfpenny' and have 'nothing to offer on science or the mysteries of creation' – the film is also said to demonstrate 'the grip that Shelley's story retains on the imagination', even if one 'can't help turning your thoughts from Shelley to Doyle.'

Consequently, it is not that Mary Shelley's novel has ceased to inspire filmmakers. On the contrary, as was suggested at the start of this chapter, the novel's influence may be so dispersed that it is almost impossible to capture. Rather than a narrative of decline, it is therefore the case that the most interesting appropriations are by films that do not explicitly invoke the novel, while those films that explicitly establish a relationship often do so in an uninspired bid for respectability or as a simple exercise in branding.

NOTES

1 Janet Maslin, 'Film: John Malkovich in "Making Mr. Right"', *New York Times*, 10 April 1987.
2 Robert Stam, 'Beyond Fidelity: the Dialogics of Adaptation' in James Naremore (ed.), *Film Adaptation* (New Brunswick, NJ: Rutgers University Press, 2000), pp. 54–79.
3 Anon, *Edison Kinetogram*, 2, 15 March 1910, 3–4.
4 F.S.N., 'At the Roxy', *New York Times*, 11 May 1935.
5 Paul O'Flynn, 'Production and Reproduction: The Case of *Frankenstein*', *Literature and History* (1983), 194–213.
6 Bosley Crowther, 'Screen: Routine Horror; "Curse of Frankenstein" Bows at Paramount', *New York Times*, 8 August 1957.
7 Clem., 'Film Reviews', *Variety*, 15 May 1957.
8 Crowther, 'Routine Horror', and Clem., 'Film Reviews'.
9 Derek Johnston, 'Genre, Taste and the BBC: The Origins of British Television Science Fiction', PhD thesis, University of East Anglia (2009), https://ueaeprints .uea.ac.uk/10565/1/Thesis_johnston_d_2009.pdf.
10 Kevin Heffernan, *Ghouls, Gimmicks and Gold: Horror Films and the American Movie Business, 1953–1968* (Durham, NC: Duke University Press, 2004).
11 Clem., 'Film Reviews'.
12 Nora Sayre, 'Screen: Butchery Binge: Morrissey's "Warhol's Frankenstein" Opens', *New York Times*, 16 May 1974.
13 Vincent Canby, 'Young Frankenstein', *New York Times*, 16 December 1974.
14 Pit, 'Film Reviews', *Variety*, 24 September 1975.
15 Robin Wood, *Hollywood From Vietnam to Reagan* (New York: Columbia University Press, 1986), p. 75.
16 Kim Newman, *Nightmare Movies: A Critical History of the Horror Movie from 1968* (London: Bloomsbury, 1988).
17 Stephen Holden, 'Screen: "The Bride"', *New York Times*, 16 August 1985.
18 Janet Maslin, 'Film Review: Frankenstein; A Brain on Ice, a Dead Toad and Voila!', *New York Times*, 4 November 1994.

19 A. O. Scott, 'Film Review: Full Moon, Romance and a Demon Rustler', *New York Times*, 7 May 2004.

20 Nicolas Rapold, 'Everyone Wants a Piece of this Wandering Monster: "I, Frankenstein" Stars Aaron Eckhart as the Lonely Ghoul', *New York Times*, 24 January 2014.

21 Manohla Dargis, 'Review: "Victor Frankenstein" Recasts a Tale that Keeps on Giving', *New York Times*, 24 November 2015.

14

DAVID PUNTER

Literature

The afterlife of Mary Shelley's *Frankenstein* is huge and complex, and includes a variety of novels, as well as 'novelizations' of films. The reasons for this impact on posterity have been much discussed; they obviously include the original novel's dealings with science and technology; the constantly reinterpreted relations between Victor Frankenstein and his creature; the obsessive nature of Victor's fascinations; and age-old myths to do with transgressive knowledge and human aspiration. It is no accident that Mary Shelley's subtitle was 'The Modern Prometheus', although even here, as in so many other aspects of the work, there is an ambiguity, even perhaps a series of ambiguities. It would seem natural to assume that the Promethean figure thus indicated is Victor himself, but the creature's own search for (self-)knowledge has also been seen as Promethean; one might also want to question the exact tone of the word 'modern' here – is Victor meant to be presented to us as a worthy successor to the original Prometheus, or rather as a downgraded equivalent, thus satirizing the whole notion of the Promethean, at least within a modern context? And it is to this vexed notion of the 'modern' that I shall return at the end of this chapter.

One of the matters, it is fair to say, that has proved most tantalizing down through 200 years of literary history has been the clash of viewpoints between Victor and the creature, which seems to have demanded constant rewriting. In Mary Shelley's text, we are on the surface presented for much of the time with Victor's viewpoint; he, after all, is human, while the creature is not, at least in the sense that he has not been born of human reproduction. Yet it has been frequently pointed out that it is often with the creature that the reader feels most sympathy, for a variety of reasons. The creature is irrationally shunned by human society; the creature is, to begin with, helpless and in need of our pity as much as our scorn; the creature evolves into a being whose attitude towards Victor, and towards wider issues of social organization, can often seem far more rational, more well-considered, indeed more articulate than Victor's increasingly frantic and rage-filled speeches.

Among the questions which arise are ones to do with paternal and filial feelings and duties; the creature, after all, like any human child, is not responsible for his own origins, and Victor's rejection of him can, on some readings, seem callous and vindictive.

But then, of course, the creature proceeds to supply what may be considered good reason for Victor's resentment; he does, after all, become a murderer, although again it has come to seem unclear whether we should consider this behaviour as innate to the creature himself, or as a response to his treatment at the hands of a world which considerers itself human and yet reacts to his intrusive presence in an exceedingly inhumane way. Mary Shelley's text thus opens for us a variety of readerly subject positions; and it is arguably this 'open-ness' which has been the cause of the apparently endless series of reinterpretations which have continued until the present day.

In this chapter, I shall look at four (out of 30 or so) recent *Frankenstein* narratives: Brian Aldiss's *Frankenstein Unbound* (1973); Dean Koontz's series of five *Frankenstein* novels, published between 2005 and 2010; Susan Heyboer O'Keefe's *Frankenstein's Monster* (2010); and Michael Bunker's *Brother, Frankenstein* (2015). These are vastly different books, appealing to vastly different readerships, which serves to show that it is not only the content of *Frankenstein* which remains open to interpretation; there are questions of genre as well. We might want to say that Mary Shelley's *Frankenstein* is a classic; but there would be critical reservation about this. It is, after all, the work of a very young author, and the text is melodramatic, to an extent two-dimensional, inexplicit about psychological complexity. We might want to say that it is Gothic, and indeed it is within the Gothic canon that it has most usually been treated; but it is an unusual, if not unique, kind of Gothic, dealing not in antiquity, the remnants of the feudal and other motifs emblematic of the 'original Gothic', but rather in contemporary fears and anxieties. We might want to consider it as a horror story, and to do that would immediately be to place it within a small, ill-regarded subgenre, characterized by instant shock and thrill rather than by any deeper engagement with the human plight.

Aldiss's *Frankenstein Unbound* has probably become the best known of the modern novelistic remakes, and it is typically generically uncertain. The plot hangs on one of the most unlikely of devices – Aldiss is, after all, best known as a writer of science fiction – a 'timeslip' whereby our hero, Bodenland, finds himself back in the early nineteenth century. While there, he meets Byron as well as Percy and Mary Shelley; perhaps remarkably, he finds himself in a sexual relationship with Mary. But he also meets Victor Frankenstein and the creature, and here is where matters become complicated.

For the essence of Aldiss's book is that Victor and the creature are not figments of Mary Shelley's imagination; rather, they too are on the same plane of reality as the circle of writers whose famous – or infamous – gathering at the Villa Diodati was supposedly responsible for their 'creation'. And matters go far further than this, because the question of the origin of the 'timeslips' which are threatening humanity in the year 2020 (which is the 'original' setting for the book) appears to take us back to Mary Shelley herself; by either inventing or recounting the tale of *Frankenstein*, it may be that she has herself effected an intrusion into the chronological ordering of the universe. Is the construction of the pseudo-myth of Victor and the creature an event of such proportions that it cannot be contained within linear time as we experience it?

In the service of these kinds of question, the original novel is, as it would need to be, substantially rewritten: perhaps most startlingly of all, the decision of Victor in the Mary Shelley novel not to create a mate for the creature, on the grounds that it would risk producing a race of monstrous beings, is here reversed, and a female creature is indeed made. Not only that, but they do indeed proceed to mate, although there is a complication: the female creature has the face of Justine:

> When she came very near, I had a clear view of her face, turned brightly to the moonlight. There I read conflicting things. It was the intent face of female in rut – yet it was also the face of Justine, impersonal with death. If anything, *his* face was even more horrific, lacking as it did all but a travesty of humanity; despite his animation, it still most resembled a helmet, a metal helmet with visor down, roughly shaped to conform to the outlines of a human face. The helmet had a tight slit across it, representing a smile.[1]

The panoply of images here is worthy of attention: the female has a 'human' face, yet it is in one crucial sense *not* human, for it is the face of a dead woman – dead, indeed, by Victor's own fault. The male does not have such a face – indeed, in a sense he does not have a face at all, but rather the 'representation' of a face – here the inhumanity of the creatures is starkly represented. Yet although the creatures are not human, they act in what we might, with some stretch of the imagination, claim to be a 'natural' way. Victor, by contrast, is clearly deranged: here is part of his speech to Bodenland, his last before Bodenland shoots him:

> '... no purpose in life on this globe – only the endless begetting and dying, too monstrous to be called Purpose – just a phantasmagoria of flesh and flesh remade, of vegetation intervening – humans are just turnips, ploughed back at the end of the winter – the soil, the air, that linkage – like Shelley's west wind – the leaves could be us – you know, you understand me, Bodenland,

"like ghosts from an enchanter fleeing, yellow and black and pale and hectic red, pestilence-stricken multitudes...". Did you ever think it might be life that was the pestilence, the accident of consciousness between the eternal chemistry working in the veins of earth and air?... we have to be above the old considerations, be ruthless, as ruthless as the natural processes governing us.'
(p. 138)

Yet if this is madness, then it is a madness, as the text suggests here, which is fully rooted in a 'romantic' view of nature and the universe; and this is typical of the book, which is replete with quotations and half-quotations from not only Mary Shelley herself but also the other major Romantic writers. And the acts of 'impersonation' which form a large part of the text go further than that. Much of the original *Frankenstein* is, after all, a tale of flight and pursuit; so is much of *Frankenstein Unbound*, but here most of the chase involves Victor and Bodenland. Moreover, as Bodenland pursues Victor across the timeslipped landscape, many of his reflections are in fact virtually identical to Victor's own reflections in the original novel; just as in Mary Shelley's work, we are constantly having to negotiate perspectival shifts between Victor and the creature, so here too we are immersed in a clash of thoughts and voices, but this time between two human figures, while the creature itself – which is, admittedly, the ultimate object of the chase – remains an indistinct figure, physically and psychologically, until near the end.

So *Frankenstein Unbound* is predominantly a work of intertextuality, almost a compendium of *Frankenstein*, and Mary Shelley-related phrasings and motifs. There are aspects to the novel's scenario which are just plain silly: for example, when Bodenland returns to the early nineteenth century, he does so in a car with a swivel-gun mounted on top, which is apparently standard hardware in the year 2020; throughout his adventures and emergencies, he always manages to hide this car in the unlikeliest of ways. But there is no denying the power of the climactic final episode, with its reminiscences of Mary Shelley's *The Last Man* (1826). Now pursuing the creature, our hero comes to a 'great plateau', with on it a 'mighty building':

From where I stood, it was hard to grasp the size of that distant structure. It appeared to be round and to consist of little more than an immense outer wall. It was certainly inhabited. From within the walls came a glow of light – almost an atmosphere of light, reddish in colour, and punctuated by intenser beams of brightness moving within the central cloud... My speculation was that this was the last refuge of humanity. The place was so remote that I could only believe the timeslips to have delivered me at a point many centuries – maybe many thousands or even millions of centuries – into futurity. So that I might be witnessing the last outpost of mankind after the sun had died. (pp. 152–3)

There are shadows of Olaf Stapledon and William Hope Hodgson here, as well as a host of unanswered questions: has Bodenland indeed been travelling through time as much as through space?[2] Is this vision of a red city not at least partly a quasi-medieval vision of hell? And these questions are mythically and theologically informed ones, reminding us of the potential consequences of human transgression in the realms of the gods.

Dean Koontz's *Frankenstein* series also contains questions, but they are for the most part of a more mundane, or at least customary, kind. Set in contemporary New Orleans, the long and complicated plot centres on two figures, Victor Helios and Deucalion. Helios is in fact our old friend Victor, who has turned his scientific prowess to prolonging his own survival, thus re-enshrining the old Romantic and Gothic theme of eternal life. Deucalion is the new name for the creature – mythologically Deucalion was Prometheus's son, as he was also responsible for the rebirth of mankind after the great flood. But what has happened over the intervening centuries is that Helios/Frankenstein has grown increasingly cruel in his search for the creation of a New Race, while Deucalion has learned much from his past misfortunes (including the loss of half of his face in a previous act of rebellion against his maker) and now occupies what we might refer to as the moral high ground as he seeks to resist Helios's attempts to replace the human race with another species, created by himself, who will have none of humanity's 'flaws' of sympathy, fellow-feeling and pity.

But the genre-crossing here occurs in relation to detective fiction, or even 'police procedural', since Deucalion is assisted, with varying degrees of success, by two members of the police, Carson O'Connor and Michael Maddison. It is also, as it were, internally crossed with another Gothic staple, also subject to numerous rewritings, namely *Dracula* (1897) – one of Helios's creations, who has been 'planted' in the police force, rejoices in the name Jonathan Harker, and has turned into a murderer. Further complications, including a man called Pribeaux who kills for the sake of body parts in the continuing effort to build himself a supremely beautiful woman to match his own narcissistic pride in his physique, are added as the series of novels proceeds; but here, for the sake of brevity, I want to focus on the first of the series, *Prodigal Son*.

Here the emphasis is very much on Helios's programme for replacing the human race with a race of super-beings, and on the difficulties he encounters while pursuing this path. For example, he is continually creating for himself the perfect wife, yet this perfection rapidly crumbles and he is forced to replace the existing model with a later one – Erika Four thus succumbs to supersession by Erika Five. The theme of overweening ambition is thus at the very heart of things; and Helios has had the good sense to implant his creations with a ban which precludes them from destroying him or themselves.

The intertextual references multiply. Deucalion, for example, who is in hiding because of his grotesque physical appearance, appears to live largely in a partly disused movie theatre, accompanied by an obese figure, known to him from his earlier years in a freak show, who is referred to by one of the detectives as bearing an uncanny resemblance to Sydney Greenstreet in *Casablanca* (1942). The decaying movie theatre itself prompts the detectives into reflections on *The Phantom of the Opera* (1910). Similarly, the longevity of his principal characters gives Koontz the opportunity to muse on a long swathe of history. Here, for example, is Helios settling down to a quiet evening of reading:

> Outside, the night was hot and humid. In Victor Helios's library, the air-conditioning chilled to the extent that a cheerful blaze in the fireplace was necessary.
>
> Fire featured in some of his less pleasant memories. The great windmill. The bombing of Dresden. The Israeli Mossad attack on the secret Venezuelan research complex that he had shared with Mengele after World War II. Nevertheless he liked to read to the accompaniment of a cosy crackling fire.
>
> When, as now, he was perusing medical journals like *The Lancet*, *JAMA*, and *Emerging Infectious Diseases*, the fire served not merely as ambience but as an expression of his informed scientific opinion. He frequently tore articles from the magazines and tossed them into the flames. Occasionally, be burned entire issues.[3]

What may be of most interest here is not the crossover with detective fiction but the relation to what one might fairly call 'conspiracy fiction', from Donna Tartt to Dan Brown, wherein the whole of human history can be subjected to a radically revisionary explanation.[4] What we are customarily told, according to this view, is but a distortion of how human affairs have really been governed and affected, whether it be by the Knights Templar, the Rosicrucians or the Illuminati. And it is indeed true that the late eighteenth and early nineteenth centuries – the period when Mary Shelley and the Romantics were writing – were a hotbed of such conspiracies. But it is also true, as the success of contemporary novels attests, that we are now again in a historical period when conspiracies appear to be all around us, as we might see from the multiple explanations continuing to be advanced for the deaths of the Kennedys, Elvis Presley and Princess Diana, to take but three examples.

So here the 'plot of history', in at least two senses, is the work of Victor Helios, albeit in association with others; and this plot continues, in the form of what we might otherwise term 'replicants' – the catalogue of equivalents is vast; the Stepford Wives would be but one example.⁵ If we think back to Mary Shelley's *Frankenstein*, then we might detect a historical shift here: whereas the original creature was distinguished by his inability to hide his appearance, and indeed his fate can be said to have been due to his perceived ugliness at least as much as to any moral failing, then the scenario in *Prodigal Son* is largely about deception and disappearance; the ease with which individuals can be replaced by their apparent equivalents, which in turn suggests another generic crossover, this time with the spy thriller, which constantly entertains the possibility of 'deep cover', the notion that it is possible to live a life of pretence, awaiting only the call from one's masters to do their bidding and thereby accomplish one's destiny.

Whether this cultural 'spy narrative' has any truth behind it or not is not my concern here; suffice to say that there is not – and cannot be – any specific evidence to demonstrate the case one way or the other; all spy trials, some would say, are rigged. My point is rather that here in *Prodigal Son*, and the rest of the series, *Frankenstein* has become adapted for our times. The two detectives, to take yet another example of cross-generic mutation, have much in common with the wise-cracking doublings of endless US detective dramas – while, of course, they also serve to ground the reader in the commonplaces of everyday life even when confronted, as these detectives frequently are, with what seem to be irrefutable manifestations of an inexplicable supernatural.

And thus we might move towards the uncanny, in terms of the relations between the familiar and the unfamiliar, of readerly positions and how those are arranged in relation to the ever-changing characters within the apparently unitary text which is Mary Shelley's *Frankenstein*. For perhaps this is the major point: that Mary Shelley's book has now mutated into something which is no longer a book, a single text, but which is instead a *world*. We are familiar with this world, or at least with versions of it – many of them filmic and with only a tangential relation to the original novel itself – and therefore within it we can, as writers as well as readers, allow ourselves permission to roam. Aldiss, for example, moves the 'frozen wastes' of Walton's expedition to a timeslipped Geneva; Koontz transposes geography with barely a word of explanation. Susan O'Keefe, in the unpromisingly titled *Frankenstein's Monster*, also takes permission to roam; but she does it in an extremely interesting way, which seems to me to deepen the impact of the original text as well as supplying a range of new readings.

Frankenstein's Monster is written almost entirely from the perspective of the creature. Victor himself has died; but the creature finds himself the object of a more or less crazed pursuit by Walton, who has taken up Victor's cause with, as it were, a vengeance. The reasons for this seem initially not entirely clear: Walton has certainly pledged himself to avenge the death of his friend, but the depth of his attachment to Victor's memory seems largely inexplicable, although this does lay bare one of the prime concerns behind Mary Shelley's original novel and behind many of the remakes, namely scenarios of attachment and loss.

For just as Victor and the creature may be seen, from the very beginning, as engaged in an unending rehearsal of thwarted parent/child relationships, here the broken attachments seem to be felt most strongly by Walton, the loner who, unable to entertain ideas of attachment outside his obsession with pursuing and destroying the creature, turns in on himself and converts his love for Victor – itself a peculiar and no doubt 'transferred' love – into hatred of the creature. Similarly, the creature himself is in search of attachment. He finds it twice, first in the form of a young woman called Mirabella, but Walton appears and the inevitable occurs:

> I stood. The captain's mouth gaped with astonishment. From the side a soldier grabbed Mirabella and pulled her away. She struggled, striking his face, trying to twist loose.
>
> And in a single dreadful moment: Mirabella's frantic movements distracted the captain. He turned toward her. She jerked free from the soldier and ran back to me for protection. Walton shook off his trance, seized the pistol from the captain, aimed at me, fired, and –
>
> Mirabella fell dead within the circle of my arms.[6]

Once again – as so often – the creature has been the unintended agent of the destruction of someone he loves, and who has seemed capable of loving him despite his appearance:

> As I write these words, faces flash before my mind's eye: Frankenstein's brother, his friend, his bride, he himself worn to fatal sickness, tracking me down; the nameless who, like the Austrian soldiers, unwittingly placed themselves in the path of my rage; even the myriad bodies that comprise my parts. All of these clamour in noisy accusation: *You are death.*
>
> And now Mirabella. I am bruised and beaten, but it is her blood that stains my hands. (p. 53)

The important connection here is between the 'deaths' that *comprise* the creature – the deaths which have preceded him, but which have been essential to the very composition of his charnel-house body – and the deaths which he is doomed to re-enact. The creature is, in John Donne's words, 'every dead thing', and thus it is inevitable that he spreads death around him.[7]

But this may, of course, be a metaphor for an apparently quite different scenario, namely that which runs through *Frankenstein* like a seeping vein, namely the rejections and struggles of adolescence. On this reading, we would want to say that as soon as a possible partner for the creature appears, the forbidding dictate of the father steps in; you are not allowed, says the Voice of the Father, to grow up, you are not allowed to leave your subaltern position; and if you try, then the punishment – by the father himself, by the whole of a superegoic society which the father represents – will be terrible; you will have visited upon you the wrath of God, and the punishment will be all the more severe – as in the past it has been for Victor – because it will actually be upon your nearest that the punishment will be visited, while you will walk free, but in the knowledge that it is you who have (again) caused death.

The creature's second relationship, however, is altogether more complex, and it is with Lily, who is, apparently, Walton's niece. This relationship is a masterpiece of subtlety: sometimes Lily appears to wish to be with the creature; sometimes she manifests a venomous hatred towards him; sometimes she leads him on sexually; at other times she professes herself repulsed by him. She herself is a mystery, although some aspects of this mystery are clarified as the novel progresses: she *needs* her frantic 'escape' with the creature, the endless journeying, the return to the Orkneys, because she herself is fleeing the wrath of her father – the inexplicable bloating sickness from which she suffers, and in which the creature sorrowfully believes, turns out to be pregnancy, and one to which she cannot own to her own family. Furthermore, however, it is revealed in the end that she is not even the daughter of this supposed father, Winterbourne, but rather Walton's own daughter: and thus the ties of family love and hatred are knotted even more ferociously together.

And they are knotted together in another way, for throughout the novel there is a theme of madness – of a very human madness, quite aside from the creature: Walton is clearly deranged, and it becomes clear that Lily has inherited this insanity, first manifested in the multiple partners whom she takes and which makes it impossible for her or anybody else to know the identity of the father of the baby who is born at the end of the book, and second in her wild, ever-changing attitudes towards the creature, who appears to her to be at once her saviour and her doom.

In a sense, then, this is the drama, like so many others, of a woman driven mad by repressive social attitudes; but this theme in turn loops back to another perennial Frankensteinian theme, perhaps expressed most fully when the creature, rejected yet again by Lily, howls his rage and sinks deeper into the animality which, he fears, is his true status:

> I was not a man? I was not a monster? At best I was an animal? Then I would be one fully; she would not take that little from me: I would glory in it. Piece by piece I shed my clothes, that poor disguise of humanity that I had worn always in vain; piece by piece I shed the mask till I ran naked. In the thick underbrush, stickers and branches made a gauntlet that would flay me of this skin, stolen from men to hide the beast beneath. I ran mile after mile, deeper and deeper into the woods, until, at last, they claimed me for their own, and I was no longer not a man, no longer not a monster; I became in my mind an animal in truth, a wondrous, undiscovered species.   (p. 210)

The ending of the novel provides a fit translation of the creature's exile, and at the same time a kind of salvation: finding himself amid a landscape of coalmines and collieries, where endless fires burn, an explosion enables him to exert his peculiar strengths and thus at last to become welcomed as a saviour of life rather than as a destroyer of it. Even there, Walton finds him; but it is a monstrous Walton, himself destroyed from within by his unassuageable lust for vengeance, and in the end it is this implacable fixation which finishes him, while the creature's ability to see more clearly the world outside his own narcissistic concerns – even if that entails recognition of the 'animal' part of himself – allows him to enter into a new kind of life.

O'Keefe's book is sensitive, subtle, intriguing and successful in providing the creature with a substantially new voice. Michael Bunker's *Brother, Frankenstein* is a very different matter, and does not deal in the original novel's characters at all, except elliptically, metaphorically. Instead, the plot concerns a doctor and scientist called Chris. As a doctor, Chris is trying to help a young Amish boy, Frank Miller, who is autistic – interestingly, a theme also picked up by Koontz – and also suffers from numerous physical disabilities. As a scientist, Chris is involved in a programme, originally funded by DARPA, to develop an ultimate weapon in the shape of a 'transformed' – and the old children's toys, Transformers, are very much to the forefront here – human body which will carry world-annihilating weaponry and be more or less impervious to attack.

Chris conceives of the idea of saving Frank's life by implanting his vital organs, including his brain, into a prototype version of this weaponized android; since this act is not sanctioned by his military bosses, he is then forced to go on the run with Frank, all the time terrified that Frank might undergo 'the change' at any moment when he feels under threat – moments which, because of his continuing autism, are not easy to predict. In this flight he is assisted by a secretive team of anti-government computer hackers; he is opposed by a pursuer figure, Dresser, who partially takes the place of Victor in the original novel and of Walton in O'Keefe, but with the added dimension of being a single-minded, supremely violent agent of the State.

Within this scenario, there is an embedding of the by now familiar set of arguments as to who is the monster – is it Frank, who is physically only arguably human; or is it Chris, who has performed a truly monstrous experiment and now finds himself taken over by the need to contain the resultant fallout? 'I ask myself – or God', says Chris at one point, when Frank has become disguised as Ben and 'hidden' within an Amish community where he can feel more or less at home,

> what is it is to be human. What is it, I ask, that makes us worthy of life?
>
> In every way that I can think of, Ben is human. Maybe he's even more human than I am. So my thoughts dwell on that for a while. Then I ask myself: 'Can I kill a man?' A boy. Can I do that?
>
> I suppose I can. I'm about as bad as a man can be. I mean, there have been serial killers and Hitler and all those epic tyrants, but in the end what did they really do? Didn't they take life into their own hands? Didn't they play God? Isn't that what I've been doing all along?[8]

Due to the nature of Frank/Ben's techno-construction, Chris holds the power of life and death over him. Frank is, in a very material sense, Chris's creation; yet within the walking super-weapon, there remains the human Frank, and to terminate the destructive power of the weapon, to prevent it from becoming 'unbound', would entail ending what is left of Frank's life, and also going against the love which burgeons and endures between them.

Man and machine, human and robot, the power to create and the feelings entailed in continuing to feel responsible for one's creation, one's creature, all of these motifs are at play in *Brother, Frankenstein*, and there are numerous other minor allusions to Mary Shelley's text and its earlier remakes; in order to calm himself through deeply autistic episodes of 'stimming', for example, Frank initially relies on gripping two bolts, just like, Chris muses, the bolt through the creature's neck in the Boris Karloff version of *Frankenstein* (1931).

An added dimension is supplied by the Amish setting, in terms both of Frank's original background and of the place where Chris hopes he can find some kind of peace. For the Amish represent, both here and in other of Bunker's work (for Bunker is of the 'plain people' himself), an alternative to technological striving, a way of life that relies on community and tradition rather than on the manic individualism associated with the mad scientist, a location where there are no monsters but where everybody can be accepted according to their gifts and their work. Ben is dubious about this:

> 'But I'm a monster', Ben said.
> 'I don't care if you're a monster. I still love you . . . Frank'.
> I called him Frank, because that's who he really is.
> Now, out here on this beautiful night, bathed in the scents and
>   fragrance of the farm,
> I know the truth.
> I'm the monster. Not Frank. *I'm* the monster.
> And I begin to cry.   (p. 251)

Brother, Frankenstein is a strange piece of work, Mary Shelley's *Franken-stein*, perhaps, crossed with *RoboCop* (1987), and behind it all a sentimental longing for a peaceful life which can be lived independently of striving, and thus away from the possibilities opened up by potentially transgressive knowledge. There is flight and pursuit here, just as there is throughout the whole corpus of *Frankenstein*-based texts, but it is not a simple dialectic between creator and created, rather it is a double flight, as in so many buddy movies, of an ill-assorted pair of people mutually dependent on each other from pursuit by a supposedly all-powerful State.

The lines of flight, then, to put it in the terms of Gilles Deleuze and Félix Guattari, are *different*; but so too are the attachments being proposed.[9] Frank is not Chris's son, any more than a father/son relationship would be strictly true of any other version of *Frankenstein*; but nevertheless questions of attachment and responsibility, beneath the patina of techno-jargon, are at the heart of the novel. It is significant that Chris is both a doctor and a scientist: he works as a doctor to help and prolong human life, but as a scientist his principal work is the development of machinery and weapons to end that life. Where do the boundaries lie? Is there any such thing as 'pure research'? Or indeed, to put it more simply and yet at the same time more devastatingly, can *any* research be done which will not in the end – if only because of funding sources – serve to entrench and prolong the power of the State?

In the end, it is difficult to know what happens, or has happened, to Frank:

> Frank doesn't speak.
>   At least for now he doesn't. He just rides along in silence and does what I say. He stims now and then, but his bolts are gone and he shows every sign that he's retreated back into the shell of autism. Back where I found him. Or maybe he's just hiding out, unwilling to deal with man's inhumanity to man. No outbursts or changing now, but he's lost something he'd

had there for a while. That spark of hope that maybe the world is worth experiencing. (p. 326)

To move towards a conclusion: it is increasingly frequently being perceived that manifestations of mental illness or disability should not be seen merely as themselves but rather as a series of protections against fear, perhaps the greatest fear of all, which is of the disintegration of the self; this certainly seems to be proposed in *Brother, Frankenstein*, but it is at least arguable that this fear is integral to the whole body of Frankenstein works from Mary Shelley onwards. Victor, after all, forms his own scientist-self around the dissolution of family ties, attachments, relationships: he forms a 'substitute-self' impervious to affection and feelings, and it is at least arguable that the creature is, at least to begin with, an externalization of that separateness, the loneliness which is the inevitable effect of cutting oneself off from human community.

And so, on this reading, the quasi-myth would not merely be about the perils of science and technology; rather, it would be about what the lust for knowledge – through scientific, alchemical, magical or any other means – represents or conceals, as it becomes a carapace over a lonely, suffering self which has given up on familial or social attachment. If this is the case, then it would go a long way towards explaining the continuing fascination with the Frankenstein scenario, for it would be emblematic of the very essence of post-industrial modernity.

The aim of the modern, if we put it in very abstract terms, is to form an alternative: a cleaner, more enlightened, better organized alternative to the messy, shadowed structures of what is taken to be 'traditional society'.[10] But there is a price to be paid, and it is a price which Victor and his many avatars are charged with paying: namely, the return of all that threatens high-level social organization – as it threatens the most basic of 'civilized' organizational structures, as Victor discovers on his wedding night. It is possible, of course, that the West is now engaged in a process of moving beyond 'modernity', as generally conceived, into a cultural condition where randomness, the continual presence of chaos, instabilities of mapping – whether it be of the universe, the planet or the atom – are more accepted: this, at least, would be the hope and trajectory of the postmodern.

But there remains that which haunts these projections into the future, and it could be said that one of these sites of haunting is the human body itself. That body can be changed, it can be subjected to all manner of prosthesis, extension, invasion, and it may well be that in the end, as various lines of argument have it, we are all in the act of becoming cyborgs; but while that transformation is incomplete, we still have to confront the fruits – and indeed the by-products – of our labour, creatures which are not fully created, humans who suspect that they are not fully human, monsters who are even capable of entertaining doubts as to their own monstrosity; and it seems as though, while we are engaging in that confrontation, that process of endless flight and pursuit, the figures of Victor Frankenstein and his creature will remain and continue to develop in our imaginations.

NOTES

1 Brian Aldiss, *Frankenstein Unbound* (London: Jonathan Cape, 1973), p. 134. Future references will be made parenthetically.
2 See Olaf Stapledon, *Last and First Men* (London: Methuen, 1930) and William Hope Hodgson, *The Night Land* (London: Eveleigh Nash, 1912).
3 Dean Koontz, *Prodigal Son* (London: Bantam, 2005), p. 62.
4 See, for example, Donna Tartt, *The Secret History* (New York: Knopf, 1992) and Dan Brown, *The Da Vinci Code* (New York: Doubleday, 2003).
5 Ira Levin, *The Stepford Wives* (New York: Random House, 1972).
6 Susan Heyboer O'Keefe, *Frankenstein's Monster: A Novel* (New York, 2010), p. 52. Future references will be made parenthetically.
7 See Donne, 'A Nocturnal upon St Lucy's Day, being the shortest day', in *John Donne*, ed. John Carey (Oxford University Press, 1990), p. 116.
8 Michael Bunker, *Brother, Frankenstein: A Novel* (Santa Anna, TX: Createspace, 2015), pp. 250–1. Future references will be made parenthetically.
9 See Gilles Deleuze and Félix Guattari, *A Thousand Plateaus: Capitalism and Schizophrenia* [1980] (Minneapolis, MN: University of Minnesota Press, 1987).
10 See my *Modernity* (Basingstoke: Palgrave Macmillan, 2007).

15

CHRISTOPHER MURRAY

Frankenstein in Comics and Graphic Novels

Frankenstein, or The Modern Prometheus (1818) has long inspired adaptations in other mediums. While much is known about the theatrical and cinematic versions of the story, much less has been written on the very diverse adaptations of the novel that have appeared in the medium of comics. This chapter will consider a number of versions of the Frankenstein story in comics and graphic novels from the 1940s to the present. There are so many examples that it is impossible to be comprehensive, but several will be discussed in detail.

Whale and Ward

One of the most influential and enduring versions of the story came in the form of James Whale's 1931 film produced by Universal Pictures, and its 1935 sequel, *The Bride of Frankenstein*. These have had a huge effect on how the story and the creature have been represented subsequently, and this is particularly true for comics. Karloff's creature has become iconic, but has proved to be a rich source of parody, especially in comics. It is also quite different from the creature encountered in the book, as seen in the frontispiece for the 1831 edition. In his illustrations for the 1934 edition of *Frankenstein* American artist Lynd Ward also takes a markedly different approach from that of Whale and Karloff. Published between the making of Whale's two films Ward's illustrations offer an image of the creature which is much closer to Mary Shelley's intentions. While not exactly a comic or graphic novel, Ward is well known for his wordless picture books which use some of the formal language of comics. His stark imagery draws on a much earlier German woodcut tradition, from the Renaissance woodcuts of Albrecht Dürer to the late nineteenth and early twentieth century Expressionist revival of woodcuts, which echoes the influence of German Expressionist film on Whale. Ward's work also contains allusions to the Romantic literary movement Mary Shelley was associated with, such as the image of the creature observing its reflection in a pond, which is reminiscent of William Blake's *The Ancient of Days* (1794), and another recalls *Nebuchadnezzar* (1795). These influences combine with Ward's surrealism, modernism and Art Deco styling, evoking several artistic and intellectual traditions. Ward was also highly influenced by the Belgian artist Franz Masereel and the German Otto Nückel, who were pioneers in the use of wordless sequential narratives in the woodcut style, and who would, like Ward, have a considerable influence on later generations of comics artists. Indeed, their wordless books are in many ways precursors to the modern graphic novel, however, Ward's illustrations for *Frankenstein* were designed to complement the novel, not to tell the whole story themselves, so they do not constitute a proto graphic novel, although his striking and surreal images left an impression on some later graphic adaptations of the story. Despite this, the early versions of *Frankenstein* in comics were largely influenced by Whale's vision and Boris Karloff's performance, rather than Ward's imagery. For this reason most of the representations of the creature in comics have followed Karloff's lumbering, inarticulate beast, rather than the tortured being written by Shelley and visualized by Ward.

The New Adventures of Frankenstein

The first appearance of Frankenstein's monster in comics was perhaps in an eight-page story in *Movie Comics* #1 (National Periodicals), which was published in April 1939 and was designed to tie into the release of the film *Son of Frankenstein*, which was a sequel to *Frankenstein* and *Bride of Frankenstein*, again starring Karloff but not directed by Whale. The *Movie Comics* story was an adaptation of the film, using an uneasy mixture of film stills and artwork, and perhaps for this reason has been largely forgotten. The earliest Frankenstein comics to make any impact came the following year, with Dick Briefer's series 'The New Adventures of Frankenstein' in *Prize Comics* #7 (Crestwood Publications, December 1940), which was the first of his many versions of the creature. *Prize Comics* 'Frankenstein' was an anthology which also had superhero and adventure stories, and Briefer's 'Frankenstein' may have been the first horror story in American comics. Briefer used the pseudonym 'Frank N. Stein' and it is stated that these stories were 'suggested by the classic of Mary W. Shelley'. Frankenstein's creature is here presented as a horrific lumbering monster with prominent scars over its face and body. Its skin is chalk white, which makes the red scars stand out all the more, and its visage is horrific, with drooping eyes, no nose, a torn lip and jagged teeth. While the creature is reminiscent of Karloff's it was much more horrific in its appearance. It is also referred to as 'Frankenstein' and the story is transposed to New York in the 1930s, where the creature is pursued by Denny 'Bulldog' Dunsan, a relative of Victor Frankenstein. In later stories the creature would fight the numerous other characters who appeared in *Prize Comics*, including its superheroes The Green Lama and The Black Owl, but, despite being an antagonist, the creature also became involved in the war effort, and in several stories battles the Nazis (as was common in comics of the time).

The rise of horror tropes and characters in comics in the 1940s may have been related to the fact that there was an effective ban on horror films during the war. The hugely popular horror films of the 1930s were displaced by uplifting or informative propaganda films. Horror was thought to be counterproductive to those efforts, but comics received less scrutiny than other media, like film, so the appetite for horror was satisfied by comics.[1] In the post-war years Briefer's Frankenstein character started to change, and in time an altogether different character and approach would emerge, along with a shift in genre, as Briefer's character became a humorous one, but there were also other versions of the story appearing in the 1940s, and some attempted more direct adaptations of the source material.

Classic Comics – Adapting the Novel

Although there were individual horror stories in the early 1940s, like Briefer's series in *Prize Comics*, and stories with an overtly horrific tone, like *Captain America*, the horror genre in American comics was not firmly established until August 1943 with the publication of *Classic Comics* #13 by Gilberton Publications. This featured a full issue adaptation of Robert Louis Stevenson's *The Strange Case of Dr Jekyll and Mr Hyde*, and is probably the first dedicated American horror comic. Two years later Frankenstein appeared in *Classic Comics* #26 (December 1945), also by Gilberton Publications. This story was later reissued under Gilberton's more famous title, *Classics Illustrated*, following the launch of that series in 1947. This comic, written by Ruth A. Roche, with artwork by Robert Hayward Webb and inks by Ann Brewster, is remarkable for several reasons. On the surface this comic draws on the popular image of the creature established by Whale and Karloff, but the actual story is quite different and the comic was created by a largely female creative team, with a female writer and inker. This was unusual for the time. There were relatively few female writers in American comics in the 1940s, but Roche was a notable exception, working as an editor and writer at the famous Eisner-Iger studio, and indeed, being a business partner of Jerry Iger, who ran the studio. It is not known why Roche undertook this particular adaptation, but it is noteworthy that at the time she wrote this Roche would have been just a few years older than Mary Shelley when she created the modern horror and science-fiction genres. Perhaps Roche felt some connection to Shelley, being one of the few women writers in comics, but it is just as likely that the reason she undertook the adaptation was that she was one of the best and most respected writers at Gilberton and this was a prize assignment.

The *Classic Comics* version, in keeping with most adaptations of the novel, took some liberties with the book (removing Walton's frame narration, for example), but in large part Roche's script is very faithful to the novel. Indeed, Roche's work for Gilberton was praised for raising the standard considerably. As William B. Jones notes in *Classics Illustrated: A Cultural History* (2011):

> The young writer displayed a command of narrative pacing in her scripts for *Classic Comics* and a willingness to trust the authors whose work she adapted. Fewer liberties would be taken with the originals on Roche's watch, and the textual matter would assume increasing importance during the Iger years, as the educational role of *Classics Illustrated* grew more prominent.[2]

Jones also notes that 'Roche's adaptation of Mary Shelley's gothic parable remained one of Gilberton's most popular titles, going through nineteen printings between 1945 and 1971', and that 'comics authority Mike Benton lauded the *Classic Comics* edition of *Frankenstein* as "probably the most faithful adaptation of the original novel – movies included"'.[3]

Roche, Webb and Brewster's adaptation is interesting for more reasons than its relative fidelity to Shelley's novel. The script by Roche and the artwork by Webb and Brewster combine to provide some surreal moments. The pages in which the monster is created adopt none of the spectacle of Whale's film, but rather allude to it with lightning being seen through a window, almost touching the creature. Some of the surrealism of Ward's illustrations is in evidence, but the creature is also certainly meant to evoke Karloff. Here the creature is coloured grey, perhaps to differentiate it from the Universal Studio's version (which readers would have known was green from posters and magazines), but the effect is to make him more closely resemble Karloff's creature, as the film was in black and white. However, as Jones point out, there was another point of similarity between the film and the comic:

> Webb and Brewster, like film director James Whale, got the period wrong, garbing the characters in something like Regency style rather than clothing appropriate to the novel's 18th-century setting. But most film costumers and, for that matter, book illustrators (Lynd Ward is a notable exception) have made that same mistake.[4]

What is perhaps most notable about *Classic Comics* #26 is the ways in which it uses the visual language of comics to great effect, and the aforementioned importance that Roche gives to the 'textual matter'. On the latter point, there are several passages and phrases from the novel that Roche is careful to work into her adaptation, capturing the dynamics of the relationship between Victor Frankenstein and his creature. Particularly effective is the way that she allows the narration to provide insights into the thoughts and motivations of both Frankenstein and the creature. The artwork also evokes aspects of the novel. There is one striking page which shows Frankenstein travelling with his companion Henry Clerval across Europe, from Geneva, to Strasbourg, to Paris, Rotterdam, then England, before making their way to Scotland (Figure 15.1). This page is remarkable for the almost full-page image of the creature, superimposed on the panels, and even cutting across caption boxes. This is suggestive of the fact that the creature is following Victor and Henry on their journey. He is ever-present, but unseen. He is on top of the panels, and in-between them, but the reader can also see through his form and read the panels and text beneath. This ingenious technique represents Victor Frankenstein's psychological state. He is oppressed by constant thoughts of the creature; where it might be, what it might be doing and the rash promise he has made to provide it with a mate, but he cannot share those concerns with his companion. This interplay between how Victor acts on the surface/what the reader is shown and what the reader knows is really consuming him is mirrored in the interplay between the panels and the image of the creature. This captures something of the feeling of Shelley's novel, which is frequently oppressive, and aims to reveal the tortured state of Victor's mind, while also revelling in the details of travel, and Shelley's treatment of time and movement, which can be quite disorienting, like a frenzied travelogue. This page replicates the effects often found in Gothic literature, which comics scholar Julia Round describes in terms of excess, doubling and performativity.[5]

The comics' treatment of death and violence is also quite daring. When Justine, the servant who is wrongly convicted and executed for the murder of Victor's young brother, William, is seen in prison awaiting her fate, the last panel on the page shows her leaning her head back in despair, drawing attention to her long neck. The first panel on the next page shows Justine hanged, the noose tight around that same long neck, and her head pulled back in an echo of the previous panel, this time not in despair but in the aftermath of her violent death. This is a shocking transition, and its sharp movement in time and space serves to stand in for the sharp movement of the execution. Here the comics medium is used to imply an action which goes unseen. Moreover, Justine's hands are tied behind her back and her

Figure 15.1 *Classic Comics* #26 (December 1945), later released as *Classics Illustrated*, written by Ruth A. Roche with artwork by Robert Hayward Webb and Ann Brewster

dress falls off her shoulder, clinging around her body with emphasis upon her breast. The effect is to provide an uneasy parallel between this and the later murder of Elizabeth, who is strangled in her bed on her wedding night. The comic's portrayal of this is unexpectedly brutal. Blood spurts from her mouth as the creature looms over her on the marriage bed, crushing her throat. When Victor discovers her she is lying on the bed, her leg exposed, with blood on the sheets in a visual allusion to the marital deflowering that never occurs, and is instead replaced with murder (with the implication of rape). He then leans over the body in an overly sexual pose. This is much more explicit than Whale would have dared in 1931, or Hollywood could have in 1945, and these effective storytelling devices go some way to demonstrating why this was such a popular and powerful adaptation. This also makes it surprising that the comic ever saw print at all, much less being reprinted through the 1950s, when attacks on the industry as corrupting the nation's youth reached their height.

It may well be because this was an adaptation of a literary text, and therefore more 'worthy' than most other horror comics, the representations of violence and sex were seen as less objectionable. The *Classic Comics* adaptation of *Frankenstein* may look on the surface like a simplified and watered-down version of the novel but the adaptation is very well handled by Roche and the artwork makes inventive use of the medium in such a way as to create a mood of oppression and to suggest extreme violence, which, given the constraints on comics of the time, makes this adaptation all the more remarkable.

Frankenstein Genres

While Dick Briefer's original version of *Frankenstein* was a rampaging monster, over the course of the war years his creature changed. In early 1945, as the end of the war was in sight, he created a humorous version more suited to an optimistic post-war world and aimed at a younger readership, but with social satire that adults could appreciate (Figure 15.2). To make his character friendlier Briefer placed his small button nose at just above eye height to suggest deformity while not making the character too terrifying. The creature had a flat head (recalling Karloff) and an enormous frame, and dressed in blue trousers, a bright yellow top and a huge red jacket. This series ended in 1948 and a third volume was launched in 1952 featuring a return to horror. Unfortunately the timing was poor, as psychiatrist Frederic Wertham's protests against the supposed effects of horror comics on levels of juvenile delinquency soon led to Senate hearings in 1954 and the comics industry would be accused of subverting the nation's youth. To defend itself,

Figure 15.2 Dick Briefer, *Frankenstein* #10 (Prize Comics, 1947)

and perhaps to put a major competitor (EC Comics) out of business, most of the American comics publishers grouped together to form the Comics Code Authority, which oversaw adherence to the Comics Code, which eliminated all references to sex, violence, crime and particularly horror. Moreover, in Britain one of the comics that prompted a similar wave of censorship was a British edition of Briefer's *Frankenstein* #2, which was one of several comics that was put before the Prime Minister, Winston Churchill, attached to a memo that recommended a ban on American horror comics.

With the Comics Code in place and the horror genre effectively banned in both America and Britain, the trend towards humorous versions of horror characters became even more popular. Humorous versions of the creature were seen in comics such as *The Adventures of Jerry Lewis* #83 (DC, August 1964) and *Bob Hope* #95 (DC, November 1965), and there were many films, television shows and comics that successfully mixed the two genres, such as the Abbot and Costello monster films (1948–1951), the Addams family cartoons (1938–1988) and TV series (1964–1966), and *The Munsters* TV series (1964–1966), with its Karloff-inspired Herman as the hapless patriarch. The Munsters also appeared in a comic produced by the publisher Gold Key in 1967, while in Britain they appeared in *TV Century 21* (City Magazines, 1966). The humour comic *Wham!*, published by Odhams Press, introduced their version of the creature, 'Frankie Stein, The Friendly Monster', in the fourth issue (July 1964). This was created by Ken Reid, one of the most gifted humour artists working in British comics at the time.

In some comics the creature made the leap into yet another genre – the superheroes. This was seen in Briefer's humour comics of the 1940s, where the creature became Blooperman, parodying Superman. In the late 1950s and 60s, with the horror genre suppressed, superheroes once again became dominant in American comics, and there were several appearances of the creature in superhero comics. Indeed, one of the most improbable of these was a superhero Frankenstein, who was published for three issues by Dell Comics. This character was an artificial being that had lain dormant in the ruins of a castle (in America) for a century and had been awoken by a bolt of lightning. Calling himself Frank Stone, he used a rubber mask to disguise his green head (the rest of his body being Caucasian), and adopted a costume to fight crime. Other versions of the creature appeared in *Detective Comics* #135 (DC, May 1948), where he met Batman, in *Superman* #143 (DC, February 1961). It is also notable that Frankenstein's creature was one of the inspirations for The Incredible Hulk (Marvel, May 1962), who was an amalgam of the creature, the werewolf, and Jekyll and Hyde. Of course, the latter is the most direct inspiration, but visually the Hulk takes a lot from Karloff's creature in the early issues. Karloff-inspired versions of the creature also appeared in *Tomahawk* #103 (DC, April 1966), and in *X-Men* #40 (Marvel, January 1968).

In the 1970s there was a resurgence of interest in horror comics following a relaxation of the Comics Code, and a revival of horror films. In response Marvel launched new Dracula, Werewolf and Frankenstein comics. *Monster of Frankenstein* (January 1973–September 1975), written by Gary Friedrich with art by Mike Ploog, was reasonably faithful to the original story, and very well executed. The style of the comic was perhaps influenced by Hammer Horror films (as was the prominent scar on the creature's forehead), and the comic came out the same year as Brian Aldiss's novel *Frankenstein Unbound* (1973), and the influence of Aldiss's time travel story could be detected in the fact that once this first story arc was completed there was editorial pressure to bring this version of the creature into the present day. As Ploog recounts, 'they wanted to bring Frankenstein up to the 20th century, and have him battle in the streets of New York with Spider-Man, and I just couldn't do that'.[6] Ploog left, but his replacement, Val Mayerik, was a worthy successor, and drew heavily from the Universal films, but with cancellation the series ended on a cliff-hanger (except for German readers, as the story was continued there for a time because it was so popular). The legacy of this version of the creature was that he received the Marvel treatment, which stressed that characters were not simply good or evil, but tortured and complicated. As Susan Tyler Hitchcock notes in *Frankenstein: A Cultural History* (2007):

> Despite the sensationalistic violence portrayed on every comic-book cover – always perpetrated by the monster – a strong element of compassion towards the creature runs through these Marvel Comics, which often managed to recapture the essential moral ambiguity of Mary Shelley's story. The drama is pitched high, but the moral message resounds. The villains who attack the monster threaten human society as well. The angry monster is a misunderstood victim of circumstances; the vengeful monster acts to re-establish the social order. The common man has more kinship with the monster on both counts than he does with the mad scientist who made him. After decades of being portrayed as the outsider and the other, the enemy and the embodiment of all that is ghastly and inhuman, the monster had become a hero.[7]

Despite cancellation, this version of the creature became a recurring character across several Marvel comics.

In 1975 a book and LP record set was released called 'The Story of Dracula, The Wolfman and Frankenstein', with a story and artwork by Neal Adams and Dick Giordano, who were at that point a highly regarded creative team, having worked together on a very popular and influential run of *Batman*. While clearly intended for young readers, the story seems to have been inspired by the popular Hammer Horror films of the time, and was even reprinted in the British magazine *House of Hammer* #18 (1978). In *Weird War Tales* #93 (November 1980) DC Comics took up the mantle of the creature in comics again, resurrecting him from his earlier appearances in 1948 and 1961 to feature in the line-up of 'Creature Commandos', a team of superhuman monsters working for the government. The creature was by now firmly established as a recurring character across comics issued by many different publishers. He transcended genre and could be a hero or a villain. Rarely has a comics character been so flexible, and shared so widely. However, one of the best versions of the creature published by mainstream comics publisher came not in the form of a comic but in the form of Marvel Comics' illustrated edition of the novel produced in 1983 with artwork by celebrated horror comic artist Bernie Wrightson.

Wrightson's series of fifty illustrations were a labour of love, which he was not paid for, and which he worked on between paying jobs for seven years. Wrightson's illustrations, like Ward's, draw on the woodcut tradition, and the descriptions of the creature given in the novel itself, rather than the influence of the films (or comics). All of Wrightson's considerable expertise in the horror genre is brought to bear to produce one of the definitive representations of the creature. Wrightson makes clear his debt to Ward in several images, some of which mirror Ward's compositions and style. In his illustrations the creature exudes menace, but also a tortured humanity, and Victor Frankenstein's pursuit of scientific discovery, and the melancholy that follows his act of creation, has rarely been captured so well in a visual medium, and within a few years several comics adaptations would refer back to Wrightson.

Frankenstein: The Graphic Novel

Martin Powell and Patrick Olliffe's 1990 adaptation of the novel is one of the best versions in comics, and approaches the story in a similar way to the 1945 *Classic Comics* version. It was published as a three-issue series by Eternity Comics, then later as a graphic novel by Pulp 20 Press in Los Angeles. Powell noted in an interview that as a child he was obsessed with Whale's films and the *Classics Illustrated Frankenstein*.[8] Olliffe's art is rendered in a stark black and white style that recalls the horror comics of the 1970s, as well as influences from Ward and Wrightson. There are some surreal panels that recall Webb and Brewster's art for the *Classics Illustrated* edition, and the same kind of eroticism conjured by that story, but overall the tone and narration of Powell and Olliffe's version is even closer to the original novel than Roche's script, largely because they have much more space to unfold the narrative, with three issues rather than one. As a result the pacing of the story is slower, and much more time is taken to establish mood and develop characters. And being created in 1990, 45 years after the *Classic Comics* edition, they had a lot more freedom in terms of the representation of sex and violence. The frame narration, with the tale being delivered to Walton by the dying Frankenstein, is maintained, and Powell's script manages to capture something of Shelley's style through a skilful and sensitive combination of paraphrase and quotation from the novel. However, the pages dealing with the creation of the monster draw on the Whale films, with elaborate technology harnessing electricity to galvanize the creature. The artwork also does a good job of representing the dualism inherent in the story, especially with its shifts in perspective and point of view.

While the *Classic Comics* version is clearly an influence, the handling of key sequences is quite different. The panels that deal with Justine's execution keep the innocent maid at a distance, heightening the sense of Victor's helplessness, and once she is dead three almost identical panels, each split by the taut rope, show the top of Justine's head covered by a sack. The first panel shows the crowd staring at the lifeless girl, with Victor among them. He does not move over the next two panels, but the onlookers slowly drift away, leaving Victor alone with her in the final panel. The 'silence' is broken by a caption expressing Victor's thoughts – "'I had failed them all'" (Figure 15.3). This breaks the carefully maintained spatial and temporal positioning of Victor in this tragic moment, reminding the reader that this is all a memory, conjured by Victor for Walton much later, and written down in letters for Walton's sister, in a ship trapped in ice in the Arctic. The effect is one that occurs throughout the comic, and which is executed with great skill by Powell and Olliffe, who also use this technique to reflect the epistolary nature of the novel. The shifts in narrative voice are subtle. For the first ten pages the narration is immediate and in the first person, giving insight into Victor's thoughts as he pursues the creature and is nearly killed in the attempt. This is not in the novel, but it does serve as an introduction to Victor's quest and his desire for revenge. This narration, being 'of the moment', rather than a testimony taken down by Walton, is not presented in inverted commas like the rest of the narration. In the last pages, once Victor is dead, the narration is suspended as the story returns to the 'present', and the creature and Walton converse. Finally, on the last page, the narration returns, and again in inverted commas, reminding the reader that these are Walton's words, recorded in his letter to his sister. The final panel offers an almost direct quotation of the last sentence from the novel, concluding the story with the same sense of melancholy and despair that Shelley achieves, with the creature

Figure 15.3 Martin Powell and Patrick Olliffe's *Frankenstein: The Graphic Novel* (1990)

consumed by the enormity of the stark natural environment of the Artic, as Walton's ship bears Victor's body, and his confession, away. Of all the comic adaptations of *Frankenstein*, this is the one that best communicates the themes and pathos of Shelley's work, while also finding medium-specific equivalents to the mode and techniques employed by Shelley, and Gothic literature more generally. This is something that this comic shares in common with the *Classic Comics* version, but this comes closer to the tone and imagery created by the novel.

Over the next few years several more *Frankenstein* comics would appear. This was partly driven by the attention brought by the 1994 film directed by Kenneth Branagh and starring Branagh as Frankenstein and Robert DeNiro as the creature. This film attempted to offer the most faithful cinematic adaptation yet seen, although there are significant divergences from the source material, including the use of Justine's body to create the creature's proposed mate, and the re-animation of Elizabeth. To tie into the film, Topps Comics released a four-part adaptation written by Roy Thomas with art by Rafael Kayanan. Topps followed this with another series, also written by Thomas, *The Frankenstein/Dracula War* (February 1995), with artwork by Claude St. Aubin. Despite Thomas's long experience with horror comics, the best thing about these comics are the covers. The film adaptation has covers by John Bolton, and the covers for *The Frankenstein/Dracula War* were provided by Mike Mignola, the creator of Hellboy. The storytelling, both in terms of the script and the artwork, is poor across both series, and the inclusion of Dracula was partly driven by the fact that Topps had the licence to produce Dracula comics based on Francis Ford Coppola's 1992 adaptation of Bram Stoker's novel, but these comics were weak attempts to exploit these rather flawed films. Equally flawed was Caliber Comics' 1994 adaptation of the novel that aimed to be a faithful version 'without the trappings of Hollywood', although the timing suggests that it was also prompted by the release of the film. This comic, written by Eric Jackson and drawn by Charles Yates, was presented with a striking cover by Vincent Locke, but as with the above examples, a good cover is no guarantee of the quality of the story. The comic is executed with nothing of the skill seen in the Roche, Webb and Brewster or the Powell and Olliffe versions, although it clearly aspires to the same goals.

A more successful relationship between a *Frankenstein*-inspired film and comic came in 2003 when writer Chris Yambar and artist Robb Bihun released a comic based on the Edison Studio's 1910 film version of *Franken-stein* directed by J. Searle Dawley. This film was the first cinematic version of the story and was thought lost for decades until a single copy was redis-covered in the 1970s. This comic stays true to the silent nature of the film by having none of the characters speak, but instead a narrator provides an explanation of what is occurring. It is also a quite faithful recreation of the film, which in 2003 was not widely available, as viewings were tightly controlled by the owner. This has some connection to the 1939 debut of Frankenstein in comics, in *Movie Comics* #1, discussed earlier, as it uses images closely drawn from the film to piece the story together, although Yambar and Bihun's work is considerably more successful. In 2010 the film was released into the public domain and has since then been freely available on the internet, but in 2003, at the time the comic was released, this was practically the only way to experience the narrative. Another unusual relationship between a comic and film adaptation of the novel came in the form of Kevin Grevioux's *I, Frankenstein* (2009). The comic was published by Darkstorm Comics, and the creation of the comic pages was actually a part of the pitching process of the film script, also written by Grevioux. The finished comic was collected as a graphic novel at the same time as the film was released in 2014.

In the early years of the twenty-first century there was a flurry of Frankenstein comics. In 2000, *Creature Commandoes* was relaunched by DC Comics, again featuring the monster. In 2004, *Doc Frankenstein* appeared, created by Geof Darrow, Steve Skroce and the Wachowski Bros (directors of the 1999 film *The Matrix*), and published by Burlyman Entertainment. Set in the future, but with several flashbacks to the past, this story shows Frankenstein as an immortal genius and the 'Messiah of Science' battling against religious fundamentalists who have taken over the world. At around the same time Scottish writer Grant Morrison brought the DC Comics' Frankenstein back into contemporary comics in his 'Seven Soldiers of Victory' storyline (DC Comics, 2005), and this version of the character has appeared in *Frankenstein: Agent of S.H.A.D.E.* (2011). Perhaps one of the strangest versions of the novel in comics came in the form of *Embalming – The Another Tale of Frankenstein* [sic], a manga series created by Nobuhiro Watsuki. The main story was preceded by two stories, 'Dead Body and Bride' and 'Dead Body and Lover', published in 2005 and 2006, and *The Another Tale of Frankenstein* appeared in *Jump SQ* magazine between 2007 and 2015, and was collected in a series of books. The idea that connects the various story arcs of *Embalming* is that over the century since Victor Frankenstein's creation of his monster, other scientists have replicated his work and the world is now plagued by such 'Frankensteins'. The bizarre story departs substantially from the novel and all adaptations of it, and draws in characters like Sherlock Holmes and historical figures like Jack the Ripper.

Frankenstein: The Graphic Novel (2008) by Jay Cobley and Declan Shalvey was yet another attempt to offer a 'faithful' rendition of the novel in comics. This is a meeting point between the 1945 *Classic Comics* edition and the 1990 version by Powell and Olliffe. Like those other adaptations, part of the aim was to create a bridge to the source material by establishing familiarity with the story and themes while also being entertaining and innovative in its own right. While the Cobley and Shalvey adaptation is less formally innovative than some of its predecessors, it serves the novel well and tells the story in a skilful and engaging way. The atmospheric use of colour and some striking use of page composition help to communicate the Gothic themes of oppression, responsibility, mortality and despair. The creature is presented as Other through the use of speech balloons and captions that look yellowed and deformed, which is a good way to suggest a monstrous, guttural voice, or at least something about his voice that sets him apart. Produced by Classical Comics, this graphic novel was designed as a teaching aid and came in two versions, one with original text and the other simplified. It was also accompanied by a teaching resource pack on CD. 2008 also saw Dabel Brother Productions start their adaptations of Dean Koontz's *Frankenstein*-inspired novels. Koontz's stories, which mix noir and science fiction, see Victor becoming immortal having turned his process on himself. In the present day he is a philanthropist, but secretly plans to take over the world with an army of creatures that he has designed, supplanting the 'Old Race'. The creature, who has taken the name Deucalion, vows to defeat him, and two New Orleans detectives are drawn into the struggle. Koontz's story was adapted by Chuck Dixon and Brett Booth, and while Dixon does a good job of streamlining the complex story, the artwork is wholly inappropriate. Booth's style is far too mainstream, and does not communicate anything of the horror or noir sensibility of the books.

Frankenstein's Womb (Avatar, 2009), by British writer Warren Ellis and Polish artist Marek Oleksicki, is not an adaptation of the story, but rather a reflection on the process of its creation, moving the focus onto Mary Shelley. The story opens with Mary in a carriage with her future husband Percy Shelley and her step-sister Claire Clairmont as they travel across Germany on their way to meet Byron in Switzerland. The story revolves around their rumoured stop at Castle Frankenstein, and sees Mary enter the abandoned castle while Percy and Claire wait in the carriage. In the ruined castle Mary encounters a vision of the creature she will create. He tells her of the infamous alchemist Johann Conrad Dippel (1673–1734) who once worked at the castle, while also revealing Mary's fate, and that of her circle. She has visions of her past, and specifically her birth, which killed her mother, and learns of the future infidelities and tragedies that await her.

Ellis's postmodern story is most likely drawn from Radu Florescu's 1975 book *In Search of Frankenstein*, which speculates that Mary visited the castle and heard tales of Dippel's infamy as a dark magician and heretic from the locals. Florescu's contention is that Dippel was the model for Frankenstein and Ellis adopts this highly disputed idea, but whether or not this actually happened is beside the point. This idea gives Ellis the pretext to dissect the various social, literary and scientific discourses that came together to produce the novel, marrying that with a consideration of Mary herself, presenting her as an intelligent, independently minded young woman reflecting on her own life, the nature of creativity and the price of literary alchemy – what it costs to achieve immortality through art. Ellis is known for intelligent story telling that also packs a powerful emotional punch and this short story does not disappoint. Added to that, the artwork by Marek Oleksicki perfectly captures the mood of Ellis's story and the novel, evoking the intensity of Ward's wood etchings, the menace of Wrightson's images and the under-stated power of Olliffe's art (Figure 15.4). This comic, despite its relatively short length, offers one of the most provocative and compelling variations on the Frankenstein story in comics.

Of course, the more serious the comics become in their adaptations of the novel, the funnier the humour versions become, and 2009 saw the creation of *Electric Frankenstein*, a comic created to promote the punk rock band *Electric Frankenstein*. This comic, produced by Eye Bank Comics and created by Mike Hoffman, parodies several Frankenstein films and comics, and has the creature, known as Franklin, wrestling with his greatest fear – the Bride's desire for children (Figure 15.5). Franklin turns to Victor, who he has imprisoned in the dungeon, for help, and soon the castle is besieged by cigar-chomping winged Franken-cherubs cloned by Victor as part of his escape plan. He also delivers a final blow to Franklin by impregnating the bride. This is one of the best parodies of the novel, and adaptations of it, to appear in recent years.

In 2012 Bernie Wrightson and horror comics writer Steve Niles created *Frankenstein Alive, Alive!* published by IDW, a sequel to the illustrated edition of the novel Wrightson produced in 1983. This finds the creature in 1920 working at a Coney Island freakshow and considering suicide. Wrightson's return to the creature was widely acclaimed by critics. Similarly, Phoenix's *She Lives!* (2014) has the Bride survive the end of *The Bride of Frankenstein* film and join a circus. Set in the late 1940s and with elements of noir, the story shows the Bride becoming disillusioned with her existence and desiring to live a normal life, but she is exposed by acts of heroism, including foiling a robbery and saving the lives of several children when their school bus is trapped by electrical wires. The book is remarkable for several reasons. Firstly the wordless story is rendered in a simple yet beautiful style, and the narrative and characterization are extremely well

Figure 15.4 *Frankenstein's Womb,* by Warren Ellis and Marek Oleksicki
(© Avatar Press, Inc, 2009)

Figure 15.5 *Electric Frankenstein*, by Mike Hoffman (© Eye Bank Comics, 2009)

Figure 15.6 Woodrow Phoenix, *She Lives!* Artist's Book (Handmade, edition of one, 2014)

handled. Secondly, the format and creation of the book are unique. The pages of the book are one metre square, and it is an original piece of comic art. The images were drawn directly into the specially prepared blank book in a singular act of creation which allowed little margin for error. It has never been published and Phoenix has declared that it never will be (Figure 15.6). These are meaningful choices by Phoenix, and reflect the themes of responsibility towards a creation, and the burden of creating such a 'monster'. Phoenix has to accompany his oversized creation wherever it goes, and has to be protective of it, like a parent would be of a child. This book is a remarkable achievement on many levels, from the story Phoenix creates, the manner in which he created it and the care that he takes with it.

In 2015 Dark Horse Comics, a prominent publisher of horror comics, produced *Frankenstein Underground* written by Mike Mignola and drawn by Ben Stenbeck. There are allusions throughout this five-part series to many of the Frankenstein comics that preceded it, and Mignola brings them all into his 'Hellboy universe'. In many ways this comic once again re-invents the creature while paying homage to the long tradition of *Frankenstein* in comics. In 2015 the Being Human festival sponsored an event in Dundee organized by Drs Daniel Cook, Jennifer Barnes and Chris Murray at the University of Dundee. This project celebrated the city's connections with

Figure 15.7 Chris Murray, Norrie Millar and Phil Vaughan, *Mary Shelley's Dundee*, or *Frankenstein Begins* (© UniVerse Publications, 2015)

Mary Shelley, who spent some time there as a teenager, when her father sent her to live with the Baxter family. The current author, along with artist Norrie Millar, and letterer and designer Phil Vaughan, produced a comic as part of this event. The story suggested that many of the things in the novel were inspired by Shelley's time in Dundee, a busy industrial city based around jute and whaling (Figure 15.7), drawing on her claims in the 1831 edition of the novel that Dundee and the surrounding area inspired her imagination. The comic playfully draws upon a range of versions of the story and the creature, and Millar's work displays the influence of many earlier comics adaptations, and like *Frankenstein's Womb*, turns its attention back on the creator of the novel.

The story of Frankenstein and his creature has become a very important modern myth, which continues to communicate vital messages about creation, life and death, responsibility, vengeance, and the relationship between intellectual curiosity and morality across its various retellings. The creature itself, particularly as portrayed by Karloff, has become iconic and ubiquitous, but comics have offered many different interpretations of the story, from adaptations that are very faithful to the tone and themes of the novel, to parodies, superhero versions of the creature, and ruminations on identity and the nature of artistic and scientific creativity.

NOTES

1 Christopher Murray, *Champions of the Oppressed: Superhero Comics, Popular Culture, and Propaganda in America during World War Two* (Cresskill, NJ: Hampton Press, 2011), p. 72.
2 William B. Jones, *Classics Illustrated: A Cultural History* 2nd edn. (Jefferson, NC: McFarland, 2011), p. 50.
3 Ibid., p. 51.
4 Ibid., p. 51.
5 Julia Round, *Gothic in Comics and Graphic Novels: A Critical Approach* (Jefferson, NC: McFarland, 2014), p. 95.
6 Mike Ploog, interviewed by Jon B. Cooke in *Comic Book Artist* #2, 1998, collected in Cooke (ed.), *The Comic Book Artist Collection Volume One* (Raleigh, NC: TwoMorrows Publishing, 2000), p. 159.
7 Susan Tyler Hitchcock, *Frankenstein: A Cultural History* (New York and London: W.W. Norton and Co, 2007), p. 226.
8 Michael Powell, in *Frankenstein: The Graphic Novel* (Los Angeles, CA: Pulp 20 Press, 2012), p. 93.

16

KAREN COATS AND FARRAN NORRIS SANDS

Growing up Frankenstein: Adaptations for Young Readers

In the author's note that accompanies the young adult novel, *This Monstrous Thing* (2015), Mackenzi Lee argues that while many people cast Mary Shelley's *Frankenstein* (1818) as the first steampunk novel, it does not fit that genre's minimal definition of posing an alternative history, or position Victor Frankenstein's scientific experiments within an industrial framework of gear-driven, clockwork mechanisms driven by steam power. Steampunk is a form which is influenced by images of nineteenth-century technology and explores how such images can be elaborated as part of an alternative account of history. Lee's steampunk adaptation of Shelley's work does all of these things, drawing the writing and reception of Shelley's novel itself into an alternate history that touches on themes of discrimination, social and personal responsibility, teen angst and romance. In *Frankenstein Makes a Sandwich* (2006), a poetic adaptation for picture book readers, Adam Rex's oversized, green-skinned, neck-bolted but still somehow friendly looking creature leaves his home in search of lunch. When his abusive neighbours pelt him with garbage, he fashions their offerings into an enormous, disgusting sandwich. In this way, Rex turns the horrific moments of mob violence in Shelley's original and its film adaptations into a humorous narrative poem that depicts resilience in the face of bullying, one of the many themes he takes in a comic direction in this and the subsequent *Frankenstein Takes the Cake* (2008). These and many other authors that we will highlight in this chapter find in *Frankenstein* a peculiarly apt vehicle through which to explore certain anxieties and trends in both children's and young adult literature. While our chapter draws mostly from titles originally published in the US, our framework for discussing them applies more broadly to texts and readerships outside that context.

Contemporary teen fiction is littered with reanimated corpses and other things that should be dead but are not, giving metaphoric voice to many of the dominant themes in the genre, such as body dysmorphia; experiencing oneself as an outsider; bullying to the point of evoking violence; and even failed or tragic romance. Bodily changes brought on by puberty may make a teen feel monstrous, clumsy, trapped in a body he or she does not understand, and rejected by peers. Social rules and conventions make this experience even more traumatic, as some teens, feeling disempowered themselves, turn their anxiety outward in bullying behaviours that isolate those whose bodies exceed normative parameters. One of the recurring themes of the middle grade and young adult adaptations of *Frankenstein* that focus on such mistreatment, interestingly enough, is redemption; either through providing a sympathetic back story for the scientist, or attending more closely to the social needs of the monster, adaptations for both children and young adults often end with forgiveness or at least understanding and empathy for their behaviours. And while the love affair between Victor and Elizabeth and the monster's demand for a mate have always featured prominently in adaptations, these elements transform in interesting ways in the middle grade and young adult adaptations; couple relationships matter, but siblings and peer friendships are as important as romance in the adaptations.

In addition, the monster's relationship to his creator offers an analogue to some teens' spiritual search; emerging out of the animistic worldview of childhood, many teens feel abandoned by a god who will not intervene in ways they can feel on an experiential level, just as Frankenstein's monster feels abandoned by his creator. The flip side of the teen reaching for a response from his or her god is the culture's fear that the teens they are responsible for creating through enforced obedience to repressive regimes of various kinds will rise up against them in the fashion of what Isaac Asimov dubbed the 'Frankenstein complex'.[1] It is a tale at least as old as the book of Genesis and Milton's *Paradise Lost* (1674), and these twin themes resurface in today's trend of teen dystopias, many of which take the Frankensteinian motifs of scientific overreach and righteous anger against an irresponsible 'parent' as their guiding lights. Death itself becomes a prominent theme in literature for this age group as well, to the point that Roberta Seelinger Trites has called it the 'sine qua non of adolescent literature, the defining factor that distinguishes it both from children's and adult literature'.[2] This is, according to Trites, because young adults must confront the fact that death represents the ultimate limit to their power. Hence, a story that challenges that limit, particularly one that replaces a seemingly absent god with an active human scientist, is bound to resonate, and indeed, both Lee's *This Monstrous Thing* and Kenneth Oppel's *The Apprenticeship of Victor Frankenstein* series (2011, 2012) focus on the desire to resurrect a beloved brother rather than create a wholly new person. But ultimately, *Frankenstein* adaptations, like so many other paranormal fantasies for teens, are stories about the terrible consequences of attempting to defy death, so they do the work Trites claims they do of forcing teens to confront the limit of their power. Given that the watchword for youth literature, for better or worse, is 'relatable', then, this nineteenth-century horror tale provides much that is relatable to the adolescent experience.

But the fact that *Frankenstein* has found its way into literature for very young children as well as adolescent literature is a bit more puzzling. To understand this phenomenon requires an understanding of the existential concerns of the developing child. Most psychological theorists believe that children develop socially, morally and cognitively in stages. The danger in thinking in terms of developmental stages, however, lies in considering them as uniform, defined and tied to particular age ranges. In addition, because we do not believe children to be cognitively able to process the full meaning of a text, we have a tendency to dismiss the complexity of their actual responses to and understanding of stories. In thinking of children's reading, we often operate out of what Marah Gubar calls a 'deficit model', which considers young children as deficient adults, lacking the skills and intellectual resources they need to understand complicated ideas.[3] A more accurate position aligns with what Gubar describes as a 'kinship model'; children are human, after all, and while they may be somewhat inexperienced and dependent, they are sensitive to themes, details and emotions that connect them in intimate ways to texts that, though written for adults, address concerns across the age spectrum.[4] In *Frankenstein*, themes and issues such as family relationships, the roles and dangers of knowledge and secrecy, and the fear of isolation are all live issues for even the youngest members of our species.

Even within a kinship model, though, developmental stage theories can offer a useful heuristic tool for understanding how and why the themes and motifs in *Frankenstein* appear and change in adaptations targeted at readers of different ages. A useful way of working with stage theories, then, is to understand that certain concerns impress themselves upon children at certain times due to social situations and developing physical and mental abilities. During these initial confrontations with new situations, children develop patterns of response that persist in similar situations throughout their lives. For instance, psychologist Erik Erikson argued that the first task of infants is to learn whether or not the world is a trustworthy place. If their environments are fairly orderly and predictable and their caregivers are reasonably responsive, they learn patterns of trust, which recur whenever they encounter a new situation, such as going to school or entering a new relationship; they will expect the environment and people in it to be kind and reasonable until proven otherwise. If, on the other hand, their situations are chaotic and their caregivers unpredictable, they will approach new situations from a position of distrust. We can see this dilemma depicted on the monster's first day out, so to speak.

From his first day and throughout his life, Frankenstein's creature knows only loneliness. The first moments of his life are narrated by Victor Frankenstein, who is disgusted with and frightened by his creation, abandoning it the moment it awakens. Later, the creature finds his way to Frankenstein's bedchamber, giving Frankenstein a second opportunity to embrace his creation. This is not the case, however. Frankenstein recounts that the creature came to him and 'muttered some inarticulate sounds, while a grin wrinkled his cheeks... I rushed down stairs. I took refuge in the court-yard belonging to the house I inhabited; where I remained during the rest of the night.'[5] Thus, in his first moments of life, even as he smiles and gurgles like an infant, the creature is both abandoned and detested by the one who should care for him most.

For the creature, this is just the beginning of his loneliness and isolation. He is left alone to learn about love and pain, and his attempts to reach out to others are consistently met with fear and revulsion. Even his best efforts, such as his attempt to resuscitate the drowning child, are violently misunderstood, causing him to lament:

> 'This was then the reward of my benevolence! I had saved a human being from destruction, and as recompence, I now writhed under the miserable pain of a wound... Inflamed by pain, I vowed eternal hatred and vengeance to all mankind.'
> (p. 116)

Thus, based on his many tragic misadventures in the earliest part of his life, the creature approaches new situations and people with distrust, and even with hatred and violence in some cases.

The creature's development continues to mirror that of a growing child. Like the creature, for instance, young children test the limits of their autonomy and bodily abilities. They learn language and its effects on others. And their behaviour, intentionally or not, is sometimes monstrous. So perhaps one reason why *Frankenstein* is so often adapted for children, and recognizable as a type even when children have no knowledge of the source text, is because of this sense of kinship between the monster and the child; he *is* a child, modelled on the view that children are born innocent and learn how to behave from the way they themselves are treated. Had the monster not been so maligned and harassed, had Victor taken responsibility to nurture him as a loving father, he might have become a hero. But therein lies the darkness: he is an unnatural child, and he intentionally kills a child when the child, William, rebukes him and acknowledges that he is a Frankenstein, that is, a naturally born member of what should have been the creature's family. In testing his strength and his limits, the creature learns that "'I, too, can create desolation; my enemy is not impregnable'" (p. 117), a realization that he embraces with child-like glee. Thus, as the creature evolves into a monster in the social world, his development suggests a sinister undercurrent with regard to childhood itself: its innocence is no protection, and may become its doom if carelessly handled.

But the trajectory of adaptations for children does not follow this path toward the creature's eventual isolation and despair. Instead, adaptations for children focus on themes of mastering fears and redeeming social relationships. Latent in all children is a deep-seated fear of rejection and abandonment by their caregivers as well as the feeling that their bodies are fragmented assemblages of parts rather than coherent wholes. And in fact, our ordinary language practice of saying things like, 'He has his father's eyes' or 'That nose comes from her mother's side of the family' probably adds to children's sense that they are made of bits and pieces that may not all be pleasing. When Frankenstein recoils in horror at his patched-together creation, and other humans reject the creature because of his looks, these unconscious fears are given imaginative form. Psychologist D. W. Winnicott lists going to pieces and complete isolation as two of the 'unthinkable anxieties' for a child's developing ego; as a text written for adults, *Frankenstein* makes these anxieties thinkable, while adaptations for children make them not only thinkable, but also enfold them in plots and images that help children overcome them.[6] If someone who looks like Frankenstein's monster can be lovable, then there is hope for the patched-together child reader.

Still, the undercurrent of incongruity between the innocent child and the monstrous child haunts adaptations for young readers, taking them in one of two directions: toward humour or horror. Children know that they are relatively weak, powerless and in need of protection; tweens and teens know that the social world is tricky to navigate. And while they may resent these generalized feelings of helplessness and/or social anxiety, being able to give them a specific form and location can make them manageable. For the youngest readers, for instance, if the monster is under the bed, he's not everywhere all around. For older readers, understanding the motivations behind unfriendly social actors may inspire forgiveness, empathy or even tactics for managing difficult circumstances. But representing either the monster or the scientist as ridiculous, friendly or even in need of the child's protection is even more empowering.

Given our cultural abhorrence for subjecting child readers to horror, adaptations of Frankenstein and his monster for very young children are always more funny than scary. One example of the funny monster is displayed in Neil Numberman's picture book, *Do Not Build A Frankenstein!* (2009), in which a child builds a 'Frankenstein' that follows him around, annoying him. The monster's annoying behaviour is comical to readers as he dresses in women's clothing, pushes the child too high on the swing, and unsuccessfully pretends that he is not actually following the child. Ironic humour is used in adapting Shelley's famous monster in Adam Rex's hilariously clever poetry picture books mentioned above. Like Rex's texts, Rick Walton's *Frankenstein: A Monstrous Parody* (2012), by the pseudonymous Ludworst Bemonster, parodies a variety of literary monsters, such as Dracula, the mummy, the wolfman and, of course, Frankenstein's monster in intertextual dialogue; Walton parodies Ludwig Bemelmans' *Madeline* in style, structure and plot. This picture book is humorous for young readers familiar with the *Madeline* series (1939–1961) because they can identify the similarities, and because the monster children, unlike Madeline and her classmates, are rewarded for bad behaviour, such as yelling, whining and walking in crooked lines.

The monstrous child in particular is expressed through humour in several ways. On one hand, the monstrous child may actually be a monster, as in *Frankenstein: A Monstrous Parody*. However, children are also often parodied through presenting the human child as a little monster in picture books, such as in Samantha Berger's *Crankenstein* (2013). In this picture book, a child becomes a 'Crankenstein' whenever he or she throws a tantrum. The Crankenstein monster, illustrated as a child with an oversized green head and a large, wailing mouth, is horrific because of his tantrums and emotional outbursts, but also humorous as the pictures depict the silly, everyday occurrences he whines about. While a child might decide that the book is overly didactic or even pokes fun at child behaviour, the book changes tones at the end when two Crankenstein children meet and begin to laugh at the other's tantrum. The book redeems the monstrous child when he looks at his own ridiculous behaviour, but it also reminds readers, young and old alike, that the Crankenstein will 'be back', suggesting that the monstrosity of children is intermittent.

While many adaptations of *Frankenstein* successfully incorporate humour to entertain child readers while alleviating feelings of powerlessness and dissipating fear, some attempts fall short, especially when the pictures introduce an element of pity for characters who are supposed to be the target of the humour. Curtis Jobling's picture book, *Frankenstein's Cat* (2001), offers an example. The story's premise is that Dr Frankenstein's first experiment, a cat pieced together from nine different cats, is lonely and wants a friend, but because he is ugly, smelly and clumsy, he repeatedly fails at making friends with different people in Frankenstein's castle, at one point even tearing up at his mistreatment by other inhabitants of the castle. Finally, he requests that Dr Frankenstein make a friend for him. What Frankenstein creates, however, is unexpected and thus supposedly humorous to readers; Frankenstein creates a dog that chases the cat around the castle 'forever and a day'.[7] The story ends with this conclusion: 'If one had to come up with a moral to this story – and I'm not sure there is one – I guess it could be this: What you get (in this case a large, vicious zombie dog) isn't always what you asked for.'[8] While this conclusion is probably meant to be wry, the blurring of sympathy, humour and horror returns the child reader to a sense of powerlessness in the face of adult didacticism.

Another way to make a fear of monsters manageable is to build an alternate world where monsters live, such as we find in Katherine Tegen's *Dracula and Frankenstein are Friends* (2003). Rather than setting the narrative in the real world, characters from the source text are transplanted into a new setting, an imaginary 'world of monsters' in which the character is in contact with other well-known characters. In this particular example, 'Frankenstein', who is actually Frankenstein's monster from Shelley's text, lives in a town of monsters. Other infamous monsters also live there, such as Dracula, the invisible man and the creature from the black lagoon. Besides displacing the monsters into a world of imagination rather than reality, these books present readers with intertextual puzzles that highlight the fictionality of the characters and allow readers to experience the pleasure of knowing the references. We find such worlds in Lisi Harrison's *Monster High* series (2010), Jon Skovron's *Man Made Boy* (2013) and Allan Rune Pettersson's *Frankenstein's Aunt* (1978), as well as the TV show *Scooby-Doo and the Ghoul School* (1988) and the film *Hotel Transylvania* (2012). The settings may be metaphorical or have details that map onto real towns and schools, but they are clearly distinct from the real world, reminding readers that monsters only exist in safely contained story worlds.

Frankenstein is not only confined to an imaginary town in *Dracula and Frankenstein are Friends*; he is also confined to his domestic space, which is presented through Doug Cushman's detailed illustrations. The first two-page spread shows Frankenstein's neighbourhood and the types of houses each resident lives in. While Dracula lives in a turreted castle and the mummy lives in a pyramid, Frankenstein lives in a spooky house, complete with loose shutters and electrical equipment atop the roof. This illustration shows that monsters not only belong here, but that they each have their own special space, alleviating the anxiety about where monsters might be. To further emphasize this idea and to make the monsters seem friendly, readers are shown the insides of Dracula and Frankenstein's houses. Dracula's home features a cosy sitting room with a roaring fire, a 'Velcome' doormat and a vampire sleeping snuggly in his coffin with his toes humorously exposed. In contrast, Frankenstein's home depicts Frankenstein working in his laboratory in the middle of the night. Yet his home is also cosy with its stone fireplace, family photos and silly lab assistants bringing Frankenstein a variety of beakers. The familiarity of these domestic spaces makes the monsters seem similar to the reader; both monsters and children have happy, but clearly separate, homes.

While the beginning of *Dracula and Frankenstein are Friends* seems welcoming and even funny as Frankenstein and Dracula play tricks on their friends and experiment with chemicals, the fun fades when conflict arises. Frankenstein plans to host a Halloween party, but when he tells Dracula about his idea, Dracula commandeers not only Frankenstein's idea but also his invitations, resulting in their mutual friends attending Dracula's party while Frankenstein sits home wondering why his guests have not arrived. The juxtaposition of illustrations comparing Frankenstein and Dracula's party preparations helps establish both homes as inviting places for a party. When all of the guests arrive and begin to enjoy themselves at Dracula's party, however, readers are likely to sympathize with Frankenstein because he can be seen through Dracula's window, sitting in his house alone. Guilt overtakes Dracula, and he decides to surprise his friend by bringing the guests to Frankenstein's house. All of the characters are shown dancing and smiling in the end, and the book ends with the idea that the friendship has been repaired, restoring the domestic sphere and emphasizing Dracula's redemption, rather than Frankenstein's. Additionally, in vilifying Dracula, this picture book follows the adaptation trend that presents Frankenstein (or rather, his monster) as a victim with whom we should sympathize; even among monsters, he is sometimes an outcast.

The social anxiety and resolution in Tegen's text address concerns characteristic of children entering the peer-intensive environment of school. Middle childhood, according to Erikson, is a time of finding out how the world works. He argues that the dilemma that children must resolve during this period is one of industry versus inferiority; they are interested in the technical aspects of how things work as well as the social respect that competence and skill will earn them. One of the reasons why this particular dilemma gains salience is because children in school are comparing themselves, and being compared through grading as well as social grouping, to their peers. Enter *Franny K. Stein* (2003), a series of illustrated chapter books designed for new readers. Franny is a scientist whose tastes and talents run toward the Gothic. Her parents do not understand or approve of her preference for bats and beakers over daisies and ponies, nor do her classmates, so, in the first book in the series, Franny feels sad, alone and unappreciated. Her sympathetic teacher suggests that she approach her problem like a scientific experiment, and her research leads her to transform herself into the kind of inoffensive girl who fits in by conforming to stereotypes. However, when the school is threatened, she lives up to her namesake by creating and animating a monster scary enough to take on the threat. Her classmates are at first stunned into silence by the revelation of her abilities and their fear of the creature, but by the next day, they laud Franny as both a hero and a friend, addressing her needs for social acceptance and acknowledgement of her particular set of 'scientific' skills. Like Frankenstein, Franny's approach to science alienates her from family and friends, but unlike Frankenstein, Franny's experiments eventually gain her positive recognition.

David Gooderham proposes that fantasy texts for middle grade readers address themes of 'invention, construction and achievement'; they are characterized by 'sustained thoroughness and painstaking rationality', even going so far as to move toward the appearance of realism.[9] In that respect, the Franny K. Stein series is transitional from an emphasis on wish fulfilment, where the science is vague and tinged with magic and silliness (her monster, for instance, is made of cold cuts), to books for older readers that take their science and their psychology more seriously. *Goosebumps Most Wanted: Frankenstein's Dog* (2013) presents science in two competing and serious ways. On one hand, the main character, Kat, loves science, loves her scientist uncle and wants to become a scientist. Introducing herself and her situation, Kat narrates:

> [Uncle Victor is] a brilliant scientist and I'm just a sixth-grade girl. But I really think we have a lot in common. He's kind of my idol. I mean, I'd love to be a scientist and inventor like him when I'm older. He spends all his time just dreaming up amazing things and then building them. How much fun is that?[10]

However, as Kat arrives at her uncle's home to spend a week with him and document his work for a school project, Kat begins to doubt her uncle and his pursuit of science, casting science in a new light that suggests that it can be dangerous and scary. As Kat discovers that her uncle is creating artificially intelligent robots that often become rebellious and even violent, Kat begins to fear her uncle and his intentions. She breaks her uncle's rules against going into his laboratory and against turning on his robot when her new friend wants to see it in action. Overall, this novel shows Kat to be balancing her own desires against the desires of her uncle and her new friend. She is trying to decide where she belongs socially, and she is testing the limits of her own agency. At the end of the novel, Kat discovers that the man she thought had been her uncle all along is actually another robot, and her actual human uncle comes home from France in the final pages. The conflict is resolved as Kat realizes that all of the rules she has broken were never really rules that her *actual* uncle gave her. Furthermore, her uncle does not seem angry at her for being in his lab and playing with his experiments. The scientist is redeemed because he was never 'mad' or dangerous to begin with, Kat is reassured that her family status and friendships are intact, and she is free to explore becoming an industrious scientist in the future.

Themes of scientific and social competition between peers, as well as testing the limits of one's power, are not confined to print; these themes are also explored on screen in children's films such as Tim Burton's *Frankenweenie* (1984/2012). Like Franny K. Stein and Kat, young Victor Frankenstein aspires to become a scientist in *Frankenweenie*. He is misunderstood by his family and classmates, and he turns to scientific experimentation to prove his self-worth to himself and others. What begins as a school science fair assignment quickly escalates to a dangerous competition between the students in reanimating their dead pets. In an ironic twist from Shelley's text, Victor's reanimated dog turns out to be the only non-violent creation, because Victor has performed his experiment out of love when his dog, Sparky, is killed by a car. The other children, however, reanimate their long-forgotten dead pets out of competition and by stealing Victor's discoveries, causing their creations to become monstrous. This dark adaptation suggests that there should be limits to scientific experimentation, and also that one should evaluate the motivations behind scientific endeavours before beginning. In reanimating Sparky, Victor reclaims his only friend, but being the smartest kid in school and competing with his peers is detrimental.

Transitioning between middle childhood and adolescence, many adaptations of *Frankenstein* and its characters explore tween and adolescent anxieties regarding social status and the changing body, which are often related. *Monster High* (2010), by Lisi Harrison, is the first novel in a popular series that follows several teen monsters as they navigate typical adolescent scenarios such as high school, first loves, friendship and physical development. The *Monster High* series has seen great popularity within a broad spectrum of young readers for several additional reasons. One clear reason is that the series has spread beyond the novels to other merchandise, including dolls, animated cartoons, a clothing line and a kid's website with the slogan, 'Be yourself. Be unique. Be a monster.' Part of the series' popularity is also due to the variety of characters that it puts on display, providing today's young girls with monster versions of stereotypes including 'the popular girl', 'the rebel', 'the pretty girl', 'the athletic girl' and so on, as characters that ironize the types while tacitly reinforcing them as possible sites for identification and imitation.

While this series follows characters including a teen wolf, vampire, mummy and lake monster, in addition to several teen human characters, arguably the most provocative character is Frankie Stein, the newly born (newly made) daughter of Viktor and Viveka Stein. Born a teenager, Frankie must work through typical teen issues like making friends at a new school, coping with body image issues and falling in love for the first time. However, because she is also a monster, these issues are even greater for her because she must hide her identity in public. Frankie is special because while others are complacent about hiding among humans (aka 'normies'), Frankie wishes to fully integrate the monsters, who call themselves Regular Attribute Dodgers (RADs), into the human population so that they can celebrate their uniqueness. Assumed a normie in the first novel, Melody joins Frankie's fight and sums up their philosophy toward integration this way: 'I don't want to give in to intimidation. I want to fight. I want people to stop being so afraid of each other's differences.'[11] The work that Frankie does along with her friends makes it clear that this novel explicitly navigates not only stereotypical teen issues but also speaks implicitly to the difficulties of racial integration, as well as LGBTQ issues as the RADs begin to 'come out'. Using a multi-voiced discourse as both RADs and normies take turns narrating this series, the series makes it clear that monsters are not only redeemable, but, perhaps even more importantly, that they have been misunderstood and misrepresented all along, marking this as a transitional series between literature for children and literature for teens.

Many adolescent and young adult novel adaptations change the gender of characters from the Frankenstein myth, sometimes to make a specific point about gender stereotypes, but more often to attract a new readership. The *Monster High* series clearly targets adolescent and teen girls, and it does this in part by turning monsters that are typically male into female teen characters. Frankie's status as a monster allows the YA reader to explore themes of embodiment, social acceptance and tolerance. While this series' main focus is not on *Frankenstein* specifically, the use of this character as the main protagonist suggests something unique about Frankenstein's monster as an original, a leader and a strong example of understanding and accepting the abject body. As the series progresses, Frankie begins to use less make-up to cover her green skin, and she begins to realize that the bolts in her neck that spark uncontrollably when she feels strong emotions are not something to hide; she learns that her bolts should be celebrated because they help her express herself. She even learns that her boyfriend finds them erotic, and she realizes they can become pleasurable to her. By the time the series ends, monsters have become part of normal society, and artificial neck bolts have become a fashion statement among normies. The *Monster High* series specifically targets a female readership, suggesting that the Frankenstein myth, and Frankenstein's monster specifically, may serve the purpose of helping young girls learn to appreciate their changing bodies.

Through humour, domestication and what we might call technological or science-based fantasy, then, very young children as well as children in the middle find Frankenstein and his monster useful tropes for managing fears of inferiority as well as fears of being a social outcast. These adaptations for younger readers are most often redemptive and reassuring, both for the monster and for the scientist. Children need to know that they can make mistakes, that they can even behave monstrously, and still be forgiven. But as they develop a more nuanced understanding of their own interiority and their often contradictory motives and feelings, they look for texts that are more character driven and psychologically complex, and this is what we find in young adult fiction.

Like children's picture books, novel adaptations for young adults represent variety in their world building. Some, for instance, focus primarily on Frankenstein and/or his monster, adapting Shelley's characters. Novels such as *Mister Creecher* (2011) by Chris Priestley and Kenneth Oppel's novels in *The Apprenticeship of Victor Frankenstein* series, *This Dark Endeavor* (2011) and *Such Wicked Intent* (2012), follow this trend. Priestley's novel and Mackenzi Lee's *This Monstrous Thing* include Mary and Percy Shelley as fictional characters themselves. In contrast, other novels build a world based on intertextuality, combining well-known literary characters, such as in Suzanne Weyn's *Dr. Frankenstein's Daughters* (2013) and Megan Shepherd's *The Mad Man's Daughter* trilogy that culminates with a focus on the Frankenstein myth in *A Cold Legacy* (2015). Some novels delve into a fantastic 'world of monsters' in which Frankenstein and his family are participants, such as in Jon Skovron's *Man Made Boy*, while other novels, such as Peter A. Salomon's *Henry Franks* (2012) brings Shelley's work into 'the real world', creating a scavenger hunt as readers are invited to investigate the intertextual connections. Regardless of how the adaptation builds its world, the majority of these works all share one important aspect: they focus on how the scientist or his creation participates in domestic relationships, often exploring why Frankenstein becomes estranged from his family, or how Frankenstein or his monster is redeemed through familial reintegration. Through an emphasis on domesticity, the adaptations for teens provide the psychological complexity that many teens seek.

Redeeming the mad scientist and his monster through their relationships with others appears a priority for today's adaptations. Chris Priestley's *Mister Creecher* exemplifies this by revealing part of the missing narrative in Shelley's novel – the duration of time in which Frankenstein and Henry Clerval are travelling throughout Europe while the creature awaits the creation of his bride. By telling the creature's side of the story through the eyes of an orphaned child narrator, Priestley shows the positive, redemptive qualities of the creature, while simultaneously revealing Frankenstein's baseness.

However, some novels, such as Kenneth Oppel's, synchronously redeem and vilify Shelley's characters through the explorations of domestic relationships. In *This Dark Endeavor*, Victor Frankenstein is revealed to be a heroic risk-taker, but also a proud and jealous twin. Set before Shelley's novel begins, the first of Oppel's two novels recounts Victor's teen years before constructing his creature, following Victor's adventures as he, Henry, Elizabeth and Konrad – his twin – discover the forbidden Dark Library in his home. When Konrad falls ill, Victor seeks a risky cure, but Konrad dies nonetheless, possibly as a result of the cure. Over the course of the novel, Victor is shown to be brave as he risks fighting wild animals, deep lake diving and disobeying his father, all for the love of his twin brother. These depictions redeem Victor before he ever begins his dark endeavours in reanimation. However, Victor is also shown to be a selfish show-off, craving attention from his parents, friends and especially from Elizabeth, his brother's girlfriend. Overall, *This Dark Endeavor* presents a sympathetic backstory for the scientist while also providing a rich investigation into Victor's domestic relationships.

Such Wicked Intent continues Victor's story in the aftermath of Konrad's death, appealing to teen interest in loss and death, showing the fallout when the teen protagonist tests the limits of his power and fails. Victor's struggle with Konrad's death is paralleled by his feelings of the loss of his personal power. However, Victor soon discovers a formula that allows the drinker to delve into purgatory and visit the dead. Once again, Victor has the opportunity to use forbidden knowledge to test the limits, and he travels to the other side to try to rescue Konrad from death, foreshadowing his future work with reanimation. Each time the characters enter the spirit world, they feel powerful and indestructible while they are there, but once they leave, they are drained, eventually learning that they are leaving bits of their souls behind each time they return to the real world. Victor, his friends and readers alike must question the best course of action: lose one's soul to save a loved one, or lose a loved one to save one's soul. Thus, this adaptation of the Frankenstein myth is satisfying in its psychological complexity that comes through the exploration of domestic relationships, science and the occult.

Man Made Boy, by Jon Skovron, brings a completely new character's perspective into consideration as it follows Frankenstein's monster's son, named Boy, in the modern world. Boy and his parents live and work with a variety of well-known monsters in a freak show as a way of hiding in the modern world. Like any teen, Boy's problems consist of issues with his parents, popularity, romance and identity formation. While the novel is entertaining because it incorporates so many well-known characters and allusions from other texts, and because it answers the question, 'What if Frankenstein's monster actually had a family?', the novel is perhaps most intriguing because of the way it introduces technology as both cure and poison. Boy is actually a cyborg, created from both human and machine parts as a nod to what Shelley's creature might have looked like had she lived in the twenty-first century. To cope with his teen angst and his domestic relationship problems, Boy 'plugs in' to the internet as a hacker to relax and chat with his online friends. However, the technology that allows Boy to unwind becomes his greatest enemy when Boy creates a sentient virus and frees it into the cyberspace. Much like Shelley's Frankenstein who creates his monster and abandons it, resulting in the creature's fury toward its creator, Boy's feminized virus is abandoned and she retaliates. Because she is a computer virus, she can control electronics, as well as humans, recreating and adapting the Frankenstein myth for a contemporary teen audience. Including a complex variety of romantic relationships, exploring the social needs of the monster, feminizing the monster and integrating modern technology puts a new spin on an old narrative, revitalizing it for contemporary teen readers.

Adaptations of *Frankenstein* for young readers address a variety of concerns across the spectrum of childhood and adolescence. For the youngest readers and viewers, both the scientist and his creature are depicted as comic stereotypes that represent children's curious and sometimes monstrous natures and behaviours, and help mitigate existential and imaginary fears. For older readers, the characters exhibit more psychological complexity, providing metaphorical expression for the social anxieties, embodiment and identity issues and spiritual questions that plague contemporary tweens and teens. Their stories are by turns cautionary and comforting, redemptive and relatable, horrific and humourous, but no matter the tone or outcome, they engage young readers in the fundamental questions posed by Shelley's text: What does it mean to be human? What does it mean to be a monster? How responsible are we toward the 'monsters' we ourselves have created? What are the ethical limits of science and technology? Such questions have achieved an even greater degree of salience in a world where our technologies have the capacity to render us both more and less human; innovative adaptations of *Frankenstein* thus offer useful guides for helping young people navigate this contemporary landscape.

NOTES

1 Isaac Asimov, 'That Thou Are Mindful of Him', *The Bicentennial Man and Other Stories* (Garden City, NY: Doubleday, 1976), pp. 61–86, p. 63.
2 Roberta Seelinger Trites, *Disturbing the Universe: Power and Repression in Adolescent Literature* (University of Iowa Press, 2000), p. 118.
3 Marah Gubar, 'Risky Business: Talking About Children in Children's Literature Criticism', *Children's Literature Association Quarterly*, 38(4) (2013), 450–7, 451.
4 Ibid., 453.
5 Mary Shelley, *Frankenstein*, ed. and Intro. Marilyn Butler (Oxford University Press, 1998), p. 40. Future references will be made parenthetically.
6 D. W. Winnicott, *The Maturational Processes and the Facilitating Environment* (Madison, CT: International Universities Press, 1965), p. 58.
7 Curtis Jobling, *Frankenstein's Cat* (New York: Simon & Schuster, 2001), n.p.
8 Jobling, *Frankenstein's Cat*, n.p.
9 David Gooderham, 'Children's Fantasy Literature: Toward an Anatomy', *Children's Literature in Education*, 26(3) (1995), 171–83, 179.
10 R. L. Stine, *Goosebumps Most Wanted: Frankenstein's Dog* (New York: Scholastic, 2013), p. 4.
11 Lisi Harrison, *Monster High* (New York: Poppy, 2010), pp. 256–7.

GUIDE TO FURTHER READING

The below references refer to the sections of the volume. Please note that all of the chapters in the book have bibliographical notes which can also be consulted.

Editions

The fullest listing of 287 editions of *Frankenstein* in chronological order from 1818 up through part of 2000 may be found in Stuart Curran's upenn bibliography now on the Romantic Circles website at: www.rc.umd.edu/editions/frankenstein/textual.

Part I: Historical and Literary Contexts

Behrendt, Stephen C. (ed.) *Approaches to Teaching Mary Shelley's Frankenstein*. New York: MLA, 1990.

Botting, Fred (ed.) *Frankenstein: Contemporary Critical Essays*. Basingstoke: Macmillan, 1995).

'Reflections of Excess: *Frankenstein*, the French Revolution and Monstrosity' in *Reflections of Revolution: Images of Romanticism*, ed. Alison Yarrington and Kelvin Everest. London: Routledge, 1993. 26–38.

Butler, Marilyn. 'The First *Frankenstein* and Radical Science'. *Times Literary Supplement*, 9 (April 1993), 12–14.

Clemit Pamela. *The Godwinian Novel: The Rational Fictions of Godwin, Brockden Brown, Mary Shelley*. Oxford: Clarendon Press, 1993.

Collings, David. *Monstrous Society: Reciprocity, Discipline, and the Political Uncanny, c. 1780–1848*. Lewisburg, PA: Bucknell University Press, 2009.

Craciun, Adriana. 'Writing the Disaster: Franklin and *Frankenstein*'. *Nineteenth-Century Literature* 65 (2011) 433–80.

Gigante, Denise. 'Facing the Ugly: The Case of *Frankenstein*'. *ELH*, 67 (2000), 565–87.

Glut, Donald F. *The Frankenstein Catalog: Being a Comprehensive Listing of Novels, Translations, Adaptations, Stories, Critical Works, Popular Articles, Series, Fumetti, Verse, Stage Plays, Films... Featuring Frankenstein's Monster and/or Descended from Mary Shelley's Novel*. Jefferson, NC: McFarland & Company, Inc., Publishers, 1984.

Hill, Jen. *White Horizon: The Arctic in the Nineteenth-Century British Imagination*. Albany, NY: State University of New York Press, 2008.

Hill-Miller, Katherine C. *'My Hideous Progeny': Mary Shelley, William Godwin, and the Father-Daughter Relationship*. London: Associated University Presses, 1995.

Hogle, Jerrold E. '*Frankenstein* as Neo-Gothic: From the Ghost of the Counterfeit to the Monster of Abjection' in *Romanticism, History and the Possibilities of Genre: Re-forming Literature 1789–1837*, ed. Tilottama Rajan and Julia Wright. Cambridge University Press, 1998. 176–210.

Levine, George, and U. C. Knoepfelmacher (eds.) *The Endurance of Frankenstein: Essays on Mary Shelley's Novel*. Berkeley, CA: University of California Press, 1979.

Lyles, W. H. *Mary Shelley: An Annotated Bibliography*. New York: Garland Publishing, Inc., 1975.

Marshall, David. *The Surprising Effects of Sympathy: Marivaux, Diderot, Rousseau, and Mary Shelley*. University of Chicago Press, 1988.

Newlyn, Lucy. *Paradise Lost and the Romantic Reader*. Oxford: Clarendon Press, 1993.

Richard, Jessica. '"A Paradise of My Own Creation": *Frankenstein* and the Improbable Romance of Polar Exploration'. *Nineteenth-Century Contexts* 25 (2003): 295–314.

Rushton, Sharon. *Shelley and Vitality*. Basingstoke: Palgrave, 2005.

St Clair, William. *The Godwins and the Shelleys: The Biography of a Family*. London: Faber and Faber, 1989.

'The Impact of *Frankenstein*', in *Mary Shelley in Her Times*, ed. Betty T. Bennett and Stuart Curran (Baltimore, MD: Johns Hopkins University Press, 2000), 38–63.

The Reading Nation in the Romantic Period. Cambridge University Press, 2004.

Veeder, William. *Mary Shelley and Frankenstein: The Fate of Androgyny*. University of Chicago Press, 1986.

Wolfson, Susan J. and Ronald L. Levao (eds.) *The Annotated Frankenstein*. Cambridge, MA: The Belknap Press of Harvard University Press, 2012.

Wollstonecraft, Mary. *The Vindications*, ed. D. L. Macdonald and Kathleen Scherf. Peterborough, Ontario: Broadview Press, 1997.

Yousef, Nancy. *Isolated Cases: The Anxieties of Autonomy in Enlightenment Philosophy and Romantic Literature*. Ithaca, NY: Cornell University Press, 2004.

Zonana, Joyce. 'They Will Prove the Truth of My Tale: Safie's Letters as the Feminist Core of Shelley's *Frankenstein*'. *Journal of Narrative Technique* 21(2) (1991) 170–84.

Part II: Theories and Forms

Bolton, Michael Sean. 'Monstrous Machinery: Defining Posthuman Gothic'. *Aeternum* 1(1) (2014), 1–15.

Botting, Fred. *Making Monstrous: Frankenstein, Criticism, Theory*. Manchester University Press, 1991.

Braidotti, Rosi. *The Posthuman*. Cambridge: Polity, 2013.

Fincher, Max. *Queering the Gothic in the Romantic Age: The Penetrating Eye*. Basingstoke: Palgrave, 2007.

Fukuyama, Francis. *Our Posthuman Future: Consequences of the Biotechnology Revolution*. London: Profile Books, 2002.

Graham, Elaine. *Representations of the Post/Human: Monsters, Aliens and Others in Popular Culture*. Manchester University Press, 2002.

Haggerty, George E. *Queer Gothic*. Urbana and Chicago, IL: University of Illinois Press, 2006.

Halberstam, Judith. *Skin Shows: Gothic Horror and the Technology of Monsters*. Durham, NC: Duke University Press, 1995.

Halliwell, Martin and Andy Mousley. *Critical Humanisms: Humanist/Anti-Humanist Dialogues*. Edinburgh University Press, 2003.

Haraway, Donna J. *Simians, Cyborgs, and Women: The Reinvention of Nature*. London: Free Association Books, 1991.

Hayles, N. Katherine. *How We Became Posthuman: Virtual Bodies in Cybernetics, Literature, and Informatics*. University of Chicago Press, 1999.

Herbrechter, Stefan. *Posthumanism: a Critical Analysis*. London: Bloomsbury, 2013.

Mousley, Andy. *Literature and the Human: Criticism, Theory, Practice*. London: Routledge, 2013.

Schoene, Berthold. *Writing Men: Literary Masculinities from Frankenstein to the New Man*. Edinburgh University Press, 1999.

Smith, Andrew and William Hughes (eds.) *EcoGothic*. Manchester University Press, 2013.

Part III: Adaptations

Allen, G. S. *Master Mechanics & Wicked Wizards: Images of the American Scientist As Hero and Villain from Colonial Times to the Present*. Amherst, MA: University of Massachusetts Press, 2009.

Chibnail, Steve and Julian Petley (eds.) *British Horror Cinema*. London: Routledge, 2002.

Gooderham, D. 'Children's Fantasy Literature: Toward an Anatomy'. *Children's Literature in Education*, 26(3) (1995), 171–183.

Grieveson, Lee. *Policing Cinema: Movies and Censorship in Early Twentieth-Century America*. Berkeley, CA: University of California Press, 2004.

Haynes, R. D. *From Faust to Strangelove: Representations of the Scientist in Western Literature*. Baltimore, MD, Johns Hopkins University Press, 1994.

Hutchings, Peter. *Hammer and Beyond: The British Horror Film*. Manchester University Press, 1993.

Jackson, A., K. Coats and R. McGillis (eds.) *The Gothic in Children's Literature: Haunting the Borders*. New York and London: Routledge, 2007.

Jones, G. *Killing Monsters: Why Children Need Fantasy, Super-Heroes, and Make-Believe Fantasy*. New York: Basic Books, 2002.

Newman, Kim (ed.) *The BFI Companion to Horror*. London: British Film Institute, 1996.

Norris Sands, F. 'Dr. Frankenstein's Hideous Progeny: A Typology of the Mad Scientist in Contemporary Young Adult Novels and Computer Animated Film.' Dissertation, Illinois State University, 2015.

Pirie, David. *A Heritage of Horror: The English Gothic Cinema, 1946–1972*. New York: Equinox, 1974.

Prawer, S. S. *Caligari's Children: The Film as Tale of Terror*. New York: Da Capo, 1980.

Rigby, Jonathan. *English Gothic: A Century of Horror Cinema*. London: Reynolds & Hearn, 2004.

Skal, David J. *The Monster Show: A Cultural History of Horror*. Harmondsworth: Penguin, 1994.

Stephens, J. and R. McCallum. *Retelling Stories, Framing Culture: Traditional Story and Metanarratives in Children's Literature*. New York and London: Routledge, 1998.

Tudor, Andrew. *Monsters and Mad Scientists: A Cultural History of the Horror Movie*. Cambridge, MA: Basil Blackwell, 1989.

William Uricchio and Roberta E. Pearson. *Reframing Culture: The Case of the Vitagraph Quality Films*. New Jersey: Princeton, 1993.

Wheatley, Helen. *Gothic Television*. Manchester University Press, 2006.

INDEX

Cambridge Companions to...

AUTHORS

TOPICS

The Actress edited by Maggie B. Gale and John Stokes

The African American Novel edited by Maryemma Graham

The African American Slave Narrative edited by Audrey A. Fisch

Theatre History by David Wiles and Christine Dymkowski

African American Theatre by Harvey Young

Allegory edited by Rita Copeland and Peter Struck

American Crime Fiction edited by Catherine Ross Nickerson

American Modernism edited by Walter Kalaidjian

American Poetry Since 1945 edited by Jennifer Ashton

American Realism and Naturalism edited by Donald Pizer

American Travel Writing edited by Alfred Bendixen and Judith Hamera

American Women Playwrights edited by Brenda Murphy

Ancient Rhetoric edited by Erik Gunderson

Arthurian Legend edited by Elizabeth Archibald and Ad Putter

Australian Literature edited by Elizabeth Webby

British Literature of the French Revolution edited by Pamela Clemit

British Romanticism edited by Stuart Curran (second edition)

British Romantic Poetry edited by James Chandler and Maureen N. McLane

British Theatre, 1730–1830, edited by Jane Moody and Daniel O'Quinn

Canadian Literature edited by Eva-Marie Kröller

Children's Literature edited by M. O. Grenby and Andrea Immel

The Classic Russian Novel edited by Malcolm V. Jones and Robin Feuer Miller

Contemporary Irish Poetry edited by Matthew Campbell

Creative Writing edited by David Morley and Philip Neilsen

Crime Fiction edited by Martin Priestman

Early Modern Women's Writing edited by Laura Lunger Knoppers

The Eighteenth-Century Novel edited by John Richetti

Eighteenth-Century Poetry edited by John Sitter

Emma edited by Peter Sabor

English Literature, 1500–1600 edited by Arthur F. Kinney

English Literature, 1650–1740 edited by Steven N. Zwicker

English Literature, 1740–1830 edited by Thomas Keymer and Jon Mee

English Literature, 1830–1914 edited by Joanne Shattock

English Novelists edited by Adrian Poole

English Poetry, Donne to Marvell edited by Thomas N. Corns

English Poets edited by Claude Rawson

English Renaissance Drama, second edition edited by A. R. Braunmuller and Michael Hattaway

English Renaissance Tragedy edited by Emma Smith and Garrett A. Sullivan Jr.

English Restoration Theatre edited by Deborah C. Payne Fisk

The Epic edited by Catherine Bates

European Modernism edited by Pericles Lewis

European Novelists edited by Michael Bell

Fairy Tales edited by Maria Tatar

Fantasy Literature edited by Edward James and Farah Mendlesohn

Feminist Literary Theory edited by Ellen Rooney

Fiction in the Romantic Period edited by Richard Maxwell and Katie Trumpener

The Fin de Siècle edited by Gail Marshall

Frankenstein edited by Andrew Smith

The French Enlightenment edited by Daniel Brewer

French Literature edited by John D. Lyons

The French Novel: from 1800 to the Present edited by Timothy Unwin

Gay and Lesbian Writing edited by Hugh Stevens

German Romanticism edited by Nicholas Saul

Gothic Fiction edited by Jerrold E. Hogle

The Greek and Roman Novel edited by Tim Whitmarsh

Greek and Roman Theatre edited by Marianne McDonald and J. Michael Walton

Greek Comedy edited by Martin Revermann

Greek Lyric edited by Felix Budelmann

SIA information can be obtained
ww.ICGtesting.com
ted in the USA
HW010349030820
2199LV00010B/184

9 781107 450608

CPSIA information can be obtained
at www.ICGtesting.com
Printed in the USA
LVHW010349030820
662199LV00010B/184

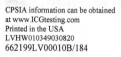